The church's secret ... a

TONY BUSHBY

THE
TWIN
DECEPTION

Michelangelo and Leonardo da Vinci
preserved a papal secret,
and the discovery of an old Bible unlocks it.

Joshua Books
JoshuaBooks.com

Joshua Books
JoshuaBooks.com

All correspondence to the publisher
Joshua Books
PO Box 1668
Buddina 4575
Queensland Australia

Copyright © Tony Bushby 2005
The rights of Tony Bushby to be identified as the moral rights
Author of this work has been asserted by him in accordance with
the *Copyright Amendment (Moral Rights) Act 2000* (Cth)

Without Prejudice

First Printed 2006

Publisher's Disclaimer
All rights reserved. No part of this book may be reproduced, transmitted or utilized in any form or by any means, electronic or mechanical, including photocopying, recording, or by any information storage and retrieval system without permission in writing from the Publisher. Whilst every care has been taken to ensure the accuracy of the material contained herein, neither the author nor the publisher or its agents will bear responsibility or liability for any action taken by any person, persons or organisations claimed to be based in whole or in part upon the information contained herein.

Category: Author: Religious & Theology: History: Ancient Mysteries

ISBN 0 9757953 4 1

Master Distribution world wide through Joshua Books
www.joshuabooks.com

TONY BUSHBY

Tony Bushby was born in Australia in 1948 and is the author of five books, all of which are regarded as classics of their genre.

In 1985 he began research into the origins of Christianity and has since revealed incontrovertible evidence of cover-ups, fraudulent activities, and forged Gospels within the established Christian church. To date Tony has written four outstanding books on this subject that have received acclaim the world over. He is also held in high regard for his writings on the subject of Near-Death Experiences, and has personally interviewed over 600 people worldwide who have experienced the phenomena.

Tony continues to research in the Middle East and Europe, seeking further evidence of Truth and gathering information that challenges the basis of our core beliefs. He has access to rare ancient writings in the Alexandrian Library in Egypt, and adopts the attitude that 'regardless of how many people may be disturbed, there is no religion superior to Truth'.

ALSO BY TONY BUSHBY

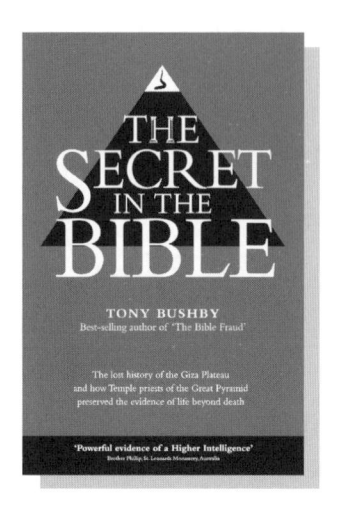

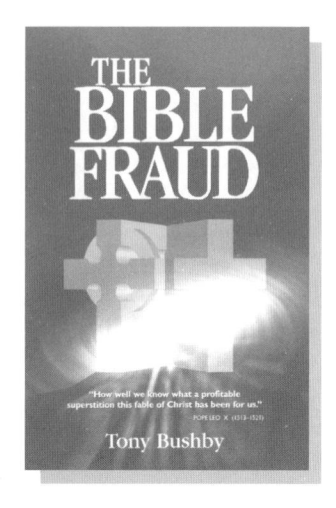

What others have said about Tony Bushby's books...

*I thoroughly enjoyed Tony Bushby's **The Bible Fraud**. Its tale ended my own research into the origins and source material of the Bible (not for a book! Just my own curious hunger to know!). This author has done in a careful and extremely well researched book, far better than most in this genre. The attention to detail, which I have confirmed myself over the past twenty years from various sources, is validated and more accurate than many academic papers found in our universities.*

It is undoubtedly the most important book on Christianity and the Roman legacy ever written, and most likely will have the least impact because it explodes the mythology and power basis for a religion which will be impossible for most to swallow. A truth that will choke rather than enlighten. I look forward to his next book and I do hope that it opens eyes to the true wonders and we finally put away the destructive toy of over simplified pacification tripe that exists in political, commercial establishment religions.

MAE, Isle of Sanday, Orkney, Scotland

The Bible Fraud. *The ramifications of this evidence are impossible to calculate.*

Rev. Herbert O'Brien, Ordained Minister of the Reformed Baptist Church, Melbourne, Australia

*I have just finished reading **The Secret in the Bible**. For some reason it doesn't take long to read any of Tony Bushby's work. Perhaps it's the fact that I couldn't put it down once I started reading it! Reading is a passion for me and I must say rarely do I get so much in a book as what Tony Bushby offers to his readers. I eagerly await the publication of his third book. I cannot thank the author Tony Bushby, or Joshua Books for making his books available, enough. Of course the service from Joshua Books was impeccable.*

Edward Sloan, International

*Thank you for devoting so many years to finding out what **The Secret in the Bible** is and for sharing it with others. I'm still in awe over the revelation.*

Charis, International

*I have purchased and read **The Bible Fraud** and **The Secret in the Bible**. I find the information in them tremendously exciting. They supply missing pieces to the historical puzzle, and lead in a much more realistic direction than traditional explanations. Truth is always better than fantasy, because it is real.*

Whitney Prescott, Stone Mountain, GA, USA

***The Bible Fraud** is a real eye opener. It is well documented and easy to understand. Everyone should read this book to understand how we have been deceived. Especially all Christians who think they know the truth. You will never think the same once you have read this book.*

JS, Jacksonville, Florida, USA

*I just received the book **The Bible Fraud** and I'm very pleased with the truths coming out in this publication. Many of the truths that Tony has spelled out in this book have been known by myself and others for a long time but never the whole story as set up in this book! Thank you Tony for putting it all together!!! I'm looking forward to the new book Tony is writing ...*

REE, Minot, Nevada, USA

*Tony has now revealed the 'Great Mystery' in his second book so all, not just chosen initiates, can experience the essence in their own way. The book is also very well referenced for those wishing to further pursue its revelations. Anyone who has a hunch that we are not being told the complete truth in life must read this masterpiece. **The Secret in the Bible** by Tony Bushby rightfully deserves a place on everyone's bookshelf beside **The Bible Fraud**. 'Tempora pattet occulta veritas' - in time, all hidden truths shall be revealed.*

Robert Adams, Queensland, Australia

*In regards **The Bible Fraud**, I must say that this is the first time in my entire life that I have read anything of this nature concerning the person of Jesus Christ. I have long loved the reading of scripture since a child and committed much to memory. To think ... that the loved and respected writings may be a fraud is difficult to receive. I will continue on the journey.*

RL, Kent, Washington, USA

*If the general public were to read **The Bible Fraud**, it would cause much angst and awe. Can it change history? Yes, I think it could.*

JF, Niagara Falls, Ontario, Canada

Thank you for your huge contribution to unravelling millennia of obscuration.

Andrew Yates, International

*I think that **The Bible Fraud** is a book that has been awaited for a very long time by so many people, and it gives everyone something to think about.*

DG, USA

*Having read both of Tony Bushby's books, **The Bible Fraud** and **The Secret in the Bible** - twice, I wish to congratulate Tony Bushby for writing two such exceptional books and to Joshua Books for publishing them.*

CJ Jones, New South Wales, Australia

*I recently obtained and read **The Secret in The Bible** and I had to write and say thank you for such a fantastic book. It was not easy purchasing in the UK but the excellent Nexus Bookshop supplied me from here. In this time we live in, things are happening at an accelerated rate both in the negative and positive arenas and the truth is a powerful necessity. Both Tony Bushby and Joshua Books have delivered one of the most powerful publications of this age and must both be congratulated by us all. It is a brave step to print such a work when I would imagine that the 'establishment' would rather it remained buried or at least only known by them.*

Danny Grant, London, UK

*I can only say that all heretofore thoughts concerning the NT have been laid to rest since reading **The Bible Fraud**. It brings a perspective to light of "religion" that should be compulsory reading for all honest people. It demonstrates how "religion" was shrewdly used by the ancient rulers much as it is today. The old thought about 'the more things change, the more they stay the same' is markedly demonstrated in this publication. Kudos to the author. Can't wait to read the sequel.*

WB, Independence, MO, USA

***The Bible Fraud** was ABSOLUTELY FABULOUS.
Tony Bushby has confirmed for me what I have thought to be true
for quite a while.*

JAM, Goulburn, NSW, Australia

*After having read your colossal book **The Bible Fraud**, I cannot find the
words to thank you enough for a job well done. Not only did you present
the historical truth concerning one of the world's foremost avatars, but
you also gave the locations where one may find these truths for themselves.
It may perhaps be years before most people will become honest with
themselves and open their eyes to the truth your work has presented
to the world, but thanks to the powers that be, the truth is now an
'open book'. I personally thank you for a wonderful, fantastic,
and noble job you've done with this work. It has been a long time coming,
but the truth has indeed set us free, and as most people know,
'you can't hide the truth', and most people 'can't handle the truth'.
Thank you again Tony, and I leave you with all good wishes
for peace profound.*

James A McCormick FRC

*On the other hand, a real truth seeker will realise that a guy who brings
his bedroll to a library so he can research night and day would be an
infinitely more reliable source than a writer whose main focus is
fame and ego enhancement.
Congratulations on **The Bible Fraud***

Claudia, USA

*Please send my congratualtions to Tony - whoever he is, wherever he is
- for **The Bible Fraud**. How simple and straightforward the truth is,
when unearthed in such a practical way. The results of his unstinting
investigation will surge across the world. I hope he keeps his head
well down.*

FB, Llandudno, North Wales, UK

*I was truly impressed with the amount of information and references supplied in **The Bible Fraud**. He deserves a lot of credit for his work.*

EP, Toronto, Ontario, Canada

*I am just as fascinated with **The Secret in the Bible** as others. I had delayed my opinion/view because of the 'unknowingly, initiated' process. I felt my mind doing an actual transformation through my entire being. For example: My yearly physical exam surprisingly baffled my doctor. When she was told I arrived for results, she rushed out, with wide-eyes ... bringing me into an inner-office with colleagues. At first I thought, 'Oh my God, something terrible was found'. Then I had this overwhelming calmness and sat, as the physician opened my records for review. She says, 'Let me congratulate you, Ms English. I wanted my colleagues to meet you. After all of your test results, of all the patients I have examined, I want you to know, not one person around your age (44 years old), is physically perfect of lab tests. Not in 20 to 25 years, have I seen such excellent results! I have told my colleagues that I have not prescribed any medications of any kind and you were not on any 'fad diets'.*

*I tell you this story because I know my physical condition is directly linked to the 'unknowingly, initiated' process of reading **The Secret in the Bible**. I feel like I am on top of the world, mentally and physically. Yes, I have carried the book with me since I received it. I can always find a moment to glance through it over and over and realise there is a 'secret of immortality'. Hey! I am convinced that each individual reader will have their own mind, body and soul revelation when they read this book. **The Secret in the Bible** is an 'interactive' guide! My deepest gratitude to you and all the team for making it available.*

Lois, International

The Bible Fraud - *How sad that we have suffered the long years of history so dreadfully deceived.*

M & MD, Hastings, New Zealand

ALSO AVAILABLE NOW

WHAT HAPPENS WHEN WE DIE?

A classic collection of stories drawn from research carried out over 30 years by the author Tony Bushby

Joshua Books
JoshuaBooks.com

ALSO AVAILABLE NOW

TONY BUSHBY
Best-selling author of
The Bible Fraud, *The Secret in the Bible* and *The Twin Deception*

THE CRUCIFIXION OF TRUTH

THE DISCOVERY OF HIDDEN VATICAN SCROLLS
AND THE FALSEHOODS THEY REVEAL ABOUT CHRISTIANITY

NEW EVIDENCE OF
FORGERY AND FICTION IN THE NEW TESTAMENT

'A knock-out blow for Christian Fundamentalism'
Michelle Daniels, Independent

*'A mesmerizing account of deceit and dishonesty
that is impossible for the church to deny'*
Mr. John Telfer, Director, Stanford Books

Joshua Books
JoshuaBooks.com

TWO SIDES TO THE STORY

Around a quarter of the world's population today is termed 'Christian' and that body of people is divided into two distinctive groups … believers and non-believers. Believers consider the church presentation of the story of Jesus Christ to be the greatest event in world history and non-believers are of the opinion that the story is an inherent priesthood deception. This book provides new evidence that Christianity has no foundation in historical fact and the story of Jesus Christ is not honestly presented.

The material presented in this volume is radical and far-reaching, and some people may find themselves at odds with the conclusions reached. Therefore it must be stated that the Author, Publisher and Associates, will **NOT** engage in time-consuming written religious argument with readers who hold different opinions. *The Twin Deception* is produced without prejudice, save that readers may find whatever pleases, displeases or instructs them, and are free to enjoy their own speculation, and hold their own opinion. Those who doubt what is revealed in this book should personally conduct their own research to verify that what is recorded is supportable in historical records and church archives.

The Author's intention is to expose doctrines and dogma falsely proclaimed by ecclesiastical authority as true and factual and is published for the benefit, wisdom, instruction and spiritual enlightenment of modern humanity. A book that gives people food for thought, which strengthens and clears their minds and enables them to grasp truths, does real and substantial good. That is the task of this volume, and may God be with those people who are on their journey.

CONTENTS

Acknowledgment		24
The gift of an old Bible		25
Introduction		30
1.	**The biblical evidence of Jesus' twin**	32
	The discovery of the 'Gospel of the Twin'	35
	The 'twin brother of Christ' is again recorded elsewhere	38
2.	**The boyhood of the twins**	42
	The father of the twins	45
	Another name given to Jesus in the Talmud	46
	Mary's story paralleled in old scroll	47
	Ignoble birth in a noble house	48
	Gospels confirm Mary's unexpected pregnancy	49
3.	**Twins raised by the Essenes**	50
	The blood relatives of Mary	51
	A damning statement	52
	The Essene's two messiahs	54
4.	**The names of the twins**	57
	The linguistic evolution of names	58
	Deified twin boys in church records	59
	The variant names of the twins	59
5.	**The suppressed records of John the Baptist**	66
	Unknown information about John the Baptist	66
	The anointing of John the Baptist	67

	An early church tradition	67
	Who was the leader of the Essenes?	68
	The 'Star of Bethlehem' mystery solved	69
	Evidence of a messianic 'Star' family	71
6.	**The life story of the first-born**	**73**
	The expectations of a messiah	73
	Many messiahs at that time	74
	Judas Thomas the Galilean	75
7.	**An apocalyptic vision**	**76**
	Forerunner of the Last Supper	78
8.	**Gospel appellations of the Galileans**	**80**
	An extraordinary confession	80
	The historical evidence	82
	What the records of Josephus really said	83
	Roman records of Khrestus	85
	Insurgents in Rome	86
	A religion of Galilean criminals	88
	Finding Judas Khrestus in the Gospels	89
	The Galilean fortress	91
9.	**The beginning of the Khrestian uprising**	**94**
	The 'misprint' in the Gospels	94
	The Roman Imperial Secret Service	94
	The tradition of a 'substitute'	96
	The Mithraic father of Rome	97
	The saving victim	98
	Destruction of the true history	99
	The removal of Simon' body	100

	One twin sold	101
10.	**Khrestians active for centuries**	**105**
	The nature of the Khrestian movement	105
	The records of Emperor Julian	107
	Hatred of the human race	109
11.	**The life of the second-born**	**112**
	The traditions of Cornwall	112
12.	**The House of Hillel**	**115**
	Jesus becomes a rabbi	116
	The prophet steps out	116
	'An unmarried man may not be a rabbi'	118
	The truth hidden in the darkness	118
	Mary Magdalene's royal father	120
	The tradition of incest	122
	The wedding at Cana	123
13.	**The books of 'magic' written by Jesus**	**125**
	'Magic' a disease of religion	126
	'Simon the magician' honoured as a god	127
14.	**The initiation of Jesus in Egypt**	**129**
	Tempted by the Devil	131
	The place of the skull	133
	Church admits 'invention of the cross'	135
	Administration of strong potions	136
	Entrance into Heaven	137
	The Third Degree	138
	Resurrected from death	139

'Thou hast become a God' 141
Origin of the Panther knowledge 141
Crucifixion unknown by Second Century historians 143

15. Bringing secret knowledge to the world 144
The Sanhedrin condemn Jesus 146
Dark and light 147
The death of Rabbi Jesus 148
The age of Rabbi Jesus at his death 150
Church fathers admit Jesus was stoned 151
Merging the two factions 152

16. The Exodus to Britain 153
The church retracts a statement 153
The precedence of the British church 156
The original British church non-Christian 157
The arrival of the Gospel of the Twin 159
No Easter in Britain 161

17. How the twins became God 163
No church councils for the first 300 years 163
Emperor Constantine's bloodline 164
Reasons for the first religious council 165
Presbyter's religions 'destitute of foundation' 167
The two gods of Christianity 168
Selecting a new god 169
The 'sons of God' 172
The two natures of Christ 173
The Sibylline Books consulted 173
The untitled manuscript 175
Manufacturing the Gospels 176

The Seraglio Bible	178
Manuscripts burnt at the Council of Nicaea	178
The use of scribal quills	179
The emergence of the Gospels	180
The British origin of the 'Roman church'	181
The sister city of Rome	182
The close of the Council of Nicaea	182
Divisions among Eastern and Western presbyters	183
The beginning of ecclesiastical councils	184

18. Twin stories in the Gospels — 185

The Secret Scrolls	185
Origin of the holiest truths	187
Disassembling the Gospels	188
Strange verses in the Bible	191
The disbelief of the bishop	193
The secret Gospel of Mark 'carefully guarded'	194
The hidden side of things	196

19. What did the first Bible really say? — 198

It is not true that the Bible is authentic	198
The letters of St Jerome	200
How the Vulgate got its name	200

20. Outside interference in the Gospels — 204

Previous beliefs nullified	204
A prostitute orders Gospels to be rewritten	205

21. A strange church statement — 210

Alcuin's twins	210

22.	**Twin powers of the church**	212
	Papal forgery	214
	The papacy sold	216
	The twin reality	216
	The militia of Jesus Christ	218
	Terrorist popes	219
	Double-trouble	220
	The attempt to kill Protestants	222
	Rabbi Jesus triumphs	224

BOOK TWO ... THE RENAISSANCE PERIOD

23.	**Twins on horseback**	226
24.	**Christianity's disbelieving popes**	228
	Papal confessions	228
	What Pope Alexander VI said	229
	Struggling with secrets	232
	The 'fable' of Pope Leo X	234
	Pope Leo's brothels	237
	The Gospel according to Marks and Silver	238
	The Easter Friday banquet	239
	Papal editing of historical records	241
	Summary	242
25.	**Cardinal Bembo's original Gospel manuscripts**	243
	The Cardinal's private library	244
26.	**The forbidden theme of twin boys**	245
	The Bible and its twin painters	245
	The use of artist's license	247

	The hidden words of Leonardo	247
	Leonardo thinking out loud	250
	The unfinished painting of Mary	252
	Michelangelo and secret information	253
	Twins in the heart of Christendom	254
	Michelangelo's lost works	256
	Raphael, the papal playboy	256
	Later forgery in 'twin' paintings	258
	Council of Trent censors artwork	259
	Many artists knew about the twins	260
	Twin iconography reaches the antipodes	261
27.	**An opposing Bible**	**262**
	Secrets in the King James Bible	262
	Differences between the two Bibles	264
28.	**Concealing special messages**	**265**
	Knights Templar knowledge not lost	270
29.	**Twins in a French church**	**276**

BOOK THREE ... THE COVER-UP

30.	**The Alexandrian scrolls**	**279**
31.	**A deliberate attempt by the church to avoid detection**	**281**
	The true purpose of the Council of Trent	282
	The Creed of Pope Pius IV	284
	An anomaly in the records of a French monk	286

32.	**Why Pope Sixtus rewrote the Vulgate**	**288**
	The church establishes a publishing house	288
	Fraud is just plain fraud	288
	Penned by the church	290
	The destruction of the evidence	292
	The Vulgate denounced 'untrue' by Pope	293
	No papal opposition to rewriting the Vulgate	295
33.	**What was the church censoring?**	**297**
	The *Index of Prohibited Books*	297
	The establishment of a church censoring office	298
	Pope Alexander orders a cover-up	299
	Forgery in historical records	301
	An order from the Inquisition	302
	False books published by the church	304
34.	**A new church history written**	**306**
	References to the twin deleted	307
	A retroactive fabrication	308
	Forging reference sources	310
	The suppression of *Diderot's Encyclopedia*	312
	Summary	313
35.	**The suppressed chapter of the Bible**	**315**
	The FIRST Vulgate translated in secret	315
	How the First Vulgate differs from modern versions	316
	The incomplete books of the Bible	316
	The author of the missing sections	317
	False speeches in the Acts of the Apostles	318
	What the missing section says	320
	The suppressed chapter of the Acts of the Apostles	320

	The manuscript from Constantinople	324
	Deletions from the Book of James	325
	The hidden dweller	325
36.	**The letter from Rome, c. 90 AD**	**327**
	Summary of Comments	335
	Overview of the 'Letter from Rome'	337
37.	**Conclusion**	**340**

Bibliography — 341

　　The Library of the Fathers — 351
　　The writings of Dr. Constantine Von Tischendorf — 351
　　Encyclopedias and dictionaries consulted — 351
　　Bibles used as comparative references — 353

Index — 355

ACKNOWLEDGMENT

The conclusion presented in this book would not have been possible without access to archival libraries, and the one owned by Julie Halligan deserves special mention. Her private collection contains eight thousand volumes, and some rare editions date back to the 16th Century. Her library is most extraordinary, and when considered in conjunction with the decades of time and personal investment involved in its establishment, it must be classed as magnificent. Standing upon ceiling-height shelving extending a lineal distance of 82 feet (approx. 25 metres) are volumes of specific research material collected by Julie containing the history and literature of every age and every country. Some volumes carry the names of people who are today but echoes in the corridor of time, and others are records of the history of entire nations.

Each of Julie's books is like the doorway to the house of an old friend, and to read them all would take a lifetime. I thank Julie for her constant devoted, intelligent collaboration with me in my work, and for privileged access to her very special collection of books, so freely granted.

THE GIFT OF AN OLD BIBLE

There was a time when to question the literal truth of the Bible was heretical and that is exactly what my earlier books did. The publication of *The Bible Fraud, The Secret in the Bible* and *The Crucifixion of Truth*, provoked a powerful response, not least a vigorous correspondence from all over the world. Christians distinguished themselves by the bitterness of their attacks and, amidst insults and accolades, groups and individuals sent in new research material in the form of old manuscripts, rare books, and ancient church decrees. Rabbinic sources provided fresh data, as did researchers and translators of medieval texts, and access to private archival libraries was offered. Of great help was the availability of an original version of *Diderot's Encyclopedia*, a volume that Pope Clement XIII ordered destroyed immediately after its publication in 1759. A monastery in Cumbria, England, supplied documentation relating to the origin of the first Gospel, and a disillusioned ex-priest revealed the church's innermost system of accounting for the twofold nature of the Gospels. Much of that material is discussed in later chapters.

Central to the argument presented in this book is the content of an old Bible gifted to me by a lady in England. This Bible is quite special, for proudly written in bold capital letters in the descriptive section in its front pages is the word FIRST. This Bible was published in 1563 at Rheims in France and is the FIRST English-language copy of the Vulgate ever produced. The Introductory Pages carry a history of its translation, and the names and circumstances of the priests involved in its publication. Its existence precedes later Vulgates that received major structural changes under the papal command of Pope Sixtus V in 1588 and nine subsequent revisions thereafter. This Bible differs greatly from today's edition and carries information about Jesus and

St Paul that is excluded from modern versions.

The following chapters demonstrate the effect of that evidence on our understandings of Christian origins and the significance of the deletions are explained. In summary, the modern-day Vulgate is a widely different Bible to that published in 1563 and understanding the nature of the changes is especially important for those who believe the Bible is the word of God. The availability of the FIRST Vulgate has made it possible to develop a new story about the circumstances surrounding the birth and emergence of the Christian religion and moves the debate on the origin of the New Testament into new territory.

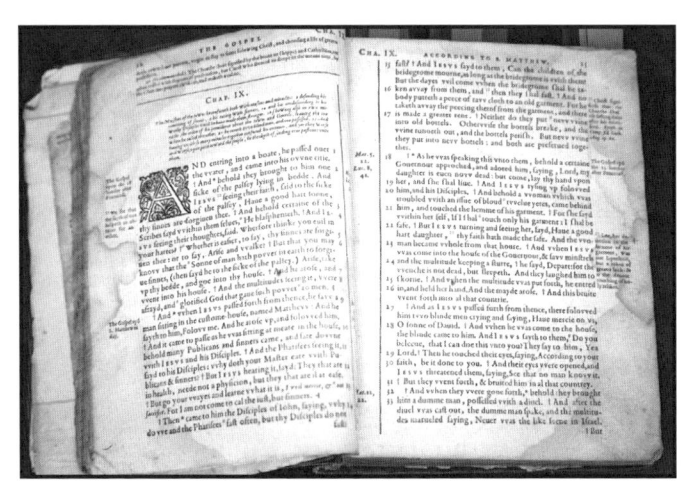

© Tony Bushby, 2005

These two pages are from the Gospel of Matthew in the FIRST Vulgate Bible

This old Vulgate Bible has now been copyrighted in readiness for photographic reproduction in its original form, and its subsequent availability to the public.

SOME PHOTOS OF THE FIRST VULGATE

Modern Bibles have deleted this Preface that appears in the FIRST Vulgate.

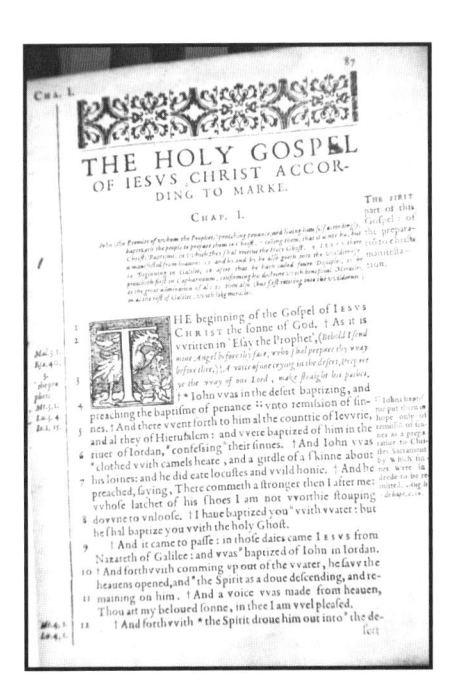

Opening page of the Gospel of Mark as published more than four hundred years ago. Note the spelling of Jesus' name at that time

THE TWIN DECEPTION

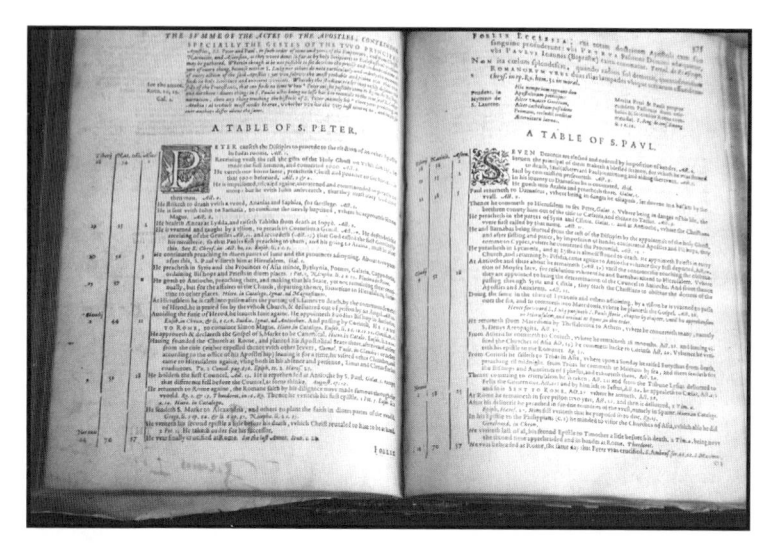

These sections called TABLES do not appear in modern Vulgates. This particular picture shows the TABLES of Peter and Paul.

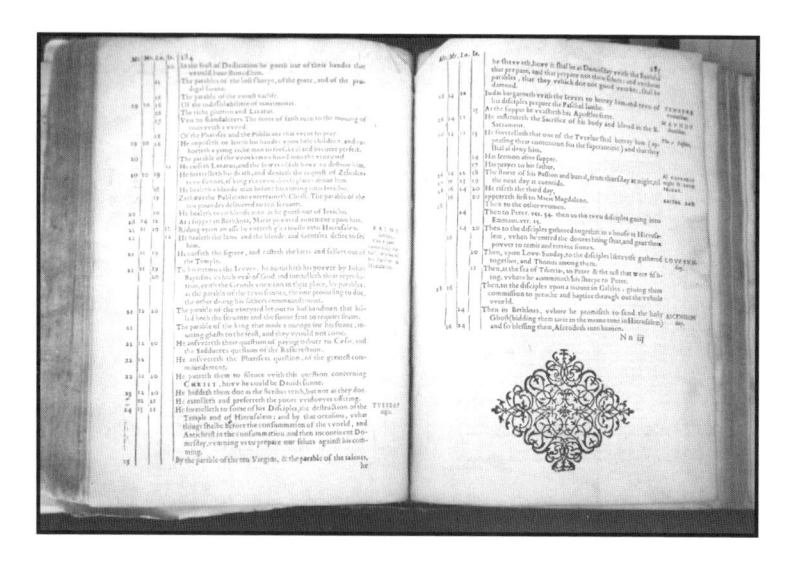

The closing pages of the TABLES.

This picture shows some deterioration starting to creep into the FIRST Vulgate after more than four hundred years of existence. It should be remembered that this Bible was printed just sixty years or so after Christopher Columbus discovered the New World.

INTRODUCTION

The records of St Lactantius (d. 328) and Bishop Ambrose of Milan (333-397), claim that the writings used by the church in their time relayed 'history mixed with religious fanaticism' (*Encyclopedia of the Roman Empire,* Matthew Brunson, 1994, Pg. 241) and their concerns were supported by St Jerome (347-420) in the following century. 'How often,' says Jerome of a monk with whom he argued regularly about the contents of the Gospels, 'he roused me with fury with his zealous talk of the fanciful and not of the fact' (*The Letters of Jerome*, XXII, and repeated in L 4). In unraveling the complex history of New Testament development, this book attempts to disentangle those two opposing aspects, and account for the dualist overlay existing in the Gospels.

By stripping away supernatural elements, the New Testament relays a confused skeletal outline of the lives of two separate men, one materialist, and the other spiritual. This work unravels those stories and shows what the New Testament really is, who wrote it, how it came into being, why it was altered, and how much historical truth it contains. Until now, this aspect of the Gospel story has never been fully developed and by co-coordinating new information with surviving records, a reconstruction of the probable course of events that eventually resulted in the religion of Christianity is presented. This end result establishes that the New Testament is not portrayed for what it really is and reveals why and how the church strived for more than 1600 years to conceal sensitive information about Jesus and his immediate family. This book questions the church's role in presenting the New Testament stories as factual and introduces previously unknown material opposing that position.

When a theologian talks of a 'higher truth'
he is usually trying to conceal a lower falsehood.

Tony Bushby

CHAPTER 1

The biblical evidence of Jesus' twin

It may seem strange to the modern reader that the New Testament provides church evidence that Jesus had a twin brother, and that he was one of the twelve disciples. It is within Christianity's own texts that the most valid argument for the existence of twin boys is found, and centuries of editing have not fully deleted what was originally written. In presenting this argument, I confine my hypothesis to a framework of acknowledged manuscripts and the probabilities and possibilities of information contained within them. What must be remembered in correlating this material is that old writings are the only source of information on Christian origins and that material has been subjected to centuries of variant translations and censorship, and much is confused or lost.

The Gospels of Matthew and Luke narrate that Jesus was the first-born of Mary and Joseph and that he had four brothers and at least two sisters. The Gospels of Mark (6:3) and Matthew (13:55) state that James the Younger, Joses (Joseph), Judas called Thomas (Jude in some later translations) and Simon, are the sons of Virgin Mary and therefore the brothers of Jesus. Although there are frequent attempts to dismiss the significance of this passage on the grounds that 'brothers' can mean friends or associates, there is evidence in the FIRST Vulgate that reveals that 'brothers' means precisely that.

Roman Catholics are obliged to hold the opinion that the brothers and sisters of Jesus were the children of Joseph by a former marriage. This conclusion stemmed from the Gospel of James (*Protevanglium*) that related to the age of Joseph at the birth of Jesus. However, the canonical Gospels state that Joseph had sex with Mary after the birth of Jesus, and a narrative in the Gospel of Matthew saying that Joseph 'knew her not until she had born a son' (Matt 1:25) eliminates church claims that Mary was a perpetual virgin. From references in the Gospels of Mark and Matthew it is clear that the brothers and sisters of Jesus were subsequent children of Mary in the fullest sense.

© Rome Press Bureau. Photo by Lorenzo Bottoli, 1963

Interior of the Basilica of St Paul's Outside-the-Walls in Rome showing the mosaic apse, originally created by Venetian artists in the 16th Century. The domed ceiling portrays Jesus (seated, centre) with his four brothers. The figure to the far right is Judas Thomas who wears a blue robe over a burgundy undergarment identical in every aspect to the design and colour of Jesus' attire.

Since James, Joses, and Simon are the brothers of Jesus, so then is 'Judas called Thomas'. The name Thomas as applied to Judas is a Grecized form of the Aramaic name, Toma or Tomas, a translation meaning 'twin'. The Hebrew form of the name is Teom (*Song of Solomon* 7:14) and corresponds to the English colloquial abbreviation, Tom. In an ancient version of the Syrian

Bible, Thomas is called Tomme (Tommy) Didymus (twin twin) and the Gospel of John (11:16; 20:24 and 21:2) also calls Thomas, 'Didymus', being the Greek word for 'twin', hence 'twin the twin'.

It is therefore a fact of Gospel scholarship that 'Judas called Thomas' is the twin brother of Jesus, and in some older Bibles he is called 'Judas the twin who is also Thomas', and 'Didymus the Twin'. Within these narratives lies a profound truth revealing the substance of historical information that the church has strived for centuries to conceal.

Another canonical text adds to the cover-up. It is a supportable fact that the Epistle of Jude carried in today's version of the New Testament is called the Epistle of Judas in the FIRST English-language Vulgate of 1563. This comparable evidence reveals that sometime after the 16th Century the church changed the title of that Epistle from Judas to Jude, thus subtly removing direct reference to Jesus' twin brother as the possible author of that document. In today's Bibles, the Epistle of Jude begins like this:

> Jude, the servant of Jesus Christ, and the brother of James ...

The same passage in the FIRST Vulgate reads:

> Judas, the double of Jesus Christ, and brother of James, Joses, and Simon ...

It was important for the church that this narrative be falsified or deleted for it unambiguously states that Jesus had a 'double' and four blood brothers, and provides direct support for the same brothers named in the Gospels of Mark and Matthew.

One of the more celebrated early Christian bishops, Eusebius Pamphilius (260-339) of Caesarea, said that the Epistles carrying the names of two of Jesus' brothers, Judas and James, were disputed by early presbyters and considered fictitious. From his records it is known that the Epistle of Judas was initially rejected from the canon because it adopted the preaching of the Book of Enoch, an Essenic writing not officially recognized by the church. After a long and bitter debate about Verse 14 that mentions the Book of Enoch, the Epistle of Judas was included into the Christian canon in 397, some 72 years after it was rejected at the Council of Nicaea in 325.

The discovery of the 'Gospel of the Twin'

Additional evidence for the existence of a twin of Jesus was supported with the 1945-46 discovery of a Coptic translation of the Gospel of Thomas in a sealed funerary urn near Nag Hammadi in Syria. It was one of fifty-two manuscripts bound in thirteen books and now called the Nag Hammadi Scrolls. The cache of writings was found literally 'buried in the desert' after a windstorm had blown away sand and exposed the urn. The academic opinion is that 'these writings may be considered to be wholly Christian in origin and largely based on the earliest Greek Bible' (*Encyclopedia Britannica*, 15th Ed. Pg. 912).

The Gospel of Thomas received its great publicity because of its sometimes-close links with the canonical Gospels and modern synopses of those Gospels often compares the parallels to Thomas. But, unlike the canonical Gospels, it is void of both narration and any discernible outline, and suggests a more mysterious route to enlightenment. It is composed of 114 sayings (or *logia*) and the possibility that Jesus knew some of the sayings it preserves is generally conceded. The church claims that this collection of mystical sayings was assembled sometime around the mid-Second Century under the pseudonym of Didymus Judas Thomas (Twin Judas Twin). However, a later chapter in this book adds new light to the origin of this Gospel and reveals that it was in circulation much earlier in the First Century.

It appears that the original collection of sayings was theologically neutral but went through an evolutionary process until it received its name and the sayings recorded in it applied to Jesus. After the laborious task of comparing the Gospel of Thomas with sayings of Jesus in the canonical Gospels, some researchers concluded that it was the template or model for the original version of the Gospel of Mark, the first canonical Gospel written (*Catholic Encyclopedia*, Vol. vi, 657). Like the Gospel of Thomas, the oldest version of the Gospel of Mark available today is void of descriptions of a virgin birth and resurrection of Jesus Christ.

The Gospel of Thomas (Tomas) was originally called the Gospel of the Twin (*The Wisdom of the Ancients*, Sir Francis Bacon, 1619, reprint by Berington, 1894), and within it, Judas Thomas is regularly identified as 'Judas Thomas the Twin'. The references are consistent and a narrative recording that 'the people united their adoration of the two persons called Christ' has tremendous implications for the church and its current presentation of the Gospels. Not surprisingly, the Gospel of Thomas (Tomas), the Gospel of Peter, and other early manuscripts referencing Jesus' twin brother, were suppressed after the first ecclesiastical council at Nicaea in 325 (*Edict of Constantine*).

© Author's own photo, 2005

This is an ancient Latin version of the Gospel of the Twin showing hand binding with leather straps and the good condition of the book. This Gospel records a discussion between Jesus and Tomas (Thomas), his twin brother, and argues for the immortality of the soul.

One thing is for sure; whoever wrote the Gospel of Thomas was an Initiate into the Ancient Mysteries, and was in possession of secret knowledge. It's introductory pages state that it is 'an arcane writing' (*Prologue, Gospel of Thomas*) and for that reason it would more aptly be called the Gospel of Hidden Knowledge, for it reveals various secret teachings of the Ancient Mystery

Schools. The Gospel opens with a short statement advising readers that it is composed of 'secret words' that were collected and transmitted by Didymus Judas Thomas (Twin Judas Twin), and persons 'who find the interpretation of these sayings will not taste death' (*Gospel of Thomas,* 1:1). That profound statement immediately suggests that the Gospel holds some form of sacred intention and its clues to the existence of an immortal status within humans has been revealed in a previous book by this author, *The Secret in the Bible* (Tony Bushby, Joshua Books, 2003). Much of the terminology of the Gospel of Thomas centres around the mysterious Kingdom of God, so cryptically referred to in both the canonical Gospels and the Dead Sea Scrolls. This important aspect of the Gospel of Thomas will have greater significance in later chapters for both Jesus and his twin claimed to know the 'Secret of the Kingdom of God'.

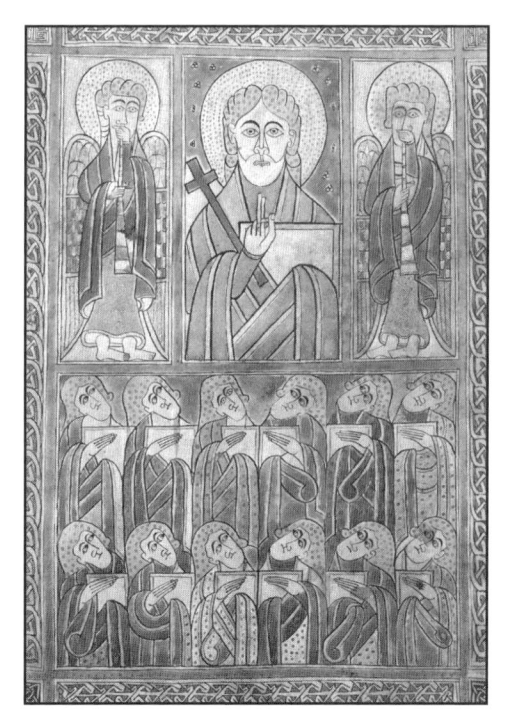

© Mrs Lucy Ogilvie's Collection

Keeping one's mouth shut. The frontispiece of one version of the Gospel of Thomas shows twins standing either side of Jesus covering their mouths with their hands, implying that they are withholding secret 'twin' knowledge.

The 'twin brother of Christ' is again recorded elsewhere

The issue of 'Judas the Twin' was further clarified in the Acts of Thomas *(Acta Thomae)*, known to scholars in both Greek and Syriac prior to the Nag Hammadi discovery. The Acts of Thomas is a long story filled with picaresque details, and is one of the most readable and intrinsically interesting writings of early Christianity. It bears the unmistakable signs of Gnostic origins and is generally believed to have been composed in Edessa by a Syrian scribe named Bardesanes (154-222) (*Homily on the Life of a Pilgrim,* Ephraem the Syrian, CPG 1, 1152-1155, TLG 1214). If the place of its origin was really Edessa, as others for sound reasons supposed (*Chronologie,* ii, 172), this would lend considerable probability to the statement explicitly made in the document saying that the remains of Judas Thomas had been brought from the East, a point clarified in a later chapter.

In the Greek version the author's name is given in two variants. At first he is named as 'Judas, who is also called Thomas', and later, also in the first chapter, he is called 'Judas Thomas who is also called Didymus'. These writings have been compared to the Coptic versions discovered in 1945, and all editions contain this narrative that refers to …

> … the twin brother of Christ, apostle to the most high and fellow Initiate into the hidden word of Christ who does receive his secret sayings.

The Acts of Thomas presents 'Thomas as Judas Thomas, that is Judas the Twin' and also 'Te'oma Christ' (twin Christ). It provides other references to twinship, with this example: 'The eleventh act introduces Thomas' twin, the other Didymus, as an identical twin who is the lord himself' (*Encyclopedia of Early Christianity,* Everett Ferguson, 1990, Pg. 899-900). Another statement narrates an incident where Jesus appeared to a young man who 'saw the Lord Jesus in the likeness of the apostle Judas Thomas'. Jesus then called out: 'I am not Judas the Twin who is also Thomas, I am his brother'.

A fragment of parchment believed to be from an earlier version of the Acts of Thomas, records Jesus saying, 'Greetings Twin, and my second messiah', and that the populous 'saw as two beings, one single Royal token consisting of two halves' (112:80), a statement supported by references to two messiahs in the Old Testament and the Dead Sea Scrolls. In thirty-three separate narratives, the Acts of Thomas presents Judas Thomas as the twin brother of the one the church now calls Jesus Christ (cap. 31, pg. 148). An intriguing narrative also preserved in the Acts of Thomas refers to Mary as 'the one who art mother of twin young ones; come forward Hidden Mother', and in a Fifth Century Syrian Bible she is called *Gemellipara,* which is Latin for 'mother of twins' (*Diderot's Encyclopedia,* 1759).

Another ancient writing in the Thomas tradition is called the 'Book of Thomas, the Contender', and it also forms part of the Nag Hammadi corpus. In that writing Judas Thomas is explicitly called Jesus' 'brother', 'double', and 'my twin and true companion' (138:7f; 138:19f).

In addition to these three documents, there is another writing that the church accredits to the authorship of Judas Thomas. It is called, *Evangelium Joannis de obitu Mariae,* that is, the 'Message of John Concerning the Death of Mary', and this book refers to Judas Thomas as 'the twin brother of Jesus the Most High' and 'Thomas, the one they call the Lord's twin'.

When referring to the Gospel of Thomas, the Acts of Thomas, the Book of Thomas, and the Message of John Concerning the Death of Mary, the *Catholic Encyclopedia* comments:

> His name (Judas Tomas/Thomas) is the starting point of a considerable apocryphal literature, and there are also certain historical data which suggests that some of this apocryphal material contains germs of truth. (*Catholic Encyclopedia,* Vol. XIV, 1912, Pg. 658)

In presenting this thesis, one must remember that the church, in a Decree of the Council of Trent in 1547, proclaimed the apocryphal writings as the true word of God. Unused Christian manuscripts were never declared 'un-canonical' but in stark contrast, the Council decreed that all apocryphal literature was of authority equal with books in the New Testament. The church admits that the writings carrying the name of Thomas contain elements of 'truth' about his life, and this reference bears unintended witness to the accuracy of the premise being developed in this book.

© Byzantine Art (Icons of Constantinople, 1972)

This Fifth Century mosaic is in the Imperial Palace at Constantinople and is titled, 'Joseph with Jesus and the Geminius', meaning literally, 'the twin'. The raven sitting on the arm of the front boy is the symbol of an initiate in some ancient Mystery Schools, and the camel locates them in Egypt.

A crucial fact to be remembered when discussing these old writings is that the texts in which Judas Thomas appears as Jesus' twin were once accepted works of scripture and widely used by early presbyters in Western congregations (*History of the Christian Church*, Dr. Schaff). This means that during the establishment years of Christianity, the idea of twinship was perfectly acceptable, and with the naivety of the times, the birth of identical twins was seen by the common populace as a miraculous and fascinating event (*Cult of the Heavenly Twins,* Rendel Harris, 1906). A multiple birth was regarded as a supernatural occurrence, one of divine origin. 'Once upon a time, in Myth, twins signified whatever dualisms a culture entertained; mortal/immortal; good/evil; creation/destruction; light/dark; day/night; it is what they believed in their minds' (*Natural History*, Pliny the Elder, Book 6). The writings of First Century classical Roman historian, Publius Cornelius Tacitus

(c. 56-126), record the birth of twins to Livilla (d. 31 AD) and Drusus (d. 23 AD), the son of Emperor Tiberius, as 'a rare event' that 'so delighted the Emperor that he did not refrain from boasting before the senators' (*Annals,* 11, 84).

Had the writings under the name of Thomas been included in the canonical collection today, Christianity would accept the twinship of Jesus. Also to be borne in mind is the fact that the Gospel of Thomas, the Acts of Thomas, the Book of Thomas, and the Message of John Concerning the Death of Mary, all escaped centuries of editing that were applied to the canonical Gospels, a claim supportable by simply comparing an old Bible with a new version. However, whatever editing the Gospels have undergone, the evidence is still there to be uncovered. Simply put, the canonical writings say that Jesus had a brother called Judas Thomas (Tomas) who was somebody's twin, for the Gospel of John adds, 'Judas Thomas, one of the twelve, called the Twin' (John 20:24).

One reason for understanding that Jesus had a twin brother lies in the fact that it was obviously a true story, for there was no advantage to be gained by ancient scribes inventing and compiling such extensive Gospel documentation around a false account. From church texts it can be established that during the developmental period of Christianity, Judas Thomas of the Gospels was considered not only Jesus' blood brother, but also his identical twin. Six centuries later, Islamic tradition maintained that the face of Judas Thomas 'was the same as that of Jesus, his double brother, who preached on behalf of the two'. Mohammad (520-632), the founder of Islam, quoted this ancient knowledge as 'Hadîs' … being traditional Islamic understanding. The one incontrovertible aspect of the matter is that the church tried to conceal the fact that the name Tomas (Thomas) is Greek for 'twin' and is still recorded as such in ancient Greek Bibles. The availability of the FIRST Vulgate, the unraveling of the coded secrets of a Knights Templar initiate, coupled with the release of ancient documentation from the Cumbrian monastery, reinstates Judas Tomas the Twin (Thomas today) to his true place within the Gospel accounts, and within history.

CHAPTER 2

The boyhood of the twins

It is known with certainty that Jesus is mentioned in writings external to church documentation. Rabbinic records, for example, are of great importance in determining Christian origins and provide invaluable, and conflicting information about circumstances surrounding the birth and death of Jesus. The Talmud enshrines within its pages Jewish oral law and is divided into two parts, the Mishna and the Gemara, but those writings do not mention Judas Thomas because he was outside the rabbinic establishment. The first document discusses such subjects as festivals and sacred things, and the Gemara is basically a commentary on these subjects. When the Talmud was written is not really known, with some authorities suggesting a date of 150-160, while others say 450. However, it will be shown in a later chapter that it was not written until after the Council of Nicaea in 325 but existed in oral tradition. Unfortunately, the Talmud received major editing by church censors (see Chapter 33) in the 16th Century, but some unedited copies survived, and they provide information about Jesus that needs to be discussed.

A common appellation for Jesus in the Talmud is Yeshu'a ben Panthera, the outcome of a widespread Jewish belief during the earliest centuries that he was the result of an illegitimate union between his mother Mary and a Roman soldier named Tiberius Julius Abdes Panthera, Panthera being the latinized version of 'Panther'. Panthera's existence was confirmed by the discovery of a tombstone at Bingerbruck in Germany with the engraving etched in the stone reading:

Tiberius Julius Abdes Panthera, an archer, native of Sidon, Phoenicia, who in

9AD was transferred to service in Rhineland (Germany). (*Jesus the Magician,* Professor Morton Smith, San Francisco, 1978; Also, *Dea. Lea.* 1973-1974)

This find added fuel to the theory that Jesus was the illegitimate son of Mary and Panthera, and *The Bible Fraud* (Tony Bushby, 2001) unlocked the coded word, 'Abdes'. Classical scholar Professor Morton Smith described the tombstone as possibly 'our only genuine relic of the holy family' (*Jesus the Magician,* San Francisco, 1978) and added that 'for the benefit of the non-Jewish reader it should be addressed by the church'.

© Film Library of Bad Kreuznach Museum, West Germany

What remains of the Bingerbruck tombstone.

In addition to the array of Jewish references to the Panthera attachment to Jesus' name, additional references are found in Christian writings. Celsus (c. 178), a well-informed late Second Century historian and author, was an acknowledged expert on the presbyter's writings, and wrote a now-lost book called *The True Discourse*. His sense of fair play won the respect and admiration of many of his contemporaries and Roman Emperors sought his advise on matters of religion. Many copies had been previously created from this work, and among the churchmen known to have read and studied them were Bishop Eusebius (*Ecclesiastical History*) and St. Augustine *(City of God)*. Some 40 years after Celsus' death an early presbyter, Origen of Alexandria (185-251), at the request of his friend, Ambrosias, wrote a refutation against the charges of Celsus called *Against Celsus*. The elaborate works consisted of eight books that took years to write and were eventually completed by persons unknown nearly 70 years after Celsus' death. But Origen's attempts to dispel the accusations of Celsus failed and the only remedy that could be found was to destroy the writings of Celsus themselves. However, about 90% of *The True Discourse* was reconstructed by Jackman (1836) and Keim (1873) using extracts, arguments and whole pages found so carefully cited word-for-word in Origen's condemnation. Origen reproduced the following verse about Mary from Celsus' records:

> Mary was turned out by her husband, a carpenter by profession, after she had been convicted of unfaithfulness with Panthera. Cut off by her spouse, she gave birth to Jesus, a bastard; that Jesus, on account of his poverty was hired out to go to Egypt; that while there he acquired certain magical powers which Egyptians pride themselves on possessing. (*Contra Celsus*, 1:28, Origen)

In a following passage (*Contra Celsus*, 1:32, Origen), Origen again added that the paramour of the mother of Jesus was 'a soldier called Panthera', an accusation he repeated in verse 1:69, sentences erased from the oldest Vatican manuscripts and other codices under Christian control (*Origen Contra Celsus*, Lommatzech, Berlin 1845), but recorded in Jackman and Keim's reconstruction.

The records of St. Epiphanius, Bishop of Salamis (315-403) confirmed the Panthera story, and his information is startling. This champion of Christian orthodoxy and saint of Roman Catholicism frankly stated that 'Jesus was the son of a certain Julius whose surname was Panthera' (*Heresies*, lxxvii, 7, Epiphanius). This is an extraordinary declaration recorded as accepted ancient history in Christian writings and is called by the church today, the 'Riddle of Epiphanius'. The Panthera legend was so widespread that these two early churchmen, Origen and St Epiphanius, inserted the name in the genealogies of Jesus and Mary some two and three centuries after the Gospel time of Jesus Christ. Enlarging on their statements is this passage from the Talmud: 'Rabbi Shiemon ben Azzai has said: I found in Jerusalem a book of genealogies; therein was written that Such-an-one (Jesus) is the bastard son of an adulteress' (*Jebamoth,* 49A). 'Such-an-one' is a well-known substitute for the name of Jesus in the Talmud, as has been proved and admitted on either side (*Jewish Encyclopedia*). Shiemon ben Azzai flourished at the end of the First and beginning of the Second Century and was one of four famous Rabbis, who, according to Talmudic tradition, 'entered Paradise' (He knew, and used, the Secret in the Bible). He was a Chassid, one of the pious Jews of Palestine, and most probably an Essene. He remained a celibate and rigid ascetic until his death.

The father of the twins

Roman Emperor Augustus (27 BC-14 AD) hoped to be succeeded by one of his grandsons but they both died before him. In 4 AD, Augustus lost his favourite nephew, Gaius, the son of Julia and Agrippa, who died as a result of battle wounds. This was the probable motive for the adoption of Tiberius, Augustus's stepson, into the House of Caesar in that same year. Tiberius subsequently succeeded Augustus and reigned as Emperor for 23 years. The Roman historian Tacitus has left a lurid and repulsive picture of Tiberius, but as far as the Roman Empire was concerned, Tiberius fulfilled and made permanent the work of Augustus.

© British Museum

Left: This bronze coin struck shortly after his death shows the deified Emperor Augustus wearing a crown of thorns. Right coin: Emperor Tiberius. The superscription reads, 'Tiberius Caesar Augustus, son of the deified Augustus'. In the mindset of the time, Tiberius was officially called the 'son of God'.

The inscription on the Bingerbruck headstone is interpreted as describing 'Tiberius Julius' with the nickname of Panthera, or Panther. The conclusion reached is that the name fully represented Tiberius Julius Claudius Nero (14 BC-37AD) who became Emperor of Rome in the year 14. Mary, as a young woman, was resident in Rome with her mother, Bernice, and was living in Augustus' palace (*Encyclopedia Judaica*, Vol. 8, Ed. Cecil Roth, Jerusalem, 1974). It is possible that she was a Temple virgin acting on behalf of Augustus as part of his drive to restore old values and Religious Orders. This premise concludes that Tiberius raped Mary in the palace on his return from a crusade, and from that encounter she bore twin sons (*The Bible Fraud*, Tony Bushby, Joshua Books, Australia, 2001). Rape was a common event and soldiers were notorious for their treatment of young women. Under the Law of Moses, a betrothed virgin who had sex with any man during the period of her betrothal was to be stoned to death by the men of the city (Deut. 22:21) unless she could prove her innocence (*Commentaries on the Law of Moses,* Jonathon D. Michaelis, 4 Vols. 1814), and it seems that Mary was able to do that.

For centuries, ecclesiastical scholars have discussed at length why Jesus was regularly called Panthera but no satisfactorily explanation has been given for the appellation. In many cases a name was a reflection of that person's character or occupation and that was the case with Tiberius Julius Claudius Nero's pseudonym, Panther. Panther was attached to Tiberius because of his association with a secret society known as the House of the Panthers, and one of his twin sons, Jesus, subsequently joined that House by initiation, and also received the appellation of Panther.

Another name given to Jesus in the Talmud

There was another, lesser-known name Jesus was called during those years and that was 'Yeshu'a ben Stada', meaning, 'son of Stada'. This name is recorded in the records of the Sanhedrin and also in the Talmud. What can also be found in the Gemara, and has embarrassed Christian authorities for centuries, is this statement:

> Yeshu'a Ben Stada was Ben Panthera, Rabbi Chisda said; The husband was Stada, the lover Panthera. Another said; the husband was Paphos ben Jehuda; Stada was Yeshu'a ben Panthera's mother … and she was unfaithful to her husband.(*Babylonian Shabbath,* 104 b, repeated in almost identical words in the *Babylonian Sanhedrin,* 67 a)

These apparently contradictory assertions can be ironed out when read in context … Stada was Yeshu'a ben Panthera's (Jesus') mother, and Panthera was his father.

Mary's story paralleled in old scroll

The name 'ben Stada' attached to Jesus is found paralleled in the ancient Mehgheehlla Scroll, discovered in a Genizah by Russian physician D. B. de Waltoff near Lake Tiberius in 1882, and now called the Safed Scroll. This old text relays the story of twin brothers called Yeshai and Judas ben Halachmee who were the illegitimate sons of a fifteen-year-old girl named Stadea. The name ben Halachmee was that of Stadea's later husband, not the biological father of her sons. Unfortunately, no mention is made of the real father's name but ben Halachmee was the adopted name given to Stadea's twin boys. The closeness of the name Stada in the Talmud to Stadea in the Safed Scroll is extraordinary and the slight difference in spelling is a variation in translation. 'The name Stada has various forms and may have been borrowed from a fanciful name that meant a scholar; or had a regional identity like Stabiae or Statila, a woman of good family' (*The Name of the Furies*, Eumenides).

According to the Safed Scroll, Yeshai and Judas ben Halachmee were taken in, raised and educated by the religious order of Essene monks. The Essenes were a perennial Jewish colony that flourished in particularly Judea around the time ascribed to the New Testament stories. Pliny the Elder in his book *Natural History* described them as 'a race by themselves, more remarkable than any other in this wide world'. An older Essene named Joseph was assigned as their 'religious father', guardian, and trustee. Subsequently one boy became a student of Rabbi Hillel's school of philosophy and the other, the leader of the Essenes. Additionally, the Safed Scroll mirrors aspects of the story in the Gospels and provides external evidence that the conclusion reached in this volume was known in ancient tradition.

Ignoble birth in a noble house

According to Jewish writings, Stada was 'the descendant of princes and rulers' (*Babylonian Sanhedrin,* 106 a) and her royal heritage directly links her as being one and the same as Mary of the Gospels. In Hebrew and Roman tradition of the times, people's names 'often appear in distorted form, particularly in rabbinic literature', and were sometimes an attempt to disguise the true personality of the person in discussion (*Mary in the Babylonian Talmud*, G.R.S. Mead, BA, MRAS, London & Benares, 1903). This type of understanding provides the key to researchers that enables them to unlock the true essence of who is being referred to in ancient writings, particularly the Gospels. For example, the name of Herodias in the New Testament is simply the female derivative of Herodes, or, 'of the family of Herod'.

The Bible Fraud revealed that Mary of the Gospels was of noble birth through her grandfather King Herod (c 73-4 BC) and grandmother Mariamne 1. Herod himself descended from a noble line of kings through his Nabatean mother, Cypros of Petra. The Nabateans were a Semitic people and the earliest sources regarded them as Arabs. Today they are generally referred to as the Nabatean Arabs. Owing to its secure location, the Nabatean kings adopted Petra as their capital city that became incorporated into the Roman Empire in 106. The Nabatean Arabs passed out of history with the advent of Islam (*Encyclopedia Judaica Jerusalem,* 1971, Pg. 740-744) in the Seventh Century. The House of Herod was founded by the marriage of Cypros of Petra to Antipater (Antipas), the Idumean, to whom Cypros bore four sons, Herod being one. The name Herod subsequently became the title of seven rulers mentioned in the New Testament and in Roman history.

Mary, and thus Judas Thomas and Jesus, had a bloodline connection to the Nabatean Arabs through her grandmother, Cypros of Petra. Curiously enough, another Arabic tradition in Jesus' family is recorded in the *Book of the Nativity of John* (the Baptist). John's mother, Elizabeth, 'hurried outside veil-less … and for this she received a bill of divorcement' (*The Book of the Nativity of John,* Hugh J. Schonfield, 1929, Pg. 35).

Gospels confirm Mary's unexpected pregnancy

The New Testament states that Joseph returned from a long trip of some months to Galilee with the intention of marrying Mary. The Gospels of Matthew and Luke narrate that they were 'betrothed' before Joseph's departure, that being the equivalent of 'engagement' in modern-day terminology. However, upon his return, it was plainly apparent that Mary 'was with child' (Luke 2:5) and it 'could not be hid from Joseph'. The Gospel of Matthew elaborates upon his sad feelings when he saw the violated condition of his bride-to-be, and being unwilling to defame her, privately discussed ending their engagement (Matt. 1:19). From the Gospel description, it is clear that Joseph was not the biological father of Mary's twins and the church agreed, adding that, in truth, there never was an 'immaculate' conception of Mary (*Catholic Encyclopedia*, 1914, Vol. 15th, Pg. 451; *New Catholic Encyclopedia*, 1967 Ed. Vol. xiv, Pg. 693). The conclusion, therefore, is that Judas Thomas and Jesus were conceived in the usual human way and despite all the grandeur that has been created around the arrival of the Gospel Jesus Christ, the twins of the New Testament arrived as any other flesh-and-blood Roman boys. The latest printing of the Oxford Bible (1995) agrees, for it calls Jesus, 'the human one'.

CHAPTER 3

Twins raised by the Essenes

Drawing upon the information provided in the Safed Scroll, the pregnant Mary went to the Bethlehem Essene community until the time of the birth of her sons. Groups of Essenes existed 'all over, as they were a very numerous sect' (*Bible Myths,* T. W. Doane, 1882, Pg. 431) and lived in country areas as well as cities. They maintained mainly secluded communities throughout the whole of the Roman occupied territory 'and in every town the Order had its respective 'house' (*Antiquities,* Josephus).

The sect was inspired into existence specifically to preserve secret information encoded into the Torah. They formulated a definite mystical understanding of some aspects of the Bible that paved the way for a far different understanding of the scriptures to that which is presented today. They cast a veil of secrecy over what they considered of the highest religious importance and concealed under the threat of death the hidden information in both the Torah and the Book of Enoch. They were guardians of hidden biblical knowledge and preserved that understanding in a coded alphabet in 'secret books'. The central aspect of their literature was its pre-occupation with prophecy and it is recorded they had an uncanny ability to successfully predict future events. Philo, the First Century Alexandrian philosopher, historian and statesman, compared them not only with the Persian Magi but also with the Indian Yogis.

Some researchers explain the Greek name Essenes as meaning the 'Silent Ones' and others as signifying 'Healers', and assert the term means 'Pious'. Some call them Seers, Performers of the Law, Retired Ones, Men of Essa,

Stout Ones, Mysterious Ones, Daily Baptists and Apron-Wearers. In the latter respect, echoes of the Essene beliefs can be found in the rituals of the Masons today. Josephus (b. 37 AD) records they 'don a white apron' before their ceremonies after which they 'then take them off, which they consider sacred clothes'.

With what is known about the Essenes, any of these names could be successfully applied. The oldest research papers variously call them Therapeutes, Physicians, Ascetics, Monks, and Ecclesiastics, which are but different names for one and the selfsame sect. The researchers best qualified explain the word Essene is nothing more than the Egyptian word for that of which Therapeute is the Greek, signifying the character of the Ascetic sect of Ecclesiastic monks as professing to the practice of healing (*Bible Myths,* T. W. Doane, 1882, Pg. 424-425).

The blood relatives of Mary

Essene missionaries established stations or colonies in Rome, Corinth, Galatia, Phillippi, Colosse and Thessalonica, and at Ephesus they had a well-established 'College of Essenes' (*Anacalypis,* Godfrey Higgins, Vol. 1, Pg. 747 and Vol. ii, Pg. 34). They also maintained at least one settlement in the Qumran area by the Dead Sea and others in Jerusalem, Antioch, Bethlehem, Damascus and Mount Carmel. 'They had a flourishing university, or corporate body, established on these principles, at Alexandria in Egypt, long before the period assigned for the birth of Jesus Christ. From this body they sent out missionaries, and had established colonies, auxiliary branches, and affiliated communities, in various cities of Asia Minor, where colonies were in a flourishing condition before the preaching of Paul. They also resided in monasteries on the lake of Parembole (or Maria) also in Egypt' (*Anacalypis,* Godfrey Higgins, Vol. 1, Pg. 747, and Vol. ii, Pg. 34; also, *Ecclesiastical History,* Eusebius, lib. 2, Chp. xvii). The Essene movement was connected to the Hasmonean bloodline through the High Priest, Mattathias (c. 166 BC), and father of the military king, Judas Maccabeus (c. 160 BC). The male offspring of the House of Herod were forced into circumcision during the reign of John Hyrcanus (c. 135-104 BC), a Hasmonean of the earlier Maccabean period. In other words, the Herod family adopted the religion of Judaism.

Towards the Essenes, King Herod the Great was favorable, maybe because they made it their invariable practice to refrain from disobedience to the political authority. Philo said they had never clashed with any ruler of Palestine, however tyrannical, up to his own lifetime in the mid-First Century. This was a passive attitude that could not fail to commend itself to Herod, and he even went so far as to exempt the Essenes, like the Pharisees, from the oath of loyalty to himself. It was due to their solidarity and the family affinity that the young Mary had her twin boys secretly raised within their community. The Essene hierarchy were her blood relatives and expounded similar principles and traditions to the Herodian philosophy. Contemporary writers, Josephus, Philo and Pliny, estimated their numbers at four thousand persons in the Palestine area during the First Century. Except when toiling in the fields, they dressed invariably in white linen robes. From the almost unanimous accounts of those three historians, it is possible to make virtually a complete reconstruction of the life and conceptions of the Essenes.

> They perpetrated their sect by adopting children ... above all the Essenes were the educators of the nobility, their instruction being varied and extensive. They cultivated obedience, truthfulness, continence, justice and temperance. The initiated members ate alone. They laid claim to magical powers and the ability to predict ... it is enough to say that between Essenism in certain aspects and Christianity there are some points of resemblance. (*Catholic Encyclopedia*, Vol. V. 1909. Pg. 546-547; also, Josephus, *Jewish Wars*, 11, 120)

They were generally celibates although Josephus indicates that they were divided within themselves and there was one particular sect that accepted a kind of marriage between men and women.

A damning statement

The discovery of the Dead Sea Scrolls found in caves at Qumran in 1947 was epoch-making because they included Old Testament texts dating back to the 3rd Century BC and covering the period up to the year 68. These are the oldest known copies of the scriptures and they revealed to analysts how many of the scribes who originally wrote them felt free to amend them at their own discretion. Interpolations were added directly to texts and without insert marks rather than footnotes or marginal glosses. The knowledge of these changes should concern those people who believe the texts to be the direct and sacred expressions of the words of God.

© Grollenberg

Qumran, looking east to the Dead Sea. This photo was taken in 1944 and before the discovery of the Dead Sea Scrolls in the dark cliffs in the foreground. Down lower, in the middle of the 'V', can be seen the remains of the Essene monastery and some nearby tents for archaeological exploration. The Jordan enters at the extreme left.

The weight of scholarship heavily supports the opinion that the Dead Sea Scrolls were products of the Essenes, although Christian apologists debate this point. It is possible that these writings were compiled (or stored) in various settlements and moved to the Dead Sea caves from other areas for protection and preservation. It is not improbable to suggest that the manuscripts were deposited in the Dead Sea area as late as 132 by the Jewish leader Simeon bar Cochba, but the general opinion is the oldest and largest of the three separate discoveries was hidden for safe keeping when the destruction of the Qumran settlement seemed imminent, sometime shortly before the beginning of the Jewish War in 66.

It has long been known there was information in the Dead Sea Scrolls damning to Christian beliefs and the church's high-level involvement with interpreting the Scrolls fostered a grave element of suspicion. Since the Scrolls were found some six decades ago, close associates of the Vatican were placed in dominant positions in every phase of the investigation and translation of the Scrolls. Priests regulated the flow of information and controlled its release. Michael Baigent and Richard Leigh discovered during research for their work, *The Dead Sea Scroll Deception* (Corgi 1992), just 'how fiercely the world of orthodox biblical scholarship was prepared to fight to retain its monopoly of available information'.

The first public access to the Dead Sea Scrolls was given in 1991 and they revealed to the world that nowhere in the cache is Jesus Christ or the Christian church mentioned. Probably the most explosive narrative (4, Q246) was that referring to the Teacher of Righteousness saying, 'He will be called son of God, and they will call him son of the Most High ... His kingdom will be an eternal kingdom' (*The Dead Sea Scrolls Uncovered*, Eisenman and Wise, Pg. 70). The existence of this narrative was kept a closely guarded secret for 32 years, and was known only to the church's team of scholars, but withheld from the public.

Neither is the term 'Essene' found in the Dead Sea Scrolls, for the Qumran community never referred to itself by that name but they did use a number of Aramaic terms. From this evidence, it is clear that the Community did not have a single definite name for itself although the term 'Ebronites' (or Ebionites, in some translations) is recorded in the later-dated scroll discoveries. These particular writings were found in the ruins of a Byzantine monastery further up the hills from the oldest and largest collection of Qumran (*The Dead Sea Scrolls*, Documents of the Jewish Christian sect of Ebionites, The Journal of Jewish Studies, Vol. ii, No. 2 (1951), J. L. Teicher).

The Essene's two messiahs
The book of the Community Rule from the Dead Sea Scrolls introduces the Essene belief of messiahs ... in the plural. This is strikingly similar to the two messiahs recorded in the Acts of Thomas and the 'two anointed ones' in the Old Testament book of Zechariah (4:14). In the context of the tradition of the time, 'messiah' does not signify what it later came to mean in Christian

preaching. It simply meant a leader, 'an anointed one', an actual or expected liberator of an oppressed people or country.

According to the Community Rule, members of the Essenes were obliged to adhere zealously to the Law of Moses 'until there shall come the prophet and the messiahs of Aaron and Israel', real or imagined. This reference is interpreted as meaning two distinct messiahs, two equally regal figures, one descended from the biblical line of Aaron, Moses' older brother, and one from the line of Israel; i.e. the biblical line of David and Solomon. In the Damascus Document there are three additional references to the expectation of two messiahs. Certain Dead Sea Scrolls' scholars expurgated these perplexing references, not knowing what to make of a plurality of messiahs, and dropped the plural endings to bring the texts into conformity with Christian concepts. The ancient belief of two messiahs constituted such a challenge to modern orthodox Christian scholarship that they were conveniently explained away.

With the birth of royal twins in the Essene community it is taken that Judas Thomas and Jesus were seen as the two anticipated messiahs, and thus fulfillment of the Essenic messianic expectations. It is concluded that Tiberius and Mary's twins were formally adopted by Augustus, circa 4-8 AD (*The Bible Fraud*, Tony Bushby, Joshua Books, Australia, 2001) and became members of the House of Caesar. Augustus was deified after his death and, in the Roman mindset, the young Caesars were legally called, 'the sons of God'. At the age of sixteen, the twins received their 'Toga Virilius', and left the Essene community. Judas Thomas subsequently moved to Galilee, while Jesus resided at Jerusalem, and later, for a time, in Egypt and Britain. From the twin concepts of Essenic writings, Judas theoretically became a reflection of the Wicked Priest, and Jesus, the Teacher of Righteousness. Judas Thomas' haunts were the red-light districts where he mixed with pimps, prostitutes and publicans, whileas Jesus entered the world of esoteric learning and spiritual teaching.

The premise for the conclusion reached in this work is that, although illegitimate, the twins were of royal birthright and legitimate contenders to the throne of Palestine and the Emperorship of Rome. Gospel appellations such as 'king of the Jews' and the 'son of God' are rightful titles because of the tradition of the time and the identities of the mother and father. There is a solid basis for such an image in the wording of the Gospels, and a wealth of commentary exists with which to work. Over thirty narratives in the New Testament refer to the twins being 'born a king' (Matt.2: 2) and this book dissects their individual life stories. Nathanael said to Jesus, 'You are the King of Israel' (John 1:49), but there is no record in world history of Jesus ever being a king. Surely King Jesus' existence would have been of immense significance to Israelite history. So why then a blank page?

CHAPTER 4

The names of the twins

It is possible to establish that Judas Thomas and Jesus were historical personages, and that Judas was the first-born. By combining First Century Roman records with New Testament narratives, extracts from the Dead Sea Scrolls, and the de-coded secret ciphers of a 16th Century Knights Templar initiate, their Roman names can be determined, and that provides evidence for a serious and penetrating analysis of the entire Christian story. The problem of unraveling the composite nature of the New Testament is compounded by the fact that Judas Thomas and Jesus had several subsidiary names supplanted on them in the course of their lives, a custom dating back to ancient Egypt. Osiris, for example, had well over 200 divine titles, and the name-giving function carried through into the Bible, with many examples provided. Jacob became Israel; Abram became Abraham; Joseph became Zaphenath; Hoshea became Joshua; Simon became Peter; Saul became Paul; and another Joseph became Barsabbas. Antiochus, King of Syria (d. c. 163 BC), adopted the surname of Epiphanes, and the acceptance of these name changes provides a certain amount of confusion. 'Names research' is an open-ended and complex domain, and one that is particularly greedy of the researcher's time. However, in summary, tradition of the time provided for a multiplicity of names, made up of Prenomens, Nomens, and Cognomens, Agnomens, sobriquets, honorary, clan, and tribal names, and it is possible to determine the variant names of the twins.

The linguistic evolution of names

Personal names were gradually assimilated from one culture to another; eg, the Celtic *Godofrido* becomes the English Geoffrey, or Jeffrey. That was the case with the divergent names of both Judas Thomas and Jesus, and over the centuries they developed a multiplicity of different designations. The ancient forms of a name are often uncertain and different dialect pronunciations have led to divergent spellings of the same name. The social pressure to use a standard spelling did not emerge until the 18th Century and earlier writers saw no problem presenting a person's name in a variety of ways. In one study, for example, over one hundred and thirty variants of the name 'Mainwaring' were found among the parchments belonging to that family (*The Rectification of Names*, E. S. Burt, Mentor Books, New York, 1949).

People's names interact with every other aspect of human life in society, and they can be understood only if considered in relation to society. With ancient Hebrew, Greek, Christian and Jewish names, it is difficult to be exactly sure of the real names of many characters with which we are dealing, and many irregularities arise. Sometimes a new name was afterwards substituted for the original one, just as Plato was originally called Aristocles (427-347 BC), and Buddha was Siddhartha Gautama Sariputta Sakyas (560 BC). In other cases restrictions or alterations were made to the names of people after they had died, thus orator Marcus Tullius Tiro became Cicero (106-43 BC) and Roman poet, Publius Maro, became Virgil (70-19 BC). In a similar manner, the Jewish name of the historian Joseph ben Matthias (b. 37 AD) became Titus Flavius Josephus when he took Roman citizenship late in life. Today we call him Josephus, the most acknowledged historian of the time, and one who wrote extensively on Roman history.

The allocation of names was unlike today's Western procedure and a great many were purposely compounded with the names of Caesars, deities, gods, and hybrid variations, such as Herodotus, Diogenes, Apollonius, and Diana at Antinious (ILS. 7212). In some cases a name was a reflection of that person's character and was applied as a description to him or her at some stage during life. A popular loan-name among Roman men was Silvanius (ILS. 7317; Silvani, plural) that developed from the Roman god 'of uncultivated land beyond the boundaries of tillage'. A man with the name of

Silvanius was depicted as 'uncanny and dangerous', as was Diocletian, the author of crimes and a deliverer of evil.

In many cases, a name was taken from personal qualities, with Modestus deriving from modest, Servus from servile conditions, and Placidus, from a person with a placid or easy-going nature. The name of an historical celebrity, Cornelia, developed into the very popular Cornelius, and the goddess Juno's name was regularly applied. In another Roman tradition, the name was sometimes a reference to peculiar circumstances at birth; eg. Lucius=born by day; Manius=born in the morning; Alphaeus, the first born, Quintus, the fifth born and Decimus the tenth born. After the death of Emperor Constantine in 337, the Senate formally named him, 'Imperator Caesar Flavius Constantinus Pius Felix Invictus Augustus'. However, Emperor Maximian (d. 305) outdid Constantine for, in death, he received ten titles: 'Imperator Caesar Marcus Aurelius Valerius Maximianus Pius Felix Invictus Augustus'.

Deified twin boys in church records

In the records of Christianity, the names of certain twin boys of 'noble Roman birth' are recorded as having lived in the First Century and, for reasons that will become apparent, records of their lives are basically non-existent and little is known of them, except that they were called Marcellian and Marcus. The twins were deified by an Emperor of the time, and today the church acknowledges them as St Marcellian and St Marcus. It will be shown in a later chapter that Marcellian was the original birth name of Judas Thomas, and Marcus was the original name of Jesus.

The variant names of the twins

Judas Thomas, like Jesus, had a variation of names and, because of the status of his father, we shall suggest that his full Roman name was Marcellian Iulus Claudius Nero. His Aramaic name was Ioudas Te'oma and his Hebrew name was Teom (*Song of Solomon,* 7:14). He was called Tomme (Tommy) Didymus by the Syrians, and is so recorded in Syrian Bibles. His English name was Cristate, or 'crested', deriving from Tomas (Twin) Khrestus, and his English name from the 16th Century onwards was Judas Thomas. His religious or circumcision name was Ioudas Khrestus and his mythological name was Mars. In Latin he was called Ioudas Khristidunus and the Mehgheehlla Scroll named him Judas ben Halachmee. The Druids believed that he was the half-brother of Jesus, and called him Manawydan.

In 1415, the church took the extraordinary step of seeking out and destroying all knowledge of two Second Century books that contained 'the true name of Jesus Christ'. In 1394, Pedro de Luna became Pope Benedict XIII (1394-1423) and a battle raged in the church as to whether he was a legitimate pope or not. He subsequently created four new cardinals to specifically single out for condemnation a secret Latin treatise called 'Mar Yesu', and then issued instructions to destroy all copies of the mysterious Book of Elxai.

No editions of these writings now publicly exist, but church archives record that they were once in popular circulation and known to the early Christian priesthood. Knowledge of these writings survived from extracts published from them by Bishop Hippolytus of Rome (176-236) and St. Epiphanius of Salamis (315-403) along with references in some early editions of the Talmuds of Palestine and Babylonia. The rabbinic fraternity once held the destroyed manuscripts with great reverence for they were the original records of the 'Life of Rabbi Jesus' (*Cardinal Bembo, His Letters and Comments on Pope Leo X*, 1842 Reprint; *History of the Papacy During the Reformation*, Mandell Creighton, London, 1882) and their availability today would solve all problems associated with Christian origins.

However, not all is lost, for in the course of this analysis it was possible to find ancient testimony that records 'the true name of Jesus Christ'. For example, his historical Roman name in the First Century was Marcus Iulus Claudius Nero. The Greek variation of that name was Damianius (or Damian, in some records), who is recorded in history as being associated with taking the Gospel to Britain with Joseph of Arimathea (*Angilicae Histories Libra*, Polydore Vergil, historian). As mentioned, his Talmudic name is Rabbi Yeshu'a ben Panthera, with a variation being Yeshu'a ben Stada. At one stage, the rabbis had a book called the Revelations of Maran (Jesus?), which the church later retitled, the Revelations of the Lord Jesus.

In the Gospel of Basilides, originally called *A True History*, Jesus was called Caulacu. Basilides' writing was burnt by the church (*Ecclesiastical History,* iv, 7, Eusebius), which makes us suppose that it contained more truthful matter than the priesthood was prepared to deny. Scholars determined from an incomplete account in Irenaeus' work *Against Heresies* (1.24. 3-7, c. 202), the essence of what Basilides wrote, thus some elements survived.

In a Fourth Century version of the Epistle to the Philippians, Jesus is called Cresceus, identical to what Polycarp, a bishop at Smyrna (d. c. 157), called him in the Second Century. His name in the Mehgheehlla Scroll (the Safed Scroll) is Yeshai ben Halachmee, in the Koran, 'Isá, and in some icons of Constantinople, Deesis. His mythological name was Cosmos, meaning 'universal', which is probably the naming origin of the 'universal' church, later called the Roman Catholic church. There is some evidence that Cosmos became St Cosmas, the Physician of history, who was the twin brother of St Damianius, and popular superstition sometimes approximated them with the Dioscuri. However, Cardinal Caesar Baronius, Vatican librarian and Catholic historian (1538-1607), claimed that St Cosmas and St Damianius were one and the same person (*Annales Ecclesiastici*, Cardinal Caesar Baronius, Vatican librarian and Catholic historian, 1538-1607), and this may have been so. Little is known of the life of Cosmas except that he was beheaded and cannibalized after a Sacred Marriage (*Hieros Gamos*), and from the Fifth Century onwards his cultus became extensive. His name reappears in a 13th Century document written by Baibars, a self-proclaimed sultan of Egypt (d. c. 1290). In 1268 Baibars captured the Christian principality of Antioch and wrote a report on the success of Muslim conquest to Prince Bohemond in Tripoli. It said, in part: 'Hadst thou seen thy crosses sawn asunder, thy garbled gospels hawked about, the tombs of the presbyters cast to the ground, the church of Cosmas rocking to and fro and going down' *(Diderot's Emcyclopedia, 1759)*.

© *Ancient mosaic of St Cosmas, circa 16th Century, in the Byzantine Museum, Athens.*

Jesus' first Druidic name was Yesu Hesus Cunobeline (*The Bible Fraud*, Tony Bushby, Joshua Books, Australia, 2001 (Website; www.thebiblefraud.com) Bendigeid Vran when he became a honorary Arch Druid (Ibid). It appears more than a coincidence that both the Druids and Christianity had a 'Trinity', and the second person was either Jesus or Hesus. His biblical name in Fourth Century Greek Bibles was Yeshoua or sometimes Yeshu'a. The name 'Jesus' is not from any Hebrew or Greek source, for there was no letter 'J' in those alphabets until around the 9th - 12th Centuries. The names Yeshoua and Yeshu'a were, in later centuries, written with various spellings such as, Yesu'a, Yeshu, Yeshai, Yeshae and Yesse. In the 12th Century the name was spelt, Jesew Cryst (British Museum, London, the 'Harleian Heraldic Manuscript, No 269', dated about 1180). His 15th Century Latin name was Iesou Iulus Xristou and his Old English name in the 15th Century was Jesu Kraist. His modern English name from the 17th Century was Jesus Christ and his religious or circumcision name was Jesus the Krst, and that deserves an explanation.

The word Krst/Christ had its origin in ancient Egypt, being the religious name applied to Horus, the God of Light. His mother was Isis, the goddess who conceived him as a virgin. The record of Horus the Krst is found inscribed in the Palermo Stone, one of six carved basalt stones discovered in Egypt and recently relocated from Palermo to the Egyptian Museum at Cairo. They were originally deposited in the tomb of a pharaoh who lived around 2470 BC, and their ancient hieroglyphic inscriptions helped archaeologists date the early pharaohs up to the Fifth Dynasty. In early Egyptian times, a particular esoteric knowledge developed and persons like Horus in receipt of that knowledge were anointed, and then called Krsts (*Facts and Speculation on the Origin and History of the Christian Church,* Jacob Bryant, London, 1793; *The Wisdom of the Ancients,* Sir Francis Bacon, 1619, reprint by Berington, 1894; *Krata Repoa (or, Initiation into the Ancient Mysteries of the Priests of Egypt),* C. F. Koppen and J. W. B. Von Hymmen, Berlin, 1782).

St. Epiphanius believed that the Krst was the spiritual Self in each and every living person (*Haer,* liii, I). He said that Alexander of 100BC was 'one of the anointed Krsts' (*Haer,* xxix, 3), a statement that established a long history of Krst figures preceding the canonical date of Jesus. 'Anointed' or Krst figures were in existence before the writing of the Old Testament for some appeared in the story of Krishna (c. 1000 BC), and later (c. 397 BC) Ezra made references to anointing in the Book of Kings, providing two separate examples in just one narrative (1 Kings 19:16; see also 1 Kings 1-53). Some Essenic manuscripts refer to Kristo, or Krist in some translations, and in the Essene mind, Kristo was a divine internal figure set forth primarily in the Book of Enoch as One eternal with God. The Book of Enoch was written sometime around 150-120BC (*Lakeland Bible Dictionary*) and its importance was established when eight copies were found among the Dead Sea Scrolls. Krst was also established in the doctrine of the Gnostics who held Kristo as the personal and immortal Spirit of man. The son of Poseidon and Meduse was called Krst and the priests of Apollo were known as Krsts. In fact, the word Kristo and its derivations, Krst, Krist, Khyst and Krish-na appear in every ancient religious system and show that the original Kristo concept was believed to be the personal and invisible mediator and guide between God and everything spiritual in man.

In a document called *Dialogue with Trypho* written by St. Justin Martyr around 160, Trypho, a Jewish academic, claimed that the early church 'invented a Kristo'. Trypho accused Justin and his associates of purposely devising a Kristo-type figure similar in concept to the Hindu Krishna (Krishna is Sanskrit for Christ). Trypho's comments show that Jesus Christ as promoted today was unknown among the general populace at that time but the Krist concept from the Book of Enoch and Kristo, the Hindu name of the Sun, were.

Trypho, again in the writings of Justin Martyr, added that the word Krst was a substitute for an ancient divine name, and its power was known only to the 'Elect' alone of the fully initiated rabbis. In other words, the most advanced rabbis were initiates of secret knowledge and knew the substance of an ancient mystery. Jesus was to become one of them.

As a matter of interest, there is another person called Jesus in the New Testament, 'and Jesus who is called Justus' (Col. 4:11). The editors of some newer printings of the Bible changed this to read 'Joshua', but the FIRST Vulgate names him Jesus.

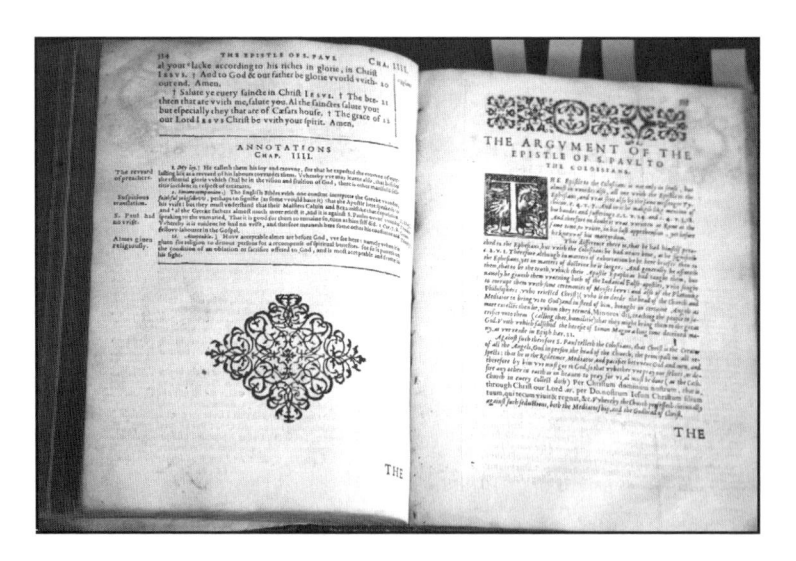

This Epistle in the FIRST Vulgate names an additional person called 'Jesus'. Note the ANNOTATIONS on the left-hand page and the beginning of the Epistle to the Colossians on the right-hand page. The ANNOTATIONS are extensive in this old Bible, but are not in today's Vulgates.

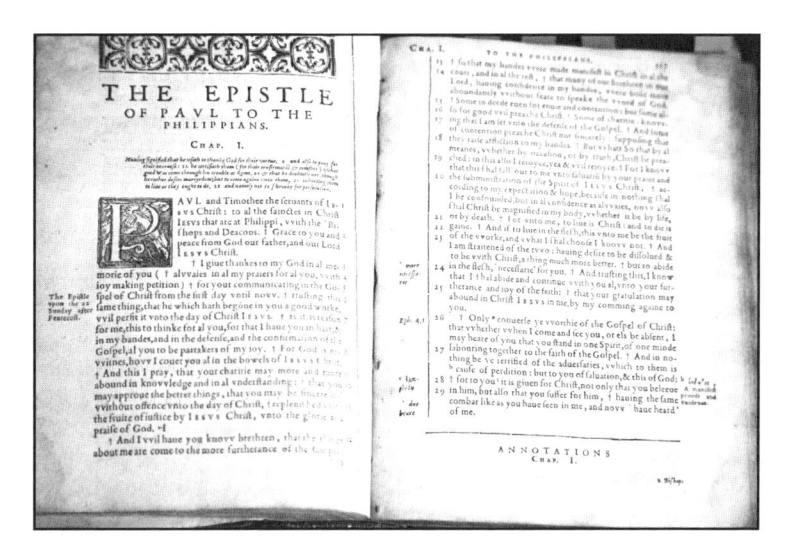

These are the opening two pages of the Epistle to the Philippians in the FIRST Vulgate. Note the commencement of ANNOTATIONS associated with this Epistle on the bottom of the right-hand page. In a Fourth Century version of this Epistle, Jesus is called Cresceus, identical to what Polycarp, a bishop at Smyrna (d.c. 157), called him in the Second Century. However, in the FIRST Vulgate his name now reads 'Iesvs'.

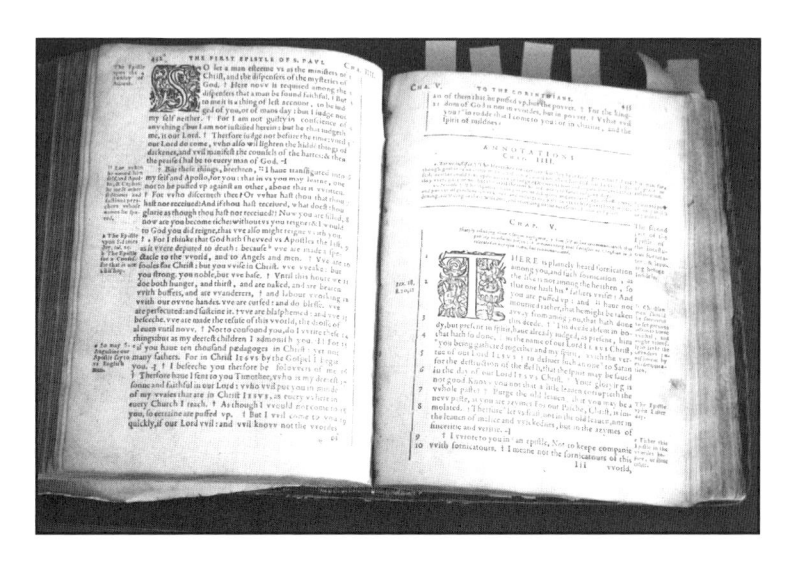

More ANNOTATIONS can be seen on the right-hand page. The FIRST Vulgate is packed with them and they attempt to clarify various aspects of the texts.

CHAPTER 5

The suppressed records of John the Baptist

Like Judas Thomas and Jesus, John the Baptist can also be connected to the Essenes. According to the Gospels, John the Baptist's mother, Elizabeth, was the sister of Judas Thomas and Jesus' mother, Mary (Luke 1:36). In some old Gospels, Elizabeth is called Enishbai and the use of this name provides researchers with a reason to look more closely at the tradition of name substitution. The Luke reference makes John the Baptist the cousin of Jesus and thus Judas Thomas, and the Gospels say that he was six months older than the twins. Elizabeth was married to a priest and this has been interpreted in some quarters as giving John the Baptist and his family Sadducee (far-right) connections. The Sadducees were yet another Jewish sect of the time, one opposed to the Pharisees. The Sadducees denied the resurrection of the dead and the validity of oral tradition. They are mentioned fourteen times in the New Testament, the Pharisees ninety eight times, mostly in the Gospels.

Unknown information about John the Baptist

A close study of the Dead Sea Scrolls has resulted in a growing consensus that John the Baptist was directly associated with the Qumran sect. The Gospels say that he was of priestly stock and lived in the Judean wilderness facing the Dead Sea 'until the day of his manifestation' (Luke 1:80). From Gospel information, John the Baptist is now generally recognized, like Paul, as an Essene. The discovery of *The Lost Book of the Nativity of John* (the Baptist) by Hugh J. Schonfield in 1929 revealed additional and striking information about him:

John the Baptist was considered by the early church as the infant messiah. Its loss (of this document) at a very early date is not to be wondered at, as the church had the best possible reasons for suppressing it. The fact that John the Baptist was regarded as the messiah by a numerous following may be a new one to many people. (*The Lost Book of the Nativity of John,* Hugh J. Schonfield, Edinburgh, 1929, Preface, Pg. x)

The anointing of John the Baptist

The Dead Sea Scrolls record that the Essenes possessed a hierarchy, an inner circle of initiated members, and their leader was known as 'the anointed one'. The practice of greasing or smearing with oil is supposed by many to be an exclusive Christian ceremony but it was in vogue by pre-Christian oriental nations. A statement in the *New American Cyclopedia* (Vol. 1, Pg. 620) confirmed that 'anointing with perfumed oil was in common use among the Greeks and the Romans as a mark of hospitality to guests. Anointing was an ancient custom throughout the East, by pouring aromatic oils on persons as a token of honor ... it was also employed in consecrating priests, prophets and kings, and places and instruments appointed for worship'.

Devotees of earlier oriental systems consecrated obelisks, images and statues with the Old Testament recording the anointing of ten stones set up by Joshua. The stone upon which Jacob slept at the time of his vision was also anointed. Aaron, Saul, David and Solomon were anointed with oil in the same way as the sick were anointed on the Sabbath (*Harmony of the New Testament,* Dr. Lightfoot, Vol. 1, Pg. 333). In ancient Palestinian tradition, kings, village heads and, in fact, any claimants to high office were anointed and hence 'anointed ones', leaders, or messiahs in the true sense of the word. Some leaders and village heads, after anointing, were called 'lord', as in landlord, or 'lord mayor'.

An early church tradition

The writings of Bishop Epiphanius of Salamis (315-403) deserve closer scrutiny for he left behind some extraordinary records about Jesus, Mary, and John the Baptist, the Gospel stories, and the Essene community. The modern-day church claims his records 'exhibit a marvelous mixture of valuable traditions' but many of those traditions violently oppose the canonical preaching of today. When St. Epiphanius wrote of an allegedly 'heretical' Judaic sect once occupying an area around the Dead Sea, he called them 'Ossenes' and said that they were sometimes called Jesseans, after either Jesse, the Old Testament father of King David, or Jesus when his name was Jesse.

Epiphanius sought to justify the latter connection of Essenes, Jesseans and Jesus by asserting in Hebrew, that the name Jesus meant 'Physician' and the Essenes were highly regarded herbal healers supporting the same doctrines as applied to Jesus Christ in the New Testament. Whether the Essenes were named for Jesus or not, the assertion that he was in some way connected with them was known and acknowledged during the earliest years of recorded Christian history. Hence it is safe to conclude the body of people today called the Essenes and the sect of Ossenes named by Epiphanius, are the same community.

St. Epiphanius said that John the Baptist was 'one of the anointed', confirming there was more than one 'anointed' person in the Gospel story, and providing a reference that corresponds with the title given to the leader of the Essenes, 'the anointed'. Origen added to the matter, saying, 'there are some who said of John (the Baptist) that he was anointed' (*Origen*, Vol. ii, Pg. 150). Emperor Julian (332-363), in his book, *The Arguments of the Emperor Julian*, introduced another factor when he said:

> At any rate neither Paul nor Matthew nor Mark dared to say that Jesus was God, but only the Krst John, they ventured to assert this.

Who was the leader of the Essenes?

A key factor in determining the significance of the Dead Sea Scrolls in relation to the twins relates to the leader of the Essenes. It is proposed that Krst John the Baptist, being 'the anointed one', was at one time their messianic leader and, as such, he was called the 'Star'. In writings available, four anointed (messiahs) leaders are recorded in association with the Essene community and Josephus added that some of the Essenes were 'involuntarily anointed', a statement not yet fully understood. Of further interest is the fact that a vial of oil was found in the Qumran caves with the Dead Sea Scrolls. It had been wrapped and sealed in a protective manner, indicating that it was precious to those who preserved it. One could be excused for thinking it was safely stored for the anointing of future messiahs.

The Community Rule outlines instructions for specific use of the 'Star', the head of the Order stating that he shall:

> … admit into the Covenant of grace, all those who have freely devoted themselves to the observance of God's precepts that they may be joined to the Council of God.

> He will cleanse him of all wicked deeds with the spirit of holiness, like purifying waters he will shed upon him the spirit of truth, and when his flesh is sprinkled with water, it shall be made clean by the humble submission of his soul to all the precepts of God.

Thus, the head of the Essene community had the authority to admit new members into the Order after baptizing them. Baptism was *not* part of orthodox Jewish tradition, so John the Baptist was at some time the head of this Order. Most likely, he had been a leader excelling in his position and surpassed the other members by being proclaimed a prophet by a large number of people. He was declared to be 'more than a prophet' by Jesus (Matt. 11:9).

That both Judas Thomas and Jesus knew certain 'secrets' is manifest from the Gospel of Mark (4:11; 4: 33-34) and they knew too much of the secret rituals of the Essenes to have been outsiders. That indicates that they had undergone the required three years of training necessary for entry into the hierarchy of the Essene Order, and then anointed as their 'token of honour' (*New American Cyclopedia,* Vol. 1, Pg. 620) before full admission into the 'inner circle of initiates'. As John the Baptist was their leader, he would have performed the anointing.

The 'Star of Bethlehem' mystery solved

As a result of his fanatical dedication to the Law of Moses, the career of John the Baptist came to a sudden and dramatic end when he was beheaded for condemning the marriage of Herod Agrippa 1 to his sister-in-law, Herodias, because 'it is against the Law (The Law of Moses) for you to have your brother's wife' (Mark 6:18).

Salome, and the severed head of John the Baptist on a platter. Painting by Sebastiano del Piomba, c. 1485-1547.

Because of the messianic family bloodline, and the tradition of the first-born, the leadership of the Essenes then passed to Judas Thomas. He became the 'Star', the head of the Essenes at their Bethlehem community, the town in which two of the Gospels record that he and Jesus were born (Matt. 2: 1; Luke 2: 15-18). As experts on the Dead Sea Scrolls have stressed, the documentation linking the messiah-figure with the word 'Star' occurs elsewhere in the Dead Sea Scrolls and is of crucial importance. Significantly the 'Star' reference is cited by sources independent of both the Dead Sea Scrolls and the New Testament, including historians and chroniclers of the First Century including Josephus, Tacitus and Suetonius. According to Josephus, the arrival of a 'Star' figure was a major factor in the revolt of 66.

Some three centuries later, the 'Star' of Bethlehem found its way into the opening chapters of the second Gospel written, that of Matthew (Matt. 2:2). Here it was retrospectively made to herald the arrival of a messiah, 'a governor who shall rule the people' (Matt. 2:6) and presented in the usual glamorized fashion of the early presbyters' writings.

The Gospel of Matthew was originally called the 'Gospel to the Hebrews' (*Adv. Haer.* 13 and 30; Also *Adv. Peleg.* 1:3), and the church admits that the first two chapters in today's Bibles were not part of the 'original Hebrew' version of that Gospel, but were structured into the writings in 'the 4th Century AD' (*Catholic Encyclopedia,* Vol. IX, pg. 527; *Ebronite Version of Matthew's Gospel,* also; Vol. IX, Oct. 1, 1910, Pg. 425; also; *New Catholic Encyclopedia,* Matthew Gospel). Those 48 forged passages, totaling more than 1200 words, were 'later apocryphal additions to the Gospels' (*Catholic Encyclopedia,* Vol. IX, Pg. 527) and were used as new opening chapters for a document that originally started its story: 'In those days came John the Baptist … and then Jesus came … to be baptized by him', when Jesus was 'at about the age of thirty years' (Matt. 3:1 onwards).

In its original form, the Gospel of Matthew, like Mark, Luke and John, did not record the arrival of the 'wise men of the East' following the heavenly Star of Bethlehem, nor any aspect of the infancy narratives carried in modern Bibles.

Evidence of a messianic 'Star' family

Of importance is the presence of Simeon bar Cochba and his troops in the Qumran area between 132 and 136. In Palestine, where 985 towns had been wiped out and 580,000 men and women had been slain in bar Cochba's revolt, the Jewish population had sunk to half its former volume, and to such an abyss of poverty that cultural life was almost wholly dead. Simeon bar Cochba claimed to be, and was acknowledged by the church, as a very popular messiah *(Oxford Dictionary of the Christian Church,* Cross, 1974, Pg. 132).

Even more remarkable is the fact that 'bar Cochba' means 'son of a Star' in Aramaic (Numbers 24:17) and was the name commonly used to describe him. Simeon bar Cochba was another in the succession of the many messiahs who have come and gone but only people who study Jewish history know anything of them. That some of bar Cochba's own documents were found in the Qumran caves suggests that he was himself an Essene leader. It would be interesting to know who Simeon bar Cochba's father and grandfather were, for it appears that the 'Star' figures were all successive and related members of one family.

CHAPTER 6

The life story of the first-born

The expectations of a messiah

The death of King Herod in 4 BC was followed by frightful social and political convulsions in Judea. For two or three years all elements of disorder were current and Judea was torn and devastated. Revolt assumed the wildest form and the celestial visions of 'a Kingdom of Heaven' were completely banished by the smoke and flame of political hate. That the common people generally expected a messiah at this time may be inferred from the records of Tacitus, who said:

> The generality had a strong persuasion that it was contained in the ancient writings of the priests ... that someone, who should come out of Judea, should attain the empire of the world; But the common people according to the influence of human wishes, appropriated to themselves, by their interpretation, this vast grandeur foretold by the fates (foretelling); nor could be brought to change their opinion for the time, by all their adversities.

An additional report came from yet another Roman historian, Gaius Tranquillus Suetonius (70-140). He served as a secretary to Emperor Hadrian (d. 117) and had access to Imperial Roman archives. His major work, the *Lives of the Caesars,* published about 120, gave accounts of the reigns of Julius Caesar and the eleven emperors who followed him. He confirmed Tacitus' record, saying:

> There had been for a long time all over the east a constant persuasion that it was recorded in the fates, that at that time some one who should come out of Judea should obtain universal dominion ... It appears by the event, that this

prediction referred to the Roman emperor, but the Jews, referring it to themselves, rebelled.

Josephus expanded upon the other reports. Probably his most famous writing was *Jewish Antiquities (Antiquities)*, a substantial tome about the same size as both Old and New Testaments combined. He also wrote *Autobiography*, *Against Apion* and *Jewish Wars* and spoke of the expectation of an actual or expected liberator of the oppressed people, saying:

> That which chiefly excited them to war was an ambiguous prophecy which was also found in the sacred books, that at that time someone, within their country, should arise, that should obtain the empire of the whole world. For this they had spoken of one of their nation; and many wise men were deceived with the interpretation.

The national mind had become so inflammable by constant brooding on this one theme, that any bold spirit rising in revolt against the Roman power could find an army of fierce disciples who trusted that it should be he who redeem Israel.

Many messiahs at that time

After Herod's death in 4 BC, Galilee passed into the hands of his son, Herod Antipas, who immediately had to deal with a local rebellion led by probably the first messiah, a certain Jude, the son of Ezekias. This developed into a full-scale battle after Cyrenius, Governor of Syria, heavily taxed the Jewish people circa 6 AD. Jude bar Ezekias declared that 'this taxation was no better than an introduction to slavery' and exhorted the nation to assert their liberty. He therefore prevailed upon his countrymen to revolt (*Antiquities,* Josephus, B, xviii, chp. 1, 1; and; *Wars of the Jews,* bk. ii, chp. viii, I) and this uprising compelled the Roman officer entrusted with its suppression to appeal to Rome for reinforcements. Subsequently 2000 insurgents were crucified and many others sold as slaves (*A Guide to the Ancient World,* Michael Grant, 1986, Pg. 261).

From the death of King Herod until the death of Simeon bar Cochba in 132, no less than fifty enthusiasts applied the ancient 'ambiguous prophecy' to themselves, obtained a following of messianic Jews, and set up as the messiah (*The Bible of Today*, John W. Chadwick, 1878). Claimant after claimant of the dangerous supremacy of the messiah then appeared, pitched a camp in the wilderness, raised the banner, gathered a force, was attacked, defeated, banished or crucified, and the frenzy did not abate.

Judas Thomas the Galilean

When Rome annexed the regions south of Galilee as the province of Judea in the early decades of the First Century (circa 30), another uprising broke out in the new provenance, led by a certain Judas who was known as 'Judas the Galilean' (Josephus). 'Judas the Galilean' is also mentioned in the Acts of the Apostles (5:37) and again involved in an uprising. The body of historical and biblical evidence currently available validates the opinion that 'Judas the Galilean' mentioned by Josephus and recorded in the New Testament, and Judas Thomas, the twin of Jesus in the Gospels, are one and the same person. Once it can be shown that Judas Thomas is simply the evangelical name of Judas the Galilean, we are no longer in the realm of fiction, but on the solid ground of history.

CHAPTER 7

An apocalyptic vision

In biblical tradition, when Judas Thomas moved to Galilee he was automatically called Judas of Galilee or Judas the Galilean, just as Mary of Bethany, Mary of Magdala and Joseph of Arimathea were named after the towns in which they lived. The possibility that Judas the Galilean headed up a division of aggressive fighting men for the Essenes does not fit the pacific and peaceful nature that Josephus, Pliny and Philo depict of them. The answer lies in one of their most important characteristics, the apocalyptic vision that was recorded as an 'end of the world prediction' in their prophetic writings.

In general, their vision foretold of an end and of a new beginning. Interpretations respecting the date of the fatal day exhibit a constant and wide divergence, and on numerous occasions, men believed the end of the world was near. Both Jesus and John the Baptist preached the end of the Age, which established their knowledge of the Essenes' prophecies. The Essenes believed the end of the world was near for they continually documented their insistence that the 'Last Times' were at hand. They were paranoid about it, and several of their texts deal specifically with the impending end of their particular world. The fact that they had a manuscript called the War Scroll among their writings attests to this, and establishes that the Essenes had readied themselves for some kind of battle.

Several copies of the War Scroll were found in Cave No. 1 and Cave No. 4 of the eleven caves discovered containing scrolls, and it is not possible to read it without recognizing that it too, like the Book of Revelation, was originally sourced from the Sibyl of Tarquin's psychic predictions. The two writings of cosmic crisis refer to earthquakes, voices from heaven and trumpet sounds and in each writing, the magic number seven is featured again and again ... seven churches, seven angels, seven seals, seven stars, seven candlesticks, seven trumpets, and so on. Parallel passages from the War Scroll can also be found in the Gospel of Matthew (5:1).

The War Scroll gives detailed directions for the conduct of combat, with the battlefield operations personally directed by priests who sound off the trumpet calls 'Advance', 'Attack', 'Retreat', 'Re-assemble', 'Pursuit' and 'Ambush'. 'When the formation was called up for that day's battle ... of the war, three formations shall stand, formation behind formation. They shall set a space between all the formations and they shall go out to battle in succession. These are the foot soldiers and beside them the horsemen' (The War Scroll, 1-3).

One specific section of the War Scroll documents a definite plan of tactics and strategy to be used in the physical encounters of man-to-man combat against the anticipated attack from invading forces called the Kittim. In the Old Testament book of Daniel (11:30) the Kittim are the Romans, named probably because they maintained a garrison on the island of Kittim in the Mediterranean Sea (Cyprus today). Later Jewish authors used the term cryptically of any victorious power. However, the important point to be stressed here is that, recorded in the War Scroll, the ultimate army leader to oppose the combatant forces of the Kittim is called, quite unequivocally, the 'messiah'. The orthodox church translators of this Scroll sought to disguise or dismantle this nomenclature by referring to the commander as 'thine anointed' which obscures the import of this passage (Ref. X: 17) in a Christian sense.

A vital aspect is to establish the date of the composition of the War Scroll. If this could be determined, we would know better whether or not it referred in any way to the now-called messiah of the New Testament and it is possible to date this scroll to within certain time frame parameters. Within the War Scroll itself, a vital clue to its dating and chronology can be found. When speaking of the Kittim, the text referred explicitly to their 'king'. The Kittim concerned cannot, therefore, be the soldiers of republican Rome, who invaded Palestine in 63BC and who had no monarchy. On the contrary, they would have to be, and could only be, the Kittim soldiers of Imperial Rome operating after the empire began in 31BC, and fell in the Fifth Century (*The Dead Sea Scroll Deception,* Michael Baigent, Richard Leigh, Corgi Books, 1992).

These soldiers invaded in the wake of the revolt of 66 that eventually saw the sack of Jerusalem by the Romans in the year 70 involving an opposing 'Star' figure. His name was Simon bar Giora and he surrendered to the Romans in dramatic fashion, dressed in a white tunic with a purple mantle, presumably to indicate royalty (*Jewish War,* 7:29, Josephus). He was taken to Rome, displayed in a victory procession and ceremonially executed as the messianic leader of the defeated Jews.

Evidence of a messiah-type figure in known operation more than 30 years after the church claimed that Jesus Christ died is the sort of information that the church contrived to suppress or, in some cases, ignore. Militarism was always associated with the 'Star' or messiah figures, and the New Testament accounts graphically confirm this in the story of Jesus Christ. Allusion is made to the violent maledictions uttered by Christ against the scribes and Pharisees, and his words of scorn and fury sound odd in the mouth of the 'meek and mild' prince of peace that the church and the exegetes have developed to portray him. 'Ye serpents, ye offspring of vipers' are not the words of a preacher of peace, but of a violent and aggressive character. In this premise, those words were spoken by Judas Thomas the Galilean, whose followers had been conspicuously involved in tumults and disturbances wherever they went.

Forerunner of the Last Supper

Among their then-secret doctrines, the Essene community believed that one of their messiahs would eventually lead them to victory over their Roman oppressors. This was the first born of the twins, Judas the Galilean, and the Essene hierarchy acclaimed him as the restorer of the Kingdom of God. One section of one Dead Sea Scroll was written in readiness for the blessing to be extended before the (hopefully) successful outcome of the radical events expected to happen when their oppressors were challenged. This outline is carried in The Messianic Rule:

> When they shall gather for the common table, the priest shall bless the first fruits of bread and wine thereafter the messiah of Israel shall extend his hand over the bread, and all the congregation of the community shall utter a blessing.

This is the blueprint of the Last Supper recorded later in the New Testament and proves that Judas Thomas the Galilean was leader of the Essenes. The New Testament records in several places that he raised the 'cup of the New Covenant' in true Essenic fashion (Mark 14:22-24; Matt. 26:28; 1 Cor. 11:25) and it is revealing to find that the word 'New' has been deleted from modern Bibles, but appears in ancient versions.

From Old Testament times, Jewish meals included a blessing over bread and wine (Gen.14: 18), and over the centuries assumed special importance as can be seen in many sections of the Dead Sea Scrolls. Josephus said of the Essenes; 'They consider it a grave sin to rest or touch food before praying'. The Old Testament changeover from simply reciting a short prayer over the bread and wine (Grace) into the symbolic ritual of eating the body and drinking the blood of a god had a long previous history and was introduced 'officially' into Christian practice during the latter part of the Fifth Century.

The earlier three known attempts to banish the Eucharist by Cyril of Jerusalem (d. 387) and Bishop Ambrose of Milan (333-397) failed miserably for the ritual was too firmly entrenched in society to be stopped. The church then formerly adopted and promoted the idea and the Apostolic Constitutions of the late Fifth Century were drawn up to provide documentation of a less 'real' way of eating flesh and drinking blood. In this way a more developed series of Eucharistic liturgies appeared. The idea the Eucharist participated in, and in some way, perpetuated the 'sacrifice' of Jesus Christ, subsequently became church dogma to later dominate Christian preaching, and gave the Eucharist a false character of a redemptive sacrifice originally having nothing to do with Jesus.

CHAPTER 8

Gospel appellations of the Galileans

From records available, it appears certain that the Nazarenes were more or less an independent Essene-derived sect and in some way were connected to the Zealots and the Zadokites. Of importance in the development of this story is the fact that the Galileans were also directly associated with the Nazarenes.

Learned Christian historian, Dr. Lardner (*Jewish and Heathen Testimonies*, Vol. ii. Pg. 102-103) established that the name 'Galileans' was the primitive appellation of the Christians (See also; *The Decline and Fall of the Roman Empire*, Edward Gibbons, 1994 Pg. 531). St and Bishop Epiphanius of Salamis in Cyprus, 'an uncritical traditionalist who rejected every kind of speculation' (*Encyclopedia Britannica*, Vol. 16, pg. 319) recorded that, in his time, the Fifth Century, 'all Christians were called Galileans' (*Epiphanius*, Ed. Petar, Vol. 1, Pg. 117). The church also said that, 'the early Christians were called Galileans' (*Catholic Encyclopedia,* Vol. V111, 1910, Pg. 539) and added that 'the word 'Galilean' is interchangeable with 'Christian'. The Galileans were the original Christians of history (*The Decline and Fall of the Roman Empire,* Edward Gibbons, 1994, Pg. 531), and therefore one would think that the name of Judas the Galilean could also read, Judas the Christian, or Judas Christian. However, the word 'Christian' was not in existence in his lifetime.

An extraordinary confession

When commenting in the Harvard Theology Review (1944) on behalf of a committee's findings, New Testament expert, Sir H. Idris Bell, exclaimed;

'There is no satisfactory evidence in our documents (world history) for the existence of a Christian community in the first century of our era ... nor is there an explanation for the non-existence of the name of the Lord Jesus Christ at that time'. That was the period when the church claimed that thousands of converts to its new religion were swarming across Europe and apostles of Jesus Christ were piously professing the 'truth of the Gospel' to a newly enlightened world.

The fact that words associated with 'Christian' or Christianity do not appear in the testimony of antiquity until much later is confirmed in the orthodox *Oxford Dictionary of the Christian Church,* and the reason put forward is one of the most extraordinary admissions ever published by the church. With over four hundred and eighty contributors consisting of Anglican, Roman Catholic, Lutheran, Presbyterian, Methodist, Jewish, Orthodox and other clerical experts, the priesthood claim in their Dictionary's Preface that they are 'the acclaimed authority on the church', and they said this about the name of their religion:

> Owing to the Pagan origin, the word (Christian) was long avoided by Christian writers. (*Oxford Dictionary of the Christian Church,* Oxford University Press, Third Edition, 1997, Pg. 333)

In trying to explain the Pagan origin of 'Christ', the church admitted that 'the name of Jesus is used in the New Testament as a synonym', that being a word having the same meaning as some other (*Oxford Dictionary of the Christian Church,* 2nd Ed., '*Name of Jesus'*, 1974, Pg. 953). In other words, the deity of Christianity was never called Jesus Christ in the early centuries.

The church said that the name 'Christian' was first used in 190 when it was recorded in the Acts of the Apostles, introduced to the world by Bishop Irenaeus shortly before his death early in the Third Century (d. c. 202). That narrative revealed that the name 'Christian' originated in the city of Antioch (Acts 11:26) and the context in which it was presented suggests that it was applied to a group of people by outsiders. However, that same narrative in old Greek versions of the Acts of the Apostles (Acts 11:26) is written 'Khrestians', not Christians, and is used as 'a term of abuse' (*Institutes of Christian History,* Johann Mosheim, Ecclesiastical historian, 1755, also; *The Birth of*

Christianity, Maurice Goguel, 1933). Taking these observations into consideration, it will now be shown that one of the appellations of Judas the Galilean was Judas Khrestus, and his messianist followers were called Khrestians.

The historical evidence

In an examination of all available existing First and Second Century documents, there are found five separate historical references to Judas Khrestus and his followers. These writings were compiled in the latter part of the First Century or early in the Second Century and the information they give about him is sparse. Probably the most controversial is found in the records of Josephus (written circa 80) and requires explaining in some detail.

A rabbi called Ekaba assembled Josephus' records towards the close of the Second Century and he was also responsible for compiling the writings of most First and Second Century historians. Shortly after the closing of the Council of Nicaea in 325, a forged reference to Jesus Christ appeared in Josephus' records and it is today called the 'Testimony of Flavius' (*Antiquities,* xviii, Ch. 3, *Testimonium Flavianum*). Theologians believe it was Bishop Eusebius who forged the passages when he admitted to rewriting a copy of Josephus' works in 329 (*On the Canon of the New Testament,* Dr. B. Westcott). As the passage is not found in any edition of *Antiquities* prior to the era of Eusebius, the suspicion fastened upon him as its author, for Eusebius personally argued that falsehood must be used to expand and develop the Roman church, saying:

> It is an act of virtue to deceive and lie, when by such means the interests of the church might be promoted. (*Ecclesiastical History*, Eusebius, Vol. 1, Pg. 381-382)

It was Eusebius who ordered the destruction of fifteen books written by an historian called Porphyry around the time of the Council of Nicaea, citing that they 'spoke badly against the Ekklesia (Ecclesia; the presbyters) and should not be made known' (*Bible Myths,* Rev. T. W. Doane, 1882, Pg. 438).

The short extravagant narrative that was forged into Josephus' records was designed to glorify Jesus Christ and is used today as evidence by Christian supporters to establish that Christ's name was recorded in a non-ecclesiastical

First Century writing, therefore that made him an historical personage. However, the church accepts the false nature of the 'Testimony of Flavius' and acknowledges that those passages are 'interpolations by Christians' (*Encyclopedia of Early Christianity,* Cross, 1997, Pg. 549) and 'should be forever discarded from any place among the evidences of Christianity' (*Life of Bishop Lardner,* by Dr. Kippis, Pg. 23).

That was not the only ecclesiastical falsification to the works of Josephus for a Third Century church record states that 'interpolations were introduced into the texts of Josephus long before his (Eusebius) time' (*Catholic Encyclopedia,* Vol. v. May 1, 1909, Pg. 620). Origen of Alexandria (185-251), one of the most influential theologians of the early Greek church, frankly admitted forging narratives into the Jewish historian's works to support his belief in the Old Testament stories (*Against Celsus,* Origen, 1.c; also, chp. xxxv, Bk. 1, also; Bishop Lardner, Vol. vi, chp. iii).

Josephus' works were subsequently published in book-form by Christian publishers, Havercamp, in Amsterdam in 1729 and at that time, the Director noted that there were other writings of Josephus in existence that were detrimental to church portrayals of its early history and therefore suppressed (*Index Expurgatorius Vaticanus,* Edited by R. Gibbings, B.A., Dublin, 1837). Havercamp openly affirmed that the other versions of Josephus's records in their possession 'did not acknowledge Jesus Christ' (*Index Expurgatorius Vaticanus,* Edited by R. Gibbings, B.A., Dublin, 1837) and thus they went unpublished. However, the church authorized the printing of the versions carrying the fabricated 'Testimony of Flavius' and issued these extraordinary orders to the publishers: 'That the corruptions of antiquity (The Testimony of Flavius) are forbidden to be excluded from the records by order of the Roman Inquisition' (*Liberty,* Bishop Jeremy Taylor, Vol ii, pg. 22, Heber's Ed., 1822; also, *Delineation of Roman Catholicism,* Rev. Charles Elliott, D.D., 1844). Thus, fake narratives are today promoted by the church as First Century evidence for the existence of Jesus Christ.

What the records of Josephus really said

There is, however, much more to the records of Josephus, and it is of a revolutionary nature. In the 15th Century, the Parliament at Paris summoned together all copies of Josephus' records and dispatched them to the Vatican for re-editing (*Index Expurgatorius Vaticanus*, Edited by R. Gibbings, B. A., Dublin, 1837). However, at that time, a hand-written manuscript of Josephus' *Jewish Antiquities* was in the possession of Bishop Rieux of Toulouse and it escaped censorship (Edmond Bordeaux Szekely, Vatican archivist, 1925). It survived unaltered to this day, and is now in this author's possession. For the betterment of mankind, this rare old document is to be published and readers can assess for themselves the revelatory new evidence that it carries about Christian origins. Its existence raises this one important question, 'Just who benefits from forging historical records'?

In its original and unedited form, Josephus' passage said that 'the tribe of Khrestians, called after him who wears the crest, has still not to this day disappeared' (*Jewish Antiquities*, 18: 63f, Josephus, Many thanks to the *Archivaliassen* of the *Bibliotheek Rijksmuseum* who made available the documentation relating to Havercamp Publishers and Josephus' records; See also, Paulus Orosius, a Fourth Century church historian who records extracts from Josephus' records that are not in the modern-day text of Josephus), and this First Century documentation explains why the later church needed to falsify Josephus' records.

The Bible Fraud expressed an alternative view on the origin of the name Khrestus, but Josephus' restored statement is from such an early period that the most probable origin of Judas Khrestus' agnomen was from the crest he wore on his head. In the early centuries, crests were made of plumes of varying colours depending on the level of ranking, and were worn with a matching mantle, like that of Simon bar Giora, mentioned earlier. Men who dressed in that manner were military priests (*Jewish War*, 7:29, Josephus), and the existence of this body of men has been censored from most church records.

© Museo Civilia Romana, 1962

The crested plumes ranged in colour from white to purple.

The special headdress and garments were originally believed to contain the power through which the leader ruled, and in higher cultures, was viewed as divine and identified with gods and goddesses. In the case of Khrestus, he was probably acknowledged as Mars, hence the origin of his mythological name.

Roman records of Khrestus

Tacitus wrote three works during his lifetime, the first being 'Agricola', the second, 'Germania', and the last, 'Annals', originally called, *After the Death of the Deified Augustus,* and that book covered the years 14-68. In 'Annals' (15:44) Tacitus records that Khrestus suffered death in Rome at the hands of Pontius Pilate during the reign of Tiberius and his captured followers were 'after having been daubed over with combustible materials (beeswax), were set up as lights in the night time, and thus brightly burnt to death'. This death procedure was known as the Roman candle and it was the forerunner of the name of one of today's fireworks. A little later, Emperor Nero (54-68) soaked Galilean criminals 'with tar before having them crucified and used them as human torches around his garden at night' (*The History of Torture,* Daniel P. Mannix, Dell, NY. 1964), complaining that 'those whom the vulgar call Khrestians are detested because of their scandalous practices' and he 'desired them to be eliminated' (*Dio's Roman History,* translated from Greek, Vol. 8 (1925), Books 61-63).

In modern times, Nero became retrospectively infamous for his persecutions of Christians but there were no Christians at that time for they were Khrestians. Tacitus and Suetonius accused the Khrestians of 'abominable practices', with Tacitus adding that they were 'warriors in constant tribal conflict'. Marcellinus Ammianus (c.330-400), the famous Roman historian, said of them in his time, 'the atrocity of the Khrestians against opponents surpasses the fury of wild beasts against men' (*Ammian,* xxii. 5, O'Neill's Trans., 1898), and St. Epiphanius added that 'the Galileans (Khrestians), were the founders of 'a new and pernicious sect, which was capable of the most horrid crimes' (*Encyclopedia Britannica,* James Moore's Dublin Edition, 1790-97).

Insurgents in Rome

In his records on the Life of Claudius (25:4), Suetonius reported that Khrestus was 'acting in Rome, the leader of insurgents' during the reign of Claudius (10 BC-54 AD), who was Roman Emperor from 41-54. Suetonius also said that Emperor Claudius expelled all Jews from Rome because of disturbances instigated there by Khrestus and his followers.

This expulsion is mentioned in the New Testament (Acts 18:2-3) in a narrative that describes Aquila, a Jew, and his wife Priscilla, being driven out of Rome by an edict of Claudius forcing them to travel to Corinth to start a building business. It is possible that the expulsion by Claudius may have been aided by Judas Khrestus's sons, Jacob and Simeon, whose combined messianic uprising was violently suppressed in 46 by Claudius's appointee, Fadus, after which they were crucified (*Encyclopedia Judaica Jerusalem,* 1971, Pg. 1118). Judas Khrestus' grandson Eleazar was also crucified after Jerusalem was taken in the year 70 (*The Decline and Fall of the Roman Empire,* Edward

Gibbons, 1994, Pg. 531).

The Roman historians' statements provide conflicting information because Tacitus citied Tiberius as Emperor at the time and Suetonius recorded that it was Claudius, thus providing a discrepancy of around eight years. Tacitus was writing around fifty years after the events he was recording and Suetonius some 40 years after Tacitus. In both cases, the two historians were writing well after the events that they described and many similar conflicts are found in their records. Suetonius, for example, said Tiberius 'was of fair complexion and wore his hair rather long at the back'. Tacitus, on the other hand, said that the emperor had a head 'without a trace of hair'.

As Tacitus was living closest to the time of the event and 'he is always careful to ascertain and record the truth' (*The Dictionary of Classical Mythology, Religion, Literature, and Art,* Oskar Seyffert, 1995, Pg. 611), his report was adopted for this work. He placed Judas Khrestus in Rome under the reign of his father, Emperor Tiberius, and described it as a place 'where every horrible and shameful iniquity from every quarter of the world pours in and finds a welcome'. This may have been the reason why Tiberius said that he 'hated the place' and spent much of his time further south on the island of Capri. There, in his 'pleasure palace', he trained little boys, whom he called his 'minnows' to lick and nibble his genitals while they all swam together in his pool. On occasion he even had unweaned babies suck his penis (*The Records of Rome,* 1868, British Library).

Until around the year 150 the records of Josephus, Nero, Tacitus and Suetonius mentioning Khrestus are four that are found in ancient historical writings having a similarity to the name of Christ. However, there is yet another reference, supplied by the Cumbrian Monastery, and published for the first time later in this book. The four known Khrestus references have been critically analyzed by researchers for decades and various opinions have been extended. Contributors to *The Encyclopedia of Early Christianity* said it was 'perhaps a reference to Christ' (Pg. 197) and the 1908 *Catholic Encyclopedia* said, 'Judas Khrestus may have been Jesus Christ', overlooking the fact that Khrestus was an 'insurgent acting in Rome', not the son of God on earth and that, according to the New Testament, Jesus Christ never went to Rome.

In referring to the records of Tacitus and Suetonius, the church argued that 'Khrestus was a Pagan substitute for Christus' (*Catholic Encyclopedia*, Vol. V111, 1910, Pg. 374-375) and is careful to use the name Christus in a favorable sense. The later priesthood assumed that the Roman historians purposely 'substituted Khrestus for Christus, or anointed, and Khrestians instead of Christians' (*Catholic Encyclopedia*, Vol. V111, 1910, Pg. 374-375). The church complained (Ibid) that the Roman records as they stand made the early Christian movement appear 'a religion of criminals', which is exactly what it was.

The Khrestians were the now-called 'early Christians' but in reality they were the followers of 'him who wears the crest', Judas Khrestus, and the so-called persecutions of the early Khrestians/Christians were due to the fact that they were criminal activists, not religious devotees. The Romans were tolerant of any religion, excluding Druidism, but very resentful of anything that savored of political rivalry. The age which the church portrays as a period of evangelical preaching was, in reality, centuries of rebellion and revolt, and much later, when the Khrestians were finally brought to bear, the field was wide open for retrospective religious propaganda.

A religion of Galilean criminals

The Khrestians were the Galilean followers of Judas Khrestus, and church scribes subsequently restructured the word to read 'Christians' in the 16th Century (*De Antiqua Ecclesiae Disciplina,* Bishop Lewis Du Pin, Catholic historian, Folio, Paris, 1686; also, *Diderot's Encyclopedia,* 1759). Therefore, any printed references to the word 'Christian' in church writings today that pre-date the 16th Century have been edited from 'Khrestian' (*De Antiqua Ecclesiae Disciplina,* Bishop Lewis Du Pin, Catholic historian, Folio, Paris, 1686) and the violent followers of Khrestus are retrospectively called 'Christians'. Judas Khrestus was the Khrestian's messiah in the true sense of the word, the anointed leader of his Galilean apostles.

'The field of Gospel history had its beginnings in remote Galilee' (*Catholic Encyclopedia*, Vol. V111, 1910, Pg. 375), the most northerly of the three provinces of Palestine (Galilee, Samaria, Judea) and included the large eastern areas of Ituraea, Trachonitis and Lysanias (Eastern Upper Galilee).

Measuring approximately fifty miles North to South and one hundred and twenty miles East to West, it was bounded in the West by the coastal plain along which ran the road from Egypt to Phoenicia. The caravan routes from the coast to Damascus and the East crossed its Southern part through the valley of Esdraelon (*Lakeland Bible Dictionary*).

In Old Testament times, King Hiram was unimpressed with the twenty Galilean towns Solomon gave him as payment for services. He called the inhabitants 'Cabul' meaning 'good-for-nothing' (1 Kings 9:13) and their 'despised' reputation endured into New Testament times with Josephus describing them as 'only representations of living things'. Galilee was known as 'the insurgent district of the country. They were a restless, excitable body of people, remote from the center of power, ecclesiastical and secular. The Romans had more trouble with the Galileans than the natives of any other province for the messiahs all started out from Galilee and never failed to collect followers around the standard' (*The Martyrdom of Jesus Christ,* Pg. 42).

Finding Judas Khrestus in the Gospels

Careful attention needs to be taken in determining which twin is being referred to in the Gospels, for by understanding the meaning and background to distinctive word formation, a differentiation can be made between the two brothers, and that goes some way to explaining the contradictory narratives surrounding the characterization of Jesus Christ. For example, the New Testament clearly states that Jesus Christ was a Galilean (Matt. 26:70) with twelve followers. In this reconstruction of the Gospels, that particular description is attributed to Judas Thomas the Galilean, the twin of Jesus, who later acquired the agnomen of Judas Khrestus during the course of his life. The church said that 'excluding Judas Iscariot, all the apostles were Galileans' (*Catholic Encyclopedia*, Vol.V111, 1910, Pg. 539) and in this restoration of the Gospels, that makes them followers of Judas Khrestus, not Jesus Christ.

'Simon, called Peter, and his brother Andrew' are clearly Galileans (Luke 22:59) and the first recruited. St. Jerome recorded that 'Simon was of mature age and Andrew was a youth'. *The Bible Fraud* established that they were both Nabatean Arabs and Simon received the appellation of Peter, which theologians, both ancient and modern, expressed difficulty in explaining.

The Gospel name of Simon Peter originated from 'Simon, originally from the rock of Petra, a fortified rock city south of the Dead Sea, the dome upon which they hoarded their wealth' (*The Keys of St. Peter,* Bunson, 1867, also; *Bingham's Antiquities of the Christian Church,* Straker's Edition, 1840). Traces of 'the Peter' or 'rock' tradition can be found in all four Gospels and they record the prominent role he played as a 'pillar' in the circle of Judas Khrestus' disciples (Gal. 2:9). The now-called first pope was really Simon of Petra and the name applied to him was in the same biblical tradition as that of Joseph of Arimathea.

John and his brother, James the Greater, the sons of Zebedee (Mark 1:19-20), were also Galileans. The brothers apparently had an excitable and quick-tempered side to their character for Judas Khrestus nicknamed them, 'sons of thunder'.

Since the term 'Galilean' was synonymous with aggression and the Zealots, it is revealing to read that Judas Khrestus was called 'one of them' three times in the Gospel of Luke (22:57; 22:59; 23:6). The Gospel of Matthew (26:73) states that the Galileans 'spoke with a peculiar accent' and warmly welcomed Judas Khrestus upon his return to Galilee from a journey to Jerusalem (John 4:45). Josephus called the Galilean followers of Khrestus 'his disciples' and Pontius Pilate later asserted (Luke 23:5) that they were rabble-rousers who set about to 'stir up the people'. Petronius Arbiter Elegantiarum, a First Century associate of Pontius Pilate, said of the Khrestians; 'They do not take daily baths and their odour is greatly objectionable, to say the least'. Ernest Renan, a 19th Century church historian, described them as 'a poor dirty set, without manners, clad in filthy gabardines and smelling strongly of garlic' (*Development of the Catholic Church,* Ernest Renan of the French Academy, 1880).

In itself, the mere suggestion of an association of 'gentle' Jesus Christ with the vicious, war-mongering Zealots (anti-Roman nationalists) is highly provocative in the church and promotes a violent reaction when raised with the more learned priests. This Gospel association immediately eliminates the meek and humble, lamb-like saviour image that Christian tradition has developed to portray Jesus Christ. But it was Judas Khrestus, not the Gospel Jesus Christ nor Jesus the twin, 'who began his ministry in Galilee and from whence he drew his apostles' (*Catholic Encyclopedia*, Vol. V111, 1910, Pg. 375). Due to Gospel falsifications clarified in later chapters, these were originally the men the church now call the 'apostles' of Jesus Christ, but they were, in reality, the militia of Judas Khrestus.

The reality of the issue is that the now-called early Christian movement was a body of brutal Galilean militants and this may explain why some modern day Christian Encyclopedias and Dictionaries fail to record an A–Z entry under the heading of 'Galilean' (See *Catholic Encyclopedias* for an example). This is a particularly strange omission, for the church proudly states that Jesus and his apostles were Galileans (*Catholic Encyclopedia,* Vol. V111, 1910, Pg. 539) yet seems reticence to fully describe their history and nature.

The Galilean fortress

During the course of Judas Khrestus's leadership of the Bethlehem Essene Community, he and his odd assortment of troops moved to the imposing fortress in the rugged hills outside Gamala in Galilee because he had 'no honor in his own country' (John 4: 44). The church said that 'he lived almost as an outlaw in the more mountainous and unpopulated regions of Upper Galilee' (*New Catholic Encyclopedia,* Vol. VI, 1967, Pg. 737). It was Josephus himself who, when as the former governor general of Galilee, equipped the fortress with ramparts and tunnels. Josephus gave an extraordinarily precise description of the site and convinced his readers that it was to all intents and purposes impregnable. 'The houses were built against the steep mountain flank and astonishingly huddled together, one on top of the other, and this perpendicular site gave the city the appearance of being suspended in air and falling headlong upon itself' (*Jewish Wars*, IV, 7).

© Photo by Alice Schalek

This desolate wilderness is traditionally identified with the location of Judas Khrestus' fortress. The monastery clinging to the side of the rock was built near the site in the 12th Century.

Here Judas Khrestus combined and developed his radical offshoot team of the Nazarenes and Zealots with the intention of advancing on Rome in a military action to free his people and claim his rightful title of King of the Jews. The people 'believed in him ... and because of his words many more became followers' (John 4: 39-41). It was Judas Khrestus, not Jesus Christ, who said, 'I have come not to bring peace, but a sword' (Matt. 10:34) and instructed his followers to arm themselves with weapons (Luke 22:36). A great variation is given in the New Testament as to the numbers of Judas Khrestus' army for the Gospel of Luke states seventy-two (Luke 10:1; 10:17; Sinai Bible), and the first book of Corinthians (15:5-8) attributes a figure of 'five hundred disciples'. In the Talmud, 'five disciples' are recorded (*Babylonian Sanhedrin,* 43 a) but they were probably the followers of Jesus, not Judas Khrestus.

The most sensitive of all Gospel documentation for later Christian tradition is that of the narratives in which the Gospel Jesus Christ is clearly made to have included Zealots among his supporters, Simon the Zealot, for example (Luke 6:15; Acts 1:13). The violent Zealots were members of an extreme Jewish sect (or political party) that resisted all aspects of Roman rule and aggression in Palestine in the First Century. They were, in today's terminology, a body of far-left militant revolutionists, fearless of death, in fact, ruthless assassins and they have a direct link with Judas Khrestus and his actions recorded in the confused narratives of the New Testament.

CHAPTER 9

The beginning of the Khrestian uprising

The 'misprint' in the Gospels

Judas Khrestus possessed a hereditary right to the throne of Judea and because of this, he rallied popular support among the Galileans, hoping maybe that he could regain land the Romans had taken. Judas Khrestus and his rebels 'started in Galilee' and came 'all the way here' (Luke 23:5) to Rome to challenge his father, Emperor Tiberius, for his inheritance.

They subsequently arrived at 'a farm called Gethsemane which belonged to a man called Joshua' (Matt. 26: 36; Syrian Bible), situated on the outskirts of the city. Some early English-language Bibles (c. 1611-1687) record the name Judas, not Jesus, in this Matthew passage (26:36), revealing the true nature of the original story and neatly accounting for the amalgamation of the two life stories in the Gospels. The later church deemed the name 'Judas' a 'misprint' and New Testament versions recording Judas' name subsequently became valuable collector's items today called the 'Judas Bible'.

The Roman Imperial Secret Service

It was at Gethsemane that the Khrestians readied themselves for battle with the Romans. Unbeknownst to leader Judas Khrestus, Emperor Tiberius had died during the long journey and Caligula (d. 41) had come into power on the 16th March 37. He became the third emperor of Rome, a dangerous and unpleasant individual. The records of Roman historians consistently paint him as a capricious and cruel young man, powerful and scheming. Suetonius, for example, said; 'So much for Caligula as emperor; we must now tell of his career as a monster' (*Life of Caligula,* XXII, Suetonius).

There was now a dynastic problem that demanded immediate and urgent action by Emperor Caligula. Judas Khrestus was the son of Mary of the Herod clan and that constituted a serious problem for Caligula. Khrestus was the rightful successor to the King of Judea but official Roman policy was now to 'rid Judea of the royal line and any other government of the sort and hand administration of the country over to the Roman legate in Syria', such was the dimensions of the hatred against Herod and his dynasty (Josephus).

It had been a long-standing policy of the Roman legion and armies of occupation to utilize informers and spies. They were called the Delatores (later, the Frumentarii), the Roman Imperial Secret Service, and were set up with the express purpose of spying on the citizens of Rome's far-flung domains (The first Delatore mentioned by name was Romano Hispo, circa 15 AD; Tacitus). They were common in the Tiberian principate and were usually Roman officials in positions, for example, of collectors of corn in a provenance that brought them into contact with locals and natives. Titus (Roman Emperor, 79-81), for example, destroyer of the Second Temple in Jerusalem in the year 70, employed special messengers and killers to carry out executions and liquidations arising from information derived from the Secret Service (*Encyclopedia of the Roman Empire*, Matthew Brunson, 1994, Pg. 164).

From information in the Gospels, it is argued that Judas Khrestus was preparing his attack but before he could get under way Judas Iscariot, an informer to the Deletores, betrayed him. On a particular night, and under Emperor Caligula's orders, the *cohortes urbanae,* the city police force of Rome and a division of the Roman Army, was assembled and in place ready to nullify Judas Khrestus' imminent uprising. There were originally three *cohortes urbane* stationed in Rome, each with 500 soldiers. This number was increased to 1000 each between the years 43 and 69. Little is known of the course of the ensuring battle but there is epigraphic evidence that a large Roman force was needed to suppress it, maybe requiring all three *cohortes.*

On that night, the Gospels state that Judas Iscariot embraced and kissed Judas Khrestus in order to identify him to the Roman military leaders (Luke 22:47-48). Judas Khrestus was obviously unknown to them and upon the signal of Judas Iscariot identifying the Galilean leader, a significant battle raged in which Simon of Petra used his sword and cut off Malchus' ear (John 18:10). It is Gospel descriptions of this episode which those who hold to the 'guerrilla leader' view of Jesus regard as watered-down accounts of a full-scale insurrection led by him. However, in presenting this thesis, that rebellion was not led by Jesus, but by Judas Khrestus, who was subsequently overpowered, arrested and removed from the scene.

At that time, large areas were under Roman occupation, and to fully understand the situation, a comparison with the occupation of France by the Germans during World War II can be drawn. There was a civil law administered by the French, and there was the law of the occupational forces, which only concerned itself with offences against the occupational authorities. This same sort of arrangement applied during the first decades of the First Century. The civil law of the Jews demanded death penalties to be carried out by stoning, in accordance with the Law of Moses. Offences against the Roman state came under the Roman authorities whose method of execution was by crucifixion. To be sentenced and executed by crucifixion, Judas Khrestus would have had to commit an offence against the Roman Empire.

The tradition of a 'substitute'

Judas Khrestus was tried on a charge of treason against the Romans, found guilty of revolutionary activity and sentenced to die by crucifixion. In his defense before the Roman Council he argued that 'he was a king' but they replied, 'we say he is not a king, but he saith it of himself' (*Acta Pilate,* 1: 1-2; 3: 98). The whole multitude called out that he was 'born of fornication' (*Acta Pilate,* Ibid), reflecting the general public knowledge that he was illegitimate. As a Roman citizen of noble heritage, Judas Khrestus then 'appealed to the Emperor', Caligula, as was his right, but to no avail. The death penalty stood and it was the year 37.

Being aware of his royal status, Judas Khrestus then exercised an age-old tradition that came with his birthright. This advantage allowed him to order the placement of a 'substitute' to take his allocated punishment. An ancient Babylonian clay tablet determined the origin of the tradition of a 'substitute'. The priests ordained a substitute should 'go to meet his destiny' and undergo, on somebody else's behalf, the afflictions in store for that person.

An echo of this ancient rite is found in the story of Barabbas offered as a substitute to Judas Khrestus (Matt. 27:16-17). Barabbas 'had been put in prison for his part in a rising in the city and for murder' (Luke 23:19). The name of Barabbas in ancient Bibles is written Jacob Barabbas (*Institutes of Christian History,* Johann Mosheim, Ecclesiastical historian, 1755), and Judas Khrestus had a son called Jacob (*Encyclopedia Judaica Jerusalem,* 1971, Pg. 1118). In Aramaic, the word 'Barabbas' means, 'son of the father', or 'son of a father', in some translations, exactly as the Gospel Jesus Christ was made to be the son of the Father.

In the 'substitute tradition', at first, it seemed, the unlucky victim had to suffer but not necessarily die. 'Therefore I have decreed that thou should first be scourged according to the law of the emperors' said the Emperor himself (*Acta of Pilate,* IX). Judas Khrestus was then 'flogged' (John 19:1) and subsequently invested with the honours of a 'purple' toga (Mark 15:17), the distinctive mark of royalty (*History of Purple as a Status Symbol in Antiquity,* M. Reinhold, Brussels, 1970). A crown called the Corona Triumphalis, among the Romans the highest distinction awarded for service in battle, was placed upon his head. Tradition records that the crowns were made from bushes and grass growing at the scene of the battle. With the official Roman formalities now completed, Judas Khrestus was led away.

The Mithraic father of Rome

The inside man in the story was a notable member of the Sanhedrin, Joseph of Arimathea, 'a secret disciple' who had met with Judas Khrestus that night and expressed his concern about 'the new Kingdom of God' (Luke 23:50; see also the prophecy of the Cumaean Sibyl in Virgil's Fourth Eclogue that predicted the coming of 'the new Kingdom of God'). In the FIRST Vulgate Bible he is described as a 'Nobilis Decurion', whereas the King James Bible calls him a 'Counselor'.

At the time the Nobilitas consisted of about 900 wealthy land-owning families who provided candidates for the 300 members of the Senate. These were the natural rulers, well educated, cultivated and influential in every facet of Roman life, territorial conquests, and politics. But Joseph of Arimathea was not just a Nobilis ... he was the 'Nobilis Decurion' and that title had a special meaning in Roman society ... he was the Mithraic Father of Rome.

The Gospel of Peter records that Joseph of Arimathea was a close personal friend of Pontius Pilate, and this narrative provides a vital reference establishing that the crucifixion took place in Rome. Christian sources, presumably motivated by a desire to place complete responsibility for the crucifixion of the Gospel Jesus Christ on the Jews, are generally sympathetic to Pontius Pilate. This is in contrast to the account in the Epistle of Agrippa 1 (Philo), which depicts Pontius Pilate as corrupt, cruel and bloodthirsty. Pontius Pilate was in Rome at this time (37) for late in 36 he had been ordered by the governor of Syria, Vitellius, to travel to the city to answer for his conduct to Emperor Tiberius (*Encyclopedia Judaica Jerusalem*, 1971, Pg. 848). However, Tiberius died on the 16TH March 37, and just before Pontius Pilate reached Rome (*Catholic Encyclopedia*, Vol. XVI, 1912, Pg. 718). Pontius Pilate remained in Rome and was still there during the reign of Emperor Claudius who died in the year 54 (*Acta Pilate,* xiii, (XXIX).

Pontius Pilate never returned to Judea but at this point he still retained the Procuratorship of Judea and the judgment responsibilities of the area still under his jurisdiction (*Pontius Pilatus,* G.A. Mueller, Germany. 1888). However he deferred to Herod Agrippa 1 (d. 44), who was also in Rome at that time having just received his commission as Tetrach of Ituraea, Trachonitis and Lysanias (Eastern Upper Galilee) from new Emperor Caligula. Those areas were mostly his late Uncle Philip 11's (d. 34) territory known also as Upper Galilee. It is no small coincidence that this was the very same territory of Judas Khrestus and his Galilean followers who had their fortress in the rugged hills outside Gamala. It was therefore opportune for Herod while in Rome to be in attendance at the trial and this is recorded in the New Testament. However, this was not Herod Antipas, but Herod Agrippa 1, and when he saw Judas Khrestus he was pleased 'because for a long time he had been wanting to see him' (Luke 23:8). Agrippa 1 was Judas Khrestus' uncle.

The saving victim

The 'substitute' for Judas Khrestus was Simon of Cyrene who was 'seized as he was coming in from the country' (Luke 23:26) and subsequently 'carried the cross to the hill of Golgotha' (Matt. 27:32). With Joseph of Arimathea's help, Judas Khrestus was exchanged for Simon under the cover of darkness and became the 'saving victim' of later church hymns. According to the Gospels, Pontius Pilate considered Jesus Christ innocent of any crime, simply because he was referring to the substitute for Judas Khrestus. Pontius Pilate remarked at the substitute's reticence to speak (Mark 15:5) saying, 'He made no reply, not even a single charge' (Matt. 27:19). Tradition gave the name of Claudia Procula to Pontius Pilate's wife, and by some she has been identified with the Claudia of 2 Timothy 4:21. She also knew the man was a substitute and advised her husband not to 'have anything to do with that innocent man' (Matt. 27:19). Later, the penalty handed to Judas Khrestus was completed with the crucifixion of the substitute.

Destruction of the true history

There were attempts by the early church to destroy documentation recording the 'substitute' of their main Gospel character and it concerned a man called Basilides. Very little is known of him, but it appears he was a presbyter in Alexandria sometime around 155-160. Of Basilides' writings only scattered fragments now survive but it is recorded that he once wrote a 24-page document called *A True History*. That document was later retitled the *Interpretation of the Gospel* (note the singular use of the word 'Gospel') and in it Jesus is called 'Caulacu'.

Scholars determined from an incomplete account by Irenaeus (*Against Heresies*, 1.24. 3-7) the essence of what Basilides originally wrote. The central act of Basilides' writing claimed that Simon of Cyrene was crucified instead of Judas Khrestus. Under the headline, 'Confession of Khrestus but not of Khrestus crucified', Basilides wrote:

> Hence he did not suffer. Rather, a certain Simon of Cyrene was found to bear his cross for him, so that he was taken for Khrestus; while Khrestus for his part … stood by, laughing at them.

> Therefore people who know these things have been set free from the ruler that crafted the world. One should not acknowledge the man that was crucified (i.e. Simon of Cyrene), but rather the one who was thought to have been

crucified; he was named Khrestus.

Basilides' report confirms the Gospel narratives about the seizure of Simon of Cyrene as the substitute for Judas Khrestus.

The Romans spoke of the Zealots as 'Robbers' in order to defame their name and whenever 'Robbers' were caught they were immediately crucified. Thus it is probable the two New Testament men called 'thieves' crucified alongside Judas Khrestus' substitute were 'Robbers' which, in centuries of translations, became 'thieves', and were arrested at the same time as Judas Khrestus. They were condemned for the same offence, as crucifixion was not the punishment for robbery. But look what one of the 'Robbers' said (Luke 23:41) about the central player in the crucifixion event:

> We are punished justly, for we are getting what our deeds deserve. But this man has done nothing wrong.

He knew the man being crucified along side him was innocent because he was substituted for Judas Khrestus. The church claimed that the Acts of Thomas contains 'an historical nucleus' (*Catholic Encyclopedia*, Vol. X1V, 1912, Pg. 658) and within it is recorded the very words Judas Khrestus was purported to have said, obviously alive:

> I did not succumb to them as they had planned, and I did not die in reality, but only in appearance; I was laughing at their ignorance.

One must also consider what information Mohammad had at his disposal when he wrote the Holy Book of Islam, the Koran, and documented this passage relating to Judas Khrestus: 'and they killed him not, nor crucified him, but so it was made to appear to them, and those who differ therein are full of doubts, with no knowledge, but only conjecture to follow, for of a surety they killed him not' (Surah 4).

The removal of Simon's body

To hide the fact from the Roman authorities, Judas Khrestus and his followers subsequently removed Simon's body from Joseph of Arimathea's private tomb (*Against Heresies,* 1.24, 3-7). Additional evidence provided in the once-canonical Gospel of Peter supports Basilides' record that Simon of Cyrene was removed from the tomb by 'two young men' (Gospel of Peter, 1: 9-10). The Acts and Gospel of Thomas, the Gospels of Peter and Barnabas, and the apocryphal writings provide eleven separate biblical sources recording that Judas Khrestus was living long after the time the church states the singular Gospel Jesus Christ died.

Examination of Roman law of the period revealed that the authorities allowed no burial rights to those who died by crucifixion and violation of this law brought severe punishment. As the penalty of crucifixion was reserved for rebels, mutinous slaves and enemies of Roman society, those guilty were simply left hanging naked and rotting, a public and prolonged agony that was a deliberate deterrent to other would-be rebels. It was a custom of the times to post centurions to prevent distressed relatives attempting to remove the bodies of the dead or near dead in defiance of the law of the time (Matt. 27:54).

According to the Gospels, Simon of Cyrene experienced crucifixion for just part of one afternoon, a few hours. He was then taken down and freely handed over to Joseph of Arimathea. Joseph's personal friendship with Pontius Pilate explains why he was able to secure the early release of Simon from crucifixion against Roman law of the time. The Acta Pilate records a long address by Joseph to Pontius Pilate with every clause beginning with the words, 'Give me this stranger'. Joseph of Arimathea arrived on the scene unannounced, removed Simon's body to the adjacent tomb 'when evening had come' (Luke 23:52; John 19:38; Mark 15:42), and then disappeared from the New Testament accounts forever.

One twin sold

By exercising the replacement option, Judas Khrestus saved his own life but this was nevertheless at a cost. He had played the 'substitution' card at the expense of his 'birthright', which now passed to the second born, his twin brother, Jesus. From the moment Judas Khrestus and Jesus were born, they encountered the ancient heritage of the 'first born' with an example seen in the Old Testament archetype of Esau and Jacob. Esau sold his birthright for a 'mess of pottage' and Jacob received his father's blessing in his place (Gen. 25:27-34).

Rabbi Jesus, 'brother second in command' (Acts of Thomas; 110:15), now received the blessing of 'the Father' and inherited the title of 'Star', the leader of the Essenes and rightful king of the Jews, but showed reluctance to assume power. The Gospels state that 'perceiving that they were about to come and take him by force to make him king, Rabbi Jesus again withdrew to the mountains by himself' (John 6:15). However, his reticence merely delayed matters for his legal obligations of royal birthright had to be fulfilled and the people wanted him 'made King' (*King Jesus* (4th Ed.), R. Graves, London, 1960). Because Judas Khrestus had drawn upon the 'substitute' advantage of his birthright, the fallen 'Star' was no longer a free man and was sold into bondage by the new 'Star', his brother and 'fellow initiate' (*Acts of Thomas*), Rabbi Jesus.

In a 'relic of the original Greek text' of the Acts of Thomas (*The Apocryphal New Testament,* Montague R. James, Oxford, 1926), Jesus 'saw a certain merchant who had come from India whose name was Abbanes, and said; I have a slave that is a good builder and I desire to sell him. And so saying he showed his Judas Thomas (Khrestus) far off and agreed with him for three litrae of silver unstamped, and wrote a deed of sale, saying; 'I Rabbi Jesus ... acknowledge that I have sold my slave Judas by name unto thee Abbanes, a merchant of Gundafor, king of the Indians' (Acts of Thomas 1: 2). They then 'sailed prosperously till they reached Andrapolis, a royal city' (The First Act: 3). The church records acknowledged the sale of Judas in the Acts of Thomas:

> Rabbi Jesus sold Judas Thomas (Khrestus) to an Indian king (Gundafor) to be his slave and to serve Gundafor as a carpenter. Judas Thomas undertook to build a palace for Gundafor, but spent the money. (*Catholic Encyclopedia,* Vol. X1V; 1912, Pg. 658)

Church records confirm the historical existence of a king by that name:

> Now it is certainly a remarkable fact that about the year 46 AD a king was reigning over that part of Asia south of the Himalayas. Despite sundry minor variations the identity of the name with the Gundafor of the Acts of Thomas is unmistakable and is hardly disputed. He began his reign during the year 20 AD and was still reigning in 46 AD. (*Catholic Encyclopedia,* Vol. X1V, Pg. 658)

THE BEGINNING OF THE KHRESTIAN UPRISING

In this phrase, written personally by Judas Khrestus in India, he expresses remorse, and reveals his royal status: 'But I could not recall my splendor; for, it was while I was still a boy and quite young that I had left it behind in my father's Palace' (*Acts of Thomas*, 'In the Country of India', 112:75).

There is endless discussion about Judas Thomas' subsequent life. According to the Acts of Thomas, he was active in northern India where he was speared to death. Another tradition in both the East and West maintained that he died of old age at Meliapore in India. This evidence is found in the writings of Ephraem Syrus, Ambrose, Paulinius, Jerome, and later in the records of Gregory of Tours (*India and the Apostle Thomas*, Medlycott. London 1905). Gregory of Nazianzus held that Judas Thomas was buried in India (Or, 25), a position supported in the Acts of Thomas (1). However, John 'golden-mouthed' Chrysostom (347-407) said that his remains had later been brought from the East to Edessa in Syria (*Homily in Hebrews*, 26), then a Roman colony that supported a royal residence (Dio Cass. 77.12).

© Madras Tourist and Travel, 1976

A shrine to Judas Thomas near Madras, India.

According to Indian legend, Judas Thomas spent twelve years in villages in the state of Orissa on the Bay of Bengal and subsequently died in Kashmir. Catholic missionaries, Francisco de Azvedo and Ippolito Desideri, brought accounts from Tibet to that effect in 1631 and 1715 respectively (*Facts and Speculation on the Origin and History of the Christian Church,* Jacob Bryant,

London 1793). The claim that Judas Thomas lived, and eventually died, in India or Tibet is strengthened at the end of the 19th Century in the documents of Russian author and researcher, Nicolas Notavitch.

He recorded that his personal friend, a Roman Catholic cardinal, confided in him that the Vatican vaults held 63 complete and near complete manuscripts written in various Oriental languages that confirmed that Judas Thomas spent many years in India and Tibet and the tomb in Khanyar Street, Srinagar, Kashmir, is his. The manuscripts, said Notavitch, were brought to Rome by missionaries from India, China, Egypt and Arabia, and suppressed. An ornate structure in the Rozabel area of Srinagar (pictured) is held in tradition to be the tomb of Judas Thomas, nee Khrestus.

© Picture Courtesy of The Great Liberation Library, Tibet

The alleged tomb of Judas Khrestus.

CHAPTER 10

Khrestians active for centuries

The nature of the Khrestian movement

To understand the New Testament and some of the beliefs it expounds, it is important to acknowledge that the people of those early centuries were semi-savages and their religious systems followed the myths of numerous earlier gods and goddesses. It was Pelops, Zeus' grandson, who, in childhood was killed and cooked by his father, Tantalus, the son of Zeus, who then served his son's flesh to the gods as the ultimate sacrifice. Thus, the eating of human flesh, particularly children, and the drinking of human blood, occupied a foremost place in the rituals of many early religions.

The 'early Khrestians/Christians' adopted this ritual, and St Justin Martyr, writing around 160, described them 'a group of atheists'. He added that 'they met in secret to eat human flesh and once the lamps had been upset, to participate in promiscuous incestuous intercourse' (*1 Apology*, 26:7, Justin Martyr). One of the great Second Century accusations made against St. Justin Martyr and other early churchmen was that they also partook in those ceremonies (*Cannibalism, The Religious Significance*, Eaton University Press, 1943). In the 20th Century, the church tried to deny the accusations; 'Justin Martyr, Irenaeus, Tertullian, Minuclus, and others are accused of it (cannibalism) but we refute it, and constantly reject it. It is an infamous thing, and is falsely reported by the Heathen of them' (*Catholic Encyclopedia*, Justin Martyr, Transubstantiation).

Around a generation later, Emperor Marcus Aurelius (c. 180) recorded that Khrestians were still seen as a strange and distinct class of people given to a 'new and wicked superstition' (*Meditations*, Marcus Aurelius). Octavius 9, a church writing attributed to a late Second Century presbyter, Minucius

Felix, confirmed the bizarre Khrestian behavior:

> ... the names of brother and sister hallow fornification as incest. Their foolish superstition makes a boast of crime; a condemned criminal is the object of their veneration. Finally there is infant murder, cannibalism and the banquet with incestuous intercourse.

The cannibalism associated with this ritual intercourse is reported under the name of Agape (*Haer*, 26:45) and was translated 'love-feasts' in the New Testament (Jude 12). This drunken cannibalistic orgy was the early Khrestian/Christian form of the Eucharist, the drinking of human blood and the eating of human corpse flesh. In the Gospel of Mary, found in the Coptic Papyrus Berolinensis 8502 and taken to the British Museum in 1896, Mary's name is given as 'Mary Eucharis'. In a similar manner, the Gospel of Mary Magdalene records 'Mary Eucharis of Magdala' as Mary Magdalene's name. The striking similarity to the names of both Marys to the word 'Eucharist' suggests that they conducted Agape ceremonies, and were called 'Eucharists', just as baptizers were called 'baptists'.

Khrestians/Christians were excluded from the princely Diocletian (c. 305) baths because of their proneness to fight, and, a little later, in the middle of the Third Century, Origen said of them:

> They heap one another unwearyingly with all manner of abuses which pass over their heads, refusing to make the least concession for the sake of peace, and animated with a mortal hatred, one of the other. They eat human flesh and practice horrid things.

Some Fourth to Seventh Century Christian bishops had personal problems with the 'love-feasts'. St Jerome, for example, expressed disgust at the Khrestians/Christians for their participation, saying it was a 'sick and degraded practice' (*Epistle* 22, Jerome). The Bishop of Hippo, St Augustine, in 395, admitted embarrassment that his own mother, Monica, engaged in the macabre festive banquets, attending what he called 'drunken carousals' in cemeteries under the cover of darkness where human flesh was eaten from the coffins of the dead (*City of God;* Augustine, 1609 translation, quoted by Mosheim, 1694-1755). Bishop Ambrose of Milan unsuccessfully forbade such practices (*Confessions,* 6:2, c. 401) and the ritual was still being condemned as late as the Trullan Council in 692. It was a widespread and on-going animalistic custom and many of the populous joined the Khrestian/Christian movement solely to partake in the 'love-feasts' (Ibid).

The records of Emperor Julian

In the Mediterranean world of the Fourth Century, where the state depended so much on religion, ecclesiastical affairs were in such turmoil that the government felt called upon to interfere in the so-called mysteries of theology. Upon the death of Emperor Constantius in 361, Julian (332-363) was acclaimed *Augustus* … i.e., Emperor, and immediately set out to restore the ancient cults.

He lived and dressed like a monk, and slept on a hard pallet in an unheated room. He loved books, carried a library with him on his campaigns, vastly enlarged the library that Emperor Constantine had founded, and established others. Proud to be an author as well as a statesman, he sought to justify his policies with dialogues in the manner of the Greek satirist, Lucian of Samosata. In a 'Hymn to a King's Son' he expounded his religious beliefs and in a book called *Against the Galileans*, he spoke of the Khrestian's/Christian's religion. 'Their Gospels', he writes, in a preview of Higher Criticism, 'contradict one another, and agree chiefly in their incredibility; the Gospel of John differs substantially from the other three in narrative and theology'. He denounced the Khrestian's Gospels, saying, 'seldom has a man composed such nonsense' and criticized the use of myths in the budding church's texts.

He presented the Khrestian's/Christian's religion as 'a system of questionable dogma' and a movement torn with scandal and schism by the Arian dispute and the divisions of the East and West factions. In 361, Emperor Julian ordered all Khrestian/Christian presbyters to centre their discourses only on the Gospels of Matthew and Luke (*Encyclopedia of Roman History*, Matthew Bunson, 1994, Pg. 21) and at that time they were void of virgin birth and resurrection narratives.

Emperor Julian bitterly opposed the Khrestian/Christian movement because they 'had slaughtered most of his family', adding that they 'slit throats with a whisper'. (*Against the Galileans*, later called *Against the Christians*, and then, *The Arguments of the Emperor Julian,* Thomas Taylor (Translator), London, 1818) They had killed his father, his brothers, and many more; and he concluded that 'there were no beasts more ferocious than Khrestians/Christians' (*Against the Galileans*). He wrote of them bitterly fighting against each other, and more Khrestians/Christians were slaughtered by Khrestians/Christians than the church today dares to discuss.

He wept when he heard of famous temples being overthrown; of the priests of Mithraism being killed and their property distributed to the Khrestian/Christian mob. It was probably at this time that he accepted initiation into the Mysteries of Eleusis, just as Emperor Augustus did some 350 years earlier. He ordered them to make full reparation for the damage they inflicted on sacred shrines and demanded the demolition of Khrestian/Christian structures that had been built upon illegally seized lands of temples and synagogues. He made Khrestians/Christians ineligible to governmental offices and provided leniency for the populace who took violence in dealing with them.

From Emperor Julian's records, it seems that the Khrestian/Christian leaders were based in Antioch and a particular event there may have some significance to a reference in the Acts of the Apostles (Acts 11:26). A famous park called Daphne, once a sacred shrine of Apollo, had been taken over and changed into an amusement park by the Khrestian/Christian movement. Julian ordered the amusements ended and the shrine restored. This had hardly been completed when a fire consumed the new structure, burning it to the ground. Suspecting Khrestian/Christian incendiarism, Emperor Julian closed their Antioch headquarters and confiscated its wealth, killing several Khrestian/Christian leaders in the battle that ensued.

© St Peter's Church, Antioch, 1979

Antioch tourist authorities present this building as the first Christian church built in that city. It is probable that the cave behind this facade was originally the site of the headquarters of the Khrestian movement.

Subsequently, Emperor Julian was speared in a battle with the Persians when a javelin was thrust into his side, piercing his liver. He died on 27 June, 363, and the Khrestians/Christians of Antioch celebrated his death with public rejoicings, praising the assassin (*The Age of Faith,* pg. 21, Dr. Will Durant, Simon and Schuster, New York).

Hatred of the human race

An extract from a record of Emperor Theodosius I (379-395) revealed that the Khrestian/Christian movement was still a menace to the population some three decades later. He said:

> The mob that gave Khrestians their name hated them for their crimes; their leader had been active at the time of Pontius Pilate, and their deadly superstition

spread throughout Judea and Rome. Some confessed their crimes and were arrested; on their testimony, multitudes were convicted of arson, but also of hatred of the human race. (*Panegyric to the Emperor Theodosius,* Pacatus)

In 384, St John Chrysotom gave a similarly valuable account in a service he delivered at Antioch:

Among the thousands of Khrestian/Christian men here there are not one hundred who will be saved, and I have doubt about these. They are worse than the Jews of old; worse than the men of Sodom. They decorate their luxurious homes with nude marble statues and have flute-girls and obscene dances at their banquets.

In 392, Marcellinus Ammianus, a retired Roman general and historian, augments our knowledge with an eyewitness account of the Roman police being driven from the Forum into Subura by the fury of the Khrestian/Christian mobs (*Records of Events,* xxvii, 12-13, Marcellinus Ammianus, in the Loeb Classical Library). This appalling picture is added to by Socrates Scholasticus (380-450), a well-known church historian from whose name the term 'scholar' derives:

Women who refused to consort with them had their breasts squeezed in a wooden frame and severally bruised. Other women had their breasts burned with red-hot irons or had hot hard-boiled eggs pressed against them. This kind of torture, which the Pagans had never used against us, was invented by men who call themselves Khrestians/Christians. (*Church History,* Socrates Scholasticus, Jenning's Trans. 1911; also vol. 67 of the Migne Library of the Greek Fathers, chp. xxxviii)

About the same time, Salvianus (d. 456), a distinguished historian of Marseilles, wrote an open letter to the church that now forms part of a book called *On God's Government* (iii, 9, Milgne Collection, vol. 53). Salvianus was no cloistered monk or overheated and unbalanced fanatic. For the age he was a writer of cultural distinction, and, living in Marseilles, he was well placed to know the extensive world that he surveys. His writings are numerous and of the Khrestians/Christians, he says:

It is a grave and painful thing that I am now going to say. The church of God, which ought to appease God, does nothing but provoke his anger. Apart from the very few who avoid evil, what is nearly the whole body of Khrestians/Christians is but a sink of vice. How many of them will you find who are not drunkards, gluttons, adulterers, fornicators, rapers, gamblers, robbers, or murderers? Which of them is not stained with human blood or foul with the slime of impurity? For to this turpitude of morals nearly their entire population has sunk, so that in the whole of their group it is deemed a sort of holiness if you are not very vicious.

In this last sentence we see the emergence of a small body of Khrestians/Christians with moral values opposing that of their larger number. They moved to live quietly in isolated areas and became known as 'vagabond monks', or 'coenpbites'. They developed a belief in the divinity of the Roman god, lived in pairs, or groups of three, and it was from this body of people that communal life in monastic settlements subsequently developed.

The Khrestian/Christian movement remained active for many centuries and its existence was the reason for the development of a military arm of the church. This aspect of Christianity's expansion is addressed after the story of the life of the second-born, Jesus.

CHAPTER 11

The life of the second-born

In order to appreciate fully the available material that can help us with our inquiry, we must investigate the records and traditions that say Jesus as a youth spent time in ancient Britain. There are four separate and independent traditions that present a consecutive story about the boy Jesus and Joseph of Arimathea traveling regularly to and from Britain. It is significant that all four traditions are entirely independent, but is synchronically achievable, and it is equally significant that no tradition exists in the adjoining shire of Devonshire.

Unfortunately, the majority of Britain's history for the first 500 years of the present era is almost entirely blank and historic evidence to support the traditions is difficult to find. Had the large collection of British archives and manuscripts deposited at Verulum as late as the year 860 descended to our time, invaluable light would have been thrown on this and other subjects of native interest. From Gildas the Wise (b. 425, *Vide*, pg. 160), the first British historian who lived in the Fifth Century, there is some data and we also glean a few scattered scraps of information from Taliesin, the Welsh Prince-Bard and authority on matters Druidical (*Book of Taliesin*).

The traditions of Cornwall

The first tradition is found in Cornwall and is recorded in Barring-Gould's *Book of Cornwall*. He states that 'another Cornish story is to the effect that Joseph of Arimathea came in a boat to Cornwall, and brought the boy Jesus with him, and later taught him how to extract tin and purge it from its wolfram. When the tin is flashed, then the tinner shouts, 'Joseph was a tin miner ... Joseph was in the trade''. For some centuries, Cornwall had almost the world monopoly of tin production. Herodotus (c. 484-430 BC), the Father of History and the World's First Travel Writer, refers to Britain as the Cassiterides or Tin Islands (Herodotus, 3:115). Aristotle (384-322 BC), Polybius (205-125 BC), Diodorus Siculus and Posidonius, both of the first century BC, all deal at length with the British tin industry and traditions still linger with considerable strength concerning Joseph of Arimathea's involvement.

© 1986. The Trustees of the British Museum

This large mosaic was found in the Fourth Century in a foyer of a house in Dorset, twenty-eight miles from Glastonbury. Because of the symbolic Chi-Rho, the church claim that this is the first representation of Jesus ever discovered. No one has been able to satisfactorily explain why this mosaic was found in England, nor why Jesus is wearing Druidic headgear.

The second and third traditions are found in Somerset and provide descriptions of Jesus and Joseph of Arimathea sojourning to a place called Paradise. A letter signed 'Glastonian' in the *Central Somerset Gazette* on 7 August 1936, revealed that 'Paradise' was also the ancient Celtic Glastonbury but the writer does not give his/her authority for the statement. It is also believed that Jesus and Joseph often stayed at the little Somerset village of

Priddy on top of the Mendip Hills, a few miles north of Glastonbury. The records of Geoffrey of Monmouth state that Emperor Augustus equipped Jesus 'with weapons' for the journey from Rome (*The History of the Kings of Britain,* Geoffrey of Monmouth, Penguin Classics, p. 119) and this reference places Jesus in Britain at least once before the age of twenty-three, for Augustus died in the year 14.

CHAPTER 12

The House of Hillel

After being raised by the Essenes, Jesus trained as a rabbi in the school of Rabbi Gamaliel Hillel (*Codex of Hillel*), the most famous Pharisee of the early first century. Rabbi Hillel became the president of the Sanhedrin in the First Century and the actual time he lived is vital in the development of this argument. Christian dictionaries document his lifespan from 60BC to 9AD with a question mark (?) indicating an uncertainty. However, synagogue sources record that 'he was born early in the 1st Century AD and died circa 72AD'. The conflictions in dating make it not improbable to suggest that the uncertain date of Rabbi Hillel's birth and death in Christian reference sources is a deliberate editorial adjustment to distance him from the time of Jesus.

Rabbi Gamaliel Hillel's father was Hillel the Elder. He was born into the House of Boethus in Babylon (present-day Iraq) about the year 75BC, and died in 23AD. Rabbi Gamaliel Hillel fathered a son also called Gamaliel who came to be known as Gamaliel of Jabneh, a town that later was called Jamnia. The birth date of Rabbi Gamaliel of Jabneh is unknown but it is recorded that he died of a great age in 115 (*Encyclopedia Britannica*, 9th Ed., Vol. XI, Pg. 59). He was the grandson of Hillel the Elder and some later historians sometimes referred to Gamaliel of Jabneh's father as Gamaliel the Elder.

It was at the feet of Rabbi Gamaliel of Jabneh that Paul/Saul of the New Testament learned the Torah (Acts 22: 3). Rabbi Gamaliel of Jabneh was one of the most important scholars of his generation, being responsible for the final version of the 'Eighteen Benedictions'. He conducted debates with Roman philosophers, Essenes and anybody interested in the Law of Moses (The Torah). That Rabbi Gamaliel's death is recorded as occurring in 115 provides a New Testament reference giving the approximate dates of the lifetime of Paul/Saul, yet this biblical connection between the two has been long overlooked by Christian analysts.

Jesus becomes a rabbi

Rabbi Gamaliel Hillel taught his students to 'seek peace, love all creatures and bring them closer to the Torah' (*Sayings of the Fathers*, 1, 12), the first five books of the Old Testament. Under Hillel's instruction, Jesus subsequently became a rabbi 'at life's half distance' in the House of Hillel. A rabbi, in Judaism, is a person qualified by academic studies of the Hebrew Bible to act as a spiritual leader and religious teacher of a Jewish community or congregation.

Rabbi Jesus was a man of pristine virtue and severity, much devoted to the maintenance of the Law of Moses carried in the Torah. From the documents available, it is important to remember that Rabbi Jesus was a Roman citizen raised by the Essenes and he taught the faith of the Jewish people in the some of the four hundred and eighty synagogues in the area at the time (Luke 4:44). To play down the importance and connotations of the title 'rabbi' given to Jesus in older versions of the New Testament, newer editions replaced the original word with the less controversial, 'teacher'. However, the word 'rabbi' is used in the oldest and most reliable texts of the New Testament and in the FIRST Vulgate.

The prophet steps out

The Essenes were famous not only as religious teachers of the Law of Moses, but were especially noted for their vast knowledge of herbal medicines. Josephus said that they …

> … have a profound knowledge of the art of healing, and study it arduously. They examine herbs and plants, which they prepare as medicine for man and beasts. They also know the use and worth of minerals as medicines, and do a great deal of good by applying these for healing the sick.

Josephus said that 'many of the Essenes have often stepped forth among the people as healers and prophets' and because of their knowledge of natural therapies they became known as the Therapeutai, 'the healers, the ones who laid their hands upon' (applying their herbal ointments). This was part of the role of Rabbi Jesus and many examples of his well meaning are found in the New Testament.

Before his official dispatch into the world as a rabbinic prophet, his cousin, John the Baptist, baptized Rabbi Jesus in the River Jordan. Baptism, or the theoretical purification from past sins by sprinkling water upon the skin, was supposed by many to be an exclusive Christian ceremony. Rev. J. P. Lundy (*Monumental Christianity,* 1876, Pg. 385) provided evidence that the rite was introduced sometime after the Babylonian captivity (circa 397 BC) and Eusebius wrote that it was 'an ancient custom' in his time (260-339).

The Essenes purified themselves frequently, using a ceremony common to many earlier religions. Once they were 'made clean from some supposed pollution or defilement', they hated to be touched.

Extreme importance was attached to ceremonial purity, and they followed scrupulously the prescriptions against Levitical defilements; even for a junior to touch a senior was pollution to the later.

There are references in the New Testament to Rabbi Jesus resisting being touched. 'Do not touch me', he demanded in the Gospels of Mark and Luke (Mark 5:30; Luke 8:45-46).

It is worth noting that the 'Messianic Rule' of the Dead Sea Scrolls records that all male members of the Essene community were, at the age of thirty years, regarded as mature and ready to serve the public. The New Testament states that, 'Rabbi Jesus, when he began his ministry was about thirty years of age' (Luke 3:23). In the canonical Gospels of Mark and John, the 'original Hebrew' version of the Gospel of Matthew, and the earliest Gospel of Luke, it was at this age that Rabbi Jesus' story began. At that time, he would have been a married man, for 'eighteen years is the age of the nuptial canopy', says the rabbinical text on the stages of life.

'An unmarried man may not be a rabbi'

Jesus is called 'rabbi' thirteen times in the New Testament and the Jewish Mishnaic Law of the time specifically states that 'an unmarried man may not be a rabbi'. Thus Jesus could not have obtained the status of rabbi if he had been unmarried, and the ramifications of this knowledge have proved embarrassing for the church for centuries. According to the Gospels, Rabbi Jesus was teaching and living the religious beliefs of the Law of Moses which provided for marriage, and under that Law, it was proper for Jesus to have had several wives at the one time (Noah's father, Lamech, was the first polygamist recorded in the Bible).

The truth hidden in the darkness

The earliest documented reference to Mary as the mother of twins appears in the Mark Gospel of the Sinai Bible (Mark 3:32) and relates to a group of people who address Jesus and say, 'Your mother and your brothers and your sisters are outside asking for you'. Modern Bibles show the three words, 'and your sisters', to be removed or indexed to a footnote. Only one of Jesus' sisters, Salóme, (Mark 15:40) is clearly defined in the Gospels but clarification that there were more appears in two other narratives, the first referring to Jesus' 'sisters' in the Gospel of Matthew (13:56).

Ancient church tradition maintained that one of Jesus' sisters was named Maria, or as recorded in some early Gospels, Margi. That this 'Maria/Margi of Christian tradition' was the 'elusive' Mary Magdalene is a conclusion that can be biblically supported, and it is possible to establish that she was Jesus' half-sister. The names of Jesus' sisters can be determined by combining the incomplete Gospel documentation with early presbyterial writings and the suppressed Gospels. But first it is important to clarify a vital Gospel statement, which claims that Lazarus and Martha were Mary of Bethany's brother and sister.

There is substantial reason for regarding Mary of Bethany and Mary Magdalene as the same person. Presbyters of the time considered them to be so as did popular tradition (*Encyclopedia Britannica*, 9th Ed, Vol. 10, 'Gospels'), and many Christian scholars today concur. Adding to the biblical construction of Mary's name, Magdalene came to be taken as meaning 'from the area of Magdala'. Today Magdala is presented as a wealthy and depraved First Century Roman holiday resort situated six miles south of Capernaum in Galilee, not far from the famous mineral springs at Tiberias. However, had Mary Magdalene moved to Bethany, she would traditionally have been called Mary of Bethany, and this is an important point in determining that Mary Magdalene and Mary of Bethany were one and the same person.

© Rothenberg

The picture shows the Sea of Galilee, with the modern town of Tiberias in the centre. The famous hot springs are in the foreground and the mountains of Upper Galilee are on the horizon.

If Mary Magdalene and Mary of Bethany were one and the same person, and the sister of Jesus called Margi or Maria in early church tradition was Mary from Magdala (or Bethany), then that made Martha and Lazarus half-sister and brother to Jesus. If so, this would mean that the so-called Virgin Mary had four paramours and nine children, including the twins. They were Tiberius, the father of Judas Thomas and Jesus (twins), the unnamed father of Jose and Simon (Mark 6:3; Matt 13:55), Philip (Herod), father of James the Younger and Salóme (Mark 3:18; Matt 10:3; Mark 15:40) and Cyrus, the father of Mary (Magdalene nee Bethany), Martha and Lazarus (Gospel of

James). When discussing the Gospel evidence of Mary's children, the very orthodox *Smith's Bible Dictionary* said: 'This is one of the most difficult problems in Bible history, and we don't know how to explain it'.

Mary Magdalene's royal father

Nowhere in the New Testament does it say that Mary Magdalene was a prostitute. More importantly, the only detrimental Gospel statement regarding Mary Magdalene's reputation is carried in Fourth Century interpolations that make up the last twelve verses at the end of the Mark Gospel today but are not in the earliest New Testaments available. For that reason most modern Bibles delete these narratives, or index them to a special footnote advising readers that they were later forgeries added to the Bible. So why did the church wish her discredited in this fashion?

Support for the fact that she was romantically involved with Jesus commenced with some Gospels suppressed early in church history. The Gospel of Mary, for example, recorded that Rabbi Jesus 'loved' Mary Magdalene and the Gospel of Philip said he 'used to kiss her often on the mouth'. In an ancient undated writing found by Reverend W. D. Mahon in the St. Sophia Mosque at Constantinople in 1883, the story is told of…

> … an old man who lived on the road to Bethany who once had been a rabbi, a man of great learning, and well skilled in the Law (of Moses), and that Jesus was often there with him reading the Law; that his name was Massalian, and that I might find Jesus there with him; But he was not there. Massalian said he was often at Bethany with his family, and he thought there was some love affair between him and one of the girls. I asked him if he had seen anything like a courtship between them. He said he had not, but inferred from their intimacy and from his fondness on the woman's part as well as from the laws of nature, that such would be the case.

Mary Magdalene is portrayed throughout the Gospels as a leader, and in the constant presence of Rabbi Jesus. All four Gospel accounts mention her first when speaking of the group of twelve women associated with the story of Jesus and, in the *Byzantine Chronicles,* she is recorded as being in Rome with Jesus at the time of the trial of Judas Khrestus. The information showed she played a leading role in his life, in fact, Mary Magdalene and other ladies, financed the ministry of Rabbi Jesus (Luke 8:3).

© Film Library of Renaissance Art, Italy

Michelangelo's Pieta shows Jesus in the arms of a young lady, obviously not of his mother's age. Was Michelangelo subtly passing on his secret knowledge that Jesus had a wife? Insert; a detail of the lady's face.

The well-established image of Mary Magdalene as a prostitute is a slander not based on fact and, like so many other stories inspired by a censorious church, has long been proved nonsense. Despite all attempts by Christian historians to cast her as a redeemed prostitute, there is no external or Gospel evidence to that effect. So who was Mary Magdalene?

From an obscure period in Christian history, her name is again found in an ancient document called *The Golden Legend,* compiled from a variety of early Gospels by the Bishop of Genoa, Jacobus de Voragine (1230-1298) and first published in Latin in 1275. It provides a reference drawn from the

Gospel of James, originally named after the brother of Jesus but re-titled under curious circumstances in 1552 to *Protevangelion*. This narrative states that Mary Magdalene, far from being a prostitute, was a woman of the noblest birth. From a 15th Century English translation of this work, we read this verse:

> Mary Eucharis Magdalene had her surname of Magdalo, a castle and was born of right noble lineage and her parents which were descendant of the lineage of kings. And her father was named Cyrus and her mother also Mary Eucharis.

Thus the church preaching of Mary Magdalene being a prostitute is contested in one of its own writings.

The Bible Fraud provided an extensive case that Mary Magdalene's father was Tenvantius, King of Britain and she was a Celtic Princess. The Druids called her Branwen, and it is probable that she was a high priestess (*Encyclopedia of Occultism,* Pg. 97). The name Tenvantius was an ancient variation of Cyrus, recorded in the Gospel of James as being a 'descendant of the lineage of Kings'. Mary Magdalene was Rabbi Jesus' second wife to whom she bore three children, Princes Cadwalladr, Prince Polydore, and Princess Anna, and that information was sensitive to the church's presentation of Jesus, and required nullification.

It is now generally understood that the story of a woman called Mary of Egypt was later adopted into the church story and applied to Mary Magdalene as the Gospel stories evolved. Mary of Egypt was a Third Century prostitute from Alexandria who solicited business among the pilgrims *en route* to Jerusalem. Subsequently she gave up her whore's life, became devout and lived as a female hermit in the Syrian Desert. She was later canonized for her alleged miracle of walking across the waters of the Jordan to take Holy Communion.

The tradition of incest

Documented twice in the Old Testament is a tradition that directly influenced all teachers or followers of the Law of Moses. This tradition accepts the act of incest to be approved by God. Moses' parents, for example, were nephew and aunt (Gen 6:20), and Abraham clearly states that Sarah was 'the daughter of my father but not the daughter of my mother; and she became my wife' (Gen 20:12). Therefore, under the Law of Moses, Rabbi Jesus could legally marry his sister or half-sister, and this may have been the reason why the later Gospel writers tried to disassociate him from Mary Magdalene by defaming her.

Therefore, it was quite proper and correct for Rabbi Jesus to marry his half-sister, Mary Magdalene, and he probably did, both parties being of 'noble lineage' through both their mother and fathers. This may have been the reason why the church tried to disassociate Rabbi Jesus from Mary Magdalene who, in this scenario, was the Virgin Mary's daughter from another marriage.

The writings attributed to Paul substantiate that the apostles and the men of Jesus' time clearly believed they had divine permission to marry their sisters: 'We have authority to lead about a sister as a wife, even as the leftover apostles and the Lord's brothers and Cephas, do we not' (1 Cor. 9:5, Sinai Bible). This narrative clearly states that Rabbi Jesus' brothers were married, probably to his (and their) two remaining sisters, Martha and Salome. If this narrative gives a correct picture of what the author of the Epistle originally conceived, then it positively reveals a family tradition of inter-marrying.

The wedding at Cana

The possibility that Christianity's Jesus Christ was a married man and fathered children causes believers to react with horror. The church defense for the suggestion is to point to the lack of documentation in the Gospels that specifically says that Rabbi Jesus was married. Just as relevant, the Gospels do not say that Rabbi Jesus was not married either. In fact, there is a deathly silence in the New Testament regarding Jesus' marital status. With the known restructuring of the Gospels, it is probable that any direct references to him being married in the earliest texts were later edited out. The numerous connotations and indirect references in the current version of the Gospels, strongly suggest the authors were under the firm impression that Rabbi Jesus was married. Whether the wedding ceremony found only in the Gospel of John was that of Rabbi Jesus' could be discussed forever, but it probably was. According to the Gospels, Mary played a significant role and a large body of people was in attendance.

© Photograph by Jacob Issacson, 1978

Modern-day Cana of Galilee.

Sex is clearly encouraged by the God of the Old Testament, particularly for recreational purposes (Deut. 21:10-14) and Judas Khrestus and Rabbi Jesus did not make celibacy a pre-requisite when choosing their followers. Many, if not all, were married (1 Cor. 9:5; Sinai Bible) and church tradition holds that Simon of Petra fathered three children while according to Paul's own statement, he himself had been married but was widowed (1 Cor. 7:8). The writings of Clement of Alexandria note that the disciple Philip, as well as Simon, brother of Judas Khrestus and Rabbi Jesus, had married and produced families. Clement's records support the claim that Rabbi Jesus' brothers married their sisters. In the Gospel of Matthew, Rabbi Jesus declared 'a man shall leave his father and mother and be joined to his wife' (Matt. 19:5). Given the traditions of the time, Rabbi Jesus practiced what he preached.

CHAPTER 13

The books of 'magic' written by Jesus

Jewish tradition invariably asserted that Rabbi Jesus learned something special on a journey to Egypt. The kernel of this persistent accusation may perhaps be reduced to the simple historical element that he went to Egypt for Initiation into the Secret Mysteries and returned with far wider and more enlightened views than those of his religious associates. At some later stage, he took it upon himself to teach his twin brother about the mysteries of eternal life, and this is exactly what the Gospel of Thomas accredited to Jesus in the opening sentences.

The accusations against Rabbi Jesus of learning 'the magic of Egypt' are numerous and one of the most enduring charges of the Jews and the early presbyters. 'They even ventured to call him a magician and a deceiver of the people', complained St Justin Martyr (*Dialogue,* Pg. 69). In another passage, Justin Martyr, giving as his authority Trogus Pompeius, showed Joseph, the 'father' of Jesus, as having acquired a great knowledge in magical arts with the high priests of Egypt (*Apology,* Justin, xxxvi, 2). This reference may be to Rabbi Jesus' 'religious father' who was appointed as his mentor during his time with the Essenes. The church again recorded the word 'magician' in relation to Rabbi Jesus, this time by Bishop Eusebius in the Fourth Century. He said that Hierocles, Governor or Bithymia (303), claimed that the First Century sage, Apollonius of Tyana, had done works far greater than Rabbi Jesus who Hierocles described as 'a magician and a robber' (*Ecclesiastical History,* Eusebius).

One of the best and most unquestionable proofs of the magician assertion is found in the so-called Museo Gregoriano. On the sarcophagus which is paneled with base-reliefs representing the miracles of the Gospel Jesus Christ may be seen the full figure of Rabbi Jesus, who, in the resurrection of Lazarus appears beardless and equipped with a wand in the received guise of a necromancer whilst the corpse of Lazarus is swathed in bandages as an Egyptian mummy. This sarcophagus is placed among the earliest productions of that particular form of art which later inundated the world with mosaics and engravings representing the events and personages of the New Testament (*Gnostics*, King, Pg. 145). 'The name of Lazarus suggests symbolism' said the *Encyclopedia Biblia* and Bishop Irenaeus agreed, saying, 'and he that was 'dead' in initiation came forth bound with bandages, feet and hands. This was symbolical of that man who had been bound in sins' (*Against Heresies,* Book V, 13).

© Catalogo del Museo Sacro IV, Vatican City, 1959; also, Prof. Morton Smith, Ph. D., The Hebrew University, Harvard

Jesus depicted as a 'magician' in the 'raising of Lazarus'.

'Magic' a disease of religion

When one seeks for clarity on the churchmen's position of the 'magic' of Rabbi Jesus, they refer the reader to the subject of 'the occult' and say that a magician is 'a person endowed with secret knowledge and power like a Persian magus' (*Catholic Encyclopedia*, Vol. XI, PG. 197). Principally, this is the intended meaning of the 'Magi of the East' in the Gospels, who were present at the nativity of Jesus, and presented gifts to the newborn baby. The church added that the Magi 'work miracles not by the power of God, gratuitously communicated to man, but by the use of hidden forces beyond mans control. Its advocates, despairing to move to the deity by supplication, seek the desired result by evoking powers ordinarily reserved to the Deity' (*Catholic Encyclopedia*, Vol. XI, Pg. 197). The church then said that 'magic' is ...

> ... a corruption of religion, not a preliminary stage of it as the Rationalists maintain, and it appears as an accompaniment of decadent rather than of rising civilization. There is nothing to show that in Babylon, Greece and Rome the use of magic decreased as these nations progressed; on the contrary, it increased as they declined. It is not true that 'religion is the despair of magic'; in reality, magic is but a disease of religion.

It is surprising to see 'magic' used as a measure for determining the level of decadence within any given society, particularly when Rabbi Jesus is recorded to have been a Magi.

'Simon the magician' honoured as a god

Simon, of New Testament fame, was also a 'magician', and in some Bibles he is called, Simon Magi. Simon was a magician because he too had been initiated into the Mysteries in Egypt, and it seems that he was an Egyptian himself. A widespread belief existed among the populous that Simon was 'he who should come' and a large amount of detail exists about him in early church records (*First Apology of Justin Martyr,* xxvi, lvi, *Dialogue,* c. Tryphonem, cxx). Justin Martyr said he 'performed feats of magic in Rome during the reign of Claudius (d. 54), was held to be a god, and honored by the Senate and people with a statue in the middle of the Tiber, between the two bridges, bearing the inscription in Latin, 'Simoni, Deo sancto ... Simon the Holy God' (Ibid). Simon's doctrine asserted 'that none could possibly have salvation without being baptized in his name' (*Adverse Haereses,* Tertullian, c.i; ANF. iii, 649), and the sentiment of that proclamation is found in Christianity today.

St. Austin (c. 380) asserted that it was generally known in church circles that Rabbi Jesus had been initiated in Egypt, and that he wrote books concerning magic (*Magia Jesu Christi*). In the Gospel of Nicodemus, the Jews brought the same accusation before Pontius Pilate: 'Did we not tell you he was a magician?' (*Codex Apocrypha, New Testament*, I, 243, Fabrius; also Tischendorf, *Evang. AP*. Pg. 214). Celsus spoke of the same charge, and in the *Clementine Recognitions* (ten books, quoted by Origen, mid-Third Century), the accusation was brought against Rabbi Jesus that he did not perform miracles but practiced magic, and carried about with him the figure of a seated skeleton.

It was with Simon that we see one of the earliest clashes between Christianity's exoteric (external) doctrines and that of the esoteric (spiritual) teaching of the Mystery Schools. An interesting legend concerns Simon and tells of his theosophical contests with Simon from Petra (St Peter today) while the two were said to have been promulgating their differing doctrines.

Simon was to prove his spiritual superiority by ascending to heaven in a chariot of fire. In the story, written some four hundred years after his lifetime, he was picked up and carried high into the air by unseen infernal spirits. When Simon of Petra saw this, he cried out with a loud voice ordering the invisible spirits to release their hold on Simon. The evil spirits, when so ordered by the great saint, were forced to obey. Simon Magi fell a great distance and was killed, which decisively proved to the 'rabble' the superiority of the Christian saint's non-spiritual powers. This story was undoubtedly manufactured out of whole cloth, as it was only one of many accounts concerning Simon Magi's death, none of which agree.

CHAPTER 14

The initiation of Jesus in Egypt

Using New Testament narratives it is possible to show that Rabbi Jesus was a full initiate into the Ancient Egyptian Mysteries. In the Gospels, his ministry terminates in a trial and sentence in which he is shown with the resolve to go through a particular 3+-day period of suffering, after which 'I shall rise again' (Matt. 27:62-63).

Before the initiatory candidate could learn the basis of the Egyptian Mysteries, he needed to have reached the mystical 'age of thirty', which did not require a passage of 30 physical years. The first 12 years required an actual passing of twelve years of time … but the candidate could attain the mystical 'age of thirty' any time following that, depending upon the measure of effort the individual candidate wished to give, which is 22 years in modern Freemasonry. The mystical 'ages' of 12 and 30 are significant in this study, for they are precisely the two ages given of Rabbi Jesus in the Gospels. He was in the temple at 12 years of age 'with the teachers' (Luke 2:42), meaning that he had completed the compulsory 12 years of training. Then, in the very next chapter of the Gospel of Luke, Rabbi Jesus was suddenly 'at about the age of thirty' (Luke 3:23), that being the mystical age of 30, and ready to commence his initiation.

The first initiatory step involved a procedure that took 40 days and included purification, not only physically, but dissolving all tendencies to evil thoughts. The candidate fasted, alternatively between vegetables, juices, and special herbal concoctions. The New Testament preserves the tradition with Rabbi Jesus being 'led into the desert … and he fasted forty days and forty nights' (Matt. 4:1-2). Jesus 'was led' by the person or guide who was to see him through his initiation.

The number 'forty' used in relation to Jesus is found many times in the Bible and its use is of particular importance. Bishop Augustine of Hippo (354-430) expressed wonder about that number when he said, 'How then, is work perfected in the number forty?' (*Commentary on the Gospel of John*, Augustine, Vol. 1, pg. 240). When analyzed, number forty is used in both Old and New Testaments as expressive of a particular period of probation or trial and probably originated with the forty-year Venus Cycle revealed by astronomers of the Mystery Schools. The Israelites, for example, wandered forty years in the wilderness, and forty years of bondage they served under the hard yoke of the Philistines. Moses spent forty days on the Mount of Sinai and both David and Solomon reigned for forty years each (2 Samuel 5:4 and 1 Kings 11:42). Elijah was in hiding forty days and for forty days the deluge fell. Then, for another forty days, Noah was shut within the ark. The men of Ninevah had a like period of probation under the preaching of Jonah. The punishment of scourging was limited to forty strokes (Deut. 25:3), so when Jesus entered into his probation period it was for forty days … it could be no other way in the mind of Gospel writers.

The trial period involved more than just fasting. The candidate was to avoid all contact with the outside world, all vacillation of mind, and all stimulation of emotions. During the forty days and nights of ordeal, he was required to study astronomical charts to supplement his skills in astronomy and to memorize charts of the heavens. He was also given a particular ritual from which to memorize certain passwords, secret signs and handclasps, skills still practiced in Freemasonry today. In a daily sacred ceremony in the temple he sipped Adibhuta, the juice of a sacred plant, and ate bread; the *Egyptian Book of the Dead* calls that ceremony Gyotishtoma Agnishtoma.

A 'private baptism' was conducted every day. The Edfu Texts record that there was once a low-lying Sacred Lake near the Great Pyramid that filled from the waters of the River Nile. Even today, adjacent to every temple of initiation in India is a lake or reservoir of holy water in which the Brahmins, the Master Teachers, and their devotees perform daily ablutions. Beside the ruins of many Mystery Temples of ancient Egypt are also found Sacred Lakes and the water was consecrated for that purpose. The holy water of the present-day Christian church is symbolic and carried-over from the baptismal rites of Egyptian Mystery Schools. Baptism was anciently called 'illumination' and some versions of the New Testament still use that word (Hebrews, 6: 4). The object of the ceremony was not to wash away material dust, but to symbolize the cleansing from one's sins, the purification of one's soul. Religious writings are replete with baptisms by immersion into certain sacred waters and such were the waters of ablutions near the initiatory temples ... to purify the consciousness and prepare it for reception into the Mysteries. For the individuals 'chosen', much was required, for then imposed upon him was a severe test designed to prepare him for the grade of 'Neocoris' (*Annobius*, liv, 5, 54: 5).

Tempted by the Devil

The forty days having expired, the initiatory candidate was then placed in an obscure chamber called 'Endymion', or Grotto of the Initiates, a room set aside for concentration and meditation, and he was there 'tempted by the devil':

> Here he was served with a delicious repast to animate his failing strength, by beautiful women, who were either the espoused of the priests, or virgins dedicated to Isis. They invited him to love them by gestures. He must triumph over these difficult tests to prove the command that he has over his passions.
> (*Crata Repoa,* or *Initiations of the Egyptian Priests*, Berlin, 1770)

Seven beautiful young women, each perfumed with a variant fragrance of the seven sacred oils of Egypt, were systematically sent alone into the room with the candidate to entice him into sexual intercourse. Had he succumbed to any of their advances, he was instantly dismissed and not permitted to proceed further into the initiatory process.

After a period of reflection came cross examination and he was interrogated as to the motives that lead him from worldliness to the sanctuary of the Hidden God. He was also examined on his fundamental knowledge of what he had learnt over the previous weeks and his fitness to progress was attained. If he answered satisfactoraly, the 'Stolista' (or Sprinkler) purified him by throwing water over his head. He had then to categorically confirm in a loud voice that he had conducted himself with wisdom and chastity.

The ceremony started at sunset and was completed at sunrise 3+ days later. The eighty-four hour duration period is determined from the *Egyptian Book of the Dead* and supported in the New Testament. The Gospels of John (19:14)) and Mark (14:2) both state that Rabbi Jesus was incarcerated on 'the preparation of the Passover' and Jewish calendars of the First Century record that the Passover was celebrated on a Wednesday, hence, Good Wednesday. Therefore, it seems that Rabbi Jesus began his initiation on Wednesday evening and completed it on Sunday morning. During that time he was permitted to sleep only on three brief occasions, called; the 'Three Hours Sleep of Osiris', the 'Four Hours Sleep of Sokar', and the 'Five Hours Sleep of Horus'.

Wearing a plain white tunic, he proceeded in the company of his guide/initiator who was magnificently clad in ceremonial Panther costume. Large numbers of unenlightened but curious passers-by gathered at that point and gazed in wonder at the candidate heading towards the hallowed premises. Appropriately, his guide carried a scourge or whip of cords by which the profane were driven back from the steps of the sanctuary. That part of the pageantry is identical in concept to the Gospel episode of the eviction of the worldly moneychangers from the holy temple of Jerusalem.

They approached the main entrance door inscribed with the following words, 'I will not let you enter through me unless you tell me my name'. That required the candidate to reveal the first password; 'The place of Light and Truth is your name'. An attendant called Keeper of the Gate stood at the South column bordering the main door and said, 'Unless you tell me your name, I will not let you past'.

The candidate was subsequently required to carry and/or drag a heavy cross through the initiatory temple. As he worked his way along the intended route, he was 'struck with reeds and fists', symbolizing the judges' pretended anger at his inferior wisdom, for he had not yet entirely departed from the lower levels of knowledge. A counterpart of the Egyptian ceremony is carried in the New Testament when the procession of Jesus was hampered by bystanders who 'mocked and beat him' as he dragged his cross. He was scourged and abused and they said to him 'who is it that struck you?'

The place of the skull

The Gospels said that Jesus 'carried his cross' and came to 'the place of the skull' where he subsequently met his demise. Taking the Gospel account and combining it with initiatory processes, a new understanding of the 'place of the skull' emerges. In one Gospel the word 'skull' is translated 'Golgotha' which is simply Greek for 'skull', but it came to mean a barren, craggy, oval shaped hilltop outside Jerusalem. In the remaining three Gospels, 'skull' is not translated 'Golgotha', but 'the place of the skull', for that was what it was in the initiatory progression. Such a physical place as Golgotha, like Nazareth, is not documented in any historical records and is only found in the New Testament where it was allegorically recorded as a location.

It appears the original translation of Golgotha was Gilgal, which is a megalithic circle of vertical stones, also called a cromlech. This structure could well be physical evidence of the survival of an ancient Old Testament cult for 'a Gilgal' where twelve vertical stone pillars was set up by Joshua after crossing the River Jordan (Josh 4:19-20). More interesting is the fact that both Elijah and Elisha were associated with 'a Gilgal' (2 Kings 2:1; 4:38) and Elijah was made to appear to Jesus Christ in the 'Transfiguration' (Matt 17:3-4; Mark 9:4-5; Luke 9:30-33).

The 'place of the skull' is a reference to the display of a human skull in the initiatory process and was used by Mystery Schools to that effect for thousands of years. For them it was symbolic, and connected the initiate with a higher awareness of his purpose that could not be reached with words. Associated with the chant, 'Remember you must die', later Egyptians adopted the concept and passed around a skull at feasts to highlight the reality of physical death. So important was the skull in mystical rites, it became the motto of the Order of the Death's Head, and one modern Secret Society is called 'Skull and Bones'.

If we wonder why 'the skull' is so important in Christianity today, it is a reflection of its vital and compulsory use in ancient (and modern) initiatory rituals. In old Christian paintings, particularly those in St Catherine's Monastery (Mt Sinai), a skull is depicted in association with famous churchmen. Orders of monks, such as Dominicans and Franciscans are always associated with human skulls and one of the several mysterious crystal skulls is called 'The Jesuit' because it had somehow been connected with the Jesuit priests of Italy. Pope Sylvester II (d. 1003) used an oracular skull to advise him on the path of Christianity (*Catholic Encyclopedia,* 'Sylvester') and the Medici popes used magical skulls in a similar manner. Paintings of St Francis of Assisi show him reverently holding a skull, and the Knights Templar worshiped a skull as their God. In old engravings of Masonic ceremonies the skull is displayed in the final stages of initiation (*The Secret in the Bible,* Tony Bushby, Joshua Books, Australia, 2003).

Before standing at the altar the candidate was told, 'put off thy shoes from thy feet, for the place whereupon thou standest is holy ground' (Ex. 3:5). He was then 'crucified'. He was firmly tied, ankle, wrist and upper arm, to the cross he had just carried and it was secured in a vertical position. He was then required to say three times, 'I raise myself to venerate God, the Master of the Great House'.

The act of 'crucifixion' was a symbol of the sacrifice of the individual self. It represented the whole of life being a surrender of the personage … a symbolic act of giving, rather than receiving. In that part of the initiation, the individual surrendered his own external will, with all its material desires and affections. It was designated the Passion because it represented the pain and stress that accompanied the process of initiation and his 'passion' to see it through; the pain of self-sacrifice, of resistance to temptation, the trouble connected with the maintenance of a constant life in the midst of a greedy and selfish world.

That particular act was a surrender consummated and demonstrated by the candidate and witnessed by standers-by. He actually presented himself and symbolically gave up his life, representing a complete, unreserved surrender, to the physical death, if need be, without opposition. He was tied to a structure that positioned him in the form of a cross. Ancient Egyptians believed that the true posture of prayer was to stand with out-stretched arms that formed a cross. That belief was later carried into Jewish tradition and written in the 'Psalms and Odes of Solomon' (pg. 42), 'I stretched out my hands and approached God … for the stretching out of my hands is a sign; my expansion is the outspread cross'.

Church admits 'invention of the cross'

The symbol of the cross originated as part of an ancient Egyptian initiatory rite and eventually found its way into Christianity. The church stated that in Christian history, 'there is no proof of the use of a cross until much later' than the Sixth Century *(New Catholic Encyclopedia*, Vol. IV, Pg. 475). It is recorded in church archives that the general use of the crucifix was ratified at the Sixth Ecumenical Council in 680 (Canon 82). The council decreed that 'the figure of a man fastened to a cross be now adopted' and the new church logo was later confirmed by Pope Hadrian 1 (772-95) (*Origin of Religion Belief,* Draper, Pg. 252).

About a century later, the first pictures of Jesus Christ standing against a cross slowly started to appear, mainly in Syrian art. In those depictions, he was of ripe age, 'utterly divested of all circumstances of suffering' (*Christ in Art*, Mrs. Jameson, Vol. 2, Pg. 317) and generally clothed in a long sleeveless tunic, called a 'colobium'. Earliest illustrations date from the end of the Eighth Century and probably the very first is called the Palatine Crucifixion, discovered in 1856 as a graffito on a wall in the page's chamber of the Imperial Palace on the Palatine Hill in Rome.

Members of the clergy consider the *Oxford Dictionary of the Christian Church* authoritative on all academic aspects of Christian theology. Its contributors include professors of ecclesiastical and church history, consultants to the Pontifical Biblical Commission and leading Christian academics. The first edition was published in 1974 under the editorship of Dr. Cross (*Oxford University Press*) and after the sell-out of the initial printing, he proudly exclaimed that 'a copy was in every parsonage in the country'.

In a remarkable disclosure, that orthodox reference work failed to record an alphabetical entry under C for 'Cross' but rather documented an extraordinary confession in bold capital letters on Page 710 called THE INVENTION OF THE CROSS (Page 842 in the 1997 Edition). The international Christian panel frankly conceded that Helena, mother of Emperor Constantine, 'invented the cross' upon which the church maintained that Jesus historically suffered and which today is 'the epitome of the Gospel'. The fraud of the crucifix logo was made official to Christianity in 1754 when Pope Benedict XIV (1740-1758) decreed that the emblem be displayed on every church and at every altar.

Administration of strong potions

The initiatory candidate remained tied in the position of a cross 'until evening', approximately three hours, during which time he was given a soporific drink. The hierophants of the Mystery Schools, the Brahmans of India in their sacred initiatory rites, the Druids in mystic ceremonies, and Greeks in their schools and academies of enlightenment all administered strong potions to their candidates to induce a supernormal experience. It was quite true that the sacred beverage, often the soma drink, was offered at certain stages of the initiatory process ... and it seemed to possess the faculty of liberating consciousness from the bonds of matter.

The Dead Sea Scrolls bore testimony of the souls of Essene initiates loosed into another world with the use of powerful fumigants, who like Egyptians, followed such practices. John Allegro, in his book, *The Sacred Mushroom and the Cross*, describes how Essenes attained higher levels of consciousness by means of Amanita Muscaria. Initiates said that the divine potion of the Mystery Schools produced not hallucinatory brain visions, but the actual freeing of the soul to journey in full consciousness into the higher realms of light; to experience true rebirth. Egyptian priests discovered herb extracts by means of which temporary clairvoyance was induced and made use of them during the initiation rituals of their Mysteries. The drugs were sometimes mixed with food given to candidates, and at other times, were presented in the form of sacred potions. The effectiveness of the narcotics is a matter of historical record.

That part of the initiatory process is reflected in the Gospels where Jesus was offered 'wine to drink, mingled with myrrh', a soporific drink (Mark, 15: 23). That august rite was a process that combined magical and *spiritual* forces to detach the candidate's soul from the heavy bondage of his fleshly body for a few hours, and sometimes for a few days, that he might ever live with the memory of that epoch-making experience and conduct himself accordingly.

Entrance into Heaven

With the candidate still tied in the 'cross-position', the initiators began to chant the three sacred syllables of the ancient mystic formula, being the word AUM. Evidence of that intriguing event is recorded in the Gospels during the crucifixion of Jesus; 'And behold, the curtain of the temple was torn in two from top to bottom' (Luke 27:51). That narrative had long puzzled biblical analysts but is explained in light of the initiatory process inside Egyptian Temples, the 'curtain' being the darkness opening up into the brightness of higher spiritual knowledge.

During the chanting the candidate then called aloud a pre-memorized question: 'Do you deny me the entrance into heaven, I who have at last learned the mystery of myself?' In that ritualistic drama, a voice then answered, 'He who is aware, *is:* behold'. The candidate was then told that the voice of the Serpent had spoken. Then the final words that concluded the performance were a thanksgiving prayer in which the candidate said, 'My God, My God, how thou dost glorify me'.

Attention is drawn to the 46th verse of the 27th chapter of the Gospel of Matthew that reads, 'Eli, Eli, Lama Sabachthani?' Translated, it says, 'My God, my God, why hast thou forsaken me?' words applied to Jesus, and further confirmation that he was an initiated man. To the unwary reader, that narrative also appears in the opening verse of one of Ezra's Psalms (22:1), curiously carrying the important number twenty-two. It reads, 'My God, my God, why hast thou forsaken me?' However, the Hebrew version of that verse translates to, 'Eli, Eli, lamah azabutha-ni?' In English: 'My God, my God, how thou dost glorify me'. That sentence rendered in its original words classified Jesus directly with the initiates of the Egyptian Mysteries.

The candidate remained in the 'cross position' (crucified) 'until evening' and then removed, now being in a semi-conscious state. He was then carried into another room where he was wrapped mummy-like (like Osiris) to the mournful groans of the assistants. At that point in the Gospels, Jesus was wrapped 'in linen' (Luke 23:53), again revealing that the Gospel writers were unknowingly recording major elements of Jesus' initiation.

The Third Degree

Jesus was now in the final stages of initiation … the Third Degree. In his drowsy state he was asked to whisper the secret word, which was 'Mah-hu-ahboni', being Ma-ha-bone in Freemasonry today. The seven highest ranking judges then entered the room wearing ritual headdresses in the form of animal masks representing Egyptian gods; Anubis, that of the Jackal; Horus, that of the hawk or eagle; Thoth, that of the ibis; Osiris, the lion; others wore their personal symbols. The headdresses of the Egyptians had great symbolic and emblematic importance, for they represented the auric bodies of the superior intelligence's of antiquity, the gods who gave them the mysteries that they preserved for centuries. They were emblematic of ancient secret truths of the first revelations of the gods to mankind.

The seven judges moved clockwise around the room seven times and then sat on the floor in the lotus posture forming a circle around the coffer. They again began to chant the mystic formula, AUM. The candidate was now rendered unconscious by three sharp blows to his forehead with a wooden mallet … that was a symbolic death. Now in the Death Trance, the judges picked up his mummy-like body and lowered it into a coffer.

That curious act symbolized a 'burial' in a 'coffin' and paralleled the Osiris ritual. Jesus endured an identical performance and was laid in a 'rock-hewn tomb' (Luke 23:53) in a ceremony that commenced with the rites of Osiris thousands of years earlier. The candidate remained in the 'coffin' until he regained consciousness. The aspirant had in fact been induced into a temporary 'death experience' with the departure from the physical body of the soul into the mysterious realms of the dead. There he learnt the 'Secret of the Dead', and the survival of the soul after death.

His removal from the 'stone tomb' after recovery provided the reason why the Gospel writers expressed amazement that the disciples of Jesus 'did not find a body' (Luke, 24: 3). The initiate had experienced the same ancient wisdom the Egyptian priests encoded into their writings ages before his time; the mystery of the human soul, of life and death; of initiation and liberation. He had learnt what the wise had sought to conceal from the masses. He knew well the penalties that awaited those who openly dared to reveal the Sacred Secret or any other associated teaching contrary to the theories of the reigning orthodox religious leaders.

Early in the First Century, Diodorus Siculus wrote, 'It is said that those who have participated in the Mysteries became more spiritual, more just and better in every way'. The same could be said of persons acquainted with a Near Death Experience, for its nature brings about extraordinary changes in the experiencer's character, turning many from materialism into believers of the existence of the soul, and henceforth a life lived with new hope and purpose.

Resurrected from death

Jesus could justly say that he had died, ascended and resurrected, awakening to discover a higher understanding of the significance of death. The same rite of 'death' and spiritual 'resurrection' for the neophyte, or the suffering, trial and re-birth, was later historicized by the Gospel writers who were not esoterically advanced enough to understand what really happened to Jesus. The nucleus of their story was built up from an outward interpretation of an inward initiation experience for they were 'simple creatures who understood nothing' (Sabinius of Hereclea c. 326, *The Bible Fraud*, Tony Bushby, pg. 212). The exoteric nature of the initiatory process provided confusion and their understanding of what had happened became externalized as an earthly event, and not the esoteric personal experience that it was. The 'ascension' of Jesus subsequently carried a false, purely material connotation, and was added into the Gospel of Mark in the Fourth Century.

The ancient civilizations inherited the Mysteries from a remote antiquity and they constituted part of a primitive revelation from the gods to the human race. Almost every people of pre-Christian times possessed its institution and tradition of the Mysteries. The Romans, the Celts, the Cretans, the Syrians, the Hindus, the Maya and American Indians, among others, had corresponding temples and rites with a system of graduated illuminations for initiates. The modern world knew little of those ancient rites yet they were conducted not only in the Great Pyramid, but also in a variety of structures, the world over. In Persian Mysteries were seven spacious caverns through which the aspirant needed to pass. Still existing today in India is the magnificent cavern of Elephanta, supported with four massive pillars, and walls covered with statues and carved symbolic decorations. The caverns of Salsette greatly exceeded in magnitude that of Elephanta, being three hundred in number, all adorned with symbolic figures that were placed in the most secret caverns, accessible only by hidden entrances.

The candidate had learnt that initiation itself involved 'dying', not a real physical death, but a symbolic one in which the soul was temporarily released or freed from the body and 'resurrected'. A journey into the realms of Beyond had been experienced by the successful initiate ... he had met with God, and now knew the highest hidden mystery ... the continued existence of life after physical death. Those who emerged from the portals of the initiatory temples belonged ever after to a secret order of exclusive Panther initiates who had glimpsed the eternal life that was lived in the heavens. That was the 'Final Revealing', and every initiate thus obtained personal proof of the immortality of his spirit and the survival of his Soul. His last 'epopteia' was alluded to by Plato in 'Phaedrus':

> Being initiated in those Mysteries, which it is lawful to call the most blessed of all Mysteries, we were freed from the molestation of evils which otherwise await us in a future period of time. Likewise, in consequence of this divine initiation, we became spectators of blessed visions resident in a pure light. There can be little doubt, then, that during a period of the initiatory ceremony, the candidate experienced visions of gods and spirits. Indeed, the most sublime part of the ceremony occurred when the initiate beheld the gods themselves, invested in a resplendent light.

That extraordinary veiled confession of one who had experienced initiation shows that the candidates enjoyed Theophany ... that is, they saw visions of gods and immortal spirits. The most sublime part of the 'Final Revealing' consisted in beholding the gods themselves, always it seemed, invested with 'resplendent light'. This statement of Proclus, another successful initiate, is unequivocal:

> In all the initiations and Mysteries, the gods exhibit many forms of themselves and appear in a variety of shapes. Sometimes, indeed, a formless light of themselves is held forth to the view. Sometimes the light is according to a human form and sometimes it proceeds into a different shape. Some of the

figures are not gods and excite alarm. These highest visions are seen only after the neophyte, through a regular discipline of gradual initiations, has developed psychical powers of clairvoyance, clairaudience and clairsentience.

When Proclus said that 'Some of the figures are not gods and excite alarm', he was referring to degraded invisible beings the initiated called, 'Inter-Dimensionals' (IDs). Those 'infernal deities' were described as grotesque creatures operating in the nocturnal shadows of the inferior sphere. It seemed that their purpose was to negatively affect the life of every human being on Earth and guide unenlightened souls to their undoing.

'Thou hast become a God'

Jesus, now dressed in a white toga, then walked out through the doorway called 'The Gate of Coming Forth by Day', into the morning sun to be met by his family and friends. His 3+-day ordeal of initiation in the Egyptian temple had ended and death held no more power over him. He had physically 'resurrected from death' and then walked among the living on Earth. He was now a Krst, and the last words he heard from his guide were: 'Farewell, thou who has experienced what thou hadst never yet experienced; from a man thou hast become a god'.

Origin of the Panther knowledge

Jesus now knew the secret Panther knowledge. In mythology, the first monster that Hercules exterminated was the Nemean Panther, and from its skin he made a long coat that when worn rendered him indestructible. Hercules' costume became the trademark of the 'Panthers' and they carried forward the special knowledge of their forefathers. The Panthers developed a confidential teaching system around the Osiris rites and their name became synonymous with 'secret information'. It was that group who were directly responsible for the advent of all later Mystery Schools and, even today, a group of people on Earth still carries the Panther knowledge (*Glimpses of Masonic History,* C.W. Leadbeater, The Theosophical Publishing House, Madras (Undated). In early ritual performances high initiates wore ceremonial costumes fashioned from Panther skins and embossed with five-pointed stars, striking garments that symbolically represented the special wisdom that they possessed.

In later times, those who achieved initiation into the highest Mysteries were awarded the appellation 'Panther', and that title was included into their family and given names. In that regard, Julius Caesar, Emperors Augustus and Tiberius, Rabbi Jesus, Joseph of Arimathea, and Agrippa, who built the Pantheon in Rome, are all recorded in history as carrying the Panther/Panthera designation, and that directly identifies them as initiated bearers of special knowledge. It is possible that John the Baptist was a Panther initiate for the Gospels describe him wearing a peculiar fur coat when he came out of the wilderness. They were 'versed in all the Wisdom of the Gods' (*Dictionnaire Egyptien*, Champollion, c. 1890) and their understanding of the Old Testament revealed that for centuries it was read by the uninitiated in a sense contrary to its intent.

The Egyptian hieroglyphic texts speak of an initiate as 'twice-born,' or 'born again' and he was permitted to add to his name the words 'he who has renewed his life', so that on some ancient tomb-inscriptions archaeologists still discover these phrases descriptive of the spiritual status of the deceased person. So little did the Gospel writers understand the initiatory process that they never perceived they were developing a story around a rabbi's experience of an ancient mystery rite in an Egyptian Mystery School.

It is probable that Jesus himself originally propounded as allegories the events of his initiation in Egypt. First Century Roman historian, Suetonius, referred to the famous old Roman adage of tradition that said; 'It is better to copy than envy', and copy they did. So intrigued were the common populous with Mystery Teachings that a body of people now called 'the early church fathers' mimed Panther concepts from their portable pulpits, and from that public re-enactment developed the word 'Pantomime' (Panther-mime). Imitating the initiatory drama became widespread on street corners and town squares throughout the Roman Empire as presbyters orated the 'good news' to the 'rabble' in eking out their living.

The sacred initiatory experience is the true secret origin of the world's major religious systems and provides answers to some of the most enigmatic mysteries of their development. It was not just Jesus who 'suffered, died, ascended and returned' in that ritualistic manner but others connected to mystical initiation were Indria, Buddha, Krishna, Quetzalcoatl, Pythagoras, Hercules and Apollonius. Those great characters were Panther initiates of the same line of teaching by degrees that arose originally in ancient Egypt. The chief feature of their lives is found to be in common, and the unmistakable sameness of the means of construction of their respective biographies is apparent … every one had passed through the trials of initiation … they knew the Secret. It was not in the course of their everyday life then, that the great similarity was to be sought, but in their inner state and in the most important events of their career as teachers of an esoteric (spiritual) principle.

Crucifixion unknown by First Century historians

The symbolic crucifixion of Jesus explains why historians of the day knew nothing of a special religious crucifixion, and the absence of a supposed stunning event is a glaring omission from the records of so many noted intellectual writers. Verification of a landmark or significant crucifixion of one Jesus Christ is absent in the writings of such highly regarded contemporary historians as Philo, Tacitus, Lucius Senaca, Pliny, Thucydides Sallustius, Suetonius, Valerius Martialis, Epictectus, Cluvius Rufus, Quintus Curtius Rufus, Josephus, Plutarch and the Roman Consul, Publius Petronius, who lived in Jerusalem at the time ascribed by the church to a crucifixion.

A crucifixion of the Gospel Jesus Christ was also unknown among the early church as late as the end of the Second Century. This was close to one hundred and seventy years after the church would like the world to believe that the brutal death of its god occurred. It must be pointed out that the modern church admits that the records of Bishop Irenaeus (d. 202) create serious problems. They said of him, 'Although of crucial importance in the development of the church's theology, Irenaeus presents problems of considerable difficulty in regard to details' about Jesus Christ' (*New Catholic Encyclopedia*, 1967. Vol. V11, Pg. 631). Irenaeus is fondly described by the church hierarchy as 'the depositary of primitive truth' (*Catholic Encyclopedia*, Vol. 11, 1907, Pg 582), but he denied a virgin birth, never mentioned a trial of Jesus Christ, said nothing of a crucifixion or resurrection, and claimed Jesus lived to an old age.

CHAPTER 15

Bringing secret knowledge to the world

It is not possible to exclude from the field of research into the story of Judas Khrestus and Rabbi Jesus any document that may hold out the faintest hope of throwing even a sidelight on the obscurities of Christian texts. Most opportunely, then, for our inquiry, is the availability of an ancient writing called The Narrative of Joseph of Arimathea. This old document has been given only brief treatment by the church in its dictionaries and encyclopedias, maybe because it presents information that opposes current doctrine. However, for the thesis presented in this book, it sheds a whole new light on the development of the Gospels, and it is too important to be denied.

As with many Christian writings, including the Gospels, there is a dispute as to the likely date when this document was written, but the general academic belief is that its composition dated to sometime around the beginning of the Third Century. The genesis of the story is much earlier and what is recorded in this document failed to capture the attention of most researchers of the New Testament. The manuscript generally relates to a fascinating account of the only Torah Scroll at Jerusalem being stolen and, because of this, the Jews were in a state of despair because they could not conduct a Passover. This is significant in our study because it was Rabbi Jesus who was accused of stealing the Torah.

A woman called Sarra publicly accused Rabbi Jesus of this act and the Jews said to her, 'We believe you' for they held her as a prophetess.

> At the fourth and fifth hours they went out and found Jesus walking in the street. Towards evening they obtained a guard of soldiers. They came to Jesus

and saying, 'Hail Rabbi'. They took Jesus to the High Priest who examined him. Jesus was held captive upon Sarra's word.

On the next day, being Wednesday, at the ninth hour, they brought him (Jesus) to the priest's hall and asked, 'Why did you take away the Torah?' He was silent.

The story of the 'missing' Torah finds a parallel account in traditional rabbinic and Jewish literature. In the Toldoth Jeschu, while we still hear of Rabbi Jesus' learning 'something special' in Egypt, its main feature is the recording of the theft of the Torah (and the Divine Name) by a 'strange device' from the Temple of Jerusalem. This 'strange device' may have simply been a cunning manoeuvre, for in the several variants of the story, we see the evolution of the tradition whereby Rabbi Jesus was said to have outwitted the guardians of the Torah Scroll. Thus, in the Palestinian Gemara we read these words:

He who scratches on the skin in the fashion of writing is guilty, but he who makes on the skin in the fashion of writing, is exempt from punishment … Rabbi Eliezer said to them: But has not Jesus brought 'magic' out of Egypt in this way? They answered him: On account of one fool we do not ruin a multitude of reasonable men.

There are several traditions of Jesus bringing writings out of Egypt on his skin and the one recorded here is the closest to the time of the original story. It is interesting to note that Rabbi Eliezer met with the objection that Rabbi Jesus brought 'magic' out of Egypt by 'marks' on the skin but not by 'scratching' (Tattoos). The marks were presumably not letters proper, that being the writing of words in Hebrew, for the discussion was not as to writing, but as to 'marks in the fashion of writing'. Did it refer to diagrams of sigils, or drawings of some kind, or to hieroglyphics? Yes it did … it refers directly to the Secret in the Bible and that information is recorded in an earlier book by this author (*The Secret in the Bible,* Tony Bushby, Joshua Books, Australia, 2003).

In discussing this complex line of tradition, all that needs be said at this time is that ancient Jewish belief plainly preserved an account of 'marks' on the skin of Rabbi Jesus. The idea in the mind of the rabbi was presumably that the Egyptians were known to be very jealous of their secret lore and did all they could to prevent it being taken out of their country. Rabbi Jesus then, according to the oldest rabbinic tradition, was said to have circumvented their vigilance by some such subterfuge as that which has been handed on in the story in the Palestinian Gemera.

The Sanhedrin condemn Jesus

In considering the preservation of these peculiar descriptions of the Torah being stolen in both Jewish and Christian tradition, it may be possible to provide an answer to a major unknown Gospel problem, that being the Romans had nothing to do with the punishment of Rabbi Jesus. No doubt it would be convenient to bring Pontius Pilate into the Jewish Talmud stories of Rabbi Jesus but they are conspicuous by their absence. It was the Sanhedrin who tried Rabbi Jesus, not the Romans (Mt. 26:3; Acts. 4.5.6.12.22.30), and the Gospels represent them as the supreme rabbinic court of justice (Mk. 14:55). They were the ultimate Jewish religious, political and legal council in Jerusalem, at and before, New Testament times. Before the beginning of the Christian era the Sanhedrin became sufficiently confident in its authority that the high priest, Hyrcanus II (63-40 BC) summoned Herod to stand trial on capital sentences he had passed without the Sanhedrin's authority (Josephus). At this particular time they had four species of capital punishment, all of which were just as cruel as Roman crucifixion ... stoning, burning, beheading and strangulation.

When Herod took Jerusalem in 37 BC he retaliated by killing the entire membership of the Sanhedrin (Josephus), but under the Roman procurators (6-41AD) the Sanhedrin's power increased once again. The chief priests were the key figures in the Sanhedrin and they were probably former high priests and members of the priestly aristocracy from which the high priests were chosen. According to Josephus, they were 'the leading men of the people, the leading people of Jerusalem, the powerful and the dignitaries'. Josephus recorded that it was the Sanhedrin who condemned James, the Gospel half-brother of Judas Thomas and Rabbi Jesus, to be stoned to death.

It seems that at this stage the Sanhedrin did not know that Rabbi Jesus has stolen the precious Torah, for they would have indeed a reason to bring him to trial on that basis alone, for the theft of their most valued document would prevent them from keeping the Passover and partaking in the consumption of the obligatory four chalices of wine. Not only would they have lost their Temple Torah, but also the sacred Secret it contained. The nature of the original grievance of the Sanhedrin is hinted at in the Gospel of John (11: 45-53) where it is said that the high priests 'questioned' Rabbi Jesus about 'his teachings' (John 18:19) and he replied that he had 'said nothing secretly' (John 18:20).

In connection with the charges against Rabbi Jesus, there is a passage preserved in the Babylonian Gemara that demands attention. It records the essence of the original charge against Rabbi Jesus, and runs as follows (in part):

> ... that thou shalt not have a son or disciple who burns his food publicly, like Jesus the Nazarene ... (*Babylonian Sanhedrin,* 103a)

The main point of the accusation is contained in the word 'publicly' for it was the doing of something or other 'in public' which apparently might not only have been tolerated privately, but which was presumably the natural thing to do in private. The main burden of Christian tradition was that Rabbi Jesus went out and taught the people the Law of Moses ... the poor, the outcast, the oppressed, the sinners, all of who, according to rabbinic law, the mysteries of the Torah were not to be expounded unless they had first of all purified themselves by the long process of initiation. These so-called 'ignorant and unclean' persons were 'Amme ha-aretz' (men of the earth) and the Secret in the Torah was certainly not for them.

Dark and light

The strict fold of rabbis charged Rabbi Jesus because 'he burnt his food publicly'. That is to say, Rabbi Jesus was about to renounce openly what he had learned in Egypt ... he was about to reveal the Secret in the Bible and, more importantly, the highly confidential Divine name of God. He said so himself:

> Nothing is covered up that will not be revealed, or hidden that should not be known. Therefore whatever was said in the dark shall be heard in the light,

and what was whispered in private rooms shall now be proclaimed from the rooftops. (Luke 12:2)

The disclosure of secret information blatantly violated the ancient rule of the order of high priests and Rabbi Jesus had to be stopped. It is evident that the whole point of the story of the 'burning food publicly' has to do with some scandal or breaking of the established rule or order of things, or with paving the way for doing so, and was the downfall of Rabbi Jesus. The main point here, however, is the question of why would Rabbi Jesus want the Torah. He said:

> Think not that I have come to destroy the Torah and the Prophets (the additional Old Testament books). I came not to destroy but to complete. (Matt. 5:17)

From the evidence of both the early church and rabbinic records, one of the most tenacious charges against Jesus was that he had learned 'something special' in Egypt. What this meant was that he had travelled to Egypt, learned the 'Secret' and returned to Jerusalem with 'marks in the fashion of writing' on his skin. With these inscriptions, he then needed the Torah, and there was only one at Jerusalem, to publicly demonstrate to the uninitiated the secret information that it held, an act stringently forbidden by Initiates. The attempted disclosure of age-old hidden information offended the priestly line 'for one is wholly forbidden to reveal their mysteries; rather one must keep them secret in silence' (*The Adepts* (4 Vols), M. P. Hall, Los Angeles, 1949 Reprint). For this reason he was arrested by the Sanhedrin, charged, and tried. 'The chief priests accused him of many things' (Mark 15:3) and found him guilty for attempting to make public the hidden Ancient Mysteries.

The death of Rabbi Jesus

Rabbinic records state that Rabbi Jesus was stoned to death by Pinhas (*Babylonian Sanhedrin,* 106b) and both Talmud's (Palestinian and Babylonian) contain a precise description that, in both cases, is appended to the following passage from the Mishna. *(Sanhedrin, 67a)*:

> … and to bring him forward to the tribunal and stone him. And thus they have done to Jesus at Lud, and they hanged him on the day before Passover.

But where was Lud? Some have suggested that maybe it derived from Lydda to Ludim to Lod (*1 Chron*. 1:11). However, this is not so for Lud (sometimes Llud) derived from 'the great burh, Lundunaborg, which is the greatest and most famous of all burhs in the northern lands' (*Ragnar Lodbrog Saga*). Both name and town alike are popularly accounted for in the wonderful legend of Geoffrey of Monmouth *(Chronicles)* that found credence in the Middle Ages. According to this story, Brutus, a descendant of Aeneas who was the son of Venus, founded this city after the fall of Troy, circa 1100 BC, and called it Troynovant, or New Troy. Some time around one thousand years later (c. 41 BC), there reigned in the same town King Lud, the father of Tenvantius, Mary Magdalene's father, who built walls and towers to his city, and renamed it Cáer Lud.

Thus Lud's Town became Londinium in the Fourth Century and then London, the capital city of England today and chief city of the British Empire (*Survey of London,* 1598. Continued by Munday, 1618, 1633 and by Strype; 1720, 1755). King Lud's name still lives in London today and is encompassed in one of the seven double gates called Ludgate, the location of St. Paul's Cathedral and the probable site of the stoning of Rabbi Jesus.

© W. Palmer; Tony Bushby, 2005

Death by stoning.

Both rabbinic accounts are part and parcel of the Lud tradition and the death of Rabbi Jesus in both writings record stoning in Britain, clearly inferred from the Babylonian Talmud. Stoning, and then hanging the body on a vertical stake, is recorded in Jewish history, and Jesus Christ 'hanging on a stake' is also preserved in the canonical Christian writings today (*Acts of the Apostles,* 5:40). The word 'stake' is found in the oldest Christian Gospels and the word 'cross' was later substituted for 'stake' in the restructuring of Christian texts in the 16th Century (*Crosses in Tradition,* W.W. Seymour, N.Y. 1898).

The age of Rabbi Jesus at his death

The Codex Nazaraeus said, 'John the Baptist had baptized for 42 years when Yesu (note the spelling of Rabbi Jesus' name in this manuscript) came to the Jordan to be baptized with John's baptism'. Assuming that John the Baptist was around twenty years of age when he commenced baptizing, this statement if reliable, would show Rabbi Jesus to be around sixty years old when baptized, for the Gospels made him but a few months younger than John. The present copy of the Codex Nazaraeus dates from 1042, but Irenaeus quoted from it and cited ample references to it. The material common to Irenaeus and the Codex Nazaraeus therefore was at least as early as the compilation of early presbyterial texts, sometime during the second half of the Second Century.

© Bibliotheque Nationale, Paris, 1980

Jesus depicted as an old and overweight man in a Byzantium ivory diptych, circa 450. Pictures of Jesus 'Enthroned' like this were in existence well before crucifixion scenes were developed for Christian artwork. Note the Celtic cross on the book in Jesus' hand.

A statement in the Gospel of John (8:57) had Jews saying to Rabbi Jesus, 'you are not yet fifty years old', a indication that the twin brothers were considered by the people who compiled the Gospel of John to be men much older than the singular Jesus Christ as portrayed in modern church literature. Bishop Clement of Alexandria said that Rabbi Jesus was sixty-three years of age when he died. Bishop Irenaeus of Lyons confirmed the elderly age of Jesus, saying that it was recorded in early Gospels and known to the Elders:

> On completing his thirtieth year he suffered, being in fact still a young man, and who had by no means attained to advanced age. Now that the first stage of early life embraces thirty years, and that this extends onward to the fortieth year, everyone will admit; but from the fortieth and fiftieth year a man begins to decline towards old age, which Jesus possessed while he still fulfilled the office of a Rabbi, even as the Gospel and all the elders testify.

Irenaeus states that Rabbi Jesus suffered in his 'thirtieth year' yet still 'possessed' the latter years of his life to fulfill the office of teaching. This suffering was the ordeal of his initiation, involving a long period of deprivation. The documentation of Clement and Irenaeus, and the internal evidence in the Gospel account, places Rabbi Jesus still alive around twenty years later than the time the church said that he died.

Church fathers admit Jesus was stoned

The early church knew the real story of Rabbi Jesus' death. Bishop Clement of Alexandria wrote: 'In his sixty-third year of his age he was stoned to death'. Writing about 197-198, the Bishop of Carthage, Tertullian, rhetorically addressed a gathering of Jews and stated: 'ye stoned him' (*Adverse Judeaus,* C. IX, last paragraph). Tertullian spoke of the stoning of Rabbi Jesus not as the invention of an enemy, but simply as a genuine piece of accepted church history.

The Jewish descriptions of Rabbi Jesus' life are totally at a variance with Christian portrayal because the references in the Talmud apply to the initiated and spiritual person, Rabbi Jesus, and record an opposing story of his life. When compared with the New Testament there is an obvious conflict of testimony because the Christian writings subsist around a crucifixion, and the Jewish writings around a stoning.

Rabbi Jesus wished to help people spiritually by disclosing the Secret he had learnt in initiation in Egypt. The rabbinic records said of him: 'In the beginning a prophet, in the end a deceiver' (*Babylonian Sanhedrin,* 106 a), the deception being his desire to disclose to the world the sacred and forbidden Secret. That information was finally revealed on Jesus' behalf in this author's earlier book, *The Secret in the Bible.*

Merging the two factions

Under the appellation of Khrestians/Christians, two distinctions of people were subsequently confounded, the most opposite to each other in their manners and principles: the Essenes (and others like the Ebronites/Ebionites) who had embraced the faith of Rabbi Jesus, and the Zealots who had followed the standards of Judas Khrestus. As the centuries rolled over both individual parties were retrospectively grouped together as one body now simply referred to as 'early Christians'. Later generations of churchmen and academics filled the words 'Christian' and 'Christianity' with complicated theological meanings until being a 'Christian' meant something entirely different than it originally was, and thus developed a new belief in a complex system of dogmas not originally existing.

CHAPTER 16

The exodus to Britain

After the outcome of Judas Khrestus's fabricated crucifixion in Rome, a series of strange events occurred, with even the most orthodox churchmen acknowledging this sensitive phase of the development of the Gospel story. The essence of what is discussed in this chapter is confirmed in the FIRST Vulgate Bible of 1563, and reproduced in a later chapter. This episode in Christian history may surprise many people, but there is substantial evidence to support what happened and its subsequent outcome.

The church retracts a statement

In 1869, the church said that Pope Clement (160-215) sent a team of missionaries out from Rome to evangelize Gaul and the Roman world at the end of the Second Century. However, in 1907, that statement was rescinded and the following admission made:

> The evangelization of Gaul has often been attributed to missionaries sent from Rome by St. Clement, a theory which has inspired a whole series of fallacious narratives and forgeries, with which history is encumbered. Most likely the first missionaries came by sea, and touched at Marseilles ... (*Catholic Encyclopedia*, Vol. VI, 1909, Pg. 395)

The first 'missionaries' were not missionaries in the modern church portrayal of the word, but a body of people called the Bethany Group. Ancient church tradition maintains that in the year 37, many of the primary Gospel characters arrived in the Southern France area with a collection of 'secret words' (*Acts of Magdalene*) and settled in various parts of Europe and England. From what records are available, everything associated with their departure points to haste.

A realistic account of events is recorded in an 11th Century manuscript (*Fonds Notre-Dame,* Paris, 1767, 101) that documents a cumulative French tradition maintaining that after the Roman authorities discovered the fabricated nature of Judas Khrestus's crucifixion, Joseph of Arimathea, Mary Magdalene, and members of her family fled by sea 'from near the city of Rome' (*The Life of Mary Magdalene,* Archbishop Maar. 6 Vols.) to Marseilles (Massilia), and some re-established their lives in that area. The church added to the information saying that 'Lazarus and some women, and some companions, landed in Province at a place today called Saintes-Maries' (*Catholic Encyclopedia,* Vol. IX, 1910, Pg. 97).

Around 1310, the church commissioned Giotto di Bondone to create a fresco called *The Disembarkation of St Mary Magdalene at Marseilles* that today is in the Magdalene Church at Assisi, Italy. It shows a body of people in a boat coming ashore in Southern France with twin youths on the wharf unloading a collection of scrolls. Quoting from the Acts of Mary Magdalene, Freculphus, an 18th Century historian, supported the tradition of Joseph of Arimathea in his writing called *The History of Literature* (*The History of Literature,* Freculphus apud Godwin), and added that the documents in the possession of the Bethany Group contained 'rites and formulations termed Celestial Judgments'.

While there are other learned minds dating from that era onward that provide a similar record of an Exodus, there is a special advantage in quoting from an eminent church historian who used Vatican records to compile a twelve-volume work called *Annales Ecclesiastici.* He was Cardinal Caesar Baronius (1538-1607), 'the most outstanding historian' of the Roman Catholic church *(Catholic Encyclopedia,* Vol 11, 1967, Pg. 105). Baronius, who turned down two offers to become Pope in 1605, became Curator of the Vatican Library in 1597 and his records say this about the Bethany Group:

> In that year the party mentioned was exposed to the sea in a vessel without sails or oars. The vessel drifted finally to Marseilles and they were saved. From Marseilles, Joseph of Arimathea and some of his company passed into Britain

and there died. These were the names of the castaways … Joseph of Arimathea, Mary the wife of Cleopas, Martha, Lazarus, Eutropius, Salome, Clean, Saturninus, Mary Magdalene, Marcella (maid?), Sara the black woman, Maximin, Martial, Trophimus, and Sidonius. (*Annales Ecclesiastici,* Vol. 1 Pg. 327, quoting from the *Acts of Magdalene,* 12 Vols. Rome 1598-1607)

Not all of the Bethany Group travelled to Britain for some settled in various parts of Gaul, with Lazarus remaining at Marseilles and reputedly dying there early in the second half of the First Century. One tradition maintained that Mary Magdalene subsequently retired to a hilltop residence at Province at a place that came to be later called La Sainte-Baume, where she lived until her death in 63 (*Dictionaaire E'tymologique des noms de Lieux en France*). A 'sister and friends of Lazarus' were said to have 'progressed up the Rhone valley' and established themselves at Lyons, 'but it was not thought necessary (for the church) to enquire why they should be found in France' (*Catholic Encyclopedia,* Vol. IX, 1910, Pg. 98). The sister traveling with Lazarus was either Martha, his full-blood sister, or Salome, his half sister. There is perhaps some interest in the fact that the church records that Irenaeus, one of the earliest presbyters, 'went to south-western Gaul' and 'began his orations at Lyons in France'.

In the Fourth Century, Bishop Eusebius recorded that the major Gospel personalities 'passed beyond the ocean to the Isles called the Britannic Isles' (*Demonstratio Evangelica,* Lib, iii). Maurus Rabanus (776-856), Archbishop of Mayence (Mainz, west-central Germany), wrote that Trophimus became the first bishop of Arles, and called himself, Eutropius of Aquitaine (south-western France). The original version of the *Book of Rabanus* was in the catalogue of Glastonbury Abbey books in 1248 and was referenced by the scribes of that time. It is interesting to note that the *Jewish Encyclopedia*, under the entry, 'Arles', records that the earliest Jewish settlers at Arles came in a boat that had been deserted by its captain. The *Recognitions of Clement* provide additional information:

The Group was made up of the family of Joseph, his servants and twelve others, including Zachaeus' (father of John the Baptist?) and Mary Magdalene. Zachaeus stopped at a place called Rocamadour; Joseph and his household continued on their way to Morlaix in Brittany, there to wait for suitable weather conditions to cross to Britain … four days sail.

The precedence of the British church

The Bethany Group was the founder of the British church (circa 37) at Glastonbury or the Isle of Avalon and that preceded the establishment of the Roman church in Britain (the church of England) by around six centuries. This unbroken claim in respect of the commencement of a new religion in Britain is constantly attested to in church records and was a subject of debate at various European church councils for decades, with the Britons being able to claim an earlier connection with the family of the twin boys long before any at Rome or Spain. At the Council of Pisa in 1409 an argument developed about whether Joseph of Arimathea or Mary Magdalene had come first to Britain. The debate continued at the councils of Constance (1417), Sienna (1424), and Basle (1434), and this record eventuated:

> The churches of France, Spain and Italy must yield in points of antiquity and precedence to that of Britain, as the latter church was founded by Joseph of Arimathea in early times.

The ancient testimony of Maelgwyn of Llandaff, Lord of Anglesey and Snowdonia (c. 450), confirmed the British connection, saying that 'Joseph of Arimathea, the noble Decurion, entered his perpetual sleep with his XII companions in the Isle of Avalon.' In the remains of a manuscript attributed to a British clergyman named Melkin (c. 450), the name 'Joseph de Marmore from Arimathea' is recorded. This may have been Joseph' full name. In some ancient writings he was also called Joseph of Abarimacie and Joseph of Dalmanutha. The tradition of Joseph of Arimathea at Glastonbury was held of such great importance that immediately after the invention of printing, when books were so scarce, his life story was published and made available. The great Wynkyn de Worde himself printed a tome called the 'Life of St Joseph', and John Pymoon, in 1516 and 1520, published two additional books on Joseph's life at Glastonbury.

In London in 1922, there appeared in a bookseller's catalogue, a 'for sale' notice of a Pamphlet published in 1642 that Lord Queensborough promptly secured for the Royal Society of St George. It was called, 'A Briefe Abstract of the Question of Precedency between England and Spain', adding that it was 'occasioned by Sir Henry Neville Knight, the Queen of England's Embassador and the Embassador of Spain'. The claim of precedence was pleaded 'before the Commissioners appointed by the French King who had moved a Treaty of Peace in two and twentieth year of the same Queen' (1579). It is of special interest that this claim was recorded in the 1642 Pamphlet at a time when nothing could be printed without a license, and that during the Commonwealth it was reprinted in 1651 in Sir Robert B. Cotton's *Posthuma* (3, 7, 77).

The Sovereigns of England publicly insisted on the precedence of the British church from the time of King Henry IV (d. 1413) till Queen Elizabeth I (d. 1602), and King Charles I (1649), and Oliver Cromwell (1599-1658) gave a license for this claim to be recorded and published … a claim based on the records of Gildas the Wise, the first British historian, who had lived for a time in Glastonbury Abbey, and had known its records and traditions.

The original British church non-Christian

The Bethany Group was never referred to as Christians, not even later when the name was in common usage. They were called Céli Dé or Culdees, as were one hundred and sixty other members of their group who arrived later. The obscurity of the origin of the Culdees has led many writers to assume that their name was derived from their life and work. The interpretation 'Cultores Dei', meaning Worshipers of God, and 'Gille De', Servants of God, are ingenious but do not solve the problem. John Colgan, the celebrated hagiologist and topographer, translates Culdees, '*quidam advanae*', meaning 'certain strangers, particularly strangers from a distance' (*Trias Thaumaturga*, pg. 156b). Further, there is the strong unvarying tradition in the West of England of the arrival there in the year 37 of certain 'Judean refugees'. It seems impossible to avoid the conclusion that Colgan's 'certain strangers' were the one and the same with the refugees who found asylum in Britain and who were hospitably received by King Tenvantius.

The British Church was first called the Culdee Church, and it was not until the Latin aggression some six centuries after its commencement that the Culdees were referred to as the British clergy in contradistinction to the clergy of the Roman church. Monasteries, or Seats of Learning, were attached to early British churches and were styled Cathair Culdich ... the Chair of the Culdees (*History of the Culdees*, Jamieson, pg. 35). The Culdees were generally expounding a particular brand of spiritual knowledge, that originally developed from Essene and Druidic traditions, being concerned with education, agriculture, an ethical code, a strong sense of fraternity among its participants, and an esoteric secret.

Their order was strictly monastic and was essentially based upon the teachings and social codes of the books brought into Britain by the Bethany Group. The Culdee Church became a hereditary institution, with the high bishops in Britain being drawn from a dynastic family, and their office passing from father to son in many instances. Certain British gods and goddesses were subsequently incorporated into the structure and the Culdee Church sponsored its own saints independent of the Roman church. Through the ages these included such well-known characters as St. Bridget, St. Patrick, St. David and St. Columba. Although now generally perceived to have been part of the overall Christian movement, the ministry and doctrines of those saints was quite divorced from the church of Rome.

© Mrs. Lucy Ogilvie's Collection

No explanation has been given as to why twins are depicted on the gates of the Church of St Giles, Wrexham, England (built circa 1715).

Surprise is sometimes expressed that there are so few records of the early British church and this is explained by the savage edicts of the Roman Emperors. They were directed not alone to the destruction of individuals who confessed the Culdee faith, but also to the literature and records of the church. In the edict of Emperor Diocletian (originally, Diocles, 285-305) the writings of the Culdee Church were to be removed or destroyed, being regarded as books of magic; in this way Diocletian was following older methods of suppression. After the Diocletian persecution died out, the Culdees rebuilt their churches and they flourished to so great an extent that at the Council of Arles in 314, four Culdee delegates were in attendance.

The arrival of the Gospel of the Twin

Polydore Vergil (1470-1555), an Italian historian living in England, wrote in his *Angilicae Histories Libra*:

> Britain, partly through Joseph of Arimathea, partly through Fugatus and Damianius, was of all kingdoms the first that received the Gospel.

Damanius was another name for Rabbi Jesus, and that Gospel was not the Christian Gospel expounded today. At the time of the arrival of the Bethany Group in Britain, the Gospels of Matthew, Mark, Luke and John, had not been written (*Catholic Encyclopedia*, Vol. V1, Sept. 1st 1909, Pg. 135-137) and therefore it was not possible for them to be introduced at that time. So what writings did the Bethany Group have?

It may be possible to answer that question. After the publication of my earlier books, the monks of an Abbey in Cumbria, northern England, sent me a series of 35 millimetre colour slides of documentation preserved in their archives that related to Christian origins in Britain. Before Henry VIII ordered the Dissolution of Monasteries in 1539, the monks moved their library into a private residence and thus their records were preserved. Notable from this material was an English translation of a writing called *Acta Cunobeline* that was presented to support the Abbot's argument that the British church preceded Roman Catholicism by 600 years. Cunobeline was a First Century King of Britain, and the father of Caradoc, the tribal leader who defended Britain from the Roman invasion of Emperor Claudius.

Acta Cunobeline was originally written by a teacher called Nidjhu who was born on 24th October 160 and died in April, 214. He spent most of his life teaching languages at a College administered by the Druid priesthood in Isca Dumnoniorum (now Exeter) in Devon. Nidjhu spent six years compiling his six-volume history of Cunobeline and during his research spoke with his progeny, some who were students in his class. Towards the end of his life he presented leather-bound versions of *Acta Cunobeline* to Cunobeline' descendants and the *Preface* in the Cumbrian Volumes confirmed that it was one from the original family collection. *Acta Cunobeline* records the esoteric principles and spiritual beliefs of the Culdee priesthood and in its original form it was a part of a First Century instructional manual called the *Palsgate Testimonies.*

The word, *Palsgate* is associated with an early Roman god and the foundation of Rome. The Latin calendar found at Anzio has inscribed opposite April 21st the entry, 'Parilia- Roma Condita' … The Festival of Pales … Foundation of Rome. Pales was the name of the divinity of flocks and herds, and April 21st is still observed as the birthday of Rome. The word *Palsgate* is a combination of *Pales* and *gate*, and means, 'Entrance to the Foundation of Knowledge' *(Acta Cunobeline).*

The Abbot claimed that it was King Cunobeline who wrote the *Palsgate Testimonies* using the writings of the Bethany Group as his exemplar. Its availability introduced new information about the religious teachings of the Culdee priests of Glastonbury and revealed some identical sayings of 'secret words' that are today found recorded in the Gospel of Thomas.

In 267, and under direct instruction from Roman Emperor Publius Licinius Gallienus (d. 268), Roman soldiers raided the College of the Druidic priesthood in Isca Dumnoniorum and, before burning it to the ground, stole the books from its library and took them to Rome. Thus a copy of the *Acta Cunobeline* ended up with Roman priests and was subsequently tabled at the first Council at Nicaea in 325 (Cumbrian Abbey records).

The conclusion is this: The Bethany Group brought into Britain the Gospel of the Twin, today called the Gospel of Thomas, a collection of initiated teachings compiled by Rabbi Jesus. The moral apothegms in that Gospel made their way into the first Christian Gospel written some decades later, that called Mark after Marcus (Jesus).

No Easter in Britain

Although considered austere by the somewhat ostentatious Roman church, the doctrine promoted by the Culdee Church, in time, became popular throughout Europe and many British priests later took up church positions in Europe. In an effort to overawe the Culdees, the Roman church officially declared Rabbi Jesus' faith to be heretical at the Fifth Ecumenical Council of Constantinople in 553 (*The Celtic Apostolic Church,* Michael J. A. Stewart).

The Cumbrian Abbey records oppose the modern-day orthodox presentation of events associated with the arrival of Christian dogma into Britain and reveal another example of church history being falsified. In 597, Augustine (Austin) was sent from Rome to Britain by Pope Gregory and failed his mission 'to bring the Culdee Church to the observance of the Roman Easter' (*Encyclopedia Britannica,* Vol. 11, 1797 Ed.; also Cumbrian Abbey records). At that time, some 600 years after the canonical time of Jesus, the scriptures and preaching of the British Church did not embrace a crucifixion and resurrection of Jesus Christ.

In 601, the Pope then sent a contingent of military priests into England and the Roman church subsequently 'extended its authority over the native British church by force of arms' (*Encyclopedia Britannica,* 1797 Ed.; also Cumbrian Abbey records). This information is profound, for suddenly the claim by the Catholic church of a peaceful spreading of its Gospel into Britain becomes untrue. Professor Geoffrey Dudley Smith, in a book called *The Religion of Ancient Britain* (1898), states that upon their takeover of the British church Roman priests burnt no fewer than one hundred and thirty volumes of writings relating to the religious affairs of the Culdees. Rome's usurpation of the pure principles of the Culdees' spiritual belief was motivated by the existence of a bloodline from Rabbi Jesus to the Caesar family, and the enigma of British philosophy (*The Bible Fraud,* Tony Bushby, Joshua Books, Australia, 2001).

Thus the Roman church forced its dogma onto the British people but the Culdees' love of their original preaching never entirely died out. Conquerors are not usually disposed to speak with much kindness or respect of those whom they have overcome or dispossessed. It was so between the successful priests of the Roman hierarchy and the ecclesiastics of the ancient church of the Culdees, whom they had succeeded in supplanting. But it is significant that the British continued to cherish the highest esteem for the memory of these men of piety who had distinguished their ancient national church; she could not eradicate from the minds of the people the principles it had imparted.

It requires but little acquaintance with British history to observe that these principles were never eradicated, and that during the reign of the Roman church in Britain, they continued to exist. Men like Alcuin in his Caroline books; John Scotus, the protégé of King Alfred; and the Archbishop Elfric with his Saxon Homily, endeavored to stem the tide of what they called 'Roman doctrinal error'.

It is on record that the Culdees officiated in the church of York up to the year 936 and according to Archbishop Raine, the Canons of York were called Culdees as late as the reign of Henry II (1133-1189). Old habits die hard, and some of the Culdee priesthood hung onto their own teachings, calling themselves 'defenders of the True Faith'. From the Register of St Andrews church we read: 'The Culdees continued to perform Divine worship in a certain corner of the church after their own manner, nor could they be removed till the time of King Alexander in 1124 so that the Culdees and popish priests performed their services in the same church for nearly three hundred years'. Ledwich states in his book *Irish Antiquities*, that at Mondincha in Tipperary as late as 1185, a Culdean abbey and church still stood 'whose clergy had not conformed to the new superstition, but devoutly served God in this wild and dreary retreat, sacrificing all the flattering prospects of the world for their ancient doctrine and discipline'.

This affected certain aspects of the Culdees' spiritual tradition and eventually led to the British church writing their own Bible, the King James Version. A common knowledge of history and a very little research would suffice to prove that the work of the Culdees, who became, from the first encroachment of Rome, the British protesters, never quite died out, and that the Reformation in the British Isles began long anterior to the date usually assigned to it.

CHAPTER 17

How the twins became God

The Cumbrian Abbey provided previously undisclosed information about Jesus Christ and the true nature of the first ecclesiastical council. The Abbey records violently oppose the modern-day orthodox presentation of events associated with that gathering and reveal priesthood deception of the highest magnitude.

No church councils for the first 300 years

The church defines its General Councils as 'an assembly of individuals professing Christianity and consisting of those who held ecclesiastical offices within the precincts of the dioceses or parish of a primitive pastor or bishop, who disclaim private judgment, and who met to deliberate on ecclesiastical matters, whether of faith, morals, or discipline'. Yet in the first 300 years of the Roman church, 'the most important time in the development of our Faith' *(Catholic Encyclopedia,* Vol. iv, 1907), the concept of convening meetings to discuss developmental aspects of religion was unknown, a fact acknowledged at the eighteen-year-long Council of Trent:

> There are so many questions to be answered and difficulties to be obviated ... with the great uncertainty of those centuries; for it is doubtful whether administrators convened, and whether diocesan councils or Synods were held. Christians ought not forsake the church of God, however, for later General Councils determined that because history transmitted to us no such account of guidelines of Infallibility, such deliberations were deemed to have been assembled in the name of Christ and considered synonymous as being assembled

by the authority of Christ.

The folly of such a retrospective decree should strike every discerning person with a full conviction of its untruthfulness, and its crude attempt to hide the fact that ecclesiastical Councils were non-existent in the first three centuries of Christianity. In 1828, Protestant Reverend, Richard Grier, D.D, wrote a book called *The Epitome of the General Councils of the Church, from the Council of Nicaea, to the Conclusion of the Roman Council of Trent in the Year 1563*, a scathing account of the development of the church of Rome through 'corrupted and pretended' church Councils. In his summary, he said: 'Do you ask me how Councils begun? I will tell you; they began in nothing and resulted in the church of Rome'.

Ecclesiastical canons conferring the right to call councils or decision-making gatherings were not part of Christian history until well into the Fourth Century and even then they were not officially ratified until the Council of Trent (*De Ecclesia*, No. 88, Petri Dens, Dublin, 1832). The whole business of the commencement and development of official assemblies was uncontrolled, irregular and without directive and it was with the person of Constantine (272-337) that a particular historic religious gathering was convened, but it was not Christian, as the church today would have us believe.

Emperor Constantine's bloodline

Constantine's father was Emperor Constantius 'the Pale', a resident of York in Britain and married to Helena, 'unquestionably a British princess' (*Epistola*, Melancthon; 1497-1560, Pg. 189). After upheavals in Lundunaborg (c. 61) under the tartan-clad Queen Boadicea, the ancient city of York became a popular resort and, from there, several Roman Emperors had functioned, deeming it a safer haven from which to rule than the vicious city of Rome. Several Roman Emperors were buried there.

Princess Helena was the daughter of King Coel 11, born at Colchester (Coel-chester?) in 248 and died circa 328. In the Vatican and British Museums are coins struck with her name, reading 'Flavia Helena Augusta' but she was best known as Empress Helena and so recorded in the annals of history. To Roman historical records, however, Empress Helena was falsely made to appear a Roman native, wife of a Roman and mother of an illustrious Roman son, Flavius Constantine, none of which is true. Empress Helena was British and so was her son.

It is not generally known that Flavius Constantine was British born and traced his Ancestries back to the New Testament family of the twins (His lineage was given in *The Bible Fraud*). Many in the church denied that fact but its own records confirmed the issue. Eminent Vatican historian, Cardinal Caesar Baronius said; 'The man must be mad who, in the face of universal antiquity, refuses to believe that Constantine and his mother were Britons, born in Britain' (*Annales Ecclesiastici*) and church knowledge is supported by over twenty European historical authorities.

Constantius died suddenly at York in 306 and Constantine, then thirty-four years old, was saluted in as leader and by hereditary right, was now King over Britain, Gaul and Spain. Of importance in this summary are the records of history that record King Constantine the Great as a direct bloodline relation to the First Century twins of Judas Khrestus and Rabbi Jesus, and that issue is probably the most important aspect in the development of Christianity.

Reasons for the first religious council

After the death of his father, King Constantine massed a powerful army in Britain, composed mainly of local British tribesmen, and began to prepare to cross the sea to the continent to engage co-emperor Maxentius (Roman Emperor 306-312) in battle. Constantine sailed with his army, landing on the shores in what is today Germany and then consulted 'the mouthpiece of God' (Irenaeus), the celebrated oracles of the Sibylline Books.

Following his interpretation of the prophecies, Constantine was confident that enemy in battle would be destroyed. After 'listening to the oracles', he accepted the advise and advanced forward for a military encounter. At Milvian Bridge (October 312), the site of the famous battle, the armies of Constantine and Maxentius clashed, and the British, under the shrewd leadership of Constantine, won an overwhelming victory. The rapacious and cruel Maxentius (d. 313) was completely routed, and his earlier seizure of Rome and the subsequent persecution of its people ended. King Constantine, with his warriors, marched victoriously on to Rome, where he received a massive welcome. Amid great rejoicing, he ascended the Imperial throne, assumed the purple, and was officially acclaimed by the Senate and the populace of Rome as Emperor. By 324, and after a series of lesser battles, the bloodthirsty and ruthless Flavius Constantine singularly ruled as King and Emperor of the entire Roman Empire, Britain, Gaul and Spain.

One of Constantine's main fears was that of uncontrollable religious disorder amongst the teeming populous. 'Roman expectations of religion's function was to maintain a stable relationship between the gods and the state and Rome's past success was its justification' (*Roman Myths*, Jane F. Gardner, 1993, British Museum). The 'peculiar type of oratory' (*The Dictionary of Classical Mythology, Religion, Literature and Art*, Oskar Seyffert, 1995, Pgs. 544-546) expounded by presbyters and their numerous gods was a challenge to the settled religious order that King Constantine desired. Presbyters manufactured religious legends, and diverse dogmas were continually developed or modified (*Catholic Encyclopedia*, iv, 498). The church said that they 'lived in an age of simple-minded credulity, and everything which they created, however extravagant and seemingly incredible or impossible, passed as perfectly good history in their receptive and uncritical minds' (*Encyclopedia Biblia*, Gospels).

In 313, a bitter argument developed between bodies of presbyters headed by Donatus, a bishop who gave his name to a schism that was later called the Donatist movement. At that time groups of presbyters and bishops violently clashed over the attributes of their various gods and 'altar was set against altar' (*Optatus of Minevis,* 1:15,19; Early Fourth Century) in competing for an audience. Eventually a Roman edict of toleration granting presbyters the right to practice their discourses was issued.

By that time, groups of presbyters had developed 'many gods and many lords' (1 Cor. 8:5) and various religious sects sprang up, each with differing Gospels (Gal. 1:6) and varying lists of apostles (2 Cor. 11:13). The 'toleration' won, however, would have no legal basis unless it had the final imprimatur of the priestly college originally established by Julius Caesar. Earlier reforms introduced by Emperor Diocletian (d. 305) reached their full development only under Constantine who gave some support to the presbyters but could not bring about a settlement between rival god-factions.

Presbyter's religions 'destitute of foundation'

Constantine 'never acquired a solid theological knowledge' about the presbyter's gods and 'depended heavily on his advisers in religious questions' (*New Catholic Encyclopedia,* Vol. X11, 1967, Pg. 576). In official Roman records, he noted that among the numerous presbyterian factions, 'strife had grown so serious, vigorous action was necessary to establish a more religious state'. His advisers cautioned him that the presbyter's religions were 'destitute of foundation' and needed official stabilization. Constantine saw in this confused system of fragmented beliefs the opportunity to create a new and combined State religion of neutral concept, and protect it by law.

When he conquered the East in 324 he sent his Spanish religious adviser, Osius of Cordoba, to Alexandria with letters to several bishops exhorting them to make peace among their own. 'For as long as you continue to contend about your various gods and insignificant questions, it is not fitting that a portion of God's people should be under the direction of your judgment, since you are divided among yourselves' (*Life of Constantine, II,* 69-71; Eusebius, N&PNF. i, 516-7).

The mission failed and Constantine, probably at the suggestion of Osius, then issued a Decree commanding all presbyters and their subordinates 'be mounted on asses, mules and horses belonging to the public and travel to the city of Nicaea' in the Roman Province of Bithymia, a country of Asia. They were instructed to bring with them the *testimonies* they orated to the rabble, 'wrapped and bound in leather' for protection during the long trip, and surrender them to Constantine upon their arrival in Nicaea. Their writings totaled 'in all, two thousand two hundred and thirty one scrolls and legendary tales of gods and saviours, together with a record of the doctrines orated by them' (Cumbrian Abbey records).

The first of three individual sittings was convened on the Summer Solstice, June 21st, 325 (*New Catholic Encyclopedia,* Vol. 1, 1967, Pg. 792) and 'held in a hall in Osius' palace ... who held the chief place there (in Nicaea) in his own name' *(Ecclesiastical History,* Bishop Du Pin, Vol. I, Pg. 598). It was a remarkable event that provided many details of early clerical thinking and presented a clear picture of the intellectual phenomena that prevailed at that time. It was at the Council of Nicaea that Christianity had it's beginning, and the ramifications of decisions made at that time are impossible to calculate.

The two gods of Christianity

The church admitted that vital elements of proceedings at Nicaea are 'strangely absent from the canons' (*Catholic Encyclopedia*, Vol. iii, 1909, Ed. Pg. 160) and the suspicion exists that documentation recording the true nature of the creation of Jesus Christ was later suppressed or destroyed. However, using records that endured (Sabinius of Hereclea, c. 326), Constantine opened the proceedings 'stiff with purple, gold and precious stones, an imposing figure, wearing weird eastern garments, jewels on his arms, a tiara on his head, perched crazily between tinted bat-wings, and a lion on his chest'. Bishop Eusebius 'occupied the first seat on the right of the emperor and delivered the inaugural address on the emperors' behalf' (*Catholic Encyclopedia*, Vol. V, May 1, 1909, Pg. 620-619). A total of 318 presbyters attended and documentation available reveals that there were no British churchmen at the Council, for most delegates were Greek. 'Seventy eastern bishops' represented Asiatic factions (*Ecclesiastical History*, Bishop Du Pin, Vol I, Pg. 598) and small numbers came from other areas.

Caecilian of Carthage travelled from Africa; Paphnutius from Egypt, Nicasius of Die from Gaul and Dommus of Stridon made the journey from Pannonia. It was at that puerile assembly, and under cult conditions, that 'bishops, priests, deacons, sub-deacons, acolytes and exorcists' gathered to debate and decide on a unified belief system that encompassed only one god. By that time, a huge assortment of 'wild texts' *(New Catholic Encyclopedia,* 1967, 'Gospels') circulated amongst presbyters, and no list of 'accepted' or canonical writings existed. Many of those Gospels, Epistles and Revelations were listed in my earlier books and some still carry the names of a great variety of Eastern and Western divinities.

The men argued violently among themselves, expressing various personal motives for inclusion of particular writings that promoted the finer traits of their own special god. When speaking of the conclave of presbyters gathered at Nicaea, Sabinius, the Bishop of Hereclea, said in an account of the proceedings:

> Excepting Constantine himself, and Eusebius Pamphilius, they were a set of illiterate, simple creatures who understood nothing.

Dr. Richard Watson, a disillusioned Christian historian and previously Bishop of Llandaff in Wales, referred to them as 'a set of gibbering idiots'. After a lifetime of research into church councils he concluded that 'the clergy at the Council of Nicaea were under the power of the devil and the convention was composed of the lowest rabble, and patronized the vilest abominations' (*Theological Tracts, 'On Councils'*, Vol. 2 (of 6), London, 1791). It was that infantile body of men who were responsible for the commencement of a new Roman religion and the subsequent creation of Jesus Christ.

A Libyan presbyter named Arius, in attendance at Nicaea, expressed concern that 'the bishops shall develop two gods' (*The Ancient World*, H.E.L. Mellersh, 1976, Pg. 377) and that ancient statement caused confusion in the church for centuries. Pious Christian historians confessed that they 'didn't understand its meaning' and described it 'to the peculiar interposition of heaven' (*The Difficulties of Romanism*, George Stanley Faber, London, 1826). However, in light of the current understanding of twin boys, it is possible to determine what Arius meant, and it provides major conflictions with the church's presentation of Jesus Christ.

Selecting a new god

Up until the Council of Nicaea, Roman aristocracy primarily worshiped two Greek gods, Apollo and Zeus, but the great bulk of common people idolized Julius Caesar. Excluding the first letter in Caesar's name, the remainder of the word had great significance in the community, 'namely AESAR is the Etruscan for 'god' … C being the Roman numeral 100' (*The Twelve Caesars*, Suetonius, pg, 104, The Penguin Classics, translated by Robert Graves, 1958). Because of that godly connection, Caesar was deified by the Roman Senate five days after his death (d. 15th March, 44 BC) and was subsequently venerated as the *Divine Julius*.

Because he was Roman and 'Father of the Empire', he was the most popular god among the rabble for more than four hundred years. His followers were called Caesareans (*Encyclopedia Britannica*, Vol. iv, Pg. 15, 1797) and so revered was the *Divine Julius* that at least three ancient provincial cities were named Caesarea in his honour: one each in Palestine, Northern Africa and Cappadocia. At the Palestinian Caesarea, Josephus described a massive structure built and dedicated in the First Century to the honour of the *Divine Julius*:

> Directly opposite the harbour entrance, upon a high platform, rose the Temple of Caesar, remarkable for its beauty and its great size. In it stood a colossal statue of Caesar, not inferior to Zeus at Olympia … and one of the goddess Roma, equal to the Argive statue of Hera. *(Jewish Wars*, 1.415, Josephus)

The Temple of Caesar stood until around mid-Sixth Century, indicating that the inhabitants proudly preserved their ancient edifice, perhaps as a revered relic to the *Divine Julius*.

Some time later, a Christian church was built on the northwestern flank of the site of Caesar's Temple, directly over the Temple foundation and using some original stones. Archaeologists at the site were puzzled by the chronological discrepancy between what they believed was the Christianizing of the Roman Empire with Emperor Constantine and the construction of a Christian church some three hundred years or so later. They wondered how the most imperial and Roman city in Palestine, the Episcopal see of Bishop Eusebius, could preserve and honour a so-called Pagan temple for so many Christian centuries. Clearly, archaeologists were accepting the orthodox presentation of Christian development and were yet to realize that there was no Christianity until well after the Council of Nicaea.

It is probable that Constantine sited the summit at Nicaea because it was the original home of Julius Caesar's clan, the Ulius (hence Julius). Remains of a temple structure exist there today and the probability is that it was originally built in honour of the Ulius family, or Julius Caesar himself. Some archaeological evidence suggested that Nicaea was called Caesarea in the Fourth Century but principal Catholic author and celebrated Doctor of the Sorbonne in Paris, Bishop Lewis Du Pin (d. c. 1725), claimed that it was called 'Number 1 Caesar' (N1Caesar) and that was later vocalized as Nicaea *(Ecclesiastical History*, Bishop Du Pin, Vol. I, pg. 598). Part of the Caesar name is still carried in the word today and enhances Bishop Du Pin's reasoning.

Because the general Roman populous adored the *Divine Julius*, he was the most fashionable god in Western presbyter's texts but was not recognized in Eastern or Oriental writings. Constantine's intention at Nicaea was to create a new god for the Empire that would unite all religious factions under one deity and presbyters were permitted to debate and decide upon whom the new god would be. Throughout the meeting, the howling factions were immersed in heated debates in attempts to promote their own divinity and the names of fifty three gods were tabled for discussion; 'As yet, the new God had not been selected by the council, and so they balloted, in order to determine the matter. For one year and five months the balloting lasted' (*God's Book of Eskra*, xlviii 26-53).

At the end of that time, Constantine returned to the gathering to discover that the presbyters had not agreed on a new deity but had balloted down to a short list of five prospects, namely, Caesar, Krishna, Mithra, Horus, and Zeus. Constantine was the ruling spirit at Nicaea and ultimately decided the new god for them. He determined that the names of his two First Century descendants, Rabbi Jesus and Judas Khrestus, be joined as one, Jesus Khrestus, and that would be the official name of the new Roman god.

A vote was taken and it was with a majority show of hands that the twins became one God ... 161 votes to 157. Following longstanding Heathen custom, Constantine used the official gathering and the Roman Apotheoses Decree to legally deify the new god for the rabble and did so by democratic consent and with the blessing of the presbyters in attendance. A new Roman god was proclaimed and officially ratified by Emperor Constantine (*Acta Concilii Niceni*, Colon, 1618).

This ancient woodcut piously reflects some of the curious scenes at Nicaea in 325.

The 'sons of God'

The adopted process for the deification of humans into gods had for centuries remained within the reserve powers of the Roman Emperor. The history of Roman religion exhibits much evidence of non-gods becoming gods and goddesses and many earlier precedents had been set. Roman writer, Ovidius (43BC-18AD), recorded the deification of Julius Caesar (*Divine Julius*) after his death in 44 BC. Augustus and others styled themselves *Divine Filius* or *son of a god* and were hailed as 'divine emperors' after their deaths. The daughter of Germanics and Agrippina the Elder, Julia Drusilla (d. 38) was also deified after her death (*Encyclopedia of the Roman Empire*, M. Bunson, 1994, Pg. 140). The story is often told about Emperor Flavius Sabinus Vespasian (d. 79) who, on his deathbed, jokingly said: 'Oh dear, I think that I am becoming a god'. Emperor Hadrian deified his handsome young companion, Antinous, after he drowned in the Nile in 112, and Marcus Aurelius (121-180), one of the greatest emperors in Roman history, deified his wife after her death. He himself later became 'a son of a god'.

The term 'son of a God' was used by several emperors to indicate their descent (sometimes through adoption or merely by pious assertion) from a previous emperor, usually an immediate or close predecessor, whose memory was held in particular respect. It was often a political statement; thus Septimius Severus assumed the title 'son of the deified Marcus' in 195 to proclaim and strengthen his legitimacy, though he had never been (nor is likely to have been) adopted by Marcus Aurelius, who died 15 years before *(Chronicle of the Roman Emperors*, Chris Scarre, 1995, Pg. 28-35).

> Roman magistrates were frequently adored as provincial deities, with the pomp of altars and temples, of festivals and sacrifices. Deification was a legal principle … and received as an institution, not of religion but of policy. (*The Decline and Fall of the Roman Empire*, Edward Gibbon, 1994. Ed. Pg. 94-95)

A ceremony was performed called 'Apotheosis' or deification. Thus, the deified ones were then called 'saviours' and looked upon as gods (*The Bible for Learners*, Vol. iii, Pg. 3). Temples, altars and images with attributes of divinity were then erected and public holidays proclaimed on their birthdays. Their surviving male offspring were officially addressed as 'son of a god', the 'god' being the new status of their deified father. Following the original example set by the deification of Caesar, their funerals were dramatized as the scene of their resurrection and immortality (*Encyclopedia of the Roman Empire*, M. Brunson, 1994, Pg. 204). All these godly attributes passed as a legal right to Emperor Constantine's new deity, Jesus Khrestus.

The two natures of Christ

That purely political act of deification effectively and legally placed Rabbi Jesus and Judas Khrestus among the Roman gods as one individual composition today called Jesus Christ, and lent earthly existence in two forms to the Empire's new deity. It also was the start of a series of bitter priesthood debates and excommunications over the dual nature of Christ that was not settled until the Council of Trent some twelve hundred years later when a Decree was passed saying that, 'We all shall unanimously teach that the distinction between the two natures of Christ is by no means done away with through the union, but rather the identity of each nature is preserved in the One'.

At the time Constantine deified his distant relatives, the Christian religion had not yet developed and the few church documents that today refer to an established Christian god previous to the Council of Nicaea are 'later forgeries, written retrospectively' (*Liberty,* Bishop Jeremy Taylor, Vol. xiv, pg. 169, Heber's Ed., 1822). That claim is supported in a later chapter.

The Sibylline Books consulted

During the course of the proceedings at Nicaea, the Sibylline Books were again consulted and another unfulfilled prophecy found. It predicted that 'an everlasting gospel to preach to them' would be written for those 'that dwell on earth until they have climbed from the pit of slime' *(Sibylline Book No. 2, 14:6)*. The legality of the Sibyl's writings was earlier established under Emperor Augustine (c. 12 BC) when he transferred a special 'pontifex' collection to the Temple of Apollo on the Palatine hill in Rome and under Roman religious policy, King Constantine had administrative license to introduce new *testimonies* for the Empire, and did.

Up until that time, a great variation of texts were in use, and presbyters preferred versions that featured stories of their favourite personal gods. Because the *Divine Julius* was 'son of god on Earth' in most Western presbyter's orations, their writings applied to him the theology of the earlier story of twin Roman boys, Romulus and Remus ... born under curious circumstances (c. 753 BC) to an earthly virgin mother with a mystical god as 'father in Heaven', the attempt by reigning King Amulius to forestall a threat to his rule involving danger to the children, a royal blood line through kingly (Venusian) descent, and the crucifixion and ascension of Romulus into heaven to become Quirinius and sit on the right hand side of God (*Anacalypis*, Higgins).

© Rubens Film Library

Flemish artist Peter Paul Rubens (1577-1640) depicts the moment when the king's herdsmen discover Romulus and Remus with the she-wolf.

The legends surrounding the life of Krishna formed the primary outline of the Asiatic presbyter's writings and they developed from the story of his fabled incarnation around 1000 BC. The life story of Krishna is recorded in the Hindu epic, the *Mahabharata,* and carries similarities to the fables built up for the *Divine Julius* (*Ecclesiastical History*, Bishop Du Pin, Vol. I, pg. 598). His virgin mother Devaki was miraculously conceived by a mysterious 'god in heaven', and his special birth 'announced by a star' (*Mahabharata*). He was depicted as a meek person who preached nobly in parables and washed the feet of Brahmans. Purity of life and spiritual insight were distinguishing traits 'in the character of this oriental sin-atoning Saviour, and that he was often moved with compassion for the down-trodden and the suffering' (*Mahabharata*). Krishna met his death by crucifixion upon a tree at the hands of his enemies, with a later variation declaring that he was tied to a cross-shaped tree and pierced with three arrows.

The untitled manuscript

However, there is another aspect to the development of the Gospels and that involves the use of Druidic philosophy. Church history records that an untitled manuscript and ten similarly untitled letters (*Adverse Marcion,* v, Tertullian, Ms.1727, Pg. 368) were in the possession of Marcellus, the son of an elderly noble Briton. Marcellus was born circa 96 and it was variously recorded that he died sometime between 164 and 168. Tertullian's reference is mankind's first record to a manuscript that can be associated with Christianity (*Adverse Marcion*, v, Tertullian, Ms. 1727, Pg. 368) and its existence throws new light on the complex nature of the contents of the New Testament.

Marcellus was a Druid at Tongres and was known as Marcellus of Britain (*Marcellus Britannus, Tungrorum episcopus postea Trevirorum Archiepiscopus; Mersoeus, De Archiepiscopis Trvirensium*). He was a descendant of Rabbi Jesus and Judas Khrestus and part of the community at Trevran in Wales which was traditionally the home of Cunobeline and his family. Marcellus exercised the chief influence in the development of the Celtic church in Southern Wales and his family was closely associated with Prince Linus, son of King Caradoc.

The premise in this work is that Rabbi Jesus (St Marcus in church records) originally wrote Marcellus' document and it recorded the esoteric principles and spiritual beliefs of the Culdees, carried into Britain by the Bethany Group. It was through the corruption of Marcellus' name (maybe) that he was later called Marcion and/or Marcus in church writings and that type of translation variation or name substitution is important to understand when unraveling presbyters' texts.

According to Tertullian, Irenaeus, and Clement, Marcellus was in Rome during 137-138 and 'narrated his *testimonies* to those that would listen' (*Church History,* Socrates Scholasticus, Jenning's Trans. 1911). That statement is taken to mean that Marcellus orated from the untitled text in his possession, and from the name of Tertullian's writing, *Adverse Marcus* (*Against Marcion*), it is obvious that the presbyterial movement was opposed to Marcellus's dissertations.

Marcellus's influence was great, as St. Epiphanius, writing in the Fourth Century, recorded that his followers were found 'throughout the whole world' (*Epiphanius, Haerieses,* Vol. xlii, Pg.1), and Bishop St. Cyril of Alexandria (d. 444), around the same time, warned his gatherers not to attend a Marcionite assembly by mistake *(Catech,* 4:4). With his brief documentation, Marcellus founded a belief system that spread rapidly throughout the Roman Empire and continued for more than 600 years after his death (*Annales Ecclesiastici,* tome ii, Fol. Antwerp, 1597, Cardinal Caesar Baronius).

Manufacturing the Gospels

From Constantine's point of view, there were several religious factions that needed to be satisfied and he instructed Bishop Eusebius to organize the compilation of a uniform collection of new writings developed from various aspects in the texts available. His instructions were:

> Search ye these books, and whatever is good in them, that retain; but whatsoever is evil, cast away. What is good in one book, write ye with that which is good in another book. And whatsoever is thus brought together shall be called the Book of Books, and it shall be the doctrine of my people, which I will recommend unto all nations, that there shall be no more war for religion's sake.' The books were written accordingly'. (*God's Book of Eskra*, xlviii 26-53)

'Make them to astonish', said Constantine. Using the philosophic teachings of Rabbi Jesus from the *Acta Cunobeline* as his exemplar, Eusebius amalgamated the 'legendary tales of all the religious doctrines of the world' from the presbyter's manuscripts at his disposal. The merging of the supernatural 'god' stories with the religious principles of Rabbi Jesus effectively joined the orations of Eastern and Western presbyters with British (Culdean) religions 'together as one' (*Life of Constantine*, iv, Attributed to Eusebius).

With a completed collection of writings that Constantine thought would unite all variant religious factions, Eusebius arranged for scribes to produce 'fifty sumptuous copies … to be written on parchment in a legible manner, and in a convenient portable form, by professional scribes thoroughly accomplished in their art' (*Life of Constantine*, iv, 36, 37; Attributed to Eusebius). 'These orders', said Eusebius, 'were followed by the immediate execution of the work itself, which we sent him in magnificently and elaborately bound volumes of three-fold and four-fold forms' (*Life of Constantine*, iv, 36, 37; Attributed to Eusebius).

They were the *New Testimonies*, and that is the first mention in world history of finished copies of what was later called the New Testament. Some of those Gospels recorded Julius Caesar, Lord Krishna and Jesus Khrestus as the Christian deity, and one of those names is found in the FIRST English-language Vulgate produced in 1563, twenty-five years before Pope Sixtus V wrote a new Bible and deleted it (*History of the Vulgate, History of the Council of Trent,* Paolo Sarpi, Translated by Brent, London, 1676; also, *Ecclesiastical History*, Mosheim, Book 6, London, 1825; also *Vicars of Christ*, Peter de Rosa, Crown Publishers, New York, 1988).

The final formatting of the name of the Christian god was not settled until after the time of the Reformation (14th-17th Centuries), for up until then it had several renditions such as Yesu Khrestus, Yeshoua Khrestus, Yeshoua Krst and Yeshu Kristos. One Fifth Century Greek New Testament records Hesus Krishna in the places now occupied by Jesus Christ in today's Bibles, revealing that a combination of the Druidic and Oriental gods was once the deity of Christianity.

The immediate relevance of the church account of the coming into existence of its New Testament is that its own records explicitly represent Constantine and Eusebius as the authors of the Christian texts. That leads to the ultimate question: 'Wherein, then, does lie the divine uniqueness of the Christian religion?'

The Seraglio Bible

In 1954, Bishop Ducati of Milan suggested that the three oldest Bibles existing today might have been among Constantine's first 50 copies. This doesn't appear so, for in 1890 a record was made of a Bible found hidden in the basement of the Seraglio library in the Topkapi Palace Museum, Constantinople (Istanbul now). It was described as being ...

> ... about two and a half by four feet square, and two feet thick, written in large Latin letters across the page. It is well bound in timber, with an inscribed gold plate on its cover, twelve by sixteen inches.

The first page contained an original letter written by Emperor Constantine in which he gave his personal approval for the use of 'a public carriage' to convey the huge book to community showings. The existence of Constantine's letter makes that 'refrigerator-size' Bible among the first written and its release today could place serious doubts on the current dating of the Sinai, Alexandria and Vatican Bibles. The huge dimensions of the Seraglio Bible are at considerable variance with those three Bibles and its Latin language conflicts with the latter columned Greek production.

The Seraglio Bible was moved to the Secret Archives of the Vatican in 1917 and nothing more was heard about it. However, in 1925, a young priest named Edmond Bordeaux Szekely was studying in Rome and may have sighted it, for he made reference to an 'intriguing Bible' that the church 'would not be willing to have go into the hands of the public' (*Christian Forgeries*, Major Joseph Wheless, Judge Advocate, Idaho, 1930). The existence of a hidden high security facility in the Catholic headquarters is confirmed on page 290 of the *Catholic Encyclopedia* (Vol. XV. 1 Oct, 1912), and Szekely's books name some of the explosive manuscripts that it holds.

For understandable reasons, nothing has been released about the contents of this old Bible but its availability to the public today would simply add further evidence that Christianity's Jesus Christ was born documentarily.

Manuscripts burnt at the Council of Nicaea

With his instructions fulfilled, Constantine then decreed that the *New Testimonies* would thereafter be called the 'word of the Roman God' (*Life of*

Constantine, ii, 21, Attributed to Eusebius) and official to all religions operating in the Roman Empire. He then ordered all presbyterial manuscripts destroyed by fire and 'any man found concealing one should be stricken off from his shoulders' (beheaded). As the record shows, previous writings of the 'pulpiteers' no longer exist, although some survived, the Gospels of Peter and Thomas being two examples. For the next two centuries, the *New Testimonies* were called the *Constantine Collection* (*History of the Bible*, Bronson C. Keeler, C.P. Farrell, 1881) and additional false narratives were built in as they developed (*Catholic Encyclopedia,* Vol., vii, 7).

The use of scribal quills

It is not recorded whether Constantine named the Gospels at this stage, or whether somebody else did later. The modern church admits that Matthew, Mark, Luke and John did not write the Gospels, saying that all twenty-seven New Testament writings began life anonymously:

> The titles of our Gospels were not intended to indicate authorship … It thus appears that the present titles of the Gospels are not traceable to the evangelists themselves … they (the canonical church writings) are supplied with titles, which however ancient, do not go back to the respective authors of those writings. (*Catholic Encyclopedia,* Vol. 1, 655, 656; Vol. V1; Sept. 1st 1909, Pgs.135-137; also; *Catholic Encyclopedia,* Vol. 6; 1910 Ed. Pg. 656)

For centuries, the Gospels bore church certification of authenticity now officially confessed in writing to be false, and while some aspects of today's Gospels had a pre-Nicene existence, they were not representative of Jesus Christ (*History of the Vulgate,* History of the Council of Trent, Paolo Sarpi, Translated by Brent, London, 1676; also, *Ecclesiastical History*, Mosheim, Book 6; London, 1825). The official clerical position maintains that 'the headings … were later affixed to them' (*Catholic Encyclopedia*, i, 117) and therefore they are not Gospels written 'according to Matthew, Mark, Luke or John', as publicly presented. The church accepts these impostures, and the confession reveals that Christianity is grounded on falsehood. The full force of the admission reveals that there are no true Gospels and the documents that are used by the church embody the very ground and pillar of Christian foundation and faith. The consequences are fatal to the pretense of Divine origin to the New Testament and expose church texts as having no special authority.

The practice of forging apostles' names to contrived writings appears to be an expedient of the late Fourth and Fifth Century church adapted to assign an 'authoritative' origin to works of people who were not 'authoritative'. It is possible that Eusebius applied St Marcus' name (Rabbi Jesus) to the untitled Druidic manuscript and it evolved from Marcus to Marc to Mark in subsequent translations, and after structural re-editing, became the Gospel of Mark known today. That writing provided the substance of two other Gospels and the essence of original Druidic truths are still embodied in them today. The Gospel of Mark was 'the second in the four canonical Gospels but the first of them in sequence of composition … and inevitably it set the standard for the later Gospels' *(Catholic Encyclopedia,* Vol. ix, Oct. 1, 1910, Pg. 674 -682). 'Matthew certainly is not first in order, and is only put first because it begins with the 'Book of the Generation of Jesus Christ' *(Catholic Encyclopedia,* Vol. vi, 657). Those virgin birth narratives were forged narratives that were not in the 'original Hebrew' version of that Gospel, but were structured into the writings in 'the 4th Century AD' *(Catholic Encyclopedia,* 'Matthew Gospel', 1909, 'Ebronite Version of Matthew's Gospel', also; Vol. IX, Oct. 1, 1910, Pg. 425; also; *New Catholic Encyclopedia,* 'Matthew Gospel').

The emergence of the Gospels

Over past decades Christian apologists consistently mislead the public into believing that the Gospels emerged between the years 65-95, but ancient literature fails to show any trace of acquaintance with, or the use of, Christian Gospels at the time of Justin Martyr, circa 160. The church agrees with the evidence of historic records, frankly stating that its Gospels 'do not go back to the first century of the Christian era' *(Catholic Encyclopedia,* Vol. V1, Sept. 1st 1909, Pg. 135-137), and the late date assigned to the arrival of Christian writings is an embarrassment for modern-day New Testament scholars. It is not possible to find in any historic writings compiled between the beginning of the First Century and the middle of the Fourth Century, any genuine references to Jesus Christ or the Gospels of Matthew, Mark, Luke and John. The reason for this is clarified in upcoming chapters.

Many people wondered at such an unaccountable omission of what the church considered the greatest events in world history. The period was rich in prolific writers and voluminous works were produced by such highly regarded historians as Pliny the Elder, Pliny the Younger, Philo, Josephus, Cornelius, Titus Livius (Livy), Porphyry, Plutarch, Lucius Seneca, Jewenal, Justus of Tiberius, Epictectus, Tacitus, Suetonius, Cluvius Rufus, Quintus Curtis Rufus, and Roman Consul, Publius Petronius, who lived in Jerusalem at the time ascribed to the life of Jesus Christ.

Those great classical scribes wrote about early religious beliefs but never mentioned Jesus Christ or the spectacular events that the church said accompanied his life. They devoted pages and pages to persons and events of no importance, but fail to make a single mention of God incarnating as a man and walking on Earth amongst multitudes to become their saviour. It was as if no such person existed to write about. However, two of those historians recorded the name of Judas Khrestus and his followers, and that was discussed in an earlier chapter.

In outlining factors explaining the late appearance of the Gospels, supporters of Christianity suggested that there might have been a First Century shortage of papyrus or leather to write upon. That opinion did not account for the availability of material used to compile the voluminous records of Roman and Jewish chroniclers of the time, and the truth of the matter is simply that the construct of Christianity had not yet begun.

The British origin of the 'Roman church'

At the closing of the Council of Niceae, Constantine transferred the use of the Lateran Palace to the bishop of Rome and ordered Marcarius of Jerusalem (d. 333) to design the 'fairest structure' and build a 'place of gathering' for the new religion (*Life,* iii, 30-33, *Constantine's Instructions to Marcarius*; also; Fabiola, Cardinal Wiseman, undated). It was British royalty through King Constantine that authorized the world's first now-called 'Christian church' for Roman religionists in Italy and that subsequently developed into the church of Rome.

The sister city of Rome

Constantine later ordered the construction of a new city on the site of ancient Byzantium, named it after himself and made it capital of the Roman Empire. No site on earth could have surpassed it for a capital; at Tilsit, in 1807, Napoleon would call it the Empire of the World. Constantinople was solemnly consecrated in 330 (*Smaller Classical Dictionary,* 1910, Pg. 161) and the transfer of empire from Rome to Byzantium was a great masterstroke in the history of civilization. By 337 it contained some 50,000 people; and in 400, some 100,000; in 500 almost a million. An official document (c. 420) lists five imperial palaces, six palaces for the ladies of the court, three for high dignitaries, 4388 mansions, 322 streets, 52 porticoes; add to these a 1000 shops, a 100 places of amusement, sumptuous baths, the Augusteum named after Constantine's mother Helena as *Augusta*, and magnificent squares that were veritable museums of the art of the classic world.

In a few short years Constantinople was the centre of the world and a later church council decreed that 'it shall now be called New Rome, and have the same privileges as Old Rome, because it is the second city in the world' (28th Ordain, Council of Chalcedon, 451).

The close of the Council of Nicaea

Some old documents state that the Council of Nicaea ended in mid-November, 326, while others said the struggle to establish a god was so fierce it extended 'for four years and seven months'. Whenever it ended, the savagery and violence it encompassed was disguised by a glossy title, the 'Great and Holy Synod', assigned to it by the church in the 18th Century. The earlier church, however, expressed a different opinion. The second council of Nicaea in 785-7 denounced the first council of Nicaea as 'a synod of fools and madmen' (*History of the Christian Church,* H. H. Milman, D.D. 1871) and sought to annul the 'decisions passed by men with troubled brains' (Ibid). If one choose to read the records of the second Nicaean council and noted references to 'affrighted bishops' and 'soldiery' needed to 'quell proceedings', the 'fools and madmen' declaration was surely an example of the pot calling the kettle black.

Emperor and King Constantine died in 337 and his decision to merge the now-called Pagan beliefs into the new religion of Jesus Khrestus brought many converts. Thus from a period of time in which 'mob rule and tyranny' (Cyril of Jerusalem, 386) reigned supreme in the new church, a series of concocted presbyter's 'commentaries filled with impositions and fables … falsely ascribed to the most holy apostles by fraudulent individuals' (*Ecclesiastical History*, Book I, Pt ii, Ch. ii (Ms. 248, Vol. 1, Pg. 93) Mosheim) became the official religious documents of the Roman Empire directly under the control of the Emperor Cult of the State.

Later church writers made Constantine 'the great champion of Christianity and it was given a legal status as the religion of the Roman Empire' (*Encyclopedia of the Roman Empire*, M. Bunson, 1994, Pg. 86). Church records show that is incorrect, for it was 'self interest which led him at first to adopt Christianity' (*Smaller Classical Dictionary*, 1910, Pg. 161) but at that time it wasn't called Christianity.

Divisions among Eastern and Western presbyters

Constantine's new god was not immediately accepted, and resistance offered by Roman custom compelled his successors to return to the earlier position (*Diondi, Diritto* rom. Crist. 3:151-187). A council of Western presbyters was held in Sardica in 347 and reinstated the *Divine Julius* as the official Roman god.

Although Constantine had earlier deified Jesus Khrestus, the new religion became official to the Roman Empire only after 381 when Emperor Theodosius (d. 395) imposed it on his subjects, and the modern church presentation of the nature of the procedure involved is unrestrained imagination (*New Catholic Encyclopedia*, Vol. X11, 1967, Pg. 563-578). In May 381 he summoned the first of three peculiar assemblies at Constantinople 'which were, as an aggregate, called by some, the second General Council of the church' (*Ecclesiastical History*, Bishop Du Pin, Vol. I, Pg. 607), and reapplied Jesus Khrestus as the Roman deity.

However, presbyterial groups were still deeply divided about the choice of god and bitterness between them resulted in only Eastern presbyters attending the first meeting (*Ecclesiastical History*, Bishop Du Pin, Vol. I, Pg.

615). There were 150 presbyters at the gathering and they were under the directions of 'Mad Meletius' a bishop from Antioch (*The Epitome of the General Councils of the Church, from the Council of Nicaea, to the Conclusion of the Roman Council of Trent in the Year 1563,* Reverend Richard Grier, D.D., 1828). The Egyptian and Western presbyters refused to attend and Bishop Nectarius, with 287 presbyters, conducted a competitive council at Aquileai in Venetia (near Venice today).

At the conclusion of deliberations, they petitioned the Eastern presbyters at the second meeting in 382 to meet for discussions between all parties at Alexandria in Northern Egypt, but the request was denied. The dissatisfied Western bishops then travelled to Constantinople and convened a third council in 383, when Nectarius demanded that Emperor Theodosius consider their majority views. However, he refused and 'issued laws that signed the death warrant' of major earlier religions, and they 'came to a sudden end' (*Catholic Encyclopedia*, x, 402). The records of the outcome of that meeting are clouded 'under the name of the Council of Nicaea to give them greater weight and authority' (*Ecclesiastical History*, Bishop Du Pin, Vol. I, Pg. 607) but what is recorded of the next council at Ephesus in 431 revealed that the presbyters' godly problems were still unsolved.

The beginning of ecclesiastical councils

The Empire gradually absorbed and adapted to its own ends the multitude of cults derived from all its parts and over the ensuing centuries coupled them together as one, the Roman universal church, today, the Roman Catholic church. Henceforth, much of the literature written from that time on was aimed at propagating a fabricated faith to the world and ensuring Roman Emperors were given perpetual places as heads of church and state. 'After Christianity had become the established religion of the Roman empire at the end of the Fourth Century, the Roman Emperors convened a succession of Councils which were called Ecumenical, Universal or General' (*Encyclopedia Britannica*, Edinburgh Ed., 1797), and thus developed a series of nineteen gatherings over the next 1200 years about which 'considerable doubt exists respecting the genuineness of their decisions, or if they actually happened' (Ibid).

CHAPTER 18

Twin stories in the Gospels

Shortly before his death in 1334, Pope John XXII issued two decretals that condemned the whole Franciscan theory of evangelical poverty. They were called *Ad Conditorem Canonum* (1322), and *Cum Inter Nonnullos* (1323), in which the Pope asserted from Gospel evidence that Jesus Christ had owned property. There is no evidence of that in the Gospels today, and this papal assurance reveals that the church writings are not a base of fact.

The Secret Scrolls

From the pope's decretals it is evident that the New Testament has had an adjustable history and this is corroborated from evidence found in the church's own files. The discovery of a cache of ancient scrolls in the Secret Vatican Archives in 1925 revealed that the Gospel of John and the book of Revelation were, in their original form, pre- Christian documents that were later plagiarized by the church writers and amended for Christian use. As the full details of the Secret Scrolls are revealed in *The Crucifixion of Truth* (Tony Bushby, Joshua Books, 2005), their discovery and contents need not directly concern us in this particular book. However, it is important to say that these ancient manuscripts provide mankind with documentation that presents a fresh starting point in uncovering the true extent of the corruptions made to the New Testament and reveals the forged nature of the Christian texts.

As incontrovertible evidence of the fabricated nature of the New Testament is now available, traditionalists and sceptics alike argue the various interpretations that the Gospel discrepancies present. Those contradictions can be brought into harmony when it is realized that the different life stories of Jesus and his twin were grafted into one under Constantine's instructions, and blended with supernatural narratives drawn from the stories of earlier god-men. Modern scholars have failed to observe the full significance of the interpolations in church texts, mainly because of the unfamiliarity of the notion of the New Testament being a human compilation in its entirety. The church knows this, and to overcome the obvious embarrassment of Jesus and his twin, trainee priests are now being told to preach that there are two different Christs in the Gospels, one in the Gospel of Matthew, and the other in the Gospel of Luke (From a personal interview with a monastic priest who is no longer in the priesthood).

Adding to the jungle of church texts, a combined committee of the United Bible Societies in 1982 acknowledged there are still 2000 disputed passages in the New Testament, and as many as 5000 ancient words are so puzzling that their true interpretation and meaning might never be known. Quoting from the Preface of the Revised Standard Version (1971) of the King James Bible, the Editorial Committee frankly admits to 'grave defects' in modern Bibles. They use such phrases as, 'these defects are so many and so serious', 'unauthorized changes' and 'tampered and corrupted texts'. The panel apologizes for the fact the Bible 'was originally based upon a Greek text that was marred by mistakes containing the accumulated errors of fourteen centuries of manuscript copying' and openly confessed that 'the text that lay before the revisers of 1611 was notoriously corrupt'. That damaging Preface has now been removed from newer printings of the Bible.

This stage of the history of the transmission of the Bible is characterized by the huge number of variant readings of the Gospels in particular, now running into tens of thousands. The author of the book *Genuineness and Authenticity of the Gospels,* Mr. B. A. Hinsdale (MA), felt compelled to stress that, 'There are 150,000 various readings of the New Testament manuscripts alone, the greater part of which must be corruptions since there can be but one original reading for any given passage'.

In defending the damaging inconsistencies in church texts, and referring to the nature of the origin and transmission of Jesus' words, the *Catholic Encyclopedia* stated:

> The sayings of Jesus did not need to be exact quotations; often they were not, since they were drawn from memories and not from stenographic reports. The words of Jesus could, and needed to be, adapted to Christian needs.

The church admits that the Gospel writers made Jesus say what they wanted him to say, and also left 18 years of his life unrecorded. Everything described in the Gospels, including the story of forty days and nights in the wilderness, can be condensed into a period of time of just a few weeks. Extracting from conflicting reports, the ministry of Jesus lasted from a few months up to a period exceeding two years, for one Gospel records Jesus attending three Passovers.

Origin of the holiest truths

Today the Christian clergy quote Gospels as if what was written in them around sixteen hundred years ago is incontrovertible evidence that those words were spoken by Jesus Christ some four centuries previous to that. However, that was not so, for the holiest truths carried through in the Gospels were inculcated by pre-Christian philosophers.

For example, centuries previous to the commencement of Christianity, Buddha quoted this advice, and the church later attributed it to Jesus: 'return good for evil and overcome anger with love'. Late in the 7th Century BC, Persian prophet Zoroaster cited guidance that was subsequently applied to Jesus in the Gospels; 'Whenever thou art in doubt as to whether an action is good or bad, abstain from it'. That statement was found in the sacred writings of the Zend-Avesta, the Avestan language being the earliest form of the Iranian language, formerly called Zend. There are some narratives in the story of Krishna that are quite repugnant to Christians, but others, such as the advice to 'give the unsmote cheek to an assailant' that is now found in the Christian Gospels and applied to Jesus. Emperor Constantine's instructions to Eusebius to search the presbyter's writings, 'and whatever is good in them, retain' is shown today in the Christian texts to have been followed by Eusebius and his scribes.

This well-known Gospel verse promoted by Christianity for centuries as being original words of wisdom spoken by Jesus, is proven not so; 'Do unto others as you would that they should do unto you'. That statement was first recorded some five hundred years previous to Jesus as a saying of the Chinese philosopher and moral teacher Confucius, and found in the records of his quotes, *The Analects of Confucius* (Pg. 76).

The Gospels reported Jesus' words when it was said that he was alone. Those conversations included sayings spoken during his lonely forty-day and night vigil in the wilderness and his prayer in the garden of Gethsemane on the night of his arrest. Both ancient and modern commentators object to those passages, saying, 'those words were put into Jesus' mouth by storytellers and should not be accepted as scripture … the Gospels, like all writings in the New Testament, are human products and should not be accorded divine status' (*The Fifth Gospel*, The Jesus Seminar, USA, 1994). Rudolf Bultman (1884-1976), Professor of New Testament studies for 30 years at Marburg University in Germany, concluded after a lifetime study of Christian texts that 'not a single line from the Gospels can be taken as certainly historically reliable'.

Disassembling the Gospels

Thus it can be established that the Gospels do not provide a literal story, and to determine the separate characters of Judas Khrestus and Rabbi Jesus from so little information, especially where much of it depends upon stray narratives, is problematical. Given the complex nature of the development and transmission of the Christian texts it cannot be said with any degree of certainty what particular elements belonged to which of the twin brothers, and in many cases, there remains obscure points. However, some particular aspects are clear, and from their different characters it is possible to attribute to each of them various Gospel narratives and therefore determine who said or did what.

Probably the most damaging of the Gospel statements refuting the church assertion that Jesus Christ was God on earth are carried in the Gospels of Matthew (11:19) and Luke (7:34). Here, Jesus frankly admits that he is 'a glutton and a drunkard', words used by him in describing how the people of the time perceived him to be.

During the research for this book, members of the Christian ministry were asked to define the church's position relating to these 'drunkard' statements. One honest answer suggested that the narratives created 'special difficulties' and others angrily claimed they were nothing more than words 'written between the lines'. However, they are words written in the Bible and presented by the church as words of God. The impression they create of Jesus Christ is embarrassing for the church in light of the divine nature in which it desires to present him. Some priests refused to discuss the subject and questioned why the verses needed to be raised, because Jesus didn't really mean what he said. To be told by the church that Jesus Christ did not mean to say what it plainly says he said in canonical texts is a simple way of getting out of the difficulty, and this particular expedient was used often by the priesthood in defending Gospel statements that are impossible to defend.

Knowing the compositional structure, and the extent of later editing the New Testament underwent, it is remarkable that these two verses were not deleted centuries ago, but the tradition current at the time of Gospel compilation allowed those verses to be recorded. There were later attempts to 'water down' the statements and some newer Bibles now say Jesus Christ was 'a winebibber', meaning 'a person who drinks a great deal of wine', while others simply say he was 'a drinker'. However, Christians the world over must accept the church presentation of the New Testament and that makes the Lord of their faith a self-confessed 'drunkard'.

In reconciling the two Gospel traditions, the 'drunkard' narratives are attributed to Judas Khrestus, not Rabbi Jesus. It is interesting to read from the Old Testament book of Proverbs, 'for the drunkard and glutton will come to poverty' (Proverbs 23:20-21). In Greek tradition 'glutton' meant 'cannibal' and is frequently used to describe 'the glutton Zeus' and 'the glutton Dionysus', both mythologically believed to have eaten human flesh. Gluttony and drunkenness were obviously condemned under the prevailing Law of Moses with an additional narrative stating that 'a glutton and a drunkard shall be stoned to death' (Deut. 21: 20-21). This belief may provide a reason why there are constant references in the Gospels to large crowds trying to stone Judas Khrestus.

The Wicked Priest of the Dead Sea Scrolls was also considered a drunkard for he 'would drink his fill' when 'the Cup of the Wraith of God' came around to him. In Dead Sea Scroll research this is generally interpreted to mean that he drank too much wine. The parallels with the two Qumran messiahs to the Gospel story of Judas Khrestus and Rabbi Jesus are extraordinary with one character in both cases represented as a military commander who wished to restore the earthly Kingdom of God, and the other of a priestly nature believing 'the Kingdom of God is within'.

Although Judas Khrestus clearly did not abstain from drinking wine, there was a good reason for his indulgence, and it was associated with the meaning of the word 'Nazarene'. The Old Testament refers to a body of pre-Christian people (male and female) called, Nazars. The word 'Nazar' signified a particular group of people who vowed or consecrated themselves to the devoted service of the Jehovah god of the Old Testament. There is more to the Nazar group than that recorded in the Old and New Testaments and by tracing them throughout the best-known works of ancient writers, they were connected with Pagan as well as Jewish adepts. Thus Alexander the Historian (311) said of Pythagoras he was a disciple of the Assyrian Nazarite whom some supposed to be Ezekiel of Old Testament fame, and famous biblical characters such as Samson and Samuel are described as Nazars. Singularly, they were called 'a Nazarite', in a group 'Nazarenes', and at the time of this story, the Nazarenes were the military arm of the Essenes.

The Nazarenes were known to have existed at least as early as 397BC and lived on the eastern shore of the Dead Sea, according to the records of Josephus (*Ant, Jud,* xiii, Pg. xv). Pliny confirmed Josephus' statements and said Nazars 'lived on the shores of the Dead Sea for thousands of ages', meaning a lengthy time. In the Old Testament they are mentioned on three separate occasions and in the Book of Numbers (6:20), it is recorded that 'a Nazar (Nazarite) may drink wine'. In the Syric Version of the Gospel of Luke (4:34) there is a reference to, 'Iasoua, thou Nazar'. Dr. Constantine Von Tischendorf (1815-1874), German biblical scholar and Professor of Theology, transcribed these words to read: 'Iesou (Yeshu'a) Nazarene', referring to Rabbi Jesus. To take the 'drunkard' references further, another narrative in the Old Testament states that the Nazars were 'made to drink wine' (Amos 2:12), implying alcohol was forced upon them by scriptural law.

Strange verses in the Bible

Judas Khrestus made this very straightforward statement when he commanded that he and his followers must 'hate our own father and mother, and wife and children and brothers and sisters and even our own life' (Luke 14:26). In the Gospel of Thomas (101/114), this concept is further supported while the Gospel of Luke (12:51) records another statement of aggression from the mouth of Judas Khrestus: 'Do you think that I have come to give peace on earth? No, I tell you, but rather division'. This Gospel verse hardly supports the church claim that Jesus Christ loves you:

> For I have come to set a man against his father, and a daughter against her mother, and a daughter-in-law against her mother-in-law, and a man's enemies will be those of his own household. (Matt. 10:35-36)

These are the words of Judas Khrestus and there are similar statements sprinkled throughout the New Testament. The Temple of Jerusalem when used by livestock merchants and moneychangers for business, enraged Judas Khrestus who, 'making a whip of cords (a cat-o'-nine-tails), drove them out, overturning the tables and seats' (John 2:15), and created a stampede of cattle and sheep. The 'whip of cords' phrase is edited out of most later editions of the Bible, but appears in the oldest manuscripts of the Gospels of Matthew, Mark, Luke and John. In some Fifth Century manuscripts, the word 'scorpion' is used in lieu of 'a whip of cords'. This weapon was a whip with leather thongs set with sharp iron points or nails, called, in Latin, 'horribilia'.

After Judas Khrestus' violent performance, the local inhabitants considered him insane and said, 'he has a demon, and he is mad, why listen to him?' (John 10: 20). There are six references in the New Testament to Judas Khrestus being 'mad' (Matt 12:24; Mark 3:21-22; Luke 19:45; John 8:48 and 10:20; 1 Cor. 14-23), with his own family claiming that 'he was outside himself'. They were in constant conflict with him, and turned him away when he 'came into his own home, and his own people received him not' (John: 1:11).

Commentators have often questioned the mental stability of the Gospel Jesus Christ and refer to some bizarre dialogue between him and the disciples, both in the canonical New Testament, and the apocryphal writings. In the

Gospel of Mark, for example, Jesus makes the claim that there are worms inhabiting hell that are fireproof and possessing eternal life (Mark 9:43-48). In the Gospel of Thomas, Jesus states that 'every woman who makes herself male will enter the kingdom of heaven.' Later, when the disciples ask Jesus, 'When will you be revealed to us?' he replied, 'When you take off your clothing, without shame, and like little children, put your clothes on the ground and tread on them'.

The Gospels reveal that Judas Khrestus could be a little peeved when awakened from sleep (Mark 4:38-39, Sinai Bible) and that he 'did not wash before dinner' (Luke 11:38). When his host commented upon his lack of hygiene, he received a full-scale verbal assault from his 'angry' guest as Judas Khrestus' uncontrollable temper flared again.

People could further question the mental stability of Judas Khrestus if they were to read a strange event recorded in the Gospel of Mark. He was hungry, and seeing a fig tree in the distance, approached it with the intention of obtaining something to eat, 'knowing it was not the season for figs'. This irrational act has intrigued biblical analysts for centuries. However, the word 'knowing' has been quietly dropped from newer editions of the Bible and subtly replaced with the word, 'for'. The passage then reads, 'for it was not the season for figs', which takes away the strange act of the Gospel Jesus Christ approaching a fig tree for a meal of figs out of season. However, the passage quoted is documented in the oldest texts of the Gospel of Mark. When only leaves were found, Judas Khrestus cursed the tree, saying, 'may no one ever eat fruit from you again' (Mark 11:12-20). The next morning, Khrestus and his followers again pass by the fig tree and noticed that it was withered away to its roots. Simon Peter said, 'Look, the fig tree which you cursed has withered' (Mark 11:20-21). The Gospel of Matthew carries a conflicting account of this verse, being, 'the fig tree withered at once'.

A Christian layman, when talking to author and translator of New Testament writings, Mr. Hugh Schonfield, made the following comment: 'If you can get around Jesus cursing the fig tree, you will have done us a great service'. It wasn't the singular Jesus Christ of today's Gospels who was talking, but Judas Khrestus. Schonfield would also have done the church a great service if he could have deleted the verse that describes the peculiar act of

Jesus Christ sticking 'his fingers into his ears, and he then spat, and touched his tongue' (Mark 7:33).

Judas Khrestus' attitude towards divorce and remarriage is made clear when he declared; 'If you divorce your wife and marry another, you commit adultery' (Matt: 19:9). In this narrative however, there is a strange anomaly. In some Fourth, Fifth and Sixth Century Bibles this passage reads, 'and he who marries a woman commits adultery and makes her commit adultery'. Here then, is a narrative full of tantalizing obscurities and uncertainties. It provides an apt example of what the researcher is up against when comparing old church texts and the surprises to be found in trying to determine the true nature of the customs of the times. Which particular version of the text is meant to be the original understanding is difficult to determine.

The disbelief of the bishop

In 1960, Anglican Bishop of Birmingham, Hugh Montefiore, suggested Jesus Christ might have been homosexual. Montefiore was motivated by Christ's unusual attitude towards male nudity in certain statements in the Gospels of Mark and John, and a reference in an Epistle to the Essenes at Colosse referring to an incident of 'complete stripping'. Montefiore suggested the 'closeness to men' in narratives associated with Jesus was supported by the Gospel passage referring to 'the disciple who Jesus loved was leaning back on Jesus' breast' (John 13:23-25) at the Last Supper. This was not Rabbi Jesus but Judas Khrestus.

The apostle John is traditionally identified as the unnamed disciple 'who Jesus loved' and this assumption was drawn from a Gospel statement applied to Jesus during his last hours in which he entrusted his mother Mary to care for John as 'her son' (John 19:25-27). Medieval devotional images of John with his head resting in an effeminate Jesus' lap and, in others, kissing Jesus' neck, gave rise to mystical texts in which John is said to 'have enjoyed the milk of the Lord,' which verbally and pictorially implies an act of oral sex with Jesus Christ (*The First Gay Pope,* Lyn Fletcher, Alyson Publications, 1992; Lists religious gay and lesbian 'firsts').

This is a detail of Jesus and St John from The Bishop's Bible, 1608 Edition. This engraving suggests that the artist who created it took the New Testament relationship between them to be one of affection and intimacy. See also, Pietro Lorenzetti's Fresco of the Last Supper (1305-1348), Lower church of San Francesco, Assisi. It provides a similar depiction.

Although a 'special relationship' between the Gospel Jesus Christ and apostle John is clearly indicated, Bishop Montefiore's theory did not find widespread Christian acceptance. Assertions that Jesus and some of the apostles were gay or bisexual are issues dismissed by the church as purely speculative. However, many homosexual elements in the New Testament are subtle and easily missed, while many forms of early Christian rites involved male nudity.

The secret Gospel of Mark 'carefully guarded'

While researching at the Mar Saba Monastery near Jerusalem, Professor Morton Smith recognized the transcript of a hitherto unknown letter from Bishop Clement of Alexandria (160-215) to Theodotus (*The Secret Gospel of Mark*, Professor Morton Smith, 1974). The main purpose of Clement's letter was to attack the teachings of the Carpocrations, a Gnostic group who flourished as early as the Second Century. Clement's correspondent had been taken back when confronted by 'heretics' who told him they had read another version of Mark's Gospel which appeared to be genuine, but of which Theodotus knew nothing. Clement frankly acknowledged the authenticity of the Gospel and said it was an enlarged version that he called 'the secret Gospel of Mark.' Clement said that 'the secret Gospel ... is now carefully guarded', and denied that the phrase, 'naked man to naked man' was recorded in association with the activities of Jesus Christ, as the Carpocrations had apparently told Theodotus.

© The Metropolitan Museum of Art

This is the Mar Saba Monastery founded by St Saba of Cappadocia in the Fifth Century. It was here that Professor Morton Smith found the Secret Gospel of Mark.

Professor Morton Smith also found a verse in the Secret Gospel of Mark that recorded the original version of the 'raising of Lazarus', found paralleled in today's canonical Gospel of Mark. It said, 'Jesus ... going to where the youth was, he stretched forth his hand and raised him, seizing his hand. But the youth, looking upon him, loved him, and began to beseech him that he might be with him ... in the evening the youth came to him wearing a linen cloth over his naked body and he remained with him all that night and Jesus taught him the mystery of God'. From the Gospels, and also the apocryphal works, comes knowledge that the instruction course for teaching the 'secret of the Kingdom of God' involved a private overnight ritual in which a young male pupil came to Jesus naked apart from a loose linen cloth about his body. A confirming episode appears in the canonical Gospel of Mark (14:52), where a young man who had been with Jesus during the scuffle at the time of his capture, 'ran away naked after a linen cloth about his body had fallen off'. These descriptions are more in keeping with the character of Judas Khrestus than Rabbi Jesus and they raise the intriguing question: 'Just what did Judas Khrestus do with these young boys in the secret nocturnal rites?'

In both the Old and New Testaments there are constant references to 'a secret' known only to initiates, and one wonders whether it had some connection with nudity or homosexuality. Leonardo da Vinci showed John the Baptist naked (Windsor, 12572; also Louvre, No. 1597) and there are numerous pictorial indications showing the baptismal candidate naked. In the earliest frescoes, the Ravenna mosaics and in a large number of later Greek Icons, the Gospel Jesus Christ is depicted naked when receiving baptism. Interestingly enough, there is no mention in the Gospels of Rabbi Jesus baptizing anyone.

The hidden side of things

The church depicts Jesus Christ as a softy, a real pushover, 'gentle Jesus, meek and mild', as recorded in Sunday school literature. But they have it wrong for the Gospels portray more the character of Judas Khrestus than Rabbi Jesus. In summation, Judas Khrestus is shown to be a man with a violent temper, an unwashed drunk carrying a sword and brandishing a whip. There are suggestions of homosexuality from a man who ate like a pig, was uncaring about family lives and was considered by many to be insane, as was also the apostle Paul (Acts 26:24). A narrative in the FIRST Vulgate of 1563 said that Judas Khrestus' followers were 'all thieves and robbers', confirmed by Ernest Renan of the French Academy who said they 'were the dregs of the nations, a poor dirty set, without manners, clad in filthy gabardines and smelling strongly of garlic' (*Development of the Catholic Church,* 1880).

Judas Khrestus constantly defended himself against verbal and physical assaults as he struggled to prove his royal identity. Did he not ask, 'Who do men say that I am?' (Matt 16:13-15). Also revealed is a man of courage, quite prepared to assert his right by force and, if necessary to employ savage physical violence against his enemies. The army of Khrestians he developed shows this, and he was the anointed leader.

CHAPTER 19

What did the first Bible really say?

Historians and theologians have speculated in the past that contemporaries or near-contemporaries of Jesus Christ wrote the New Testament and that its transmission to today is without error. Bearing in mind that 'knowledge of past times adorns and nourishes the intellect', it is important to reveal that the recorded history of the development of the Vulgate is very different to what the church would have us believe. As might be expected, the validity of the Vulgate today depends upon earlier manuscripts, and they are recorded in church history to have been constantly altered during centuries of transmission, and slowly references to Jesus' twin were deleted.

It is not true that the Bible is authentic

To cover-up the true nature of the composition of the Christian texts, an extraordinary decision is found in the records of the First Council of Constantinople of 381-3 convened by Roman Emperor Theodosius (d. 395) just forty-four years after Constantine ordered the production of the first New Testaments. What was decided at that assembly presents an historical record outlining an extraordinary episode in Christian history little known today and involved Pope Damasus (366-384), who was in attendance. He was a man so stained with impiety and so notorious with women that he was called the Tickler of Matron's Ears (*Lives of the Popes*, Mann, c. 1905). When he found that the Roman people would not walk before him in processions, he had them beaten, and many were killed. He was charged with adultery in a Civil Court, and only the intervention of his friend, the

Emperor, averted the scandal of a trial. He returned to the church and in a candid personal confession frankly admitted that the Gospel manuscripts of his day were so 'full of errors and dubious passages' (*The Library of the Fathers,* Damasus, Oxford, 1833-45) that copies coming from scriptoriums were different and conflicting. To prevent the writings being seen by the wrong eyes, and hide the evidence that Jesus had a twin brother, Damasus came up with a solution that was brilliant in its simplicity ... he banned the Bible.

The basic New Testament canon was no sooner set (between 381 and 397 generally) than the laity was strictly 'forbidden to read the word of God, or to exercise their judgment in order to understand it' (*The Library of the Fathers, Damasus,* Oxford, 1833-45). Damasus recorded that 'bad use of difficult passages by the simple and poor gives rise to hear-say' and the general populace was denied access to the compilations. The word 'hear-say' developed into 'heresy' and people who opposed church opinions were subsequently called 'heretics.' It was with a resolution of that council that the ban was officially established but some members of the priesthood had trouble understanding the new terminology. The unreliability of their explanations of heretics and heresies is illustrated in the case of St. Epiphanius, who mistook the Pythagorean Sacred Tetrad (The number 4), for a heretic leader.

After he suppressed the Bible, Damasus created an array of formidable penances and additional anathemas 'designed to keep the curious at bay' (*Early Theological Writings,* G.W.F. Hegal). Today 'anathema' means a curse or denunciation pronounced with religious solemnity by ecclesiastical authority, simply being a convenient way of disposing of proofs. Its original purpose was to 'frighten the rabble' (Ibid) and during the next fifteen hundred years anathemas were strictly enforced at bizarre public ceremonies where the 'evil' were punished or 'burnt for doubting' what the church said about the Bible (*Pastoral Theology,* Professor J. Beck, 1910). The chief tendency of the priesthood was to keep the Bible away from people and substitute church authority as the rule of life and belief. With Christian texts safely preserved from scrutiny by Decree, the church endorsed the suppression of all Bibles for 1230 years, right up until well after the printing of the King James Bible in 1611, and supported its ban with an array of severe penalties.

The letters of St Jerome

One year after he concealed the Bible, Damasus sanctioned a complete restructure of every book in both the Old and New Testaments, and it was St. Pope Damasus who was given the job. His real name was Sophronius Eusebius Heironymus, with his byname of 'Jerome' deriving from 'Yar of Rome'. He was born in the town of Stridon on the north coast of Italy and was a man of contradictions ... generous towards his friends yet merciless with his enemies. His opponents described him as 'free with his tongue, uncharitable, sly, a hypocrite, the arch monk' (*Genesis of Christianity*, Plummer, Edinburgh, 1876). Today he is called 'the Most Holy One' and, like St. Augustine, 'Doctor of the Church' (*Catholic Encyclopedia*, Vol. XV, 1912, Pg. 515; also; *Biblitheca Sanctorum*, Rome 1965, V1, 1132-7).

The information about Jerome revealed in this work is extracted from his own letters (*The Letters of Jerome*), many of which are abusive, confrontational and teem with bitter invective. His language is coarse, and a book he wrote about sex was so vile his associates destroyed it (*Diderot's Encyclopedia*, 1759). Jerome lived in a cave for many years on the barren plains of Chalcis in Syria where he was taught to read and write Hebrew by an old monk. Jerome's desert years ended unhappily, with him at the centre of a religious dispute in nearby Antioch, accused of heresy because he 'preferred Pagan literature' (*Ciceronians es, non Christianus*). Jerome was seduced by the older culture, proudly stating, 'I am a Ciceronian, not a Christian'.

How the Vulgate got its name

Because of his knowledge of Hebrew, Damasus offered Jerome the commission to restructure the Bible, the purpose being to end the great differences in the wording of the Gospels. Jerome, 'urged on by Pope Damasus' offer of wealth' (*Jerome,* Prof. Isaac Muir, A Summary of his Three Writings, 1889), travelled to Rome in 382 and commenced work on a new Bible called the *Versio Vulgar*, or 'verses for the vulgar' (*Verses for the Vulgar*, Chapter vii, *Genesis of Christianity*, Plummer, Edinburgh, 1876, also; *History of the Vulgate,* S. Berger, 1893). Before he commenced his task, Jerome wrote to Pope Damasus, saying:

> It was useless to correct the New Testament for versions of scripture which already exist in the language of others show that their additions are false.

The period before Jerome produced the *Versio Vulgar* is a tangled piece of church history and the origin and contents of the manuscripts he used to reconstruct the Gospel stories are not known. For reasons unidentified, Jerome's construction of the *Versio Vulgar* proceeded intermittently and in some instances, he 'argued and refused to act at all' (*History of the Christian Church,* Philip Schaff, D.D., Ms. No. 283, Chicago Public Library). Jerome was ordered to supplement the new Bible with a collection of narratives that he called 'peculiar additions', given to him by Pope Damasus and included the resurrection and virgin birth stories (*Adversus Helvidium* (PL 23:201, *The Letters of Jerome*). The church confirmed Jerome's statement that the virgin birth narratives were not based on the conclusion of fact:

> There seems to be no doubt that the infancy narratives of Matthew and Luke were later additions to the original body of the apostolic catechesis. (*New Catholic Encyclopedia*, 1967 Ed. Vol. xiv, Pg. 693)

Those 'later additions' revealed another doctrinal forgery perpetrated in the development of the New Testament and provide additional and ongoing evidence that the Gospels are fallacious.

Jerome's Bible was 'purposely wrote in Latin, that it might serve for the instruction of the clergy only, and not come to the knowledge of the laity' (*De Statu Mortuorum,* Dr. Burnet, English author, c. 1840). After two decades of intermittent work, Jerome eventually created the *Versio Vulgar,* a Bible that was renamed the 'Vulgate' at the Council of Trent, and one so special to Roman Catholics today. According to Jerome's personal records, that Bible was written for 'public readings to the mass of vulgar rabble and demented mobs' and expressed 'in a crude language which most of them appreciated' (*Letter 53, 10,* Jerome). Jerome called them 'Asses with two legs' (*Letter 27.1*, Jerome) and reading out 'verses for the vulgar' to the masses provided the origin of the 'mass' into Christianity.

By the time Jerome finished rewriting the texts (c. 405) Pope Damasus was dead, but his new Bible included a Preface addressed to Damasus. Jerome explained in a covering letter to Chromatus, Bishop of Aquileia in Northern

Italy (d. c. 407), that he used a combination of existing Greek texts developed after the Council of Nicaea as the basis for his new version of the Gospels. He emphasized that 'where the variations had been extreme' he treated the text as conservatively as possible, and 'made changes to meet the popular outcry' (*King James Version of the Teacher's Bible*, Appendix). He stated that he included Damasus's 'peculiar additions' in the opening of the Gospel of Matthew (the virgin birth) and opined that they were 'frankly ridiculous'.

Jerome complained of 'errors of copyists more asleep than awake' and spoke of a number of 'passages, which are in themselves false, absurd, and incredible'. He described some manuscripts before him as 'dull in perception, frivolous in expression, sleepy in sense … rubbish' and commented on 'blundering alterations of self-assured and extravagant supporters'. He stated that he did not use the original Aramaic and Hebrew versions, although he had previously translated a Hebrew version of the Matthew Gospel into Greek. Jerome admitted that he supplemented the Vulgate with this restructured verse from the Old Testament book of Job (19:25):

> I know that my Redeemer lives,
> And at the last day I shall rise from the earth,
> And again shall be surrounded with my skin,
> And in my flesh I shall see my God.

Jerome's new Bible had many critics with some saying he built-in too much of his own phrasing and took excessive liberties with earlier writings that he embraced. Others suggested that he added too definite a Christian slant to the Old Testament, 'being unafraid to depart from the original' (*Weber, N.A.*, Professor of Fundamental Theology and Church History, Washington, contributor to 1911 *Catholic Encyclopedia*). Jerome's revision of the Bible earned him the reputation of 'forger' with his friend, Rufinius Aquileus (d. c. 428), and St. Augustine bitterly condemned it, saying, 'It was so ill-done, it crosseth me, I desire it to be burnt'. Jerome retaliated, saying to Bishop Chromatus; 'If he (Augustine) did not like it, he didn't have to read it'.

The Old Testament and the Gospels of the Vulgate were thus complete. However, Jerome rejected the twenty three writings that made up the Acts of the Apostles, the Epistles and the Book of Revelation, saying that they were 'not versions, but perversions' and were 'depreciated by glosses and additions'. There is substantial scholarly opinion that the remainder of the New Testament shows no trace of Jerome's style (*Oxford Dictionary of the Christian Church,* Cross, 1997, Pg. 1710).

However, there is something unanswered about the origin of the Vulgate. In the 'Approved Holy Catholic Bible' of 1875, a comprehensive section is provided in the front of the book called the 'History of the Holy Catholic Bible', being a detailed account of the passage of the Vulgate through time. It says of its origin; 'we may date its birth about the end of the fifth century, in or about the last ten years of that century'. St Jerome died in 420, leaving a gap of 70 years before the Vulgate officially came into being. Even the most hard-line biblical scholars are grudgingly prepared to acknowledge that they don't know what changes were made to the Vulgate in those lost decades.

CHAPTER 20

Outer interference in the Gospels

Around a century and a half later, the Vulgate received more editing, and at this time the alterations that were made were documented. For understandable reasons, the world of biblical scholarship is reticent to discuss in detail the recorded events associated with the council that made the changes. To do so may give rise to the loss of confidence that the church publicly places in the New Testament, but the truth of its composition is swiftly dashed when we turn to historical Roman records. There is the inescapable evidence that not only did the church constantly alter its texts, but people outside the priesthood also rewrote the Gospels deliberately to suit their own ideas. In this part of the book we discuss a development that was to have profound consequences for the whole character of later Christianity.

Previous beliefs nullified

Previous to this time, the early church fathers accepted the concept of reincarnation and recorded their personal thoughts on the subject. St. Jerome, for example, left extensive passages outlining his beliefs on the subject, saying:

> As to the origin of the soul, I remember the question of the whole kuriakos (church); whether it be fallen from heaven, as Pythagoras and the Platonists and Origen believe; or it be of the proper substance of God; or whether they are kept in a repository formerly built by God; or whether they are made by God and sent back into bodies according to that which is written in the Gospel.

But it is not 'written in the Gospel' or any Gospels known today.

In several verses of his work called *Confessions* (c. 401), Bishop Augustine personally wrestled with his expression of the 'unexplainable' concept of pre-existence. The belief in reincarnation was so strong in his time that wealthy families preserved the bodies of their dead relatives by pickling them in salt water before burial in a sealed sarcophagus. That strange act was a result of a literal interpretation of the Old Testament book of Leviticus for they believed by following biblical instructions the soul would return and re-enter a complete and perfectly preserved form. The early Christian method of preparing the dead was less elaborate than the mummification process employed by Egyptian morticians, which involved the removal of all internal organs.

A prostitute orders Gospels to be rewritten

As the records of St. Jerome reveal, the concept of reincarnation was originally part of early Christian dogma but was censored at a special council meeting in 553. A notorious prostitute was responsible for those far-reaching changes and her name was Theodora (c. 499-559), wife of Byzantine Roman Emperor, Flavius Justinian (483-565).

An historian named Procopius of Caesarea (490-562) is our chief authority for the period, and his primary works are *De aedificiis* (*Buildings*) and *History Arcana*. From what information he recorded about Theodora, we may reasonably conclude that she began as not quite a lady, and ended up every inch a queen. She was the daughter of Acacius, a bear trainer, and grew up in the odor of the circus at Constantinople's Hippodrome. Later, she became an actress and a prostitute and shocked and delighted Constantinople with her lewd pantomimes. She practiced abortion with repeated success, but gave birth to an illegitimate child. She became the mistress of Hecebolus, a Syrian, was deserted by him, and then disappeared for some time into the brothels of Alexandria.

She reappeared in Constantinople as a poor woman, earning her living by spinning wool. Justinian met and fell in love with her, made her his mistress, then his wife, and then his queen. Two years after their marriage in 525 Justinian was crowned in St Sophia; Theodora was crowned Empress at his side; and 'not even a priest' says Procopius, 'showed himself outraged'.

She became the most powerful woman in Byzantine history and her acumen made her Justinian's most trusted, and unscrupulous, adviser.

© Film Library of Byzantine Art

A Byzantium mosaic of Empress Theodora wearing her tiara and attended by courtesans, displayed in the Church of S. Vitale, Ravenna, Italy.

From whatever she had been, Theodora became a matron whose imperial chastity no one impugned. She was avid of money and power and sometimes gave way to an imperious temper. Occasionally, she intrigued to achieve ends opposed to Justinian's. He had invested her uxoriously with sovereignty theoretically equal to his own and did not complain when she exercised her power. She took an active part in diplomacy and in ecclesiastical politics, made and unmade popes and patriarchs, and deposed her enemies. Theodora exercised considerable influence during her reign, and her superior intelligence and deft handling of political affairs caused many to think that it was she, rather than the Emperor, who ruled Byzantium. Her name is mentioned in nearly all laws passed during that period, including church Decrees.

She was an amateur theologian and debated with her husband about the duality in the Gospels (*Roman State and Christian Church* (A collection of legal documents, 3 Vols. Vol. 3 contains translations of all Emperor Justinian's religious legislation, with full discussions), London, 1966). Justinian, at that time, was labouring to reunite the Eastern and Western factions; unity of religion, he thought, was indispensable to the unity of the Empire. Theodora disapproved of the Gospels, and severally criticized the reference to souls being 'sent back into bodies' (Jerome). The debate that ensured became known as The Three Chapters and it referred to particular chapters in the Gospels. Those narratives essentially taught that all humans are equal and that created difficulties for Theodora who wanted to convince the common people that the nobility were of a higher standing in the community and therefore superior.

Her influence in religious affairs was decisive, as illustrated in what became known as the Fifth Ecumenical Council of Constantinople that opened in the Hagia Sophia on 5 May, 553. That gathering was specifically called to settle once and for all, the questions of The Three Chapters. It was the second of four councils held in Constantinople, the next being in 680 and the last in 869. The first council of Constantinople was that of 381 when Papa Damasus officially banned the Bible and introduced 'curses' into Christian tradition. Theodora convened the council to raise the difficulties that the reincarnation verses presented, and she herself was the chairperson, with Emperor Justinian taking only a casual interest (*Ecclesiastical History*, Bishop Du Pin, Vol. I, Dublin, 1783).

The express purpose of Theodora's gathering was to obtain a majority vote from the 68 ecclesiastics in attendance to condemn The Three Chapters and approve new anathemas (curses) that she issued against the Gospel doctrine of pre-existence of the soul. The matter is of considerable import from the purely historical standpoint, and therefore desirable to publish the very words of her Decree by which the early church deleted the doctrine of reincarnation out of its theology. This datum of Christian history is an item quite obscure and was difficult to locate, therefore many people should appreciate its inclusion in this book. The Decree was couched in the following sentence:

> Whosoever shall support the mythical doctrine of the pre-existence of the human soul, and the consequent monstrous opinion of its return to earth, let him be anathema (cursed). (Decree of the Second Council of Constantinople; 553; *Index Expurgatorius Vaticanus*, An exact reprint, Edited by R. Gibbings, B.A., Dublin, 1837)

An additional fourteen similar anathemas were published as part of the proceedings of the same council and all aimed at pre-existence, but included references to reincarnation. The occasion and timing of the Decrees are evidence that indicated that the belief in reincarnation was deeply ingrained in general early Christian doctrinism.

Theodora then decreed that if persons who had spoken against the Gospel alterations came forth privately 'and confesseth and forsake his sins, he shall have mercy'. With that decree the doctrine of 'confession' was established in church law and it was later developed to cover a large array of transgressions. Pope Vigilius of Rome (d. 555), who had been summoned to Constantinople, opposed the council, so Theodora locked him away from May to December. There had been intense conflict between Empress Theodora and Pope Vigilius since 543, when Theodora and Justinian, at an earlier local synod, condemned the reincarnation teachings of Origen of Alexandria. Origen was one of the shining lights of the early church and a man today regarded as one of the original pillars of the faith. To nullify earlier church decisions, the council confirmed the right of later generations to declare dead people heretics, and immediately condemned Origen as such.

When released, Pope Vigilius formerly ratified the council's verdicts and, under pressure, personally condemned The Three Chapters, but some time later he started a campaign against the Decrees and declared Theodora a heretic. 'At the instigation of Vigilius, the Council Decrees were contested in some Eastern churches and a fearful schism arose that lasted one hundred and fifty years' (*Encyclopedia Britannica*, 9th Ed., Vol. 10, Pg. 783 onwards).

On February 26, 554, 'Theodora of the Brothel', as she was called even in her imperial days, issued instructions to the scriptoriums of Constantinople for the Gospels to be rewritten and The Three Chapters deleted (*A Treatise of the Corruption of Scripture*, Thomas James, D.D., London, 1611, London 1688,

Cambridge, 1843; *Index Expurgatorius Vaticanus*, An exact reprint, Edited by R. Gibbings, B.A., Dublin, 1837). As a result, the church today preaches resurrection, not reincarnation.

CHAPTER 21

A strange church statement

The early priesthood claimed that the Bible was 'divine', but knew it was false, and said so. Bishop Victor of Tunnunum (near Carthage?), who died about 589 and whose work, said the church, 'is of great historical value', made this statement:

> In the consulship of Messala, at the command of the Emperor Anastasius, the Holy Gospels, as written by *Idiota Evangelista*, are corrected and amended. (*Chronica*, p. 89-90, Victor of Tunnunum, cited by Dr. Mills, Prolegom to R.V., p. 98)

In the Sixth Century Byzantine Emperor Anastasius II (652-721) recognized the authors of the Gospels were 'idiots' and again external parties authorized the rewriting of church texts, a never-ending process, even in the 21st Century.

Alcuin's twins

In 790, Holy Roman Emperor Charlemagne (d. 814), instructed Anglo-Latin clerical scholar, Alcuin, to rewrite the Vulgate (*Encyclopedia Britannica*, 9th Edition, Vol. 1, 1875, pg. 230; also, *Diderot's Encyclopedia*, 1759). The task was unfinished when he died 14 years later (d. 804) and persons unknown, living at Aachen, subsequently completed the work. Late in Alcuin's lifetime, he wrote a short story about twin knights called Amis and Amiles that came to be called the Charlemagne Legend in the 13th Century. The essence of the story was based on an older and widespread legend that relayed the lives of twin brothers who were totally different in their characters and lifestyles. Maybe Alcuin allegorically preserved the original story from the Gospels before he rewrote them. How great were Alcuin's changes at that time is impossible to determine, but later papal statements revealed that the church itself disbelieved its texts and eventually set up a commission to officially validate its writings in the eyes of the believer.

From around that period in history followed the long and depressing Dark Ages, a thousand or more year period (to 1850) that achieved its name from the intellectual darkness resulting from church rule. During that age, schools of learning were abolished and teaching people to read and write was unlawful. 'In those Dark Ages, as the period of Catholic ascendancy is justly called, men were credulous and ignorant and they therefore produced a religion which required great belief and little knowledge' (Lecky, *History of European Morals*, ii, 14). That religion developed from a merging of the spiritual beliefs of Rabbi Jesus and the militarist attitude of Judas Khrestus.

CHAPTER 22

The twin powers of the church

After the reign of Constantine, a series of weak successors allowed the gradual dissolution of the Roman Empire and the reins fell from their hands. During this time the church expanded in two distinct directions, with a pious element developing an austere monastic life in dedication to the created Jesus Christ, and the militant faction increasing its power by wars and persecutions. The differences stress independence rather than different origin, for the pious followed the spiritual teachings of Rabbi Jesus, and the popes, like Khrestus and his followers, 'took up swords' (Matt. 10:34) and instructed their followers to 'arm themselves with weapons' (Luke 22:36). For centuries the church maintained a mighty military force and, in later times, the soldiers 'who wore the crest' (*Diderot's Encyclopedia*, 1759) were retrospectively called the Knights of St Thomas (Judas Thomas/Khrestus, the twin).

In discussing matters associated with the development of Christianity, the church said: 'One might indeed be curious about the interval between the time of Constantine and the beginning of the ninth Century AD' (*Catholic Encyclopedia*, Vol. Eleven, Pgs. 652-668, June 1^{ST,} 1911). In that 500-year period, there is very little documentation available to determine the course of the church, but what is accessible reveals extreme militarism, extensive fraud, and very little piety.

The records are sparse and in most cases nothing at all is documented. For example, in 881, Pope John VIII (d. 882) founded a papal navy (*Encyclopedia Britannica*, Vol. 6, 1973, pg. 572), but details of its size or missions do not publicly exist. However, from a solitary reference to 'the Pope's fighting fleet' existing in 1043 (*Diderot's Encyclopedia,* 1759), it is clear that it was still operational at that time. This record was drawn from documentation once belonging to the powerful Crescentis, a Roman family who played an important part in the papacy from the middle of the 10th Century to the beginning of the 11th Century. Then, in the 16th Century, some 700 years after its inception, Pope Gregory XIII (1502-1585) commissioned Giorgio Vasari (1511-74) to record the extent of the Vatican fleet while it was moored at Messina in Sicily.

© Film Library of Renaissance Art, Italy

Giorgio Vasari, Italian artist and historian, travelled to Messina and painted this picture on site. It reveals approximately 200 moored Christian ships that had returned to port shortly after Pope Pius V (d. 1572; succeeded by Pope Gregory XIII) organised the last Crusade against the Turks in 1571. Vasari studied under Michelangelo, and wrote a history of many of the famous Renaissance painters.

As a framework of policy, the church modeled itself after the old Roman state. The cast-off purple togas and shoes of Roman emperors became the clothing of the bishop of Rome, the presbyters wore the 'toga picta' bearing a red stripe and their followers opted for either black or brown togas. Until the transfer of the seat of empire by Constantine to Byzantium, the emperor reigned in Rome; from that time forward, there reigned also the popes.

The emperors were elective; so were the popes. When elected, the emperor was the fountain of all religious and military authority; so were the popes. In all the countries which lay under the shadow of his scepter, the emperor had his subordinates, and these again had theirs, down to the lowest office of the state; so did the popes ... cardinals, archbishops, bishops, priests, deacons, canons, monks, friars, are but the higher and lower constabulary of the pope, through which he sought to collect into his own hands the reins of universal government, and to hold in allegiance the nations to his church, as the Caesars held them in Rome.

During the Fourth and Fifth Centuries the church sought to incorporate with itself the strong elements of other religious systems, and by twining and twisting them together, produced a dogma that had both its strong and weak points. This compound of various elements, cemented together by the priesthood and the cunning of the ages, is called 'the body of the church' which military priests would palm onto the world as the church of God.

Papal forgery

Most Catholics go through life and never hear in school or church a word of reproach for any pope or member of the clergy. Yet the recorded lives of these men bear no resemblance to the modern-day portrayal of them and the many centuries of decadence and immorality that existed among them. For some 1600 years the church maintained a comprehensive written account of the depraved conduct of its clergy, and official records provide scandalous and disgraceful confessions of wickedness insidious in the church. The pretended holiness and piety of the priesthood is not represented in their own official records, which provide proof of the dishonesty of its own portrayal.

The foundation of Christianity was built on 'the dissemination of falsehood, error, scandal, unrighteousness and iniquity' (*The Church of Rome,* Rev. Charles Elliott, D.D., 1844, Pg. 462) and the church's own records reveal the curious character of the men involved. The modern-day presentation of the nature of the overall body of churchmen is entirely undermined when any one page of a Christian Catechism is read. The glowing light in which the church presents itself is not reflected in its own records and, in creating the desired image, its representatives overlook an exceedingly deceptive, corrupt and debauched history.

Starting with the Symmachian Forgeries (501), the Deception of Sylvester (508), the False Isidorian Decretals (Ninth Century), the remarkable and immense Pseudo-Areopagitell Forgeries (*Catholic Encyclopedia*, xii, 768), and with disinformation founded on false documents, the church perpetuated itself and consolidated its Khrestus-concepted powers. Over the centuries it amassed amazing wealth with a series of secular frauds unprecedented in human history, with probably the greatest being introduced around 850. A false document appeared that is now called the Donation of Constantine, supposedly written by Emperor Constantine, by which privileges and rich possessions were conferred on the pope and the Roman church. This comment from the *Catholic Encyclopedia*:

> It is addressed by Constantine to Pope Sylvester I (314-35), and consists of two parts. Constantine is made to confer on Sylvester and his successors the following privileges and possessions: the pope, as successor of St. Peter, has the primacy over the four Patriarchs of Antioch, Alexandria, Constantinople, and Jerusalem, also over all the bishops in the world. The document goes on to say that for himself the Emperor has established in the East a new capital, which bears his name, and thither he removes his capital, since it is inconvenient that a secular emperor have power where God has established the residence of the head of the Christian religion. The document concludes with maledictions against all who violate these donations and with the assurance that the emperor has signed them with his own hand and placed them on the tomb of St. Peter. (*Catholic Encyclopedia*, v, 118, 119, 120; *Catholic Encyclopedia*, xiv, 257)

Yet this was not all. The church went on to record the following information about the Donation of Constantine:

> This document is without doubt a forgery, fabricated somewhere between the years 750 and 850. As early as the 15th century its falsity was known and demonstrated. Its genuinity was yet occasionally defended, and the document still further used as authentic, until Baronius in his *Annals Ecclesiastici* admitted that the 'Donation' was a forgery, where-after it was soon universally admitted to be such. It is so clearly a fabrication that there is no reason to wonder that, with the revival of historical criticism in the 15th century, the true character of the document was at once recognized. The document obtained wider circulation by its incorporation with the 'False Decretals' (840-850).

At about the same time that the Donation of Constantine appeared, the first

European monastery called Eulogomenopolis was built in Italy (c. 866). As the papal armies fought their wars, pious monks developed their own little communities and lived under particular religious vows emanating from the preaching of Rabbi Jesus. Abbeys and monasteries grew from the earlier streets of hermits' huts or *lauras,* and later, walls were built around a group of buildings for defense. Small accommodation cells were then constructed against the walls, leaving a central space for chapels, fountains and a communal dining hall, or refectory. Since the territorial organization of the early church followed that of the Roman Empire, the 12th and 13th Centuries saw the development of communities living in seclusion established across Italy, France, Spain, Germany, Austria, England, and Scotland. In France, the monastic movement flourished to a greater extent than in any other country, and the monasteries became hiding places for many popes being pursued by their enemies (*Diderot's Encyclopedia,* 1759).

The papacy sold

On one hand, pious practices and Gospel belief slowly developed, and, on the other, nothing was taken on faith. In 1032, Grottaferrata Theofilatto (Theophylact, in some records) was in the murderous scramble for the wealth of the papacy and became Pope Benedict IX (d. 1065). He immediately excommunicated leaders who were hostile to him and quickly established a reign of terror. His violent and licentious conduct provoked the Romans, and in January 1045, they elected John of Sabine to succeed him as Pope Sylvester III. But Sylvester was quickly driven out by Benedict's brothers and returned to the Sabine hills. Benedict then sold the papacy to his godfather, Giovanni Graziano who assumed the papal chair, but Benedict bought it back again in 1047 (1047-1048).

The twin reality

In 1096 the legacy of Judas Khrestus' militancy created the first of eight Crusades, and they continued unabated for nearly 200 years (1096-1270). A Crusade was a war instigated by the church for alleged religious ends, and was authorized by a papal Bull. The Crusades resulted in the deaths of hundreds of thousands of people and the church today incorrectly says that they were necessary to recover Jerusalem and the Holy Lands from the Muslims. During that time, Pope Gregory VII (1020-1085) declared; 'The killing of heretics is not murder', and decreed it legal for the church and its militants to kill non-believers in papal dogma. The third canon of the Fourth Lateran Council (1215) was specifically developed to restrain opponents, with the Pope exclaiming; 'This tremendous canon will root out with fire and the sword whatever the church of Rome pronounces to be heresy'. By the judgment of the Council of Constance, it became church law for adversaries to be 'consigned to lawful flames in settling controversies' (*Decree of the Fourth Lateran Council, 1215*) and the hierarchy of the church of England sought urgent clarification that 'the term heretics' did not apply to them (Protestantism had not then a name).

We find it hard today to realize the commotion raised by Christianity, and the ardor of the Popes' campaigns. In 1182, for example, Pope Licius III (d. 1185) gained control of the official apparatus of the church and immediately instigated a forty-year attack against the Cathars (the Pure Ones), a religious sect often called the Albigensians that flourished in Western and Southern Europe in the 12th and 13th Centuries. They were a pious group who denied the divinity of Christ and opposed church preaching. They argued that Jesus Christ did not die or rise again, there was no hell or purgatory, and condemned Christian/Khrestian practices involving the use of material things, claiming they were vain and sacrilegious. For their criticism of the worldliness and corruption of the Catholic priesthood, the military sword of the church was soon to fall upon them.

Their extreme asceticism made them a church of the elect, and in France and Northern Italy, it became a popular and expanding religion of piety. 'Their leaders save souls, they do not eat meat, they do not touch women', said Alazais, an informer to Pope Innocent 111 (d. 1216), who continued the slaughter. The Cathars held that good and evil had separate creators (Rabbi Jesus verses Judas Khrestus), and the premise in this book is that Mary's twin boys were the initiators of the twofold nature of Christianity. The Cathars professed that there are two principles, one good and the other evil; that the material world of the church was evil, but the spiritual teachings in their intriguing version of the Gospel of John, was good. The medieval religious sects of the Paulicians and Bogomils held similar views in the Balkans and the Middle East, and the Cathars were closely connected to these sects.

St. Dominic depicted destroying the religious books of the Albigensians, by Pedro Berruguete (c. 1450-1504).

The militia of Jesus Christ

In the 13th Century, Pope Innocent III ordered Dominic de Guzman (1170-1221) to develop a troop of merciless followers called 'the Catholic army' (*Catholic Encyclopedia,* Vol.V, 1911, Pg. 107) who were specifically established to cut the throats of disbelievers when the priesthood was preaching the 'Lord's Gospel' (*The Lives of Saints,* Rev. Alban Butler, London, 1926). It consisted of 30,000 troops, and the general populace labeled them the 'Throat-cutters'. However, Dominic deemed them the 'Militia of Jesus Christ' (Ibid), and the 'Crested Servants of the Lord'. It is possible that those words originally read the 'Militia of Judas Khrestus, he who wears the crest', and were changed in later times when the church rewrote its records (*Diderot's Encyclopedia*, 1759). Earlier in this book, Emperor Julian (d. 363), recorded that the Khrestian/Christian movement in his time 'slit throats with a whisper', and from the available records, it is apparent that the church was still enforcing its dogma in the same gruesome manner some 800 years later.

Dominic was a ruthless killer and his activities in southern France and northern Italy continued with the persecution of the Cathars contributing eventually to their total extermination. To Dominic was ascribed the foundation of the Inquisition, with its terrifying armory of tribunals, secret police, informers, tortures, and fiery executions. The title of the first 'Inquisitor-General' was later applied to him and the introduction of the Inquisition was the only time in Christian history when the church was united in purpose and spoke with one voice. The Inquisition was concerned with the detection and destruction of people not in agreement with Khrestian/Christian doctrine and guidelines were formulated over the ensuring centuries and became fully established. Its structure developed into official church law that lasted for 599 years (1221-1820) and was vigorously upheld to specifically suppress opinions contrary to church dogma. For his successful efforts, Pope Gregory IX (1227-41) was later to canonize Dominic, and the church today falsely portrays him as a devout and holy man.

Terrorist popes

Towards the end of the Twelfth Century, the Forged Decretals of Gratian (d. c. 1159) were released (*Catholic Encyclopedia*, iv, 671) and they provided for an expansion of the church's military arm, while its spiritual arm fell further behind. This decline was due to the clergy itself, confirmed by Pope Innocent III (1161-1216): at the Fourth Lateran Council in 1215, he said:

> The corruption of the people has its chief source in the clergy. From this arises the evils of Christendom; faith perishes, religion is defaced, justice is trodden under foot, heretics multiply, schismatics are emboldened, and the faithless grow strong. (*Inquisitions in Middle Ages*, Lea, I. 129)

It is a simple matter to gather, from twenty centuries or so of Christian history, some fascinating examples of church pronouncements. This is another informational example ... Bishop Grosseteste (d. 1227), one of the most judicious prelates of the age, expressed concern when he said to Pope Innocent that 'the Catholic population, as a body, was always incorporate with the Devil' (*From St. Francis to Dante*, G.G. Coulton, pg. 56, 1908).

For the ensuring centuries, and across the territories of the theocratic (religious) 'State', terrorist popes authorized the murder and burning of their opponents. When in 1224 Frederick II ordered that heretics in Lombard should be burnt at the stake, Gregory IX, then Papal Legate, approved and published the imperial law. In 1231 the Pope enacted another law for Rome that 'heretics condemned by an ecclesiastical court should be delivered to the secular power to receive their 'due punishment' ... death by fire for the obstinate and imprisonment for life for the penitent' (*Catholic Encyclopedia*, vi, 797). He advised his clergy not to discuss the Christian religion with Jews and said that, 'the layman, when he hears any speak ill of the Christian faith, should defend it not with words but with the sword, which he should thrust into the other's belly as far as it will go' (*Chronicles of the Crusade*, pg. 148, Villehardouin, G. de). Pope Gregory was extremely severe on heretics, who he called 'traitors', and reveled in attending as many burnings as possible (*Lives of the Popes*, Mann, c. 1905).

Double-trouble

In February 1296, Pope Boniface VIII (1234-1303) issued the first of two of the most famous bulls in Christian history. Its opening words, *Clericis laicos*, gave it a name, its first sentence made an unwise admission, and its tone recalled the papal bolts of Pope Gregory VII (1020-1085):

> Antiquity reports that laymen are exceedingly hostile to the clergy, and our experience certainly shows that this to be true at present.

Distaste for the clergy probably reflected a secret doubt as to its claim of a divine origin to their religion, and the true horror of their Campaigns. With the stolen 'Patrimony of Peter' the church under Boniface was now a worldly ruler over vast territories it called States of the Church and 'Catholic, and citizens of the State', became identical terms.

On November 18, 1302, Boniface issued his iniquitous Bull of 'Two Swords' and it formalized the internal framework of Christianity's core structure for centuries to come. The Pope's bulletin declared that the church controlled 'two swords', that is, two powers; 'Both swords are in the power of the church, the spiritual and the temporal; the spiritual is wielded in the church by the hand of the clergy; the secular is exerted for the church by the hand of the military ... and the spiritual power has the right to establish and guide the secular power, and also to judge it when it does not act rightly ... Consequently, whoever opposes the powers of the church ordained of God, opposes the law of God' (*Bull Unam Sanctam,* Boniface VIII, Nov. 18, 1302; overview in *Catholic Encyclopedia,* xv, 126). The activist power originated from Judas Khrestus, and the spiritual power from Rabbi Jesus.

© Artworks da Firenze, Roma

The two principles of Christianity.
Christian artist Andrea da Firenze (Andrea of Florence, today) created this fresco at the height of the church's warring campaigns in 1385. It is called 'The Church Militant and Triumphant' and is today in the Spanish Chapel of the church of Santa Maria Novella, Florence. It depicts the pope enthroned as supreme authority in the centre of the portrayal with his elegant clergy grouped to his right. To his left, the laity is directed to pay homage to the priesthood under the threat of sword-bearing soldiers wearing clerical attire. 'The white and black hounds are visual puns on the Dominicans

… *'domin canes,' meaning 'hounds of the Lord' (Encyclopedia Britannica, 1973, pg. 882).*

With the late 20th Century model of the papacy in one's mind, it is difficult to imagine what it would have been like in the 14th or 16th Centuries, let alone the ninth or the seventh. The now-called expounders of 'Christian virtue' were brutal killers and 'crimes against faith were high treason, and as such were punishable with death' *(Catholic Encyclopedia*, xiv, p. 768). The church ordered the 'secular arm' of the State to force its religion upon humanity by mass murder, and 'the clergy, discharging in each district the functions of local state officials, seem never to have quite regained the religious spirit' (*Catholic Encyclopedia*, i, 507). The church painfully confessed its gruesome record, saying: 'The role of heresy in history is that of evil generally. Its roots are in corrupted human nature … it has rent asunder the bonds of charity in families, provinces, states, and nations; the sword has been drawn and pyres erected both for its defense and its repression' (*Catholic Encyclopedia*, vii, 261).

The attempt to kill Protestants

The massacre by St Bartholomew (d. c. 1560) was followed by fearful civil wars in which one million men were killed. The Edict of Nantes (Brittany) published by Henry IV in 1598 brought these wars to a close in the short term. Then there was the Irish St Bartholomew of 1641, who in his attempts to kill all Protestants massacred 200,000 men women and children. Later, there were the persecutions of Italy, Spain, Poland, Austria, Bavaria, and in the early 19th Century, Zillerthal, Madeira, Florence, Naples, France and Ireland.

Christian historian and author, Dr Will Durant (c. 1950), made the following summary comment about the action of the popes:

> It was inconvenient that for centuries the heads of the church should have to lie, break faith, steal and kill; but by the common consent of kings these procedures were indispensable to the preservation of a state.

After the fall of Napoleon in 1814, Pope Pius VII returned to Rome, revoked Napoleon's decision to write a new Gospel and create a new messiah, and set about reinstating Christianity by a series of Concordats with other countries. An official policy to aggressively re-impose church dogma in Europe was now pursued ... and existing media records reveal the horrific methods priests developed in upholding their oath of persecution. Instances of probably the most glaring examples of extremism in enforcing Khrestian/Christian concepts are found in newspapers of the day:

> Witness the horrible crucifixion of females so minutely detailed by Baron De Grimm, who was an eyewitness of them during his residence at Paris, and which were suppressed not by the interference of the clergy, but by order of the Lieutenant of Police. Let anyone consult the *Edinburgh Review* of September 1814, p. 302, *et seq.*, and he will find detailed instances of the most horrible fanaticism, which occurred in the streets of Paris. (*Delineation of Roman Catholicism*, Rev. Charles Elliott, D.D., London, 1844, Pg. 27)

Additional instances of church persecutions are found in 19th Century newspapers held in the British Library Newspaper Division at Colinsdale in London, and were rampant in countries where the Bible stood foremost in the list of heretical books and the authority of the Roman church was predominant.

SS. MARTHA ET MARIA VIRGINES. *In Februario.*

S. VVILGEFORTIS VIRGO. 20. *Iulij.*

© Mrs. Lucy Ogilvie's Collection

These are two of eight engravings produced by Hieronymus Wierix (1553-1619) showing the crucifixion of young women. Along with eight similar depictions of children being crucified, they appeared as part of the frontispiece of a Bible published in 1608.

Rabbi Jesus triumphs

The historical evidence of centuries of brutal church-instigated events provides a different representation of the principles of Christianity than that offered by its modern-day advocates. The church's attitude towards persons opposing its doctrines was fully and accurately ascertained by its wars of extermination waged against differing religions, and opposing views. This murderous aspect of Christianity, it is concluded, originated as the legacy of Judas Khrestus, and as the church developed, his militarist lifestyle was upheld and became the essence of Catholicism well into the 20th Century.

It was with modern times and Pope John XXIII (1881-1963) that the militaristic side of the church finally waned. He travelled around Rome freely, breaking with the tradition that the pope, now derived of his former revolutionary power, was a 'prisoner of the Vatican'. In an attempt to depoliticize the church, he played down his position as ruler of Catholicism and emphasized his role as 'servant of the servants of God', a title that slowly bought the spiritual aspect of the church to the front.

BOOK TWO

THE RENAISSANCE PERIOD

CHAPTER 23

Twins on horseback

Late in the period of the Catholic Crusades (1096-1270), the Knights Templar, a religious military Order, came into being, and subsequently attained extensive power and wealth. An ancient book called *Resuscitatio* records that the true history of early Christianity was known to initiated members of the Knights Templar movement, having originally been …

> … imparted to Hugh de Payens (Grand Master, d. 1136) by the Grand-Pontiff of the Order of the Temple (of the Nazarene sect), one named Theocletes, after which it was learned by other Knights Templar in Palestine. (*Resuscitatio* or, 'Bringing into Publick Light, Several Pieces hitherto Sleeping', Dr. William Rawley, 1657)

It is possible that the Knights Templar was inspired into existence to maintain the secret of Mary's twin boys and developed their official symbol around the hidden knowledge. The Templar' seal shows twin knights riding a single horse, a symbolism that depicts the essence of their initiated knowledge. They built a circular fortress in Spain with twin towers and called it Tomas, a translation meaning 'twin'.

The seal of the Knights Templar.

The church eventually declared the Knights Templar heretics and successfully annihilated most of the Order in another attempted mass slaughter concluding in 1314. However, many escaped, moving to safe areas such as Britain, and then regrouping. Around that time, they established and funded an art school called Scopetine, and developed a system of initiation for members so inclined (*Diderot's Encyclopedia,* 1759). Subsequently, enlightened members passed on the secret knowledge, and depictions of Mary with twin sons then subtly started to appear in works of art. Probably the first was by Italian artist Pacino da Bonaguide around 1320 and other early and rather obvious symbolisms are the frescos of the church of St George in Switzerland that have been recently dated to around 1370-90. From these early examples, it is obvious that the artists purposely intended to depict Mary with twin boys and thus the special knowledge of the Knights Templar was preserved.

Ghirlandaio (1449-1494), in his relatively short life, was obviously aware of the Templar secret, and painted a number of large frescos in various Florentine churches as well as one in the Sistine Chapel of the Vatican. One work was called the 'Two Innocents' and clearly defines Mary with twin boys. Various other artists cleverly portrayed the twins as a disguise behind which they could subtly present the knowledge without fear of repressive action from the church and its dreaded Inquisition. This suppressive power was gaining momentum, and then three consecutive popes of particular interest to our dissertation, uncompromisingly acknowledged the speciousness of Christianity.

CHAPTER 24

Christianity's disbelieving popes

The idea of twin boys survived in a small number of artistic depictions well into the 15th Century and then, suddenly, as though from nowhere, there was an unexpected and explosive rebirth of interest in Jesus' twin brother. All the evidence for this crucial resurgence of twin imagery, and its emergence from hidden sources into more direct representation, points to the life of three particular popes ... Alexander VI (1431-1503), Julius II (1443-1513), and Leo X (1475-1521). What they, and their professional clergy said is almost unbelievable, and from the existence of a series of unusual discourses, it is clear that they knew about Jesus' twin.

Papal confessions

It was these three popes who commissioned the creation of a considerable number of artworks and sculptures by Italian artists Leonardo da Vinci (1452-1519), Michelangelo Buonarroti (1474-1564), and Raphael Sanzio (1483-1529). Catholic theologian and renowned papist, Johann Eck (1466-1529), argued against persistent rumours amongst the intelligentsia of Rome that alleged a papal secret had been confided to Leonardo, Michelangelo, and Raphael, by firstly the Borgia pope, Alexander VI, then Pope Julius II, and later confirmed by Pope Leo X.

At some period in their lives, all three artists lived in luxurious quarters at the Palazzo del Belvedere (British Museum, 279, v), a villa on the Vatican Hill, and worked on private commissions for various popes. They dined regularly with the popes and had the help of theological experts to assist them with their creative designs. But it was a series of documented papal confessions that strengthened the suspicion that Leonardo, Michelangelo and Raphael were confidentially told about Jesus' twin brother, and they surreptitiously secreted that information into their sculptures and paintings.

© Florence Film Archives, 1961

The village of Vinci at which Leonardo was born.

What Pope Alexander VI said

Rodrigo Borgia was elected Pope Alexander VI in 1492, and the Romans said of him that had his mother foreseen his nature, she would have strangled him at birth. He was a member of the infamous Borgia family, who derived their prominence and power in Italian politics. It is from the diaries of German chaplain, Johann Burchard, Pope Alexander's Master of Ceremonies, that we learn the most about the character of the Borgia pope. Burchard personally eyewitnessed Alexander's debauchery and wrote the famous comment saying that 'the Pope's Christianity is a pretense'.

Alexander VI was so notoriously infamous and his history so large and well known that he has proved a great embarrassment for the modern church vainly trying to portray a pious past. With his twelve bastard children (*Collins*

Dictionary), including Don Cesare and Donna Lucrezia, and his numerous mistresses, the 'Vatican was again a brothel' (*The Records of Rome*, 1868, British Library) and his debauched Papal Court was compared to the ancient 'fleshpots' of Caesarea in which St. Augustine reveled.

Pope Alexander VI.

Pope Alexander VI was a sexual pervert and lurid stories were bandied about by the intellectual underworld of Rome. It was claimed that he had sex with Lucrezia who was his daughter by Vanozza Catanei. One wit of Rome called Lucrezia 'the Pope's daughter, wife, and daughter-in-law', and he fathered a daughter with her. Alexander consorted in the Vatican with mistresses and prostitutes and this one example recorded by Burchard depicts the nature of the Christian leader:

> On Sunday evening, October 30, Don Cesare Borgia gave a supper in the apostolic Palace, with fifty decent prostitutes or courtesans in attendance, who after the meal danced with the servants and others there, first fully dressed and then naked. Following the supper, lampshades holding lighted candles were placed on the floor and chestnuts strewn about, which the prostitutes, naked and on their hands and knees, had to pick up with their mouths as they crawled in and out among the lampshades. The Pope watched and admired their noble parts. Don Cesare and Donna Lucrezia were also present and later all three took a prostitute of their liking for further dalliances.

Against this backdrop, and because of his debauched lifestyle, he could not escape the satirists, pamphleteers, and other wits who sold or distributed their deadly epigrams to his opponents. This was one of them, and, after its release, the city of Rome shook with cynical laughter:

This broadsheet was distributed in the streets of Rome in 1501 and presents Pope Alexander as the Devil and the Antichrist.

This pamphlet speaks of Alexander dabbling in black magic and other Pagan rituals. He had a Venus inlaid in his emerald Christian cross and an 'offensive' painting of Isis naked in his papal bedroom *(Lives of the Most Eminent Painters, Sculptors, and Architects*, Giorgio Vasari, 1907 Ed.). At that time, witchcraft was an ecclesiastical, rather than a civil concern, and the documented evidence reveals that the Pope's personal beliefs were not that of Christian orthodoxy. This remark, buried away in a collection of once-suppressed papal pronouncements called *Anecdota Ecclsiaia Histories,* or *Secret Church History* (Vienta, Paris, 1822), and confirmed in *Diderot's Encyclopedia,* revealed what Pope Alexander VI really thought of Christianity:

> Almighty God! How long will this superstitious sect of Christians, and this upstart invention endure?

When one of his bastard sons 'was fished out of the Tiber with his throat cut ... that it was a warning from Heaven to repent, no one felt more keenly than the Pope himself. He spoke of resigning; and proclaimed his determination to set about that reform of the church 'in Head and members' for which the world had so long been clamoring' (*Catholic Encyclopedia*, xiv, 32, 33). But his grief was assuaged by the attentions of his lady loves, notably pretty Guilia Farnese, niece of a cardinal, and whose picture as Virgin Mary now adorns one of the great frescos of the Vatican.

In 1501 Pope Alexander VI re-established censorship of publications by an edict ordering that no book discussing the Christian religion be printed without the written approval of the local archbishop or 'bearing the personal permission and privilege of the Pope'. This was the beginning of what was to be called the *Index of Prohibited Books*, and in 1559 the suppression of books became official Christian policy.

Soon after Alexander died his body became black and fetid, lending colour to rumours that he was poisoned. Historically, the church of Rome bears the heavy burden of the murder of up to forty popes, many of them by poison. Undertakers and porters, 'joking and blaspheming' says Burchard, had trouble forcing the swollen corpse into the coffin built for it. Gossip added that a little devil had been seen at the moment of death, carrying Alexander's soul to hell.

Struggling with secrets

It was at this juncture that Pope Julius II entered the picture. He was not deeply disturbed by a delegation of monks who approached him expressing criticism of the clergy and the morals of cardinals. He had heard the like before; people for centuries past had complained that popes, cardinals, and priests lived immoral lives, and that the popes loved sex, power and wealth more than being the Vicars of Christ.

The reign of Julius was controversial. After he said that 'Christians are the unstable, unlettered, superstitious masses' (*Diderot's Encyclopedia,* 1759), he was generally regarded as an embarrassment by the church and modern Christian historians. The Florentine historian, Guicciardini, remarked at the time that Julius II had nothing of the priest but the dress and the name. He was a willful, coarse, and bad-tempered man. He advised his secretary to take three mistresses at one time 'in memory of the Holy Trinity', and frankly admitted that he could not contain any secret confided in him, saying, 'It will kill me if I don't let it out'.

© Picture courtesy of the House of Castiglione, Italy

For his tyranny, Matthew, Mark, Luke and John are allegorically depicted stoning Pope Julius II to death. This painting once belonged to King Henry VIII.

He had tired of seeing Giulia Farnese playing Virgin Mary; he wished to move into the four chambers once used by Pope Nicholas V; and he wanted these rooms decorated with paintings congenial to his self-perceived heroic stature and aims. In the summer of 1508, he summoned Raphael to Rome, and around the same time, commissioned Michelangelo to create an array of works.

Michelangelo subsequently carved a statue of him, and Julius II examined it with a puzzled expression, asking, 'What is that under my arm?' 'A book, your Holiness', replied Michelangelo. 'What do I know of books?' roared the Pope. 'Give me a sword instead'. His Holiness' preference of a sword to a Bible had its effect in Rome. He became known as the 'dreadful' or 'terrifying' pope and earnt the name of 'the Warrior of Rome'. He led his army into battle in full armour and at one stage he was almost captured, and nearly taken prisoner.

Michelangelo despised Julius for canceling a major commission to build a marble family tomb and subsequently reflected his feelings in this rare sketch created shortly after the Pope's death in February 1513. It shows the pope dead and naked on the toilet wearing his mitre, and being removed by a servant.

The 'fable' of Pope Leo X

Perversions, forgery, pornography and prostitution, continued in papal circles. On 11 March 1513, Giovanni de Medici was elected pope and took the name of Leo X. He was not yet a priest, but this defect was remedied on 15 March at a Vatican celebration for the anniversary of the death of *Divine Julius*. Guicciardini, the historian of Florence, recorded that the new pope accepted the Pagan enjoyment of life and was 'exceedingly devoted to the flesh, especially those pleasures which cannot, with decency, be mentioned' (*Diderot's Encyclopedia*, 1759). This statement implies that the pope was homosexual or an adventurous bi-sexual.

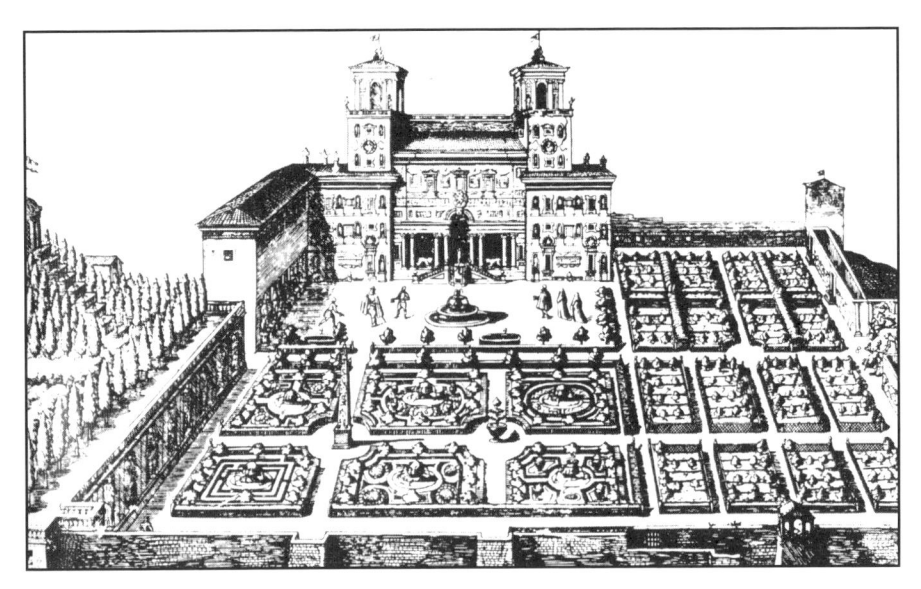

The Villa Medici, Rome, where Pope Leo X grew up.
Engraving by Gottefred de' Scaichi, 16th Century.

Modern churchmen praise him as 'a person of moral life and sincerely religious' (*The Oxford Dictionary of the Christian Church*; Cross, 1963, Pg. 799; *The New International Dictionary of the Christian Church,* 1974, Pg. 591), and add that his pious qualities were responsible for his unanimous election by the cardinals. However, historical records reveal a different story. In Volume IX of the 1797 Edinburgh edition of the *Encyclopedia Britannica* (Pg. 788) the following passage is recorded:

> When Pope Julius died, Leo was very ill of venereal disease at Florence and was carried to Rome in a litter. Later, an ulcer broke, and the matter, which ran from it, exhaled such a stench, that all the cells in the enclave, which were separated only by thin partitions, were poisoned by it. Upon this, the cardinals consulted with physicians of the enclave, to know what the matter was. They,

being bribed earlier (by de Medici himself), said the cardinal de Medici could not live a month; which sentence occasioned his being chosen pope. Thus Giovanni de Medici, then 38 years of age, was elected pope on false information and as joy is the most sovereign of all remedies, he soon recovered his health, so that the old cardinals had reason to repent.

A hale and hearty Pope Leo X now filled the Pontifical chair and his first declaration was, 'God has given me the papacy, now let me enjoy it' (*Encyclopedia Britannica*, 13th Ed. xix, pg. 926-7). That was an indication of what was to come from the man who fully developed 'the sale of indulgences' into Christianity. The church said this about him:

> As an Ecclesiastic, his deficiency in professional knowledge, his utter indifference to the restraint of his character, the reputed laxity of his principles, his proneness to dissimulation, his deeply rooted voluptuousness, and his fondness for the society of musicians, jesters, and buffoons, rendered him contemptible, or something worse. By a course of lavish expenditure in the indulgence of his own taste for luxury and magnificence, by the part, which he took in the troublous politics of the day ... Leo completely drained the papal treasury. (*Annales Ecclesiastici*, Folio iii, Antwerp, 1597, Cardinal Caesar Baronius)

The church had scarcely a pope more dedicated to expensive pleasures, or to whom money was so anxiously sought than Leo X. Pope Julius 11 had earlier bestowed indulgences on all who contributed toward building the church of St. Peter at Rome, and Leo X expanded upon the doctrine. To replenish the coffers and to maintain his 'luxuriant abundance' he speedily adapted the sale of indulgences as a major source of church revenue. In forming his plans, he was assisted mainly by his relative Laurentius Pucci, whom he made Cardinal of Santaquatro, and John Tetzel, a former officer of the Teutonic Knights in Prussia and avid seller of indulgences.

© From 'The Collection of the Masters', Milan

Pope Leo X. This is a portrait by Raphael. The figure on the left is his cousin Giulio de Medici who would go on to become Pope Clement VII. The other person is Luigi Rossi, another cousin. It is interesting to note a series of Tarot Card depictions on the face of the book in front of the pope. The church said of Leo: 'He was not a handsome man. His fat, shiny, effeminate countenance with weak eyes protrudes in this picture' (Catholic Encyclopedia, Vol. ix, 1910, pg. 163).

Pope Leo's brothels

To finance his lifestyle Leo borrowed prodigious amounts of money from bankers at 40 per cent interest. The booming brothels simply did not bring in enough tax money, even though there were 6800 registered prostitutes servicing a citizenry of 50,000. His gifts to relatives, friends, artists, writers, and musicians, his lavish maintenance of an unprecedented court, the demands of the new St Peter's, the expense of the Urbino war, and the preparation for a crusade, were all leading him to bankruptcy. In Rome the bankers despoiled themselves. The Bini firm had lent Leo 200,000 ducats, the Gaddi 32,000, the Ricasoli 10,000; moreover, Cardinal Pucci had lent him 150,000 and

Cardinal Salviati 80,000, the cardinals would have first claim on anything salvaged; and Leo died worse than bankrupt. As security for some of his loans he pledged the freehold of some churches, the Vatican's silverware, tapestries, valuable manuscript collections, and jewelry.

To replenish his treasury Leo created 1353 new and saleable offices, for which appointees paid a total of 889,000 ducats (US$11,112,500 in 1955). He nominated 60 additional chamberlains and 141 squires to the 2000 persons who made up his ménage at the Vatican, and received from them a total of 202,000 ducats. In July 1517, he named 31 new cardinals, chosen 'not of such as had the most merit, but of those that offered the most money for the honour and power'. Cardinal Porizetti ... physician, scholar, author ... paid 30,000 ducats and altogether Leo's appointees on this occasion brought in another half a million ducats for the treasury.

Even blasé Italy was shocked, and in Germany the story of the Pope's financial transactions shared in the anger of Luther's revolt (October 1517). Some cardinals received an income from the church of 30,000 ducats a year and lived in stately palaces manned by as many as 300 servants, adorned with every art and luxury known to the time.

The Gospel according to Marks and Silver

All in all, Leo spent 4,500,000 ducats during his pontificate (US$56,250,000 in 1955) and died owing 400,000 more. A favourite satire that developed around him was called the *Gospel According to Marks and Silver*, which began:

> In those days Pope Leo said to the Romans: 'When Jesus, the Son of Man, shall come to the seat of our majesty, say first of all, 'Friend, wherefore art Thou come hither?' And if He gives you naught in silver or gold, cast Him forth into outer darkness.

It was Pope Leo X who made the celebrated quote about Christianity that revealed his knowledge about the church's false presentation of Jesus Christ, and his comments revealed that he was fully aware of Jesus' twin brother.

The Easter Friday banquet

At a lavish Easter Friday banquet in the Vatican in 1514, and in the company of 'seven intimates' (*Annales Ecclesiastici*, Cardinal Caesar Baronius), Leo made a declaration that the church has since tried hard to invalidate. Raising a chalice of wine into the air, Pope Leo toasted:

> How well we know what a profitable superstition this fable of Christ has been for us, and our predecessors.

The pronouncement was recorded in the diaries and records of both Cardinal Pietro Bembo (*His Letters and Comments on Pope Leo X*, Reprint 1842) and Cardinal Jovius, (*De Vita Leonis X*, originally published in 1551) two associates that were witnesses to Pope Leo's celebratory confession.

Portrait of Cardinal Pietro Bembo by Titian, circa 1540. He was the Pope's secretary and witness to Leo's confession.

Cardinal Caesar Baronius was Vatican librarian for seven years and wrote a twelve-volume history of the church called *Annales Ecclesiastici*. He was the church's most outstanding historian (*Catholic Encyclopedia,* Vol. 11, 1967, Pg. 105) and his records provide vital inside information for anybody studying the rich depth of falsification in Christianity. Baronius, who turned down two offers to become pope in 1605, added the following comments about Pope Leo's declaration:

> This pontiff has been accused of atheism, for he denied God, and called Christ, in front of Cardinals Pietro Bembo, Jovius and Iacopo Sadoleto, and other intimates, 'a fable' ... it must be corrected. (*Annales Ecclesiastici*, Folio viii and xi, Antwerp, 1597, Cardinal Caesar Baronius, 1538-1607)

The church devoted two and half pages in its first edition of the *Catholic Encyclopedia* to nullify the most damaging statement ever made by the head of Christianity, basing the essence of its argument on the assumption that what the pope meant by 'profitable' was 'gainful', and 'fable' was intended to be 'tradition'. Hence Catholic theologians reasoned that what the Pope really meant was, 'How well Christians have gained from this wonderful tradition of Christ'. But that wasn't what he said.

It was from Christianity's own records that Pope Leo's statement became known to the world. The diaries of Cardinal Pietro Bembo, the Pope's secretary for seven years, added that Leo 'was known to disbelieve Christianity itself. He advanced contrary to the faith and that in condemning the Gospel, therefore he must be a heretic; he was guilty of sodomy with his Chamberlains; was addicted to pleasure, luxury, idleness, ambition, un-chastity and sensuality; and spent his whole days in the company of musicians and buffoons. His Infallibility's drunkenness was proverbial, he practiced incontinence as well as inebriation; and the effects of his crimes shattered his constitution'.

On behalf of the church, Cardinal Baronius officially defended Pope Leo's damaging declaration saying it was 'an invention of his corroded mind', but in applauding the pope's tyrannical conduct, supported the essence of his testimony on the grounds of the Infallibility of the church of Rome:

> Of his wicked miscarriages, we, having had before a careful deliberation with our brethren and the Holy Council, and many others, and although he was unworthy to hold the place of St. Peter on earth, Pope Leo the Great (440-461) originally determined that 'the dignity of Peter suffers no diminution even in an unworthy successor' (289, 294, passim.). In regard to the keys, as Vicar of Christ he rendered himself to put forth this judgment truly; and all do assent to it, so that none dissent who does not fall from the church; the infamy of his testimonial and conduct are readily pardoned and forgotten.

Later, John Bale (1495-1563) seized upon Pope Leo's confession and the subsequent Vatican admission that the Pope had spoken the truth. Bale was an Englishman who had earlier joined the Carmelites but abandoned the order after the Inquisition slaughtered his family (*Of the Five Plagues of the Church, Count Antonio Rosmini,* Catholic priest, 1848). He became a playwright and in 1538 developed a lampooning pantomime to mock the pretended godliness of the Catholic church and 'parodied its rites and customs on stage' (*The Complete Plays of John Bale*, ed. Peter Happe). After the public disclosure of the hollow nature of Christianity, 'people were rejoicing that the papacy and the church had come to an end' *(Of the Five Plagues of the Church*, Count Antonio Rosmini, 1848) and later Christian historians acrimoniously referred to the popular theatrical production as 'that abominable satire', dishonestly claiming that it was the origin of Pope Leo's admission (*De Antiqua Ecclesiae Disciplina,* Bishop Lewis Du Pin, Catholic historian, Folio, Paris, 1686).

Papal editing of historical records

There is an extraordinary story associated with the historian Tacitus' 'Annals' and it involves church editing at the highest level. Soon after he captured the papacy, Leo announced that he would reward any person who should procure for him unpublished manuscripts of ancient Pagan or Christian authorship. Sometimes he dispatched envoys for the sole purpose in co-operating in the search or removing old texts already known to exist. His agents, on occasion, stole manuscripts or asserted papal pressure for their removal when they could not be bought. This was the case with the first six books of Tacitus' 'Annals', originally found in the monastery of Corvey in Westphalia in 1455 and removed under Leo's instructions in 1518. In the same discovery was a full collection of Pliny the Younger's letters and they too were taken to Rome.

Leo gave the purloined manuscripts to Filippo Beroaldo, with directions to censor and correct the texts, and then print them in a convenient form. Existing today is a letter written by, or for Leo, to his agent Heitmers after 'Annals' and Pliny's letters had been rewritten and published, saying:

> We have sent a copy of the revised and printed books in a beautiful binding to the abbot and his monks that they may place them in their library as a substitute for the manuscripts taken from it.

Leo had the perfect chance to delete Judas Khrestus' name from Tacitus' 'Annals' but he obviously did not think it necessary to do so. However, there are six missing pages in Tacitus' records that cover the early years of Emperor Claudius' reign (41-54 AD), and the reader should wonder why it was necessary to delete those particular pages (*Diderot's Encyclopedia*, 1759). The possibility exists that Pope Leo certified their removal, for maybe they carried information about Khrestus that connected him with his twin brother Jesus. Leo obviously thought that his personal judgment should determine what literature would be available to mankind for at this time (1518) he reinforced Pope Alexander's earlier edict for episcopal censorship of all books challenging Christianity. Leo died on December 1, 1521 and Rome experienced one of the worst financial crashes in its history.

Summary

The three popes mentioned in this chapter are among dozens who had no belief in the Gospel story, and a brief summary is given of them because they were associates of the 'twin' artists. Such men are clearly a long way removed from the church's modern-day presentation of their character and their lives are today brazingly misrepresented. Catholic historian and author, Bishop Frotheringham (1877), provided this additional overview of the popes of history … and their clergy:

> Many of the popes were men of most abandoned lives. Some were magicians; others were noted for sedition, war, slaughter and profligacy of manners, for avarice and simony. Others were not even members of Christ, but the basest of criminals, and enemies of all godliness. Some were children of their father, the Devil; others were heretics. If the Pope be a heretic, he is *ipso facto*, no Pope. The cardinals, 'mighty to drink wine', were distinguished by pride, luxury, avarice and other crimes. The morals of the bishops, priests and other clergy were equally depraved.(*The Cradle of Christ,* Bishop Frotheringham, 1877; see also, *Catholic Encyclopedia*, xii, 700-703, passim.)

There is a concise historical account of one and a half millennium of papal Christian disbelief recorded in a comprehensive book entitled *Delineation of Roman Catholicism,* written by Reverend Charles Elliott, D.D., and first published in London in 1844. This book was immediately suppressed by the church and listed on its *Index of Prohibited Books.* The author drew his information from 'authentic records of the church of Rome, namely her Creeds, Catechisms, decisions of Councils, Papal Bulls, and the records of history' … this book is startling reading.

CHAPTER 25

Cardinal Bembo's original Gospel manuscripts

Not only did the popes disbelieve the 'official' Christian story, so did the cardinals, and said so in writing. They ridiculed in private what they inculcated and taught in public, and this is evidenced in the records of Cardinal Bembo. For seven years he was an ornament of the papal court, an idol of society, an intellectual father to Raphael, a favourite with millionaires and generous women. In church terminology he was only in minor orders, and accepted the opinion current in Rome that his trial marriage with the church did not forbid him a little gracious sexual indulgence. Vittoria Colonna, purest of the pure, doted on him. Papal secretary, Cardinal Bembo, advised his associate Cardinal Sadoleto not to read the Epistles of Paul, saying:

> Put away these trifles, for such absurdities do not become a man of dignity ... they were introduced on the scene later by a sly voice from heaven.

Cardinal Sadoleto replied, saying that from the outset of his religious career 'he sharply distinguished between hearsay and eyewitness reports and classified the variety of deceivers who have written the story of Christ'. He recorded the account of an unnamed priest who was reproved by another for careless celebration of the Mass. 'When asked whether his critic really believed in transubstantiation, the incarnation, the virgin birth and resurrection, the priest concluded in saying that this story had been invented by cunning ancients to hold men in terror and restraint, and was now carried on by hypocrites' (*Diderot's Encyclopedia*, 1759). His final comment is interesting for priests were referred to as hypocrites some 1100 years earlier. In 386, St Augustine complained of 'hypocrites in the garb of monks who trade in body parts of martyrs, if martyrs they be' (*Five Centuries of Religion*, G. G. Coulton, iv, 116, Cambridge University Press, 1923).

The Cardinal's private library

Cardinal Bembo had a polished style and wrote Latin poems, many frankly Pagan. When he retired his papal post in 1520 he had developed a private library rich in original Gospel manuscripts, and said this about them:

> There are many incidents of the story of Jesus which tend to throw doubt upon it; and the existence of similar stories in history points to their origin in the fanatical and in common superstition, now wholly discredited.

Upon his death in 1547, his unique collection passed to Urbino, thence to the Vatican.

CHAPTER 26

The forbidden theme of twin boys

Anyone approaching the Italian Renaissance for the first time will usually have some ideas on the matter already. Renaissance is a word that is generally misunderstood ... it means 'rebirth' and French historian, Michelet, recorded the term for the first time in 1855. In general, the Italian Renaissance covered a period from 1420 to 1539 and is associated with the idea of a new beginning. During this time, a series of sculptures were fashioned, a particular form of architecture developed, and 2033 paintings were produced, the overwhelming majority religious in concept.

The Bible and its twin painters

The more important of these artworks for our premise were created by Leonardo, Michelangelo, and Raphael, and were completed within four decades of each other. Around that time, various popes commissioned these and other painters and sculptors to create images from the Bible stories that would help the uneducated and illiterate people of the time visualize the church's presentation of its texts (picture writing). It was not the church's fault that the commonality could only think in pictures. Many of the works were designed to promote interest in New Testament narratives and provide a visual rendering to illustrate to the common and unlettered people themes particularly from the Gospels. Michelangelo confirmed the concept, saying:

> For the principle of painting is this: Those who do not know their letters shall read from it ... again and again. The picture shall take the place of the book.

The church understood that paintings spoke a language more easily understood by the simple people, in colours that seized the eye, and in scenes that told tales. Paintings moved the people more quickly, touched their hearts more intimately than a reading of the Bible, a carving of cold marble, or a casting of somber bronze. For this reason, the papacy was a powerful patron and, by the end of the 15th Century, more than one hundred artists were working for the church in Rome on Christian paintings (*Lives of the Most Eminent Painters, Sculptors, and Architects,* Giorgio Vasari, 1907 Ed.). Churches, convents and monasteries needed frescos for their walls and panel pictures for altars. Chapels in large churches, which belonged to private families, also required suitable painted decoration. Italian art of the Renaissance period, even when treating a classical subject, is entirely Christian in its roots and meanings, and the new images strengthened the superstition of the people in a way that benefited the authority of the church.

Members of the papal court and wealthy and powerful cardinals and other clerics also employed artists and reveled in displaying their completed commissions. Artists' clients often stipulated in written contracts that their particular commissions be more beautiful than previous works made for other patrons. The Medici family commissioned Benozzo Gozzoli (1420-1497) with the task of decorating their private chapel in the Palazzo Medici. With elegant dimensions, he created portraits of the whole family in the guise of the Magi and their train. Sandro Botticelli (1445-1510) did the same thing in his Adoration of the Magi, circa 1475. Within a religious setting, he painted a collection of family portraits of living persons, in addition to recently deceased members of the Medici family. The same concept is seen in Brother Fra Angelico's interpretation of the Last Supper where the angelic Dominican could not resist placing a few living Franciscan friars in hell.

Much of the finished artwork was publicly displayed and when Leonardo revealed his painting, 'The Virgin and St Anne', the response, according to the 16th Century artist-historian Giorgio Vasari, was huge:

> For two days it attracted to the room where it was exhibited a crowd of men and women, young and old, who flocked there, as if they were attending a great festival to gaze in amazement at the marvels he had created.

Leonardo's conceptions of New Testament characters were so magnificent that they 'stupefied all the intelligentsia' and 'caused much talk among the general public'.

The use of artist's license

In researching the lives of the artists of the Renaissance, it is not possible to ignore the writings of Vasari for he personally knew many of the people he wrote about and recorded their stories in a book called *Lives of the Most Eminent Painters, Sculptors, and Architects*. Vasari talks of them conceiving 'inventions of the Madonna', 'the creation of poetic fantasies of Christ' and 'speaking with imitative pictures of imagination that seem appropriate for the people of the day'. For example, painter Giovanni Bellini, in a reply to a letter dated 19 October 1505 from Isabella d' Este Gonzaga, Marchesa of Mantua, reassured her that he would 'paint a fantasy in his own way' and portray 'Madonna with John the Baptist and other fantasies'.

Not all artists used the New Testament as a source book for some created their works outside traditional Christian symbolism, but within a conventional Christian setting. For example, Leonardo, in a reply to a request by Pope Julius II (1503-13) to include John the Baptist as an adult in a commissioned painting of the 'Nativity', stated, 'I will paint what seems appropriate to me, not you, and you shall pay me handsomely'. His words reveal that the masters of the time had artistic license to paint what they personally conceived from the Gospels … and many of them depicted Mary with twin sons.

The hidden words of Leonardo

Because Leonardo created beautiful Christian artworks the modern-day church described him as 'obviously a pious man chosen by God Himself, a good Christian, of great understanding, miraculously wrought to convince the world of the virginity and perpetual purity of the Mother'. However, this is not true, for historical records say something entirely different about him. Vasari, in the first edition of his book, wrote that Leonardo was of 'so heretical a cast of mind that he conformed to no religion whatever, accounting it perchance better to be a philosopher than a Christian' (Muntz, II, 32n). For some reason, this passage is now deleted from modern printings of Vasari' writings. But there is more.

Leonardo was extremely critical of the clergy. He called them Pharisees, accused them of deceiving the simple people with bogus miracles, forged writings, and smiled at the 'false coin' of celestial promissory notes that they exchanged for the genuine coinage of the time. He said that 'he took no more account of the wind that came from their mouths than that which they expelled from their lower parts' (*Literary Works of Leonardo Da Vinci*, Richter, I, # 10).

© Film Library of Renaissance Art, Italy

An impression of Leonardo as a young man. The original is in the Uffizi Gallery in Florence and is described as being created by a 'Tuscan Master' of the 15th Century.

He wrote 5000 pages but never published one book. He speaks of having composed 120 manuscripts of which only 50 remain. They are written from right to left in a half-Oriental script that almost lends colour to the little-known legend that at one time he travelled in the Near East, served the Egyptian sultan, and embraced the Mohammedan faith (*Literary Works of Leonardo da Vinci*, J. P. Richter, II, 385-92).

On one Good Friday he wrote:'today the Christian world is in pretended mourning because one man died in the Orient (*Literary Works of Leonardo da Vinci,* Richter, II, P. 302, 363-4, 369). He disbelieved the story of the peasant maid who bore a god and laughed at the churchmen for worshipping dead saints, saying that they were incapable of hearing prayers addressed to them (*Codex Atlantico*, B 70, r.a. *Notebooks*, II, 504). His opinion of Christianity was not very favourable:

> I could wish that I had such power of language as should avail me to censure those who would extol the worship of men above that of the sun. Those who have wished to worship men as gods have made a very grave error. (*Notebooks*, I, 295)

He took more liberty with Christian iconography than any other Renaissance artist, stating that 'the imitation of the Gospel stories is subtle speculation'. He suppressed halos, put the Virgin Mary across her mother's knee for a spanking, painted the apostles in positions suggestive of homosexuality, showed Mary scandalously naked and, on more than one occasion, depicted Jesus with a twin brother.

The true beliefs of Leonardo can be assessed more from his numerous drawings than from his few paintings. Their number is legion; onemanuscript alone, the Codex Atlantico in Milan, has within it 1700 sketches and many show Mary with twins. Here is one example:

Leonardo thinking out loud

Leonardo was the oldest of the Leonardo-Michelangelo-Raphael triumvirate, being twenty-two years the senior of Michelangelo. In 1495, Cardinal Lodovico commissioned him to paint The Last Supper on a refectory wall in the dining room of the Dominican convent of Santa Maria delle Grazie in Milan. Leonardo drew up a contract but the church argued about his fee and his insistence upon a large advance. After four months of negotiations, a financial agreement was reached. Then, for more than two years Leonardo laboured. Bandello, an author of the time, reported that Leonardo 'would spend several hours each day examining the painting and criticizing the figures to himself. I have also seen him give a few touches to one of the figures and then suddenly he would leave for the day'. The monks grew impatient, even threatening to lock him in the room until he finished. The Dominicans so annoyed him with their pressure that, according to tradition, he painted Judas Iscariot in the image of the prior.

By 1556, the finished work had turned into 'a muddle of blots'. Re-touchers clouded it when they firstly restored it in 1746; monks cut a door through Christ's feet; Napoleon's men stabled horses there. In 1943, bombs unroofed the monastery, shaking its sandbagged treasure. Saved by seven post-war restoration efforts, it miraculously endures and modern restorers have methodically peeled away layers of debasing repairs by inept painters. But much of the magnificence has vanished forever.

© Film Library of Renaissance Art, Italy

Leonardo da Vinci's 'The Last Supper', before restoration. The insert is an enlargement of the person fifth from Jesus' right who has a remarkable similarity to Jesus, particularly in the oldest coloured versions.

However, in his famous interpretation of The Last Supper, Leonardo again subscribed to the ancient belief that Jesus had a twin brother. He depicted one of the disciples (fifth from Jesus' right) bearing an uncanny resemblance to Jesus, not only in physical appearance but also in the matching design and colour of his clothing, complete to the fine detail of the width and shading of the narrow neckband on his costume.

Again, in his 'Madonna and Child and St Anne', Leonardo depicts Mary with twin boys, and a satisfactory orthodox explanation of yet another double portrait has yet to be given.

© Film Library of Renaissance Art, Italy

Madonna and Child and St Anne' by Leonardo da Vinci.

The unfinished painting of Mary

Leonardo had a specific purpose in mind when he painted one particular picture, and its concept is intriguing. Now called The Adoration of the Magi, this painting is incomplete with Mary's right arm and shoulder appearing distorted. However, John Everett Millias (1829-1896), a 19th Century art expert and Renaissance researcher, claimed that the area in question originally contained a second boy, and a later artist brushed it out by over-painting.

© Film Library of Renaissance Art, Italy

In and out of the picture? Did Leonardo originally paint a twin in Mary's arms, or did he intend to? The strange structure of Mary's right arm has puzzled art experts for decades. Note also that Mary is looking to the area where the second child would have been.

Michelangelo and secret information

The supreme sculptor and painter, Michelangelo, also avidly preserved the 'twin boys' theme in many of his famous works of Mary. The first line of a sonnet that Michelangelo wrote to himself mentioned a 'double treasure' existing in his works, and that may be understood to refer to the Jesus twins.

The entire idea that Jesus had a twin brother is anathema to the church and anyone openly expressing such a suggestion in those times would be promptly branded a heretic. Thus, artists risked persecution in order to reveal a church secret in a form that very few people would be able to understand. Yet Michelangelo's first ever sculpture shows Mary in the company of twin boys, one of them curiously hidden by her mantle. Called The Virgin of the Stairs, it an extraordinary work, carved in low relief from Carrara marble, defies conceptual description.

'Virgin of the Stairs'. Michelangelo shows one child partially hidden by his mother's costume, with his back to the viewer. Mary responds to the second child. One gets the sensation from this creation that the covered child is purposely meant to be concealed, yet revealed. This is the earliest existing work by Michelangelo and was created while he was a guest of Lorenzo the Magnificent, about 1490.

Here are two more depictions by Michelangelo showing Mary with twin boys. Left: Madonna Pitti; About 1505; Florence; Museo Nazionale del Bargello. Right: Madonna Taddei; About 1504.

Twins in the heart of Christendom

The Sistine Chapel was constructed between 1475 and 1481 and decorated during the following years. The architect was a young Florentine named Baccio Pontelli, who designed the building's proportions to match exactly those given in the Bible for the Temple of Solomon (*Michelangelo and the Pope's Ceiling*, Ross King, Random House, London, 2002). In 1508, Pope Julius II commissioned the then thirty-three year-old Michelangelo to paint the ceiling but he was reluctant, considering himself a sculptor rather than a painter. Nevertheless, for the next four years he and a hand-picked team of assistants laboured over the vast ceiling, making thousands of drawings and spending back-breaking hours on a scaffold fifty feet above the floor. The result was one of the greatest masterpieces of all time.

Michelangelo's 343 frescos on the ceiling are among the wonders of the art world and hide within themselves a great deal of symbolism. The immensity of the work demonstrates the scope and power of Michelangelo's genius and illustrates his personal vision of the biblical world. At first he worked according to a plan provided by the pope, since Julius had requested a specific pictorial theme for the vault. However, they argued about the concept and late in 1508 Michelangelo wrote that the pope 'has given me a new commission to do what I like'. Hence, Michelangelo had permission to paint whatever subject or theme he wished, and he elected to openly deal with the subject of twin boys.

For example, in one depiction, Mary carries a young Jesus on her knee, and he holds his left arm towards another and identical boy. In this illustration, the second child has turned his torso and head away from the spectator in an attempt by the artist to imply mystery or intrigue. Michelangelo also illustrated the majority of the Old Testament prophets with twin boys, and again, in some cases, one twin has his head turned away from view. The meaning of these concepts is both theologically and philosophically obscure, as is the significance of the naked young men in the background of many of Michelangelo's works.

© The Michelangelo Collection

One of forty-eight sets of twins on the Sistine Chapel ceiling.

Michelangelo also depicted two identical 'assisting genii' looking down upon the open pages of the writings of the Cumaean Sibyl in a central position on the Sistine ceiling. Known as the Sibyl of Tarquin (c. 500 BC), she was the author of the original version of the pre-Christian Book of Revelation, reproduced in its unique and pristine form in *The Crucifixion of Truth* (Tony Bushby, Joshua Books, Australia, 2005). Michelangelo depicted four other Sibyls on the Sistine Chapel ceiling. They are the Delphic, Persian, Libyan and Erythraean Sibyls, the latter being highly regarded in the Middle Ages. Her prophecy of the Last Judgment is preserved in the terrible Dies Irae or 'Day of Wrath' of the Requiem, a sequence sung in the Mass of the Dead. It is a fifty-seven-line poem divided into nineteen three-line verses. 'Authorship of the Dies Irae has been the search of historians over the centuries' (*Our Sunday Visitor's Catholic Encyclopedia,* Pg. 308, 1986 Ed.). That search is now over ... the Erythraean Sibyl wrote it.

Some twenty years after he commenced the Sistine Chapel ceiling, Michelangelo again depicted Mary with twin boys in his statue for the Medici Chapel. A number of art experts have commented on the unconventional iconography of that sculpture but have never been able to explain the existence of the second boy. One has the impression that the twin is concealed to symbolize the fact that the truth about Jesus Christ is still hidden from the majority of humanity, and those that wish to understand must adjust their thinking to see it.

Michelangelo's lost works

There are a series of works attributed to Michelangelo that are lost, destroyed or were planned but not executed. Historical records list the names of some as; the Temptation of St Anthony, Hercules, the Young John the Baptist, Sleeping Cupid, the Stigmatization of St Francis of Assisi, the Bronze David, the Twelve Apostles, a bronze statue of Pope Julius II, Christ Holding the Cross, and the Resurrection of Christ, originally planned for the Sistine Chapel for which there are several drawings still in existence.

Of particular interest is a marble statue once carved by Michelangelo and called, Mary with Two Children. In the 16th Century, this work was formerly in the possession of Lorenzo di Pierfrancesco de Medici in Florence, but its whereabouts today is unknown.

Raphael, the papal playboy

Raphael was another of the Renaissance artists who quite openly portrayed twin boys with Mary on a single canvas. He was born in Urbino in 1483 and died in 1529. About 1508 he was summoned to Rome and there he received the great commissions that gave him the chance to develop his genius to its fullest extent. Here, the untried provincial ... he was then about twenty-six ... was given the commission to decorate the Vatican Stanze by Pope Julius II, a task not much inferior to that which Michelangelo had just begun in the Sistine Chapel.

THE FORBIDDEN THEME OF TWIN BOYS

Raphael was a womanizer and a personal friend of Pope Leo X. Vasari suggests that Raphael hoped to be made a cardinal. He grew rich on papal commissions and painted idealized portraits of sovereigns who had deserved well of the Vatican. He spent most of his working life in the service of the church during which time he painted more than fifty Madonnas, all different and directly derived from living women. When Castiglione asked Raphael where he found the models for the portraits of Mary, he replied that he created them in his imagination out of the diverse elements of beauty present in the many women he knew, and from 'the embraces of other ladies which my lively imagination strongly pictured, particular the one with the big black eyes who ravished me'.

On occasion, his wit was sharp. Two cardinals visited his studio and amused themselves by picking flaws in his pictures. They criticized him, saying that the faces of the apostles in a particular painting were too red. Raphael replied; 'Do not be surprised at that, your eminences; I painted them so, deliberately; may we not think that they can blush in heaven when they see the church governed by such men as yourselves' (*Raphael*, Muntz, p. 420).

© Film Library of Renaissance Art, Italy

Madonna of the Chair, by Raphael. This is one of Raphael's most popular Madonnas and shows the mastery of the tondo, or circular form. See also a painting by Raphael; La Belle Jardiniere, Musee du Louvre. It also shows Mary with twin boys. Also, 'Madonna and Child with Saints', by Raphael. It is a thinly disguised representation of the twin boys.

However, it is possible that Raphael's depiction of twins was copied directly from the works of Michelangelo or Leonardo, for Michelangelo complained that 'everything he (Raphael) had in art, he had from me'.

Later forgery in 'twin' paintings

It seems strange that Leonardo, Michelangelo and Raphael constantly portrayed twin boys. These artists clearly created identical twins, and in some cases one boy appears slightly unfinished, shaded or partly covered as if implying something is being held back or is unknown. Who is the twin, and why is he sometimes uncompleted, as though to unveil his identity would be to reveal a mystery?

The church reasoned that one of the boys is Jesus Christ and the other John the Baptist. That is clearly not so, for artists of the time identified John the Baptist by means of one of three symbols ... a cross in his hand, a hairy coat, or a scroll. In some instances, later church artists who wished to cover-up the twin symbolism in the paintings of the masters added Christian symbols to mislead the onlooker. Leonardo's painting, The Virgin of the Rocks, was altered in this way when a cross was added to the National Gallery of London version of the picture in an obvious attempt to make Jesus' twin appear as John the Baptist.

The technique of lesser hands brushing out or adding sections from the works of Renaissance painters may seem unbelievable to the modern mind, but it was the church that originally certified the practice. After the ruling on need for standardized biblical images by the Council of Trent during the first Provincial Council (1565), Cardinal Charles Borromeo, manservant to Pope Sixtus V, moved a motion forbidding the painting of popular Christian subjects without official approval from the church. The motion was carried and from that time on, artists needed written documentation from certified ecclesiastical authorities on matters pertaining to the creation of Christian iconography. Bishops were appointed to instruct artists on the standardized presentation of particularly Gospel subjects and they were not to proceed without church permission.

© Film Library of Renaissance Art, Italy

The existence of two versions of the 'Virgin of the Rocks' has been a source of debate among historians for centuries. The first version was commissioned in 1483 (left picture) and is void of a cross in the arms of the child to the right of Mary (right picture). A later hand added the poorly painted crucifix to the London version of the picture to make the twin appear to be John the Baptist. The forgery was discovered when the crucifix started to flake off and needed reinstatement.

Council of Trent censors artwork

In 1570, Cardinal Molano edited and published an official Vatican treaty called, *De pictures et imaginibus sacris,* which provided the guidelines required for the orthodox presentation of scriptural topics or ecclesiastical subjects certified by the church. From that time on it was commonplace for later artistic hands to add or remove details to existing paintings that conflicted with church dogma.

A late example of one artist who escaped the church's decrees is found in the work of Pierre Puget who placed twin boys at the feet of Mary in his Immaculate Conception, which he completed around 1670. There is nothing in this theme, or in the symbolism associated with it, that explains why the immaculate Virgin should be represented with twin boys.

It was after the Council of Trent that many of the Renaissance artworks were given a title. It would be foolish to think that the church would allow a picture or sculpture to be publicly displayed with a caption like, for example, 'Jesus and his Twin Brother'. Few artists of the period were inclined to give *any* titles to their creations although Ghirlandaio called one of his paintings, The Two Innocenti, and Cristofano Robetta named his first work, Madonna with Two Children. However, with the introduction of heretical notions into their works, they portray the twins in suggestive guises thus covering their tracks so as to be beyond the grasp of church censors and heresy-hunters. It is for this reason that many of the pictures that are related to the twinship of Jesus portray his twin behind a veiled facade.

Many artists knew about the twins

There are only a few records of artists being persecuted for their paintings mainly because the majority of them stuck to familiar and acceptable Christian concepts. Indeed, if the Albigensian and Knights Templar massacres taught people anything about the church of Rome, and its values, it was the wisdom of keeping silent about ideas that did not meet the approval of the priesthood. The semi-concealed symbolism was a convenient way for a school or artist familiar with the knowledge of Jesus' twin brother to obscure an heretical idea, and their works were prototypes for the composition of later carvings and paintings.

The knowledge of Jesus' twin found a sure footing in artwork and over the decades, as many as twenty-five artists subtly revealed the knowledge in their works. After the death of Leonardo there were others who had worked in his studio and learned to imitate his grace of line without reaching his subtlety or depth. Among those were Cesare Magni (c. 1534), Cesare da Sesto (d. 1523), Mario d'Oggiono (d. 1530), Andrea Solari, Gaudenzio Ferrari, Bernardino de Conti, and Francesco Melzi, whose depiction of twins was carried over from Leonardo's original portrayal. However, some art schools didn't know the secret of Jesus' twin brother and painted Mary with a single child, as portrayed by church dogma.

Today there are around two hundred works of art portraying Mary with twin boys displayed publicly in some of the world's largest galleries. A large proportion are from the studios of Leonardo, Michelangelo and Raphael and the presence of twins leaves the onlooker with no doubt that twinship was exactly what the artists intended to portray. No one has adequately explained the presence of twin boys in these creations, and today many of their works appear in the most conspicuous sites in Christendom.

Twin iconography reaches the antipodes

As late as the 19th Century, the church of England was probably unknowingly revealing the twinship of Jesus in many of their churches. For example, a prefabricated glass window built in East London in 1858 and shipped to a church in Canterbury, New Zealand, depicts twin boys facing each other.

© Authors own photograph, 2005

Twins on a stained glass window in St Anne's church, South Canterbury, New Zealand.

CHAPTER 27

An opposing Bible

Once the theme of twin boys was developed, the idea spread rapidly through that loose collection of states called the Holy Roman Empire, and then to Britain. English dramatists began to disclose oblique references to a hidden knowledge and it was not lost on the small groups of individuals who understood the import: 'One face, one voice, one habit, two persons', wrote William Shakespeare in the *Twelfth Night*. Scores of volumes have been written to establish that Sir Francis Bacon (1561-1626) was the real author of the plays and sonnets popularly ascribed to William Shakespeare and that controversy is still current today. While living in Europe as a young man, Bacon was initiated into the Order of the Knights Templar and learnt the secret of Jesus' twin brother.

Secrets in the King James Bible

It was the 'wisest fool in Christendom' (*Declaratio Pro Iure Regio*, W. McElwee, 1615; also Sully), King James I (1566-1625), who encouraged the translation and publication of a special Bible for British churches. He authorized an entirely new edition, one he thought would unite Protestants and Catholics in Scotland and England. As their exemplar, committee members used a German-language Bible that had originally been translated from a Latin Vulgate. For that reason, there are no more references to Judas Thomas than what is in the Catholic Bible. James issued a set of personal 'Rules' that the translators were to follow, although he never contributed a farthing to its cost. Work began in 1607 and a committee of 47 men (some say 54, others say 50) took two years and nine months to write a new Bible and make ready for the press. Each man was paid thirty shillings per week and was required to work fifty-six hours. Upon its completion, the revised manuscripts were turned over to Francis Bacon for final editing.

Bacon worked on the new Bible for nearly a year during which time 'he hammered the various styles of the translators into the unity, rhythm, and music of Shakespearean prose, wrote the Prefaces and created the whole scheme of the Authorized Version' (*The Martyrdom of Francis Bacon,* Alfred Dodd, Pg. 141, undated, but c. 1940). Regarding the months of restructuring, Bacon's biographer, William T. Smedley, said:

> It will eventually be proved that the whole structure of the Authorised Bible was Francis Bacon's. He was an ardent student not only of the Bible, but also of early manuscripts. St. Augustine, St Jerome, and writers of theological works, were studied by him with industry. He ciphered in narratives of a hidden nature to add force to his initiated knowledge. (*The Mystery of Francis Bacon,* circa 1910, Pg. 128)

At the completion of editing, Bacon and King James 1 had a series of meetings to finalize editorial matters associated with their new Bible. It was at that time that King James ordered a 'Dedication to the King' to be drawn up and included in the opening pages. He also authorized the phrase 'Appointed to be read in the Churches' to appear on the title page. That was an announcement clarifying that King James had personally given the church 'Special Command' for that particular version of the Bible to be used in preference to Greek and Latin Bibles current at the time.

His reason was personal, for King James had previously instructed the revisers to 'defend the position of the king' in their restructuring of the texts. In their translation of 1 Peter 2:13, for example, they changed the phrase 'the emperor, as supreme' to 'the king, as supreme'. Because the King James' Bible was written to support the authority of a king, not a Roman Emperor, the later British church often referred to it as the one from 'authority', and it was presented to the public as if officially 'authorized'. In subsequent revisions, the word 'authorized' found its way onto the title page and was later printed on the cover, giving King James' new Bible a false sense of authenticity.

Robert Barker subsequently purchased the original English-language version of the King James Bible. He was the King's printer and records exist establishing that he paid £3,500 for the manuscript, the price including the Copyright. He died in 1645, and the whereabouts of this documentation is currently unknown.

In 1881, the King James Bible was rewritten and the Committee responsible for the Revised Edition admitted that they made 36,190 editorial changes before certifying publication. Their reconstructed New Testament carried alterations that changed the sense of 1600 passages and produced a text that must be viewed by every person with absolute suspicion.

Differences between the two Bibles

Among Christian churches for which Old and New Testaments together constitute the Bible, there was never complete agreement on what the Bible really was, and this confusion was probably inherited from its twin development. The variation between Bibles is extraordinary for the Protestant Book of Daniel, for example, carries twelve chapters, and the Catholic version, fourteen. Bishop Eusebius quoted Daniel 13 as scripture (*Demon, Evang.*, vi; 19) and so did Ephraem (306-373), but in Protestant Bibles, Daniel doesn't have a 13th chapter. The Protestant and Jewish versions of the Bible are a good deal thinner by seven books than the Catholic version, and the church has never explained this dramatic variation.

CHAPTER 28

Concealing special messages

Francis Bacon was a master of concealing in cipher secret information in his writings and, despite centuries of editing, some of his methods are still found in the Bible today. He took delight to hide his works, to the end they might be found out, and stands a self-confessed Teacher of Concealed Principles. Cryptography, or the art of writing in cipher to conceal the meaning of what was written from all except those who possessed the key, may be traced to remote antiquity, possibly to the Spartans. Kings and Generals communicated their messages to officers in distant provinces by means of a pre-concerted cipher; and the system was employed wherever there was a desire or a necessity to conceal the meaning of a written document. Emperor Augustus in the First Century wrote in secret ciphers and his particular system was revealed in *The Bible Fraud* (Tony Bushby, Joshua Books, Australia, 2001). Aponas, an astrological writer of the 13th Century, revealed some old ciphers that were used originally by Cabalists, and among others, a particular alphabet called 'the passing of the river' which is referred to in some high degrees of Masonry.

The most famous of all later literal cryptograms is the famous bilateral cipher described by Bacon in his *De Augmentis Scientiarum*. He originated the system while still a young man in Paris and that particular cipher required the use of two styles of typeface, one an ordinary face and the other especially designed. The differences between the two fonts were in many cases so minute that it required a powerful magnifying glass to detect them. Today, the knowledge of that simple system would no longer serve any purpose of concealment due to modern computerized forms of printing and easy detection. Originally, the cipher messages were concealed only in italicized words, sentences or paragraphs, because the italic letters, being more ornate than Roman letters, offered greater opportunity for concealing slight but necessary variations. Sometimes the special letters varied a little in size, at other times in thickness or in their ornamental flourishes.

Alphabets secretly adjusted were not entirely satisfactory, however, for although they rendered unintelligible the true nature of the writings, their very presence disclosed the fact of concealed information. Through patience or persecution, the keys to those alphabets were eventually acquired and the contents of the documents revealed to the unworthy. That was not satisfactory and necessitated employment of more subtle methods of concealing divine truths. The result was the appearance of cryptic systems of writing designed to conceal the presence of both the message and the cryptogram.

Thus having devised a method of transmitting their secrets to posterity, Bacon, and other initiates like him, encouraged the circulation of certain documents specially prepared through incorporating into them ciphers containing the deepest secrets of religion, mysticism and philosophy. Thus, medieval Masons and Rosicrucians disseminated their secrets throughout the land unsuspected by 'the uninstructed world' (*The Martyrdom of Francis Bacon,* Alfred Dodd, 1945, Pg. 32), since volumes containing those cryptograms could be subject to scrutiny without revealing the presence of the hidden message. It was a time of severe repression and of harsh government, and free speech was impossible. Able men could only dissemble and speak in allegory. 'If they had expressed their opinions openly they would have been sent to the Tower and the Block' (*The Rise of English Culture,* Edwin Johnson, Preface).

During the Middle Ages scores of 'concealed authors' (*The Martyrdom of Francis Bacon,* Alfred Dodd, 1945, Pg. 149) and members of secret political or religious organizations published books and letters containing codes and ciphers. Secret writings became a fad; every European court had its own diplomatic cipher, and the intelligentsia vied with one another in devising curious and complicated cryptograms. Some were as simple as writing words of a sentence backwards. The literature of the 15th, 16th and 17th Centuries was permeated with ciphers, few of which have ever been decoded. Without a key, the works are unintelligible, except by the art of the decipherer or one skilled in literary matters. Many liberal churchmen used cryptograms, fearing excommunication or a worse fate should their researches become suspected. Had they failed to conceal their discoveries under complicated cipher, they faced the possibility of persecution as heretics. Some ciphers were so intricate that they may forever baffle attempts at their decipherment. In those susceptible of a solution, sometimes the 'a's and 'b's need to be exchanged; at other times only every other letter was counted; and so on.

A particular pictorial design with dogs, rabbits and archers is found over the address, 'To The Christian Reader', in the 1612 edition of the King James Bible. That identical design is also found in the folio edition of Shakespeare and connected both books. However, it is the 1612 quarto edition of the Authorized Version that is of most interest, for on the title-page of the Genealogies are two complex head-piece designs both of which were used by Bacon in previous books he wrote and published in 1593 and 1594. The selection of those designs was not made by chance but was deliberately chosen to create similitude between certain books and mark their connections with each other. Most noticeable was the light and dark capital A's (A.A) in the lower design which was also used on several Shakespeare quartos and elsewhere. That direct connection between the Bible and the Shakespearean plays is long overlooked and the fact that hidden ciphers appeared in both the King James Bible and the Shakespearean plays arrests attention. Those writings contain cryptographically concealed information that is purposely encoded into the actual text and is still there today.

An impartial consideration of the Shakespearean documents cannot but convince the open-minded of the verisimilitude of the theory of Bacon being author of the plays. Those enthusiasts who for years struggled to identify Bacon as the true 'Bard of Avon' might long since have won their case had they emphasized the most important angle. That was, Bacon, the Knights Templar initiate, wrote into the Shakespearean plays the secret teachings of the Order, and major clues to unlock the hidden story in the Gospels. A sentimental world, however, disliked giving up a traditional hero, either to solve a controversy or to right a wrong. Nevertheless, the Bacon/Shakespeare controversy, as its most able advocates realize, involves the most profound aspects of science, religion and ethics; he or she who solves its mystery may yet find therein the key to the supposedly Lost Wisdom of Antiquity.

Abundant proof exists that Bacon was concerned in one way or another with the production or editing of the Shakespearean Plays. He redrafted the original Nine Degrees of the Knights Templar into Thirty-Three, and chose Thirty-Three as the highest degree of initiation because Thirty-Three was the numerical signature of 'Bacon'. The Masonic order of degrees was divided into Thirty-Three symbolic sections (33°) and the number was used in a variety of Mystery Schools.

It was probable that Bacon's cipher number coincided with an old Cabalist teaching employed in the Old Testament. The Torah used the Divine Name thirty-two times in the Creation story at the beginning of Genesis. Of that, Cabalists said that through those thirty-two paths, the soul descended to be clothed in the physical body and the thirty-third path was the ultimate return to stand before God's presence at the end of life on Earth.

Thus, thirty-three became his personal cipher number, and whenever it appears in the Shakespearean Plays, the Gospels or the Old Testament, a cleverly concealed cipher can be discovered associated with it. In the 'First Part of King Henry the Fourth', for example, the word 'Francis' appears thirty-three times on one page. To attain this end, awkward sentences were required, such as: 'ANON FRANCIS? No Francis, but tomorrow Francis; or Francis; on Thursday; or indeed Francis when then will; but Francis'. Here we see one example of the concealed use of the mystical number thirty-three in the Shakespearean Plays.

It was suggested that Bacon created his own Secret Society, by the agency of which he carried through his works, but it is difficult to find any concrete evidence that such a Society existed. Books came from his pen at a rate which, when the truth is revealed, will literally 'stagger humanity' (*The Secret Shake-speare,* Alfred Dodd, MCMXLI). He made translations of ancient classics and histories and his 'Good Pens' (other writers) wrote books under his direction. He saw them through to the press, and every book published under his direction carried his favourite secret cipher, stylized light and dark capital A's, side-by-side (A.A).

The double 'A.A' was Bacon's hidden signature cipher for 'AthenA', known in mythology as Pallas Minerva, Athene or Athena, which meant Virgin. The letters making up PALLAS MINERVA, ATHENE OR ATHENA, VIRGIN number thirty-three, and she was the esteemed Goddess of Bacon's Mystery Schools. The initiates dedicated themselves in her honour and vowed to uphold her ideals.

Athena was the Goddess of Wisdom and usually depicted in art wearing a helmet and holding a spear in her right hand in readiness to strike at a serpent near her feet. She was known as the 'Spear-shaker' among the ancient Greeks because when the morning rays of the sun glinted on the spear, the common people were in the habit of saying smilingly; 'Athena is shaking her spear again'; hence her name, 'Spear-shaker'. She was the Goddess to whom the Rosicrosse Brethren swore allegiance when they were initiated in the Secret Literary Order, the Knights of the Order, and Bacon was the head of the Spear-shakers. Side by side with the Rosicrosse arose the Lodge of the Freemasons and the College of the Rosicrucian Fraternity, which persist to this day.

In both Masonic and Rosicrucian rituals, there is a certain point in learning where the candidate is challenged by a 'spear-shaker' who menacingly threatens the candidate to the chest, shaking and pointing a spear or a sword at him. The design on page thirty-three of Henry Peacham's *Minerva Britannia* (1612) shows a hand holding a spear as in the act of shaking it. It represents the great secret of Bacon's life and gives the clue to the construction of the word, 'Shakespeare'. That volume is full of literary devices that would amply repay a careful study, but it establishes that the word, 'spearshaker', when reversed, becomes 'Shakespeare'. The 'spearshaker' also receives a mention in Bacon's restructuring of the New Testament. In the final narratives of the Gospel of John, Jesus was prodded in the side by a spearshaker.

Both Masons and Rosicrucians threateningly 'shake spears' at the candidate during the trials of his initiation. 'It was Francis Bacon's secret symbol to represent that he was 'The Spear-shaker's' representative known by the name of Shakespeare. Thus the 'Spear-shaker' wrote under the name of Shake-speare and was Sir Francis Bacon' (*Bacon and the Rosicrucians,* W. F. C. Wigston; Also, *The Mirror of Pallas*).

Bacon used the first and last letters of Athena's name (A.A) as headpieces to subtly mark particular books connected with the Secret Orders of the Knights Templar, the Rosicrucians and the Masons. 'In these books Francis Bacon had the opportunity to secrete his personal secrets which he dare not write openly about' (*Francis Bacon's Cipher Signatures,* Frank Woodward). There were many different designs of the 'A.A' cipher and numerous books that bore the coded signal were connected, including the Authorised Edition of the King James Bible and the Shakespearean Plays.

One 'A' was printed light and the other 'A' dark to indicate that while there was much open and straightforward in the designated book, there was also much in the shadow which could only be discovered by searching. (*The Secret Shake-speare,* Alfred Dodd, MCMXLI; Also, *The Martyrdom of Francis Bacon,* also by Alfred Dodd).

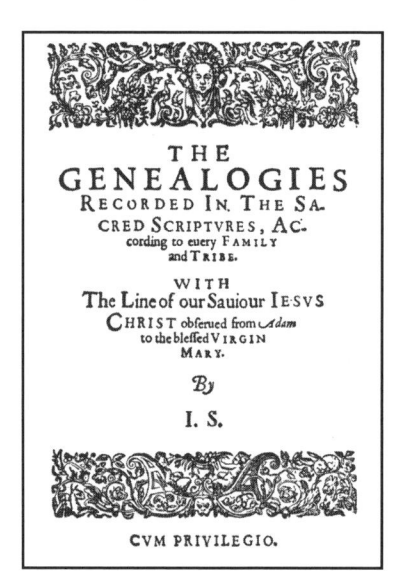

Hidden Information. This is the title page of the 1612 edition of the New Testament. The design at the head of the page was also used on the title page of the first edition of 'Venus and Adonis', 1593, and the first edition of Lucrece, 1594. Note the use in the lower panel of the light and dark 'A.A' secret cipher that indicates hidden knowledge. The same design was used on several Shakespearean quartos and elsewhere.

Knights Templar knowledge not lost

Throughout the Shakespearean Folios and Quartos are scores of hidden acrostic signatures, some of which are ingenious in their design. The simplest form was called the Capital Initial Code (CIC) whereby Bacon's name is concealed in the first few letters of consecutive lines. In 'The Tempest', Act 1, Scene 2, is an example:

> Begun to tell me what I am but stopt,
> And left me to a bootelesse inquisition,
> C O N cluding, stay; not yet …

Here, the first Initial letters of the first and second lines, together with the first three Initialed letters of the third line form the word 'Bacon'. It is not so much BACON that concerns us here, but the shape in which those letters are formed. When a line is drawn around the design of the code, the letter 'L' is revealed:

B| egun to tell me what I am but stopt,
A| nd left me to a bootelesse inquisition,
|C O N| cluding, stay; not yet …

This letter then connects with following coded letters until thirty-three consecutive ciphers are combined and spell out full words that create a statement. This code appears in both the Shakespearean Plays and the Bible, and some examples of its application are now given.

The full name that Bacon constructed to appear on title pages of his writings was 'William Shakespeare', and was created (maybe) without reference to him of Stratford, who possible bore, or had assigned to him, a somewhat similar name, possibly Shakspur. There is good reason to suspect that was exactly what happened, for Bacon created a superstructure of numbers built up on the exact spelling of the words 'William Shakespeare'. Anybody looking closely at Bacon's clues will see also the year 1623 was specially selected for the issue of the complete volume of the plays, because of the extraordinary relations which the numbers composing it bear to the combined names William Shakespeare and Sir Francis Bacon. Simply put, the total number of letters of the two names added up to thirty-three, Bacon's cipher number (WILLIAM SHAKESPEARE, SIR FRANCIS BACON = 33 letters).

The letters of the year 1623, when written in words, also add up to thirty-three (SIXTEEN HUNDRED AND TWENTY THREE YEARS) and, according to a mathematics expert, the chances of that letter/word/number combination happening are 4.8 million to one. The intriguing relationship of numbers is also carried through to the year 1561, in which the birth of Francis Bacon was registered and, curiously enough, to 1564 and 1616, the reputed dates of the birth and death of the Stratford man.

The Shakespearean plays and the authorised Bible of 1611 contain hidden messages about Jesus, Mary Magdalene and the substance of the Gospel story. Bacon knew the secret of Christian origins and concealed his knowledge in both the Shakespearean Folio of 1623 and the New Testament. His biographer confirms, saying:

> And whosoever would understand the Lord Bacon's Cypher let him consult that accurate Editione in Latine, Anno 1623 (*Advancement of Learning*) for the form of the Letters of the Alphabet, in which much of the Mysterie consisteth. (*Baconiana*, T. Tenison, 1679, Pg. 28)

Bacon's secrets were encoded in a system of letters and numbers that revealed to the initiated the presence of concealed information. He purposely coded the hidden information of the Knights Templar, Masons and Rosicrucians into those texts and several of his complex and revealing ciphers were decoded in *The Bible Fraud* and *The Secret in the Bible*.

Grace, Honour, vertue, Learning, witt,
Are all within this Porture knitt.
And left to time that it may tell,
What worth within this P:ere did dwell

"THE MIRROUR OF STATE AND ELOQUENCE"
(*Facsimile*)
A Rare Title Page in a 1656 tract

Can you see the Capital Initial Code in this rare title-page tract of 1656 of Francis Bacon?

Bacon's cipher number is found several times in the Bible. The famous Temple of Solomon stood (in biblical terms) for thirty-three years in pristine splendor and that number is the clue enabling the hidden information to be deciphered. Likewise, King David was made to rule thirty-three years in Jerusalem and Gospel writers had Jesus Christ crucified in the thirty third year of his life, those numbers again drawing attention to deeper truths.

The name of King Solomon is

not recorded by Herodotus or Plato, or by any earlier writer of standing, and, like Moses, appeared originally, and only, in the Bible. It is extraordinary that the Jewish nation, over whom the mighty Solomon had reigned in all his biblical glory, and with a magnificence scarcely equaled by the greatest monarchs, spending nearly 'eight thousand millions' (1 Kings, 8-10) of gold on a Temple, was overlooked by historians. Not only with Solomon, but there were no proofs of the twelve tribes of Israel having ever existed, and Herodotus, the earliest and most accurate of historians, never mentioned the Israelites at all.

The best-informed Masonic writers agreed that the biblical description of Solomon's Temple is 'veiled in allegory and clothed in symbols' being, maybe, a fanciful description to hide the fact that the Bible writers were talking secretly about a real Temple at Giza. New Testament writers also knew that the Old Testament stories were not historical but allegorical, having symbolic meaning only (Gal. 4:24).

Bacon learnt many truths from his initiation into the Order of the Knights Templar and coded his understanding into Psalm 46 of the Old Testament, the Gospels, and the Shakespearean Folio of 1623. It is difficult to approach any phase of his life without being confronted with what appears to be evidence of careful preparation to reveal, yet conceal, secret information. That observation does not result from imagination or prejudice. Much of his coding was centred directly on his personal cipher number, being intentional and having a cryptic meaning that concealed specific information he wanted discovered later.

Hidden in the Shakespearean Folio of 1623, in Bacon's favorite cipher system, is found thirty-three consecutive letters on page 330 (the zeros being irrelevant in ciphers, for the primary number is harmonic) that spell out: TEMPLE OF SOLOMON HIDDEN UNDER PYRAMID. That information provided the first of three clues to the history and whereabouts of the celebrated golden Temple and the full story was revealed in *The Secret in the Bible*. Directly associated with the Temple of Solomon, and also found in thirty-three consecutive letters (on page 33) are the words, JESUS CHRIST, INITIATION, GREAT PYRAMID.

The clues continue. In 'Hamlet', for example, the page numbered 100 has been omitted, 257 follows 156 and other errors are clear, obviously made in order to deliberately obtain a particular result on the last page. One could go on, but the most startling example of 'Bacon's Code' affecting the current work is found on page 111 of the Shakespeare Folio 1623. The ingenuity displayed in the manipulation of words and numbers to create this cipher is almost beyond belief. The thirty-three letter coded message is intentional, having a cryptic meaning that concealed specific information that Bacon wanted discovered at a later time. It says: JESUS CHRIST STONED DEATH LUNDUNABORG.

The fact that the name Jesus Christ is found secreted into the Shakespearean writings is not the only amazing thing about the coding of Bacon. Other examples are found in the Old Testament, that he began editing upon his appointment as Solicitor-General in 1607, and an example is found in Psalm 46. By counting 46 words from the beginning until arriving at the word, 'Shake', and then by counting 46 words from the end, the word found in that position is 'spear'. There are 111 words between Shake and Spear, which was the numerical signature of 'Bacon' by the method numerologists call, the 'K Count'. 'Shake-speare' Bacon was 46 years of age when he structured in this cipher and the year was 1607.

During the months of work involved in unraveling Bacon's ciphers, this enigmatic thirty-three-letter statement was uncovered: THE PLACE OF THE SKULL WAS THE HOME OF GOD. At the time, it was taken to be associated with Mystery School initiations for the 'place of the skull' is a reference to the symbolic display of a skull near the end of an initiation. However, the material supplied by the Cumbrian monastery places a new perspective on this phrase, and its importance is addressed in a later chapter.

Bacon's coding is centred directly on the number thirty-three and other examples are found in the SHAKESPEARE FOLIO OF 1623, THIRTY-THREE that he 'Dedicated' to 'The Pair of Brethren' (Mary's twins?). The vital clue is the thirty-three letters making up this sequential coded statement, and that points the enquirer directly to page thirty-three. When unraveling 'Bacon's Code' in this Folio, it is almost impossible to comprehend what can be found, but this sentence is there for all to see: CONSTANTINE WROTE THE NEW TESTIMONIES. Again, hidden in Bacon's cipher system is another thirty-three-letter message that spells out, RABBI JESUS AND JUDAS THOMAS WERE TWINS. Just as importantly, and in the usual thirty-three successive letters, this cipher is found: MARCELLIAN, MARCUS WERE JUDAS AND JESUS.

These statements provide valuable clues that help unravel the New Testament, but this cryptogram is also found, and it unlocks previously unknown information about the Christian religion: MAGDALENE'S CASTLE LOCATION SEGONTIUM. This cipher provides the essence for a new book that introduces stunning information about the development of the New Testament that has never before been revealed.

CHAPTER 29

Twins in a French church

The suggestion that Jesus was one of two identical twins was again supported by the discovery of four antique parchments in an old church in the hilltop village of Rennes-le-Chateau, in Southern France. There, around 1886, the parish priest Berenger Sauniere, uncovered the concealed scrolls while removing the altar stone during restoration.

At the time of their discovery it was said that the parchments were of immense importance and contained 'incontrovertible proof' that the crucifixion was a fraud and Jesus was alive as late as 45 (*The Holy Blood and the Holy Grail,* Michael Baigent, Richard Leigh and Henry Lincoln, Corgi Books, 1990). Written in Latin, two of the texts were rumoured to be genealogies of the messianic family attached to coded excerpts from the New Testament (Matt. 12:1-8, Mark 2:23-28, Luke 6:1-5 and John 12:1-11). The most damaging information, however, may have simply been a record of the existence of Jesus' twin brother Judas Thomas, and Sauniere's scrolls may have similar in content to the FIRST English-language Vulgate in this author's possession.

Sauniere later travelled to the church of St Sulpice in Paris and surrendered the parchments to an unknown party. At that time, he seemed to have been introduced into esoteric circles and subsequently returned to Rennes-le-Chateau with three paintings, one being of Pope Celestine V. From that time on, Sauniere received an unending supply of funds until his death and spent large sums of money, much more than his income as a priest allowed (*The Holy Blood and the Holy Grail,* Michael Baigent, Richard Leigh and Henry Lincoln, Corgi Books, 1990). Some of it he used to continue the renovation work in and around his church. About this time Sauniere and his housekeeper, Marie Denarnaud, started to dig in a nearby cemetery at night. The local villagers were so concerned they lodged an official complaint in writing with their mayor. Sauniere destroyed an ancient tomb and defaced its headstone that was, for nearly 100 years, the last resting place of a certain Marie Negre Dables Dame de Hautpoul. He was searching for something, and some say he was looking for the mortal remains of Jesus Christ. Others think that he was treasure-hunting for one of the gold-hoards believed hidden in the region and maybe once belonging to the Knights Templar, the Cathars, or the Visigoths who all once occupied the area at one stage (*The True Language of Rennes-le-Chateau*, by M.G.E.H. Neyman, Belgique, Books on CD-Rom).

Whatever secret he knew, he left behind an intricate and elaborate system of clues including veiled references to Mary Magdalene. He built a luxurious villa named Bethanie and in 1902 started a four year construction project to build a tower he called Magdala (named after Mary of Magdala?). He also had carved an enigmatic bas-relief of Mary of Magdala and a statue of the demon Asmodeus supporting the holy-water font. These items are in the church today. For some reason, he chiseled a cross into a stone pillar and then erected it upside down (*The Horse of God*, by M.G.E.H. Neyman, Belgique, Books on CD-Rom).

For inside the restored church, Sauniere commissioned special decorative plaques and statues to be created, each characterised by some odd, but subtle contradiction of the church presentation of the birth and death of Jesus Christ. One decoration portrays a body being carried from a tomb in a night-time scene with a full moon in the background. Another depicts a person in kilts watching the crucifixion, and a human skull resting at the feet of Mary Magdalene. Two statues of Mary and Joseph stand each side of the altar, each holding an identical baby boy, twins, as recorded in the canonical Gospels, the Gospel of Thomas, the Acts of Thomas, the Book of Thomas, Renaissance paintings, and the ciphered writings of Sir Francis Bacon.

BOOK THREE

THE COVER-UP

CHAPTER 30

The Alexandrian scrolls

During the research for this book, a British Professor of Theology made contact claiming that he had incontrovertible documentary evidence that Christianity was unknown in its present form until 1439 and was created shortly after Cosimo de' Medici (1389-1464) obtained a collection of scrolls from Alexandria and Constantinople. The Professor contends that the presbyter's manuscripts, and earlier church councils, were originally dedicated to Mithraism, having nothing to do with Jesus Christ, and the now-called popes were the Mithraic fathers of Rome. The few presbyterial writings that survived, he claims, were totally restructured under papal orders around that time, and contain unhistorical interpolations, a fact confessed by the church and revealed later in this section. His opinion is supported in a book called *Antioch, the Mithraic City,* which aroused the church to hostile activity when it was published in 1921. Written by Rev. Leonard B. Ralston, it argued that Christianity grew out of Mithraism, which was centred at Antioch, a city that is repeatedly recorded in Christian texts to have played a major role in the development of the early church. In the upcoming chapters, the Professor's comments should be seriously considered, for there is substantial and growing evidence to support his view, and the existence of a church cover-up of sensitive information adds to his opinion.

Cosimo de' Medici spent a large part of his considerable fortune collecting classic texts, so that the most costly cargoes of his ships were in many cases manuscripts gathered from various parts of the world. He engaged forty-five copyists, under the guidance of the enthusiastic bookseller Vespasiano da Bisticci, to transcribe such manuscripts as could not be bought.

All these 'precious minims' he placed in rooms at the monastery of San Marco, in the abbey of Fiesole, or in his own library. When his friend Niccolo de' Niccoli died (1437), leaving eight hundred additional manuscripts to Cosimo, he divided the collection between San Marco's library and his own.

Upon Cosimo's death, the collection passed to his son, Lorenzo de' Medici (1449-1492) who was known as Lorenzo the Magnificent. He was the father of Giovanni de' Medici who became Pope Leo X in 1513, and an earlier chapter revealed Leo's role in editing the writings of Roman historian, Tacitus. Lorenzo had sedulously supervised Leo in his education and addressed him as 'beloved in Plato' and he burned candles before a bust of Plato, and adored him as a saint (*Machiavelli*, Villari, I, 132). It was probably knowledge derived from the manuscripts in the powerful de' Medici family that encouraged Leo, as Pope, to endorse Jesus Christ as a 'fable'.

In 1489, Lorenzo the Magnificent invited Michelangelo to study sculpture in the Medici Garden among the collections recently installed there under the supervision of sculptor, Bertoldo di' Giovanni, a pupil of Donatello. The young Michelangelo, then fifteen years old, moved into the Palazzo de' Medici where he lived for two years (1490-1492). During that time, he met the circle of friends who surrounded the Magnificent ... Poliziano, Ficino, Benivieni, Landino and Pico. It was then that he created his first marble relief, the Virgin of the Stairs, showing Mary with twin boys.

CHAPTER 31

A deliberate attempt by the church to avoid detection

While it is far from easy for the church to explain why great artists created twin boys in their works, it is fairly easy to explain why the knowledge was later suppressed. The church knew that Jesus had a twin brother and, during the Reformation, took extraordinary steps to conceal the truth of its origins.

In May 1536, Pope Paul III (Alessandro Farnese, 1468-1549) published a bull of convocation for a proposed church council to be held in Mantua, northern Italy. Because unrestrained behavior and extremes of papal power fostered waves of distrust and suspicion throughout Europe, he authorised a select group of cardinals to draw up a report on the predicament and problems of the church (*Lignum vitae*, later called, *Catholic History*, Dom Arnold Wion, a Benedictine historian, 1596). Guided by Cardinal Gasparo Contarini, this group subsequently denounced the selection of incompetent bishops, the accumulation of benefices, doctrinal conflicts, the decadence of religious orders, the deficient state of the New Testament, and expressed concern about internal conflicts developing amongst the priesthood who were demanding papal clarification on the 'two natures of Christ'.

© Antonio F. Buttazoni, 1978

Pope Paul III on a medallion in the coin collection of the Vatican Library.

The report, however, fell into Protestant hands and was used by Martin Luther (1483 1546) in a violent attack on the papacy and its ever-changing code of belief. Despite charges of paganism leveled at his pontificate for its worldly extravagances ... with clairvoyants admitted to the papal court as consultants ... Pope Paul was determined to conduct a council, scheduled to open on May 23, 1537, at Mantua. However, there was violent opposition to his plans, for the changes he intended to make to priesthood privileges were unacceptable to the Curia and their powerful families. Cardinals, bishops, and priests prorogued and postponed the council's opening again and again over the course of the ensuing nine years. Finally, after the death of some of the major opponents, the pope succeeded in having it inaugurated by his legate, Cardinal Giovanni del Monte, in Trent on Dec. 13, 1545.

The true purpose of the Council of Trent

The Council of Trent's overall objective was to legislate for a thorough reform of Catholicism in answer to the challenge of the Protestant Reformation, accurse and condemn all doctrines proposed by their opponents, and quash its critics. In its early sessions, precedence was given to establishing official recognition and legalization of the church's texts. Jerome's *Versio Vulgar*, or 'verses for the vulgar' was renamed the Vulgate from *Editio Vulgata*, meaning 'common version' (*Verses for the Vulgar,* Chapter vii, *Genesis of Christianity,* Plummer, Edinburgh, 1876; also; *History of the Vulgate,* S. Berger, 1893), and the following decree was then couched:

> Now, if anyone reading these books (the Vulgate) in all their parts ... does not hold them for sacred and canonical and does industriously condemn them, let him be anathema.

Their curse effectively forbade any individual opinion on the authenticity of the New Testament and, from that time forward, criticism or private judgment was viewed as an act of heresy. In this particular sitting of four sessions there were thirty churchmen 'among whom there was not one distinguished for historical learning' (*On the Canon of the Bible*, Dr. B. F. Westcott, 474, 446), and by introducing fear and dread into the minds of people, they effectively concealed the essence of the truth of the origin and fabrications of the texts.

Pope Paul III then declared to the assembled delegates that the Latin Vulgate was, 'adequate for the proofs of Christianity' and imposed his opinion as obligatory on the entire priesthood. He supported the Damnation Decree originally established at the Council of Toledo in 632, and adopted a newer 'fatal decree' (*On the Canon of the Bible*, Dr. B.F. Westcott, Ms. 489) declaring once again 'everlasting punishment in a lake of fire as penalty for non-belief in dogmas taught from the New Testament' (Session 4, Council of Trent). Because the church claimed that the Bible was 'the word of God', Christians doubtless regard the testimony as true, but the church is a body of theologians, not historians, and the discovery of the FIRST English-language Vulgate shows that they falsely present the origin of the canonical writings.

On 8th April 1546, the fourth sitting of the Council then pronounced the Vulgate 'the only authentic text' and arranged for the preparation of a 'standard' version from the Latin variants then in circulation. In church terms, 'authentic' means that believers can be sure that the Vulgate is free from doctrinal and moral error and substantially faithful to the earliest versions available. The Council delegates pledged that 'the manuscripts of the Fathers were the Oracles of God, unanimous and infallible, handed over to the church and stamped with her Imprimatur'. Gospel 'wonders' reputed as having occurred long before their times, the foundation of the church, and the 'miraculous fundamentals' of the Christian religion rested solely upon the restructured writings of the earlier presbyters whose public prominence was retrospectively elevated to lofty heights by later church decrees.

Pope Paul died in 1549 and after a ten-year period without a pope, Giovanni Angelo De' Medici was elected on December 25th 1559 as Pius IV. He took over control of the Council of Trent and immediately clarified another doctrine that declared that no matter if the genuineness of the Christian texts had been challenged or disputed by earlier councils, the fact that later councils had since accepted them made it wrong for any person, Christian or otherwise, to dispute their authenticity.

The Vulgate then again received official church blessing when the Council declared that the 'received manuscripts and all their substantial portions to be sacred and canonical' and since then Christians have not been permitted to question the inspiration of those writings (*Catholic Encyclopedia*, iii, 274). The Council then defined the Vulgate as official to the church and Catholics are obliged to 'believe whatsoever the Church teaches from it which shall be called an Act of Faith' (Ibid). But faith is not knowledge.

After 18 years of deliberations fraught with religious disputes resulting in a new Catholic belief officially termed the 'New Learning' (*Catholic Encyclopedia*, Vol., v, Pg. 442; and *Catholic Encyclopedia,* Vol. Xv, Pg. 376) the Council of Trent closed in December 1563, making it the longest ecclesiastical meeting held in the history of the world. Just three months prior to its completion the FIRST English-language Vulgate was printed, and it reveals the effect of church decisions that expunged vital sections about Jesus and his 'double' from newer printings of the Catholic Bible.

The Creed of Pope Pius IV

In his Bull, *Benedictus Deus* of January 26th 1564, Pope Pius IV confirmed the decrees of the council, thus making them official to the church. But the importance of public acceptance of the Vulgate was paramount for the development of Catholicism and the next eleven months were spent in developing a Creed in an attempt to convince the world that the Vulgate was indeed the word of God. A Creed was a personally recited summary of religious dogma prepared by theological authority, and was originally developed for the defense of Christianity against opponents. It took the form of binding by a declaratory or promissory oath usually commencing with the words, 'I believe', or, 'We believe', intended to increase the solemnity and reverence of the act, with the affirmation resting solely on faith.

Perhaps in no other papal pronouncement is found the extraordinary method by which a pope contrived to authenticate the church's texts than that defined in *The Creed and Oath of Pope Pius IV, bearing the date November 1564.* The Creed was forced onto the whole church and since that time it has been promoted in every part of the Christian world as an accurate and explicit summary of the Roman Catholic faith. A papal Bull made it 'binding upon all Clergymen, Doctors, Teachers, heads of universities and of monastic institutions and military orders, with all reconciled converts' and the 'profession of this Creed, under the solemn sanction of an oath, is obligatory on the whole body of the Roman church' (*The Creed and Oath of Pope Pius IV, bearing the date November 1564).* The Creed became a church instrument for legalizing and maintaining a body of writings originally won by fraud and forgery.

The following passages are extracted from Dr. Charles Butler's translation of the original Latin version, and relate to part of the Creed associated with the New Testament (*Book of the Roman Catholic Church*, Charles Butler, London, 1825). To overcome the known falsifications of its texts, Pope Pius IV swore upon an oath, and declared on behalf of the church that:

> (Part 1) The original Scriptures, Hebrew and Greek, are of no authority in the Church of Rome: for they are omitted in the decree, and a translation is submitted.

> (Part 3) The Latin Vulgate is put in the place of the originals, and is authorized as authentic in all churches, sermons, expositions, public lectures, and disputations.

> (Part 5) Tradition, both written and unwritten, is added to the Vulgate, and made of equal authority with the Vulgate.

> (Part 6) The Church, that is, the Clergy, are the only interpreters of Scripture, tradition, and the Vulgate.

The central part of this Creed is the movement to 'tradition', and making it of equal authority to the Vulgate. That is to say, the church, being unable to trust its written words, resorted to the concept of the delivery of oral information from the past to give it protection when the New Testament is revealed for what it really is. Unfortunately, the case is not conclusive either way, for church tradition stemmed directly from the New Testament itself, and that came into being when Emperor Constantine amalgamated the names of Rabbi Jesus and Judas Khrestus, and instructed Gospels to be written combining their lives.

Pope Pius concluded his Creed with the words, 'I promise, vow, and swear … that the Scriptures are authentic and the rule and only rule of faith and practice … these include the holy Gospels of God … when the Roman Catholic speaks of Scripture, he does not mean the Hebrew and Greek of the Old and New Testaments, but the Latin Vulgate edition only'. The pope declared that those writings were 'a safe guide in the way of salvation, notwithstanding the numerous objections raised against them', and to disbelieve the priesthood's presentation of the Vulgate was 'to risk one's salvation' (Pope Pius IV).

The pope then again confirmed the Decrees of the Council of Trent and issued another Bull to the effect that authorized burning at the stake the penalty for any person disbelieving the church's presentation of its texts. This kind of trickery and pretense became an important ingredient in the church's maintenance of the deception that led to millions of people being deceived, for twenty-four years later, a new version of the Vulgate was written, and Catholic belief changed again.

An anomaly in the records of a French monk

The Roman church consistently claimed that only the Latin version of the Vulgate was official to Catholicism. They denied the earlier Hebrew and Greek New Testaments, and replaced them with a later Latin translation compiled by Jerome. The reason for this is clear ... Jerome confessed to introducing 'peculiar additions' into his Latin Vulgate that derived from a collection of narratives given to him by Pope Damasus ... they included the virgin birth and resurrection stories (*Adversus Helvidium* (PL 23: 201). In summary, Jerome introduced fictitious narratives into his Vulgate that were not part of earlier versions of the Hebrew and Greek Bibles, and the Roman church supported the fabrications.

That raises the important question as to when the oldest Greek New Testaments available today were really written, and a case exists to challenge the church dating of these Bibles. In the first year of the papacy of Pope Alexander VI (1492), a French monk, criticizing the Christian clergy, recorded this intriguing statement:

> They have now found out a new language called Greek; we must carefully guard ourselves against it. That language will be the mother of all sorts of heresies. I see in the hands of a number of priests a book written in this language called 'The New Testament'; it is a book full of brambles, with vipers

in them. As to the Hebrew, whoever learns that becomes a Jew at once. (*History Des Francaise*, XVI, 364, Sismondis)

The implication is that the Roman church had Greek versions of its writings at the end of the 15th Century and comparisons reveal that they differed considerably in content from Latin versions. The oldest Greek Bible known today is called the Sinaiticus (the Sinai Bible) and is displayed in the British Library in London. That Bible's version of the first Gospel written, Mark, starts its story of Jesus at the time he was baptized, 'at about the age of thirty' and makes no reference to Mary, a virgin birth, or the now-called Old Testament 'messianic prophecies'. Words describing Jesus as 'the son of God' do not appear in the opening narrative (Mark 1:1) as they do in modern Bibles, and the family tree tracing a 'messianic bloodline' back to King David is non-existent.

The Sinai Bible carries a different version of events surrounding the 'raising of Lazarus' and reveals an extraordinary omission that later became the central doctrine of Christian faith … the resurrection appearances of Jesus Christ and his subsequent ascension into heaven. The church claims that 'the resurrection is the fundamental argument for our Christian belief' (*Catholic Encyclopedia,* Vol. X11, Oct 1, 1911, Pg. 792), yet no supernatural appearance of a resurrected Jesus Christ or reference to ascension was ever recorded in the earliest Christian Gospel.

The resurrection and ascension of Jesus Christ is the 'sine qua non' of Christianity, 'without which, nothing' (*Catholic Encyclopedia,* Vol. X11, Oct. 1, 1911, Pg. 792). Apostle Paul agreed, saying, 'if Christ has not been raised, your faith is in vain' (1 Cor. 5:17), and the Pope knew that Paul was right. Subsequently the Roman church adopted Jerome's Latin Vulgate and his forged additions became official to the church. Pope Pius IV then issued his Bull and a Creed denouncing all other versions of the Bible as 'demonic' (*Book of the Roman Catholic Church*, Charles Butler, London, 1825).

CHAPTER 32

Why Pope Sixtus rewrote the Vulgate

The church establishes a publishing house

Formerly a swineherd and Inquisitor General, Felice Peretti (1521-1590) was elected Pope Sixtus V on April 24, 1585. In 1587, he established an official Vatican publishing press, and we catch the spirit of the times when we read the Pope's own words recorded in *Diderot's Encyclopedia*:

> The press will combat the deceit of heretics and the malice and ignorance of printers and publishers, and literature that has been the cause of much evil to us. Authors are everywhere, and they are worse than their own writings, which I don't mean as a compliment to either ... they must be interpreted into harmlessness.

> We shall seek to print our own account, a logical analysis of the books which deserve to hold the attention of the public. Church history will be established and will be a considerable part of our report. In general, we shall let nothing escape us, which is worthy of the curiosity of people.

Fraud is just plain fraud

In April 1588, the Pope put into motion one of the most infamous papal deceits in Christian history ... he rewrote the Vulgate, and, along with creating yet another Catholic belief (another 'New Learning', see previous chapter), covered up the biblical evidence of Jesus' twin brother. It was a strange feat of literary dishonesty and proof of its execution is found in the church's own records. After issuing a Bull declaring that he was the only appropriate person to provide a 'proper' Bible for the Roman church, Sixtus took up the task to rewrite all biblical texts official to the church. He claimed that the New Testament was without a god, saying:

> In the Gospel and the whole of Holy Scripture, there is not one word of Christ spoken of as god. Therefore, by the fullness of apostolic power within me it must be amended as to be unquestioned by the upper ten thousand, and in all public and private discussions.

Sixtus revealed a problem with the Christian texts that had plagued the church for centuries, for early tradition preserved no trace of Jesus being called 'God'. In 312, scribes being trained in the school of Lucian of Antioch noticed the fact that the presbyterial writings later used by Eusebius did not know of Jesus Christ or of him being called God (*Encyclopedia of Early Christianity,* Everett and Ferguson, Lucian of Antioch). The Editorial Committee of the *Catholic Encyclopedias* admit that the Gospel references to Jesus being called God are later glosses to earlier writings:

> The few instances of the use of God as a title for Jesus came from the later New Testament writings.

Those 'few instances' are only two, and they are found in the Gospel of John (20:28) and the Epistle to the Hebrews (1:8).

Excluding the problems with translations and interpretations of verse 1: 8, the entire Epistle to the Hebrews was established as a Third Century forgery under the name of Paul (*The Ante Nicene Library*, A collection of all the works of the early churchmen prior to the Council of Nicaea. Edited by the Rev. Professor Roberts, D.D, and Principal James Donaldson, L.L.D, St. Andrews, 24 Vols. circa 1900). Hippolytus (170-236) said it was compiled well after Irenaeus' death in 202 and Amphilochius, Bishop of Iconium (365), wrote that 'all four versions of the Epistle to the Hebrews are spurious' *(Iambi Ad. Seleucum).* While one version appears in the Bible today, in early centuries it was moved in and out of various canons solely upon the whims of individual churchmen.

The Gospel of John (20:28) reference to Judas Thomas saying, 'My Lord and my God' is of no relevance either for it is mentioned in a verse in which Jesus is made to appear to Thomas in resurrection. The church admits that those resurrection descriptions are fictional narratives which …

> ... may be explained as a deliberate alteration of details for theological purposes or else as an invention. (*New Catholic Encyclopedia*, Gospel of John, Pg. 1080 onwards)

There is no reference to the use of God as a title for Jesus in any New Testaments preceding the 16th Century, and its application from that time on was a gloss introduced by Pope Sixtus V. Professor John Knox of the Union Theological Seminary, whose standing as an authority is certified by the fact that he was chosen to edit the technical sections of the New Testament in the monumental Interpreter's Bible, confirms this knowledge, saying:

> There is no evidence that Jesus was called 'God' in the first centuries, and indisputable evidence that he was not generally called by that name.

On the most rational grounds, therefore, we may be confident that the church's presentation of the existence of a divine Jesus Christ in the First Century is untrue.

Penned by the church

Sixtus set to and personally rewrote both the Old and New Testaments in his own hand. For eighteen months he laboured night and day, imposing his personal theological views and 'adding new concepts and sentences to his liking' (Cardinal Robert Bellarmine, the Pope's Jesuit adviser). He passed days and nights in a continued frenzy, for he was insomniac. He lay with his eyes open, without speaking, eating or stirring. He was obsessed with his new creation and blatantly ignored the advise of his Jesuit consultant, Cardinal Robert Bellarmine, that the changes to church belief were 'inadvisable and difficult to understand'. The Pope created a new version of the Jesus Christ story that later caused even pious churchmen to lie on its behalf.

Strangely enough, Sixtus's new Vulgate was not sourced from Jerome's Fourth Century version, for the Gospels he referenced were from a corrupted medieval text (*Encyclopedia Britannica*, 9th Ed. Vol. 13, Pg. 631). Sceptics laughed at his professions of the then accepted Christian orthodoxy and at his literal interpretation of Genesis. One prior at an abbey in Rome sent Sixtus a note saying:

> I have received, Holy Father, your new Bible against the human race. I thank you for it. In reading your work one is seized with a desire to walk on four paws.

In 1988, Roman Catholic scholar, Peter de Rosa, published a powerful book called *Vicars of Christ*, and added this comment:

> A Bible had been imposed with the plenitude of papal power, complete with the trimmings of excommunication, on the whole church … and it was riddled with errors. The academic world was in turmoil. Protestants were deriving much pleasure and amusement from the predicament of the Roman church. *Vicars of Christ*, Peter de Rosa, Crown Publishers, New York, 1988

The Pope then issued a command that no printer, editor, or bookseller was to deviate by one jot from his new Vulgate. Anyone contravening the Bull was to be excommunicated, and only the pope could absolve him.

The harassed printers cautioned Sixtus to suppress the knowledge of the forging of church texts, saying, 'that the pope and his cardinals should be protected from exposure' (*Annales Ecclesiastici,* Cardinal Caesar Baronius). The Sixtine Vulgate Bible, as it became known, was subsequently printed and issued along with another papal Bull threatening excommunication for violations of the commands that variant readings should not be printed in subsequent editions, and that the edition must not be modified. This Bull demanded that the new Bible 'be received and held as true, lawful, authentic and unquestioned in all public and private discussions, readings, preaching and explanations'. Sixtus's own words raises serious ethical and political questions about the propriety of deception by a church leader. A false new born-again religion had been created, and perhaps Catholicism survived by absorbing it.

Sixtus' Bull was subsequently ignored, for in 1592, Pope Clement VIII (1592-1605) pronounced the Sixtine Vulgate Bible 'untrue', and 'appointed scholars called *correctores* to amend the Gospels in the interest of what he considered orthodox' (*Annales Ecclesiastici,* Cardinal Caesar Baronius). He added this extraordinary comment:

> The Bible published in vulgar tongues ought not be read or retained. Perhaps

it had been better for the church if no scriptures had been written. An ideal state of the texts never existed and probably never will. (*History of the Vulgate; History of the Council of Trent,* Paolo Sarpi, Translated by Brent, London, 1676; also, *Ecclesiastical History*, Mosheim, Book 6, London, 1825)

The Pope publicly admits to disbelief in Jerome's *Versio Vulgar*, doubts the divine inspiration of the church's texts, and the authenticity of the Gospels. In this statement we see artificiality in the modern-day presentation of the New Testament, and note that the church promotes it as the very words of God.

The destruction of the evidence

For Clement, one problem remained … how to get back copies of Sixtus' Bible that had already been distributed. Instructions went out to the Inquisition in Venice and to the Jesuit General to search printing houses and private homes and buy back every copy of the Sixtus Vulgate they could find. Clement called upon his priests to burn all copies found in churches and monasteries, but not every version was destroyed. In 1611, Dr Thomas James found a copy of Sixtus' Vulgate in the Bodleian Library in Oxford and wrote a book contrasting it with the new edition published by Clement VIII. He observed:

> The two popes did notoriously differ amongst themselves, not only in the number of verses, but also in the story itself, and in the Prefaces and Bulls. Are the popes that write and circulate these legends worthy of trust, for each Bible is different to the point of absurdity? They cannot believe them themselves, and they write and propagate them for the very reasons that Xavier wrote a special New Testament to suit the Emperor Agbad.
>
> Permit me to ask whether these legends form the best religious literature for the people of the Roman church, for will not the people that believe these things, believe anything? That Roman bishops believe this religion of legends themselves is impossible; but maybe their stories overwhelm the ignorant and foster superstitions.

But the papal deceit did not stop by recalling Sixtus' Vulgate. Pope Clement

VIII then issued instructions for a new 'authentic' Clementine Vulgate to be written with 'Sixtus' passages retranslated in order to support the peculiar dogmas of the church of Rome' (*The History of Popery,* Vol. 2, London, 1735). Cardinal il Vecchio (d. 1608) wrote that Clement and Robert Bellarmine added to Sixtus' interpolations, mixing 'religion with fiction'. At that time, the Pope said in his own name, 'There are no miracles in the Gospels which we can take literally without abandoning good sense. Who will venture to tell me how many eyewitnesses are required to make a miracle credible?' (*Diderot's Encyclopedia*, 1759).

On behalf of all Roman Catholics, Clement VIII subsequently issued another version of the Vulgate 'with some 3000 corrections' (*Oxford Dictionary of the Christian Church,* 1997 Cross, Pg. 1710), and forbade any questioning of the new updated edition by Papal Decree. Clement then declared that 'no person shall speak against the authentic version' and any layperson found with a Vulgate was to be sent to the galleys for life. It was that same pope, Clement VIII, who burned Giordino Bruno (1548-1600) at the stake.

With the origin of the New Testament unimportant, the church declared that even though 'it need not be denied that the Bible is perverted' (*Annales Ecclesiastici*, tome vi, Fol. Antwerp, 1597, Cardinal Caesar Baronius) it was its sole source of authority and the constant threat of an awful death for denying church dictates hung heavily upon people's shoulders.

The Vulgate denounced 'untrue' by Pope

The fabrication of the Vulgate did not stop there. 1n 1749 a succession of reports arrived across Europe saying that the Vulgate was again to be rewritten, and it was. Then, under papal command, it was restructured again in 1750, 1752, 1764 and 1772. Again the Vulgate, which was denounced as untrue by the church itself (Pope Clement VIII (1592-1605), *Religion of the Romans*, New York ed. 1826, Adams (on Cardinal il Vecchio)), was given sanction of divinity by Pope Pius IX (1792-1878) at the first Vatican Council I (1869-70), under the Curse of God against anyone who questioned its authenticity.

The European circulation of the Bible depended entirely on the church of Rome and was strictly controlled until the story it contained was fine-tuned. In defending itself from criticism associated with on-going reconstruction of the Vulgate, the priesthood that made up the Vatican Council I of 1869, caused to be published this solemn statement of disinformation:

> The church holds them (the books of the Latin Vulgate) as sacred and canonical, not because having been composed by human industry alone, they were afterwards approved by her authority; nor only because they contain revelation without error but because having been written under the inspiration of the Holy Spirit, they have God as their author, and as such, have been handed over to the church.

There were more changes yet to come, and they were of a significant nature. The clerical trick of tampering with the 'Word of God', and amending its plenary Divine Inspiration and Inerrancy, went into the 20th Century, even to the extent of putting a veneer of civilization on the barbarian Hebrew God and warping his words so as to make a semblance of a 'God of Mercy' out of the self-confessed 'jealous God' of Holy Writ. In 1902, Pope Leo XIII appointed a Commission of Cardinals, known as the Pontifical Biblical Commission, to further amend the Vulgate. In 1907, 'the Commission, with the approval of the sovereign pontiff, invited the Benedictine Order to undertake a collection of the variant readings of the Latin Vulgate as a remote preparation for a thoroughly amended edition' (*Catholic Encyclopedia*, ii, 557).

Then, 23 years later, Associated Press dispatches published to the world the news that 'the Vatican's International Commission on the revision of the Bible was taking steps to correct one of the most famous biblical passages, Exodus 20: 5, now believed to have been 'mistranslated' (*New York Times*, May 18, 1930). The actual text, and what the Vatican Commission thought it should read, is quoted here so that all may judge the extent of the falsification. Exodus 20: 5, originally said:

> For I the Lord thy God am a jealous God, visiting the iniquities of the fathers upon the children unto the third and fourth generation of them that hate me.

Ditto, as falsified by the Vatican Commission:

> For I, the Lord thy God, am a God of loving-kindness and mercy, considering the errors of the fathers as mitigating circumstances in judging the children unto the third and fourth generation.

No set of words, humanly or divinely devisable, could bear such enormity of contrary translation as Vatican re-interpretation of its texts. Even present translations into modern languages made apparent the correctness of the familiar or original rendering, and the Protestant church decided to retain the original statement in its version of the Bible.

No papal opposition to rewriting the Vulgate

Ninety-six years after Vatican Council 1, the church contradicted the earlier Council declaration that said that the Bible was 'without error'. An announcement carried in the Vatican's official newspaper, the 'L'Osservatore Romano' on December 1st, 1965, listed the names of persons appointed by Pope Paul VI to a special commission charged with 'the revision of the Vulgate ... that would bring corrections to such passages in the Vulgate text as may be found to be unfaithful to the original'. From 1969 to 1977, the commission, under Cardinal Augustinus Bea of Germany, prepared a new translation of the Vulgate in Latin ... one that the majority of the public could not read.

Not one pope for over fifteen centuries opposed rewriting the Vulgate and this recorded fact reveals a hostile literary tradition associated with the descent of Christian texts. If the Vatican priesthood is genuinely serious about correcting the Vulgate, they need only go downstairs into the subterranean vaults and retrieve the first edition, for in 1925, Edmond Szekely, studying in the Vatican archives, recorded that the original manuscripts of Jerome, believed lost in the Fifth Century, had survived, and 'a copy called the Amiatino Gospel' exists in the church's Secret Archives (*The Lost Scrolls of the Essene Brotherhood*, E. B. Szekely, International Biogenic Society, 1989 Edition).

In drawing the arguments in this chapter to a close, it is important to address a serious question ... what did Constantine's Seraglio Bible of 325 say about the twinship of Jesus, and what was in Jerome's Amiatino Gospel (*Versio Vulgar*) written some 90 years later? In analyzing the descent of the *Versio Vulgar* through the centuries, it can be shown that references to Jesus' twin brother were gradually deleted and a papal cover-up later instituted to conceal the existence of that knowledge. However, the essence of the knowledge is carried in the FIRST Vulgate of 1563, and that exposes all modern versions of the Bible as forgeries.

CHAPTER 33

What was the church censoring?

The *Index of Prohibited Books*

Perhaps the most dramatic form of censorship known to the world was the *Index Librorum Prohibitorim* (*Index of Prohibited Books*), by which the Roman Catholic church for centuries policed the literature available to educated people. Compiled by official Vatican censors, the *Index* was a catalogue of forbidden reading which continued to have official church sanction well into the 20th Century. The decree of Pope Gelasius I about 496, which contained lists of recommended as well as banned books, has been described as the first Roman Index.

The re-establishment of the *Index* in 1501 by Pope Alexander VI was strengthened at the first period of the Council of Trent in 1546. More comprehensive rules were developed, and books and manuscripts were condemned under ten separate headings. Seven years later, a Congregation of the Index was set up in Rome that for centuries regularly issued catalogued lists of new editions of books forbidden by the church to be read. Thus, regulated reading was established, and hardly a classic escaped. Then, in 1559, Pope Pius IV drafted and issued a Bull instructing the Christian public to buy and burn any books that were named on the *Index*.

Generations of students, scholars, the general public, the faithful, bishops and cardinals too, were forbidden to read or own books listed on the Index on pain of excommunication. That fearful restriction kept truthful and important knowledge away from the mainstream general populace and restricted public access to truths that had survived. Printers and bookshops were at mortal risk of discovery by the Inquisition whose leaders were always vigilant for any sort of public theological impropriety.

Thus, books written challenging the history and validity of Christianity, never reached a mass-market audience and many valuable tomes were destroyed. However, in the larger centers, ecclesiastical surveillance could be evaded by dissident printers and publishers and there was a silent spread of suspicion in the intelligentsia, even in the clergy themselves ... for many, despite papal Bulls, were secret disbelievers, and read what was being published (*Confessions of a French Catholic Priest*, New York, Mathers, 1837).

The last edition of the *Index* appeared in 1948 and it contained the names of more than 4000 banned books and a similar number of authors. In 1966, Pope Paul VI finally discontinued the *Index* after more than four centuries and it was relegated to the status of an historical document. In January 1998, the Vatican opened the archives of the department once known as the Inquisition and at the same time revealed the infamous *Index*. The church then publicly admitted that the Bible was once on its own black list, being originally decreed banned by Pope Damasus at the First Council of Constantinople of 381-3.

The establishment of a church censoring office

On July 22nd, 1548, Nicholas, Archbishop of Westminster, published a book called *Out of the Flaminian Gate,* being a powerful attack upon the Catholic clergy and the development of the Roman church. It was distributed widely in Europe and the resultant furor led to a rising demand in the hierarchy of the Roman church for the suppression or editing of all writings critical of it existence. Archbishop Nicholas added another aspect to church dishonesty saying that 'the forging of whole Council records was deemed corrupting humour, and upon examination of the pages of ecclesiastical lore, one must first determine whether the volume is a genuine production or individual exertion'. The church itself admitted that the records of the council of 275 bishops under Pope Sylvester at Rome in 334 are entirely fictitious (*Catholic Encyclopedia*, ix, 225; xiv, 370-371: see also Bishop Jeremy Taylor's book, *Liberty*), revealing that all church council records must be viewed with grave suspicion.

The Council of Trent responded to the embarrassment caused by *Out of the Flaminian Gate,* and during the second period of 1552, a commission was established to set up an official censoring office exclusively for church use. A new building was allocated as its headquarters and the few papal censors then employed were increased to over eighty people (*De Antiqua Ecclesiae Disciplina*, Bishop Lewis Du Pin, Catholic historian (Folio, Paris, 1686), English translation by J. H. C. Hopkins, D.D.; also *Diderot's Encyclopedia*, 1759). Suppressing free thought had become more difficult after 1450 when books started pouring off the new printing presses, creating problems for the church and the presentation of its dogma. A new crisis had developed, for printing was the greatest aid to democracy the world had yet seen and, since 1471 when presses first came to Rome, books circulated in editions of a thousand or more copies.

By 1544, the censoring office was in full operation and the Inquisition was responsible for overseeing the department. In early editions of the *Catholic Encyclopedias*, the church freely discussed its roll in the development of its censoring department, saying that it was designed to assist in the 'perversion of the truth originating in publishing surreptitious or supposititious papal bulls, briefs and transcripts originating in the deceitfulness of some parties' (*Catholic Encyclopedia*, Vol. V, May 1, 1909, Pg. 781). That, and similar statements, were removed from later printings of church encyclopedias and those falsifications made Christianity what it is today.

Pope Alexander orders a cover-up

The first complete edition of the Talmud was published by Daniel Bomberg in Venice in 1490 and then ensued across Europe a great industry in printing Hebrew books. Some writers called it the 'Golden Age of the Talmud' but it was not to last. In order to cover-up conflicting references to the life of Rabbi Jesus, Pope Alexander VI ordered all copies of the Talmud destroyed and fierce persecution followed for the next seven decades. The Council of the Inquisition required as many Jewish writings as possible to burn, with the Spanish Grand Inquisitor, Tomas de Torquemada (1420-98), responsible for the elimination of 6000 volumes at Salamanca. He had previously burned over 2000 heretics at the stake after the Inquisition was revived in Spain in 1483.

In 1550, Cardinal Caraffa, the Inquisitor-General, procured a Bull from the Pope repealing all previous permission for priests to read or own the Talmud that he said contained 'hostile stories about Jesus Christ'. Bursting forth with fury at the head of his minions, he seized every copy he could find in Rome and burnt them. In Cremona, Vittorio Eliano bitterly testified against the Talmud, and 10,000 Hebrew books were burned under his rage. His brother, Solomon Romano (1554) also burnt thousands of Hebrew scrolls and in 1559, every Hebrew book in the city of Prague was confiscated.

The mass destruction of Jewish books included hundreds of copies of the Old Testament and caused the irretrievable loss of many original handwritten documents. The oldest text of the Old Testament that survived, before the discovery of the Dead Sea Scrolls, is believed to be the Bodleian Codex (Oxford), which is dated to circa 1100. In an attempt by the church to remove damaging rabbinic information about Jesus from the face of the earth, the Inquisition burnt at least 22,000 volumes of the Talmud.

© *Burning Bibles and other Jewish books shown in a 17th Century etching.*

With printing presses running night and day in hidden locations, it was not possible to destroy all Talmuds so the church then forced the Jews as co-religionists to submit it for editing. At that time it was committed to the mercies of Vatican censorship whereby every sentence that was thought to refer to Christianity was expunged:

> In the Basle edition (of 1578), which has remained the standard edition almost ever since, that amazing creature, the Censor stepped in. In his anxiety to protect the faith from all and every danger, for the Talmud was supposed to hide bitter things against Christianity under the most innocent words and phrases … this official did wonderful things. When, for example, he found some ancient Roman man in the book swearing by the Capitol or by Jupiter of Rome, the Censor's suspicious mind instantly misgave him. Surely this Roman must be a Christian, the Capitol the Vatican, Jupiter the Pope. And forthwith he struck out Rome and substituted any place he could think of. A favourite spot seems to have been Persia; sometimes it was Aram and Babel. So that this worthy Roman may be found unto this day swearing by the Capitol of Persia or by Jupiter of Aram and Babel. (*The Talmud in History*, G.R.S. Mead, B.A., M.R.A.S., London and Benares, 1903)

At the end of 1578, the Basle edition was then officially 'licensed' in conformity with earlier censorship decisions of the Council of Trent and was no longer considered 'wicked'. Knowing that people and place names in the Talmud were purposely garbled, a modern study of its contents in light of that knowledge may reveal an interesting unknown history, for its wide sense remains true until the present day.

Forgery in historical records

After the creation of the Vatican's publishing house by Pope Sixtus in 1587, all became possible. In 1595, Pope Clement VIII used the facility after issuing a Decree declaring that 'the writings of all Catholic authors since 1515 should now be corrected, so as not only to blot out doctrines not approved, but to add to where necessary' (*Delineation of Roman Catholicism,* Rev. Charles Elliott, D.D., pg. 89, 1844). Church history written during the previous 80 years was then falsified to match the altered belief and the ongoing restructuring of the Vulgate.

An order from the Inquisition

As was the case of the New Testament, so also were the more damaging writings of the early church fathers modified in centuries of copying, and many of their records were intentionally rewritten or suppressed. The term, 'church fathers, commonly applies to the church writers of the first six centuries' *(Encyclopedia of Early Christianity,* Everett Ferguson, 1990, 'The Ancient Fathers'), and many of their writings are almost unreadable. They are full of crass fallacies, ignorance, and limited credulity, and by stripping away the naivety behind their writings the documents become simply a series of curious passages 'full of the silliest superstitions' *(Church History,* Socrates Scholasticus (380-450) Jenning' Trans., 1911). The phrase 'church fathers' is a vague generalization only and does not elaborate on what those men really wrote in texts that are now authoritative to Christianity.

Adopting the decrees of the Council of Trent, the church subsequently extended the process of erasure and ordered the preparation of a special list of particular information to be expunged from original church writings *(Delineation of Roman Catholicism,* Rev. Charles Elliott, D.D., pg. 89). Among that information was any reference to Judas Khrestus and the twinship of Jesus and this is supportable by the fact that his name is now not found in any available church writings of the first four centuries.

A special censoring office called *Index Expurgatorius* was established in 1562 and its purpose was to suppress or prohibit publication of 'erroneous passages of the early church fathers' that carried statements opposing developing doctrine. When Vatican archivists came across 'genuine copies of the Fathers', they corrected them according to the *Expurgatory Index' (Index Expurgatorius Vaticanus,* Edited by R. Gibbings, B.A., Dublin, 1837. For a full and accurate account of the *Indices,* both *Expurgatory* and *Prohibitory,* the reader is referred to Rev. Mr. Mendham's work, *The Literary Policy of the Church of Rome,* Second Ed., 1840), and that official church directive provides grave doubts about the value of all patristic writings that have been released to the public.

WHAT WAS THE CHURCH CENSORING?

© Film Library of Renaissance Art, Italy

This is the Vatican Archives (circa 1482) 'drawn on the spot' by Cardinal Calandrini who later served Pope Innocent VIII (1484-1492). It shows how easy was the job of restructuring church writings when translating and printing, for there are less than fifty volumes in the collection, each handwritten in large characters. It is upon these records that Christianity stands.

The Office of the Inquisition was in charge of editing, and rigidly oversaw the restructuring of early documents before unrestricted release. The Inquisitor General issued instructions saying that, 'the writings of the Fathers be read backwards and modified, so that the passions of thoughtful men will be subdued, and the national mind will be stimulated, for it is the true way of perpetuating our institution' (*Liberty,* Bishop Jeremy Taylor, Vol ii, Pg. 22, Heber's Ed., 1822; also, *Delineation of Roman Catholicism,* Rev. Charles Elliott, D.D., 1844).

As a result, the writings St Augustine were 'forbidden to be read, by order from the Roman Inquisition, confirmed after by the Council of Trent' (*James' Treaty of the Corruption of Scripture*, London, 1688, Pg. 108, 109), but the suppression of his writings 'did not keep men from reading them, but gave them rather occasion to seek more earnestly after them' (Ibid). The works of Augustine were subsequently printed at Antwerp in 1700 and because they were earlier 'corrupted by Bishop Fulbertus, they are now little read at this time, except by the clergy' (*Encyclopedia Britannica,* Edinburgh Ed. Vol 11, 1797, Pg. 686). Even though they came into the public forum severely edited, they still carry revealing information. Augustine is presented as one of the main Fourth Century exponents of Christianity, 'an opinion that is universally held in the church' (Ibid), and the priesthood today professes great reverence for his falsified records.

Likewise, the Inquisition originally prohibited the publication of St. Jerome's 'genuine' works but during the Reformation they came into the possession of humanitarian and biblical scholar Desiderius Erasmus (1466?-1536). After translation, Erasmus published Jerome's letters and, to the embarrassment of church hierarchy, they were openly read to the intelligentsia. The church of Rome was so angry at the exposure that it declared Erasmus, *auctor damnatus,* a damned author (*Index Expurgatorius Vaticanus,* Edited by R. Gibbings, B.A., Dublin, 1837) and publicly defamed him. Those letters still exist today.

False books published by the church

The Council of Trent pledged that 'the manuscripts of the Fathers were the Oracles of God, unanimous and infallible' but by sleight of hand the church later ...

> ... put words into the mouths of the Fathers in the first person to give the earmarks of authenticity to its forged utterances. In some instances entire treatises were falsely written and issued in the names of ancient bishops, and churchmen cited forged passages from the Fathers in vindication of their doctrine. It would require a volume to rehearse the names of those tractates, which have been falsely bred by men who, if they were now alive, would be deposed that they were never privy to their begetting. (*Confessions of a French Catholic Priest,* New York, Mathers, 1837)

Bishop Jeremy Taylor (d. c. 1825), in a pious attempt to clean out forged church records, demanded that the forgeries 'be removed, and let God's voice sound alone'. He continued:

> Many false books were issued in their names (early churchmen) … and they were made to speak, not what themselves thought, but what other men pleased. In the books attributed to St. Basil, containing thirty chapters, *De Spiritu Sancto,* fifteen of them were written by another hand … this is clear from the Preface of Erasmus to his commentary of Basil's works. Scarcely any Father who is the author of a number of books has escaped the injustice of the times. I omit other corruptions of antiquity which were listed elsewhere (*De Christian, Eccl. Success of Statu*, vii. pg. 58, 217, anno 1613) wherein the dishonesty of these men, in handling the writings of the Ancients, is laid open, by confession of their own mouths. A good face must be put on the matter, one devise or another must be invented to evade the testimonies objected. (*Liberty,* Bishop Jeremy Taylor, Vol ii, pg. 85, Heber's Ed., 1822; also, *Delineation of Roman Catholicism*, Rev. Charles Elliott, D.D., pg. 78 and 79, 1844)

Dr. Constantine Von Tischendorf (1815-1874) added to the evidence of an ongoing cover-up of true Christian history and revealed further examples of forgery in church writings. The brilliant and pious German biblical scholar and Professor of Theology spent his entire life studying church texts. His research revealed that Bishop Irenaeus' reference to 'twelve apostles' was forged into his records by a 17th Century editor, and '668 new words of a Christian flavour' were added to the Book of Revelation in 1780 (*When Were Our Gospels Written*, Professor Constantine Tischendorf, British Library). Other patristic documents of the same century were prefaced with false letters assuring the faithful that Jesus, accompanied by his mother and a band of angels, came to earth and received the souls of the church fathers at their death.

The later church admitted that records left by Justin Martyr, Clement of Alexandria, Origen and others, make 'false quotations' (*Catholic Encyclopedia*, i, 225-226), and confessed that forged narratives written into their works were 'fathered upon them' (Ibid). The writings of the Fathers in their original form were fatal to the existence of Christianity, and the establishment of the *Expurgatory Index* to fudge ancient information reveals that church records used today to vouch for the truth and credibility of its existence are forgeries.

CHAPTER 34

A new church history written

From around the time of Pope Leo X (c. 1513) until more modern times, popes and cardinals employed internal priestly writers to expound false church claims. 'The Pontiff employed interested or mercenary writers to advocate his claims ... he transformed many points of divinity so as to satisfy his thirst for power, reputation, and gain' (*Book of the Roman Catholic Church*, Bishop Charles Butler, 8 Vols. 1825, pg. 664). As a result, the priesthood unashamedly authorized the publication of hundreds of concocted books that were written to defend and support untrue church allegations. 'Several of these forged books are frequently cited and applied to the defense of Christianity by the church as true and genuine pieces' (*A Dictionary of Universal Knowledge for the People,* Lippincott and Co., 1877). Much of Christianity's defense material is painstakingly presented in long wearisome discourses drawn from inappropriate texts and taking to task, in a general sense, the body of disbelievers.

Evidence from church documents reveals that any references to Jesus Christ or Christianity in church writings pre-dating the Council of Nicaea of 325 are priesthood forgeries, applied retrospectively, and included in a new and false history especially written. The church confirmed that knowledge, saying:

> The history of some ages was composed solely by the servile agents of the Pope; and for a long time none dared to question his pretenses without being stigmatized as a heretic, and actually treated as such. (*Book of the Roman Catholic Church*, Bishop Charles Butler, 8 Vols. 1825, pg. 664)

The concept of surreptitiously orchestrating church history was an ecclesiastical scheme intentionally perpetrated to provide a past for itself that was publicly presented as factual, adding that the concept was, 'any story, by being often told, obtains currency' (Ibid). By the invention and adoption of false documents the church provided itself with a legal system suited to any emergency that gave it unlimited authority throughout the Christian world in causes spiritual and over persons ecclesiastical.

The church 'Forgery Mill' ground away for centuries and the falsifications it produced were, in many cases, taken as truth and thus the very soul of Christian history is vexed. Around every hundred years or so disintegrating and fading monastic records were regularly re-copied, and old versions then stored in Genizahs or destroyed. 'In addition to their prescribed studies, the monks were constantly occupied in copying the texts' (*Catholic Encyclopedia*, v, 303; vi, 485; and i, 696) and how often the writings were altered over the centuries is not known but the church itself admitted that there were 'many opportunities for change' (Ibid). One glaring example of premeditated adjustment to the New Testament was the 'real name of Jesus' that was altered to read 'the Lord' in subsequent revisions.

References to the twin deleted

Scribes added and subtracted to the Bible and 'the text became very corrupt during the Middle Ages' (*Encyclopedia Britannica*, 9th Ed., Vol. 13, Pg. 631). Dr. Tischendorf recorded that during that time the Gospels 'underwent such serious modification of meaning as to leave us in painful uncertainty as to what had been actually written' (*Codex Sinaiticus,* 8th Ed., The Letterworth Press). Robert Young, author of one of two better-known Concordances of the Bible, said that in the New Testament 'there are scarcely two consecutive verses where there is not some departure from the original', and 15th and 16th Century popes authorized much of those falsifications. During that time, most references to Jesus' twin brother were deleted and the texts were slowly brought into some form of standardization.

It was not until the 17th Century that the story of Jesus Christ evolved uniformly and until that time clauses, sentences and whole paragraphs in church records and New Testaments were changed, omitted and inserted with astonishing freedom wherever it seemed that the meaning could be brought out with greater force and definiteness. The church confessed that, 'It was the public character of all scribes to mold and bend the sacred oracles until they complied with their own fancy, spreading them ... like a curtain, closing together or drawing them back as they pleased' (*Catholic Encyclopedia*, Vol. 4, Pg. 498).

A typical example of scribes falsifying texts is found by simply comparing old Bibles with modern-day versions. Recorded is the tale of a leper who called out to Jesus and said, 'If you will, you can make me clean'. The verse continues, 'Jesus, angry, stretched out his hand and touched him' (Mark 1: 40-41). In the centuries of editing, the word 'angry' was changed to read, 'moved to compassion' in modern Bibles, a deliberate falsification, the purpose of which is evident.

A retroactive fabrication

Apart from official *Catholic Encyclopedias*, rare editions of *Encyclopedia Britannica* were also sourced for this work, as they carried large sections on subjects associated with Christian development. Volumes consulted extended back to 1790 and are listed in the Bibliography in the end pages of this book. None of the religious material provided in those Encyclopedias was sanctioned by the hierarchy of any Christian denomination but was privately solicited by owners of *Encyclopedia Britannica* for which contributors received payment. The priests who accepted the commission supplied the Encyclopedists with historic facts and publicly-unknown information that had the potential to overturn the whole previously-accepted history of Christianity, and, in turn, Western civilization itself.

The original encyclopedias produced under the name of *Britannica* probably provided the first and last opportunity for unaffiliated biblical specialists outside church control to release factual information about the development of Christianity. In the 1895 version alone, 344 Christian experts contributed to articles associated with the biblical sections in the 8th, 9th, 10th and 11th Editions. The knowledge they provided was subsequently printed, and the priesthood had endowed the Encyclopedists with disclosures that shocked the Christian hierarchy. The Catholic church, in particular, was horrified by revelations that were printed and realizing something had to be done, circuitously arranged for a group of Catholic businessmen to purchase the *Encyclopedia Britannica* (*History in the Encyclopedia,* D. H. Gordon and N. L. Torrey, (NY. 1947); also, *The Good News of the Kingdoms,* Mr. Norman Segal, Australia, 1995).

After the publication of the 11th Edition in 1898, the change of ownership was complete, and in a few years new editions void of 'offending' material superseded earlier versions that were then ordered destroyed. With these late and necessary corruptions to historical records the church's story is instantly disproved. In due course (1943) the *Encyclopedia Britannica* was assigned to the Roman Catholic University in Chicago (*Encyclopedias: Their History Throughout the Ages,* 1966, two editions. The 2nd Edition paid particular attention to *Encyclopedia Britannica*) and in subsequent decades, church missionaries went door to door the world over selling the sanitized *Encyclopedia Britannica* into millions of unsuspecting households. In May 1995 *Encyclopedia Britannica* was offered for sale at around US$450 million after suffering three consecutive years of losses and dwindling sales.

People with access to libraries holding older pre-edited copies of *Encyclopedia Britannica*, particularly the Ninth Edition, Volume 10, will be shocked to read page 783 onwards under the heading of 'Gospels'. It confirms what church leaders knew of the crooked nature of the early Christian bishops, the Fourth to the Twentieth Century restructuring of the Gospels, later inclusion of forged narratives into earlier texts, suppression of Gospels once used in the early church (The Gospel of the Twin), contradictions between Gospels, the falsification of church history, and the anonymous nature of fictitious Gospels now in the New Testament.

With the discovery of the Dead Sea Scrolls, the 'Vatican scrolls' and the Nag Hammadi Scrolls, that earlier knowledge was reinforced and revealed that the church of the day knew that the origin and authenticity of its Gospels was falsely presented. Persons in a position to compare earlier editions with 'under church management' editions should do so for personal confirmation that a fictitious Christian history was written, omitting previously available information about Jesus' twin, and providing the final expression of its New Learning (*Catholic Encyclopedia,* Vol., v, Pg. 442; and

Catholic Encyclopedia, Vol. Xv, Pg. 376).

Because no historical records or external archives of any kind existed to support priesthood claims of a revelatory origin to Christianity (*Annales Ecclesiastici,* tome vii, Fol. Antwerp, 1597, Cardinal Caesar Baronius), the church retrospectively compiled a false history for their own encyclopedias and used it as evidence to support their claims. Other church groups later assembled additional encyclopedic editions using earlier fabricated versions as reference sources, and thus expanded the falsified history into every modern Christian dictionary and encyclopedia published today. Simply put, in attempting to provide verification to protect and maintain its institution, the church wrote its own references and created an untrue record that falsely presented itself as an illustrious body of pious people sincerely expounding the 'wonderful works of Christ'. The relentless evasion and lawyering of the truth produced a body of writings designed to give historical credence to the church and its story, and provides untrue versions of events that are presented as factual.

Forging reference sources

The cover-up of sensitive information by fabrication is insidious in church history and an example associated with 'Succession' was perpetrated in the 16th Century. It took the form of a famous, or infamous, *Book of the Popes (Liber Pontificalis),* notorious for its spurious accounts of early and mythical 'successors of St Peter'. The *Liber Pontificalis* purports to be 'a true history of the popes, beginning with St Peter and continued down to the fifteenth century, in the form of biography's of their respective Holinesses of Rome' (*Catholic Encyclopedia,* ix, 224). It is an official papal work, written and kept in the Vatican archives, and preserves for posterity the 'holy lives and wonderful doings of the heads of the church universal' (Ibid).

In recent times, however, church officials admitted that 'historical criticism has for a long time dealt with this ancient text in an exhaustive way ... especially in recent decades' (Ibid, ix, 224), and it established that the *Book of the Popes* is an unauthentic record. The church confessed that it was forged by Vatican priests and compiled in the typically fraudulent manner of clerical writings:

> In most of its manuscript copies there is found at the beginning a spurious correspondence between Pope Damasus and St. Jerome. These letters were considered genuine in the Middle Ages. Duchesne has proved exhaustively and convincingly that the first series of biographies, from St. Peter to Felix III (d. 530) were compiled at the latest under Felix's successor, Boniface II (530-532). The compiler of the *Liber Pontificalis* utilized also some historical writings, a number of apocryphal fragments (e.g. the Pseudo-Clementine Recognitions), the Constitutum Sylvestri, the spurious Acts of the alleged 'Synod of the 275 Bishops under Sylvester', etc., and the fifth century Roman Acts of Martyrs. Finally, the compiler distributed arbitrarily along his list of popes a number of papal decrees taken from unauthentic sources, he likewise attributed to earlier popes liturgical and disciplinary regulations of the sixth century. The authors were Roman ecclesiastics, and some were attached to the Roman Court. (*Catholic Encyclopedia*, ix, 225)

The falsity of the *Book of the Popes* is thereby shown and the use of it as an historic reference source by later Christian writers was revealed when the church added: 'In the *Liber Pontificalis* it is recorded that popes issued decrees that were lost, or mislaid, or perhaps never existed at all. Later popes seized the opportunity to supply a false pontifical letter suitable for the occasion, attributing it to the pope whose name was mentioned in the *'Liber'* (*Catholic Encyclopedia*, v. 774). Thus, confessed forgery and fraud taint to the core the official record of church 'histories' and the actions of Popes of the primitive and adolescent years of the church reveal that Pope Peter and his 'Successors' are priesthood fabrications.

Frauds like this were not confined to the 16th Century, but began at the beginning of Christianity. They infested every period of its history for 1600 years and defiled nearly every document put forward, both of scripture and church aggrandizement. Professor Collins, in his celebrated *Discourse of Free Thinking*, said:

> In short, these frauds are very common in all books that are published by priests or priestly men. For it is certain they plead the authority of the church fathers that were forged, corrupted and mangled, with more reason than for any of their Articles of Faith (p. 96).

Investigation of the church's own records shows that the priesthood's claim of a continuous ministerial succession from the apostles of Jesus is false. There never was any form of ordination from a supernatural Jesus Christ or Simon Peter to church presbyters and then down to popes today. The popes are not successors of Peter, but of Emperor and King Constantine. The priesthood appointed itself and today uses false 'Successors' to support its story. The church confessed that direct lineage 'was interrupted by repeated periods; after Nicholas 1., eight years, seven months, and nine days, &c., &c.' Those interruptions are piously called 'vacations' and recorded by church historian Bishop Platina (c. 1600) to amount to 'a total of 127 years, 5 months and 9 days'. Erasmus concluded that 'succession itself is imaginary' (*Erasmus, Desid*, in *Nov. Test. Annotations*, Fol. Basil, 1542), simply because Jesus Christ was not created until the Fourth Century.

The suppression of *Diderot's Encyclopedia*

The church has a history of opposition to Encyclopedias published outside its control and that was revealed when Pope Clement XIII (1698-1769) moved quickly to suppress a major volume compiled by French Encyclopedist, Denis Diderot (1713-83) (*Oxford Dictionary of the Christian Church,* Cross, 1997, Pg. 545). The church was appalled, for his Encyclopedia stood in violent opposition to its claims, 'with forty pages against Christianity, among the boldest ever known' (*Catholic Encyclopedia,* vol. vi). Thereupon, Pope Clement ordered:

> The said volume is impious, scandalous, bold full of blasphemies and calumnies against the Christian religion. These volumes are so much more dangerous and reprehensible as they are written in French and in the most seductive style. The author of this book, who has the boldness to sign his name to it, should be arrested as soon as possible. It is important that justice should make an example, with all severity, both of the author and those who have shared in printing or distributing such a volume.

Accordingly, late in 1759, the church ordered all volumes to be burned, prohibited their sale, and decreed arrest for Diderot should he ever enter Rome (*The Censoring of Diderot's Encyclopedia and the Re-established Text* (NY.

1947), D. H. Gordon and N. L. Torrey; also, *Oxford Concise Dictionary of the Christian Church,* E.A. Livingstone, 2000, pg. 191). His Encyclopedia was placed on the *Index of Prohibited Books*, and a ban of excommunication was pronounced on any who should read it. However, not all copies were destroyed, for a Rare Books collector made a version available for the research of this book. Later, in 1764, Diderot learnt with great disappointment that his publisher, Andre Le Breton, had, under instructions 'from a team of priests', removed 'compromising' material from the corrected proof sheets of ten folio volumes of a scheduled reprint of his Encyclopedia (*The Censoring of Diderot's Encyclopedia and the Re-established Text* (NY.1947), D. H. Gordon and N. L. Torrey).

© Photo by Pierre Luiggi, 1958, in the Louvre, Paris

A bust of the French Encyclopedist, Denis Diderot.

The suppressive actions of the church draws remarkable parallels to the controlled publication of disinformation used by the 'Ministry of Truth' in George Orwell's book, *Nineteen Eighty-Four* (Penguin, 1954). For a better understanding of efforts to uphold information that supports the orthodox Christian tradition, it is interesting to note that institutions of higher education fail to offer degree courses allowing people to gain knowledge and attain university qualifications opposing Christianity.

Summary

Church history was knowingly falsified with deliberate fabrication of a whole Christian literature, manipulated to hide the existence of Judas Thomas the Twin. It is inevitable that the composers of the church's encyclopedias and dictionaries are either Christians, or persons in their service, acting strictly in Christian interests. In this manner, the church was active in concealing the essence of the truth of its origins and matters where self-interests of the priesthood were concerned, and for 1600 years perpetrated the frauds herein revealed. When researching the New Testament it must always be remembered that we are dealing with a body of edited material, not only in the New Testament itself, but also in any church-prepared writings designed to support it. Theologians and historians complacently accept the biblical postulate and have given it their official stamp of approval.

CHAPTER 35

The suppressed chapter of the Bible

The FIRST Vulgate translated in secret

The church said that the 'traditional English translation of the Latin Vulgate Bible is called the Douay Rheims, or Douay Bible. It was named after Douay, northern France, where the Old Testament was published in 1609 and 1610; and Rheims, France, where the New Testament was first published in English in 1583'. It was produced by Roman Catholic scholars in exile from England at the English College in Douay (then in the Spanish Netherlands, but now part of France). A group of former Oxford men undertook the work in order to provide English-speaking Roman Catholics with a readable Catholic version of the Bible. Vatican practice theretofore had effectively restricted personal use of the Latin Bible to its clergy. One hundred and fifty seven years later, and to make it conform to the Clementine version of 1592, Bishop Richard Challoner spent 23 years of his life revising the Douay Bible (1749 to 1772), and published the first of many revisions.

However, unknown to church historians today, an English-language version of the Vulgate was secretly published 20 years previous to the 'traditional' version mentioned in church records. In 1559, four Catholic bishops stole a Latin Vulgate from the Vatican in Rome during the turmoil preceding the election of Pope Pius IV in December that year. They took it to a safe house in Rheims, France, and began the long task of translating it into English. It was published four years later in 1563 and is the FIRST Vulgate ever printed in the English language. It is finished with a chamois leather cover, and contains both Old and New Testaments.

How the FIRST Vulgate differs from modern versions

In light of the evidence discussed so far is one question ... how does the FIRST Vulgate differ from today's version ... and what does it say about Jesus' twin? Despite the church's long-standing attempts to suppress the most damaging information about its past, it provides comparative evidence that discredits every modern version, and a few variations are given here.

Linking the church's cover-up activities together, it is revealing to note that the Acts of the Apostles and the Book of James are the only New Testament books not ending in the word 'amen'. This has led biblical scholars to believe they are incomplete in their present form and a comparison with the FIRST Vulgate proves them right. In modern Bibles, the Acts of the Apostles ends abruptly at Chapter 28, but the FIRST Vulgate has a 29th Chapter consisting of 26 verses totaling approximately 865 words. That concluding chapter mentions the Gospel of the Twin, the exodus of the Bethany Group, Paul's journey to Britain, his discussions with Druids, his preaching at Mount Lud (Ludgate) in Londinium, and a reference to the 'double' of Jesus.

The incomplete books of the Bible

The Acts of the Apostles is the fifth book of the New Testament and although 'not original to the document' (*Catholic Encyclopedia*, Vol. 1, 1908, Acts of the Apostles), the title suggests that it is about the apostles but it shows very little interest in them as a group. This and other biblical writings gives an account of the life of Paul and his extensive journeys, and the church accepts the document as authentic. However, a serious and penetrating analysis of the Acts of the Apostles reveals many problems and they must be addressed in order to understand the nature of Christian texts.

In perusing a list of old church writings, the observer will notice that there are five ancient documents that carry the title of the Acts of the Apostles. Irenaeus was the first presbyter to mention a writing by that name (c. 190), but it is not clear which version he was quoting. Early in the Third Century, Clement of Alexandria also cited a narrative from a version of the Acts of the Apostles, and Origen recorded several sayings from some versions but was vague about their scriptural status. Hence it is impossible to be precise regarding the date, origin, or authorship of the version of the Acts of the Apostles in the New Testament. Some Christian academics date its composition around 185, but they themselves say it could have been written from a combination of all five versions and compiled in the Fourth Century. A narrative in the second half of Acts stresses that the church and Rome were not in conflict, suggesting that sections were written or revised after the Council of Nicaea in 325.

The author of the missing sections

The canonical version of the Acts of the Apostles contains 1007 verses with only one statement attributed to Jesus and that is an acknowledged Sixth Century interpolation (*Catholic Encyclopedia*, Vol. 1, 1908, Acts of the Apostles). The writing consists of two dramatically different sections joined together as one, and the author of the first half of the document was of the 'same character' as the author of the Gospel of Luke (*Catholic Encyclopedia*, Vol. 1, 1908, Acts of the Apostles). That person was an Egyptian presbyter named Cerinthus, the same person responsible for writing early manuscripts that were later used by Constantine to become the Gospel of John and the Book of Revelation (*Old Christian Literature*, Van Manen of Leyden (contributor to *Encyclopedia Biblica*, c. 1860; also, Eusebius, *Ecclesiastical History*).

Cerinthus was educated in Alexandria and was an associate of Rabbi Ebron's faction of Ebronites who 'numbered among their sect all the surviving relatives of Jesus' (St. Epiphanius of Salamis, 315-403). He was directly associated with the Essenes and Nazarenes and was active between the years of 160-190.

The existence of interpolated material in modern versions of the Gospel of John and the Book of Revelation substantiates the claim that the original documents were written without reference to Christian understandings, and statements accredited to Jesus were added when Constantine reconstructed the exemplars at the Council of Nicaea in 325. At that time, Eusebius recorded that Cerinthus had 'written over' the original documents 'after his own fashion' and that admission revealed the start of centuries of falsifications to writings that were to become official to Christianity. Of the Gospel of John, the *New Catholic Encyclopedia* added to Eusebius's record, saying 'there was a series of subsequent authors who added material to the body of the Gospel narrative' (*New Catholic Encyclopedia,* 1967, Pg. 1080 onwards).

The Bishop of Rome, Callistus (217-222), knew of the pre-Christian existence of the original substance of the writing that eventually became the Gospel of John for he personally declared that it was discovered sealed in an earthenware urn 'in a cavern under the Temple of Jerusalem, having been placed there in secret long anterior (previous) to the presbyterian era' (*The Edict of Callistus,* Victor Germaine's Trans., 1822). That original exemplar of the Gospel of John was a 100 BC Essene religious direction embodying the views of the monks of the Order of the Essenes and was one of the 'secret scrolls' found in the Vatican. What remains of that originally untitled writing was published in *The Crucifixion of Truth*.

Cerinthus' impact on Christian development was strong for the Gospel of Luke was originally called the Gospel of Cerinthus. From the formal evidence, we read the words of indignation from Eusebius: 'Cerinthus wished to put his book under a name which would bring him credit, so he stole another man's signature'. Extracts were drawn from it at the Council of Nicaea and it subsequently became part of Constantine's *New Testimonies*. At the Council of Constantinople in 381, it received the name of Luke, a physician (Therapeute), described in ancient Syrian New Testaments as 'Asaia, the Essaian' or Essene (*Ecclesiastical History,* Bishop Du Pin, vol. i, pg. 607-615).

False speeches in the Acts of the Apostles

Some speeches applied to Paul in Acts were consciously modeled on the earlier speeches of Apollonius of Tyana, a First Century Greek sage and wanderer from Tyana, and are documented in the records of his life (6:3). The church conceded that the authors of the Acts of the Apostles were not present at any speeches they recorded and said that they followed 'the custom of ancient historians in writing the speeches themselves' (*Catholic Encyclopedia*, 1909 Ed., Acts of the Apostles). In other words, the speeches in Acts and other New Testament books are free compositions in which later authors put into the mouth of others, words they considered suitable to the earlier speaker, and the occasion.

Another notable instance of intentional perversion also appears in the Acts of the Apostles and relates to Paul's use of a carved dedication 'to an unknown god' on the altar of a statue on Mars' Hill in Athens (Acts, xvii, 23). Upon this inscription is based Paul's famous tirade to the Athenians: 'What therefore you worship as unknown, this I proclaim to you', with the intended implication that Paul was declaring the statue to be Jesus Christ. However, that passage is fraudulently presented, for in modern Bibles the inscription is not wholly recorded.

The falsification was challenged by Catholic Bible-writer, Erasmus, who first slammed the 'clerical propensity to warp scripture,' and then angrily disclosed the dishonest presentation of the passage. Churchmen today proudly preach that when Paul saw the inscription, he drew from it an argument for proof of the Christian religion. However, the inscription never mentioned Jesus Christ and read in its entirety it said: TO THE GODS OF ASIA, EUROPE, AND AFRICA, TO ALL FOREIGN AND UNKNOWN GODS (*The Praise of Folly*, p. 292, Erasmus). Marginal notes in the King James Bible reveal that the earliest Greek text of the Acts of the Apostles used the original plurality of gods and forging the passage was a calculated clerical attempt to usurp the statue and falsely establish in Christian texts that Jesus Christ was known in the Third Century.

A version of the New Testament known as Codex Laudianus is variously dated 14th to 16th Centuries and is the earliest known version that contained verse 37 in the 8th chapter of the Acts of the Apostles. That narrative is a forgery, saying: 'And Philip said, 'If you believe with all your heart, you may ... and he replied ... I believe that Jesus Christ is the son of God'. That narrative is clearly intended as an *apologia* for Jesus devised by a later age.
'Evidence of the forged nature of the Acts of the Apostles is confirmed by a passage preserved in the records of St. Jerome. He said that a disciple of Manichaeus (Mani) named Seleucus ...

> ... wrote falsely the Acts of the Apostles, which exhibited matter not for edification, but for destruction; and that this book was approved in a synod, which the ears of the church properly refused to listen. (*The Letters of St. Jerome*, v; 445; also, *Sod, the Son of the Man*, Pg. 46)

Such confessions cause grave doubt about everything presented by the church, and Jerome mentioning Seleucus's authorship (d.c. 280) provides the most probable dating of the commencement of the fabrication of the New Testament version of the forgery. However, we should recall the words of St Lactantius (d. 328) and Bishop Ambrose of Milan (333-397), who both claimed that the Christian writings relayed 'history mixed with religious fanaticism' (*Encyclopedia of the Roman Empire*, Matthew Brunson, 1994, Pg. 241). Therefore, in analyzing the suppressed chapter of the Acts of the Apostles, an attempt is made to extract what may be historic.

What the missing section says

Following is Chapter 29 in its entirety and a commentary on aspects important to this work is included. The church said that there is a gap between the years 62 and 65 in St Paul's history ... the discovery of the suppressed Chapter of the Bible completes his life.

The suppressed chapter of the Acts of the Apostles

Verse 1. *And Paul, full of the blessings of Jesus, and abounding in the spirit, departed out of Rome, determined to go into Spain, for he had a long time proposed to journey thitherward, and was minded also to go from thence to Briton.*

Verse 2. *For he had heard in Phoenicia that certain of the children of Israel, about the time of the Assyrian captivity, had escaped by sea to the 'Isles afar off" as spoken by the Prophet, and called by the Romans ... Briton* (This is a previously unknown biblical reference to the Bethany Group and their departure for France and Britain. It seems that in Paul's time (c. 62-65), the Exodus of the main Gospel personalities to Europe was general knowledge).

Verse 3. *And the Lord commanded the Gospel of the Twin to be preached far hence to the Gentiles, and to the lost sheep of the House of Israel* (The Gospel of the Twin is today called the Gospel of Thomas, and was later used in part to compile the Gospel of Mark).

Verse 4. *And no man hindered Paul; for he testified boldly of Jesus before the tribunes and among the people; and he took with him certain of the brethren which abode with him at Rome, and they took shipping at Ostrium and having the winds fair, were brought safely into a haven of Spain.*

Verse 5. *And people gathered together from the towns and villages, and some from the hill country; for they had heard of the apostle.*

Verse 6. *And Paul preached mightily in Spain, and multitudes listened, for they perceived he was an apostle sent from God.*

Verse 7. *And they departed out of Spain, and Paul and his company finding a ship in Armorica sailing unto Briton, they were therein, and passing along the South Coast, they reached a port called Raphinus* (Raphinus was the Roman name for Sandwich in England today. It is on the east coast of Kent, about ten miles north of Dover and ten miles east of Canterbury. Sandwich is now two miles from the sea, so much has the estuary of the River Wantsum silted up. In Saxon times (c. 919-1024) there was a house there called the Home of the Apostle, as tradition then held that Paul was one of the apostles).

Verse 8. *Now when it was voiced abroad that the apostle had landed on their coast, some inhabitants met him, and they treated Paul courteously and he entered in at the Gate of the East of their city, and lodged in the house of a Hebrew and one of his own nation.*

Verse 9. *And on the morrow he came and stood upon Mount Lud and the people listened at the gate, and assembled in the Broadway, and he preached the testimony of Jesus to them* (Mount Lud and its gate are references to Ludgate Hill in London where St Paul's Cathedral stands today. At the time of Paul's visit, the Temple of Diana stood on the site (*History of the Druids*, J. Toland).

Verse 10. *And at evening the Holy Ghost fell upon Paul, and he prophesied, saying, Behold in the Last Days the God of Peace shall dwell in the cities, and the inhabitants thereof shall be numbered; and in the seventh numbering of the people, their eyes shall be opened, and the glory of their inheritance shine forth before them. The nations shall come up to worship on the Mount that testifieth of the patience and long suffering of a servant of Jesus.*

Verse 11. *And in the latter days new tidings of the Gospel of the Twin shall issue forth out of Jerusalem, and the hearts of the people shall rejoice, and behold, fountains shall be opened, and there shall be no more plague.*

Verse 12. *In those days there shall be wars and rumors of war; and a king shall rise up, and his sword, shall be for the healing of the nations, and his peacemaking shall abide, and the glory of his kingdom a wonder among princes.*

Verse 13. *And it came to pass that certain of the Druids came unto Paul privately, and showed by their rites and ceremonies they were descended from the Jews which escaped from bondage in the land of Egypt, and the apostle believed these things, and he gave them the kiss of peace* (In considering the evidence of St Paul in Britain, it is of consequence to note that his journey there has been accepted by numerous writers, including bishops Ussher and Stillingfleet (*Church of the Cymry*, Rev. W. Hughes, pg. 15). In the Fourth Century, Bishop Theodoret of Antioch (d. c. 452) wrote, 'Paul journeyed to the Isles in the ocean' and mentioned the Druids among the groups that he was associated with. In the same century, Jerome recorded that Paul's travels 'extended to the western parts of the Isles', supporting another tradition maintaining that during his time in Britain, Paul travelled to Glastonbury and Anglesey (Mona) in Wales. Well-known hymn-writer, Venantius Fortunatus, Bishop of Poitiers (c. 530), wrote of Paul 'crossing the ocean to Britain and the extreme West.' A piece of church ground at Glastonbury is today called 'Paul's Field' and tradition also holds that Paul founded the monastery at Bangor, Northern Wales).

Verse 14. *And Paul abode in his lodgings three months confirming in the faith and preaching Jesus and his double continually* (Here Paul makes a reference to the 'double' of Jesus in the same terminology used in the Book of Thomas. In that writing Judas Thomas is called Jesus' 'brother', 'double', and his 'twin and true companion' (138:7f; 138:19f).

Verse 15. *And after these things Paul and his brethren departed from Raphinus and sailed unto Atium in Gaul.*

Verse 16. *And Paul preached in the Roman garrison and among the people, exhorting all men to repent and confess their sins.*

Verse 17. *And there came to him certain of the Belgae to enquire of him the new doctrine, and of the man Jesus; and Paul opened his heart unto them and told them all things that had befallen him' and they departed pondering among themselves upon the things which they had heard.*

Verse 18. *And after much preaching and toil, Paul and his fellow labourers passed into Helvetia, and came to Mount Pontius Pilate.*

Verse 19. *And immediately a torrent gushed out of the mountain and washed his body.*

Verse 20. *And Paul stretched forth his hands upon the water, and prayed unto the Lord.*

Verse 21. *And while Paul was yet speaking, behold there came a great earthquake, and the face of the waters changed.*

Verse 22. *And a voice came out of heaven, saying, Even Pilate hath escaped the wrath to come for he washed his hands before the multitude.*

Verse 23. *When, therefore, Paul and those that were with him saw the earthquake, and heard the voice of the angel, they glorified God, and were mightily strengthened in the spirit.*

Verse 24. *And they journeyed and came to Mount Julius where stood two pillars, one on the right hand and one on the left hand, erected by Caesar Augustus*

(This verse draws a parallel to the familiar Masonic emblem of two vertical columns named Jachin and Boaz, and referred to in the Old Testament (1 Kings 7:21). Their significance, use and mystical meanings are highly respected by Masons).

Verse 25. *And Paul, filled with the Holy Ghost, stood up between the two pillars, saying, Men and brethren these stones which ye see this day testify of my journey hence; and verily I say, they shall remain until the outpouring of the spirit upon all nations, neither shall the way be hindered throughout all generations.*

Verse 26. *And they went forth and came unto Illtricum, intending to go by Macedonia into Asia, and grace was found, and they prospered and had peace. Amen.*

The manuscript from Constantinople

There is another version of the concluding portion of the Acts of the Apostles and it varies from the version in the FIRST Vulgate. This manuscript was found in 1793 interleaved in a book written by C. S. Sonnini called *Travels in Turkey and Greece* and was purchased at the sale of the library and effects of the late Right Honorable Sir John Newport, Bart, of Ireland. Sonnini had originally translated the document from a Greek text found in the archives at Constantinople that was subsequently gifted to him by the Sultan Abdoul Achment. The contents of the title page of Sonnini's work in which the English translation of the document was found, says: 'Travels in Turkey and Greece undertaken by order of Louis XVI (Louis XVI reigned from 1774 to 1793), and with the authority of the Ottoman Court by C. S. Sonnini, member of several scientific societies. *'Mores mulorum videt et ubes';* HOR., London; Printed for T.N. Londman and O. Rees, Paternoster Row, 1801.'

This version of the suppressed section of the Acts of the Apostles has been Christianized, differing from that in the FIRST Vulgate of 1563. The late Major Samuels refers to this chapter in his book, *Far Hence Unto the Gentiles* (Chpt. 29) and, for the benefit of researchers, he states that 'a full translation of this manuscript may be seen in the British Museum, No. 3227, D. 9.'

Deletions from the Book of James

Not only is a major section of the Acts of the Apostles missing from modern Bibles, but also the closing section of the Book of James is absent. In current Bibles, James terminates at 5:19 but in the FIRST Vulgate there are three additional verses, being 20, 21, and 22. In the canonical Galatians (1:19) James is called 'the Lord's brother' with the verse extending into 1: 20 and saying, 'In what I write to you, before God, I do not lie'. In the closing verses of the Book of James in the FIRST Vulgate, the Galatians passage is extended upon and all the brothers of Jesus are again named. This is what is recorded in Verses 5: 20-22:

The hidden dweller

Verse 5: 20. *Now we brethren, like Jesus, are the children of promise. In what I write to you, before God, I do not lie. Then after seven years I went again to Jerusalem, taking with me the blessings of the brothers of Jesus; Judas the twin, the hidden dweller; James, Joses and Simon* (Jesus' blood brothers are again named, and Judas is explicitly called, 'the twin').

Verse 5: 21. *And I laid before the people the gospel which I preach among the Gentiles. When they saw that I had been entrusted with the gospel, they perceived the grace that was given to me.*

Verse 5: 22. *And let the grace of the secret words of Rabbi Jesus be with your spirit, brethren* (The 'secret words' of Jesus is again mentioned, confirming that the author of the Book of James is talking about the Gospel of the Twin that opens with a statement saying that it is composed of 'secret words', collected from Jesus and transmitted by Didymus Judas Thomas).

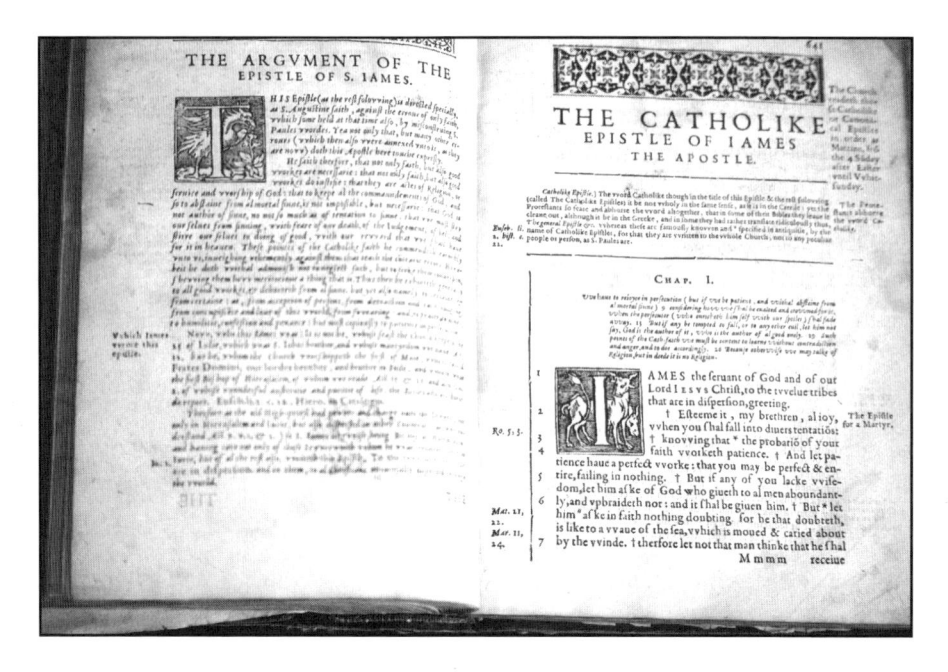

In the FIRST Vulgate, a section called an ARGUMENT generally preceded the Epistle that follows. This picture shows the ARGUMENT of James on the left page and the beginning of the Epistle on the right-hand page. This edition of the Epistle of James includes three closing verses that fail to appear in today's Vulgates.

CHAPTER 36

The letter from Rome, c. 90 AD

The following pages are extracts from a letter written by Arch-Druid Brí Leith from Rome in 90 to Brân Adamnán, Abbot of Mona (Anglesey today). This document was supplied by the monastery at Cumbria and presented with other material to support the Abbot's cause that the British/Celtic church preceded the Roman church by 600 years, a position maintained by Magna Carta. The Abbot vouches for its authenticity, adding that it was translated by Gelhi Arihyuid, bishop of the church of Llandeilo Fawr in South Wales in the 18th Century, and then held in the Cumbrian Archives. It confirms much of what is written in this book.

Dated this Calend of Sixtilis

'Sir, I have just reached this degraded city after a tedious voyage. Everything struck me as new, strange, and peculiar. I have spent several days in visiting the many buildings here erected in worship of the gods, and in enquires as to the civil and social state of the people; and I now proceed to detail you what I have seen and learned.

Domitian has just brought to a close the Dacian war, having secured a peace on very humiliating terms. This, instead of humbling him, has greatly excited his turbulent passions, so that no man is now safe here, unless he would degrade himself to flatter the capricious tyrant and his tools. The philosophers are expelled, Stoic aristocrats are killed in an awful manner, and a widespread fear of Domitian is among all the people. Rumours of conspiracies against his life are very frequent, and those who are suspected as enemies are cruelly torn from their families; but what is done with them none even conjecture. The unseen hand of tyranny is everywhere felt, and every person is in hourly dread of its chains or its daggers.

I first mingled with the people of Roma and that you, sir, may not esteem this as an exaggeration, ponder the following observation; there are many charnel-houses here and strange people linger near to them; some have the countenance of dogs and others are prominently huge in their bodies, double my tallness and statue (Comment 1). Beggars gaze around, and pester you at every turn. Prostitutes in bright garb and of the lowest class grovel on their knees for favourable acceptance for a few obols, and are full of complaints when abandoned. Very few Khrestians are to be found here. They have been purged, and have set up new headquarters at Antioch-on-the-Orontes where they are numerous (Comment 2).

© Folio 128 Verso by Leonardo da Vinci

Herodotus recorded the existence of a race of dog-headed people in his time, and Leonardo da Vinci may have preserved their likeness in this sketch.

The houses erected to the gods are many and beautiful and as you enter, they strike a stranger as one of great peculiarity. These are called Temples, and some are called Houses, like the House of Romulus. The most frightful immoralities prevail among the wretchedness of the masses of people, although the altars and images of the gods are everywhere to be seen, and although their sculptured temples are multiplied and gorgeous, and their worship is maintained with many and imposing ceremonies. And what seems to me surpassing strange is, that the more immoral the people, the more they are attached to their religious rites.

There is a huge array of priests filling the temples, and to be met with in the streets. Some wear a three-cocked hat, and some no hat. These are frequently to be seen leading in processions in honour of the gods, which processions are calculated to please the people and render them superstitious. One of these I have just witnessed. The magistrates in their robes were there; the priests in their surplices were there; with were candles in their hands, and carrying the images of gods, finely dressed, and wearing a cone on their heads. They all looked extremely fantastical and self-satisfied, and lit up candles to their god as if he lived in the dark. The walk, the look, the whole appearance of the priests seemed to testify that they belonged to the better class of society. These were followed by young men in cream vestments, singing in honour of the god whose festival was celebrated; and these, again, were followed by crowds of all kinds of people, with candles and flambeaux in their hands. The whole scene seemed superfluous but the common people are said to be fond of these things, and they are multiplied by the priests on that account.

The priests here are very numerous, and wield a vast power. I will, therefore, give you some account of them. The chief and head of them is called Pontifex Maximus of the Seven Hills, or sovereign pontiff. This man is the visible head of their religion, and is the chief of a body of priests, which, in their collective capacity, is called collegium or college. This college is the final judge in all matters relating to religious things; and where there is no written law, they prescribe what they think proper. This college is a body of vast influence, and always sits in secret. When the pontiff dies, it elects a new one, and usually from their own number. The pontifex is worshipped as a god; indeed, he is sometimes called God, and he claims to be the vicegerent of Jupiter. He says he exercises the authority of Jupiter … he lives in royal state … he levies taxes upon the inferior priests, upon the people, and also the slaves, and he claims a respect from the people, which, to me, is just like adoration or worship. Men bow before him as he passes, and none can approach him without kissing his feet.

He is the interpreter to whom the people resort; and while he punishes others at discretion, he is not himself amenable to the judgment of the senate or people. All priests, and almost all things are subject to him. He regulates the year and the public calendar. He wears a gorgeous robe bordered with purple, and a huge dry fish on his head; it is the most peculiar thing. In secret, where the eye of tyranny cannot see them, he is called cod-head (God-head?). He holds a rod in his hand wrapped around with wool, and is always surrounded by stooped assistants, common and dirty. He calls them 'little fishes', and their low foreheads; their shaven pates; their unwashed faces and uncombed hair; their coarse and filthy garments, and their unwashed feet, bore evidence against them (Comment 3). But you should come to Roma yourself to understand the power of this man, and the splendour with which he appears in public, and in which he lives in private.

These two ancient seal-cylinders shows fish-clad priests associated with the rites of the Babylonian fish-god, Oannes. This early tradition provided the origin of the headgear worn by the Christian priesthood today. Other reproductions of fish-clad priests may be found in W. Hayes Ward's 'Seal-cylinders of Western Asia', Washington, 1910, fig. 686-689, and in Dölger's, 'Ichthys', p. 119, fig. 4.

In the train of the Pontifex Maximus there is always a numerous priesthood, divided into several classes. Some of these are called Augurs, some Quindecemviri, some Septemviri; these are the chiefs. But, beside these, there are the fraternities of priests less considerable, though quite influential. These, in the language of this country, are called Fratres Ambervales, Curiones, Feciales, and Sodales. Beside these, there are priests of particular gods, and the priests of Jupiter, of Mars the Avenger, of Pan, of the Persian Sun-Runner (Mithras?), of Hercules, and of Cybele, 'the mother of the gods'. There is an order of priests here called the Repellers of Wolves, and they wear peculiar robes tied about their loins (Comment 4). And all these priests have servants, who wait upon them when they are performing rites at the altars of the gods, and offer unmeaning sacrifices.

There are also here women they call Virgines Vestales (Vestal Virgins), who are consecrated to the worship of Vesta, and who enjoy singular honour and privileges. These all wear peculiar garments, by which they are distinguished from one another, and from all the people. Their various coloured veils tells who and what they are, wherever you meet them, and you meet them everywhere.

There is a large building here that is devoted to the care of poor young girls, who are deserted by their parents, or have no parents. This building is capable of containing between one and two thousand girls, and is usually full; and all of these are compelled to be female monks (nuns?). The fact that they are taken from the very lowest walks of life accounts for the commonness of their appearance, for more common or ugly women no man might wish to see. The great vulgarity of their appearance put to flight all the images of beauty, and delicacy, and modesty, which my mind had ever associated with them.

Nothing here more sorrowfully impresses a true mind than their great multiplication of gods and goddesses. They have thirteen superior gods and goddesses being; Aesar, Jupiter Ulto, Pales, Lupercus, Apollo, Jove, Mars the Avenger, Janus, Quirinus, Pan, Venus Genetrix, Sulis-Minerva, and Juno; and they have hundreds of gods inferior, which they multiply without end. These later are persons selected for divine honours from the ranks of men, and who, for their virtues, merits or birthrights, are placed among the gods when they die. When the collegium, of which I have already spoken, has resolved to deify any person, they proclaim his apotheosis, which proclamation places him among the gods. Immediately the ignorant people begin to pray to him, and to invoke his aid (Comment 5).

First they make a god of him, and then they make him pay for the honour conferred! (?) From these small gods it is customary for classes and professions to select a patron. Musicians have selected Apollo; sailors, Neptune; farmers, Ceres; equestrians; Epona, soldiers, Mars; cities, towns, and persons select their guardian gods. Roma has selected Jupiter Capitolinus, and Athens, Sulis-Minerva; and families have their gods in their houses, and individuals carry their patrons in their pockets. And to these gods they give the honour and prayer which are due only to the only true god. I saw a poor sailor the other day who had escaped drowning at Ostia, hang up his coat as a votive offering in the temple of Neptune, and prostrate himself before his image as if it were Cernunnos!

If, sir, you have not heard of the Place of the Skull, there it stands most perfect and magnificent, with gold and stars on its falcate ceiling. Built by Agrippa, the son-in-law of the *pater patrum* Augustus (he is describing the Pantheon), it is dedicated to the god Aesar. Although various are the interpretations of its name, for some call it the Oracle, others the Star Chamber of *Ianvs* (Janus), Arx, and some say it is the Celestial Chamber, yet it is the home of Aesar, and in this temple many gods are worshipped; and sometimes initiations are held at night-time in veiled secret, and the participants wear feline skins (The Panther priesthood?). It contains many things that strike the beholder with wonder; Aesar is a bearded human head, sitting on high in the centre on black and white stones directly under the dome of light, and the twelve major gods and goddesses face it in a semi-circle … they are called Disciples, and Janus looks both ways. But sir, can it be that Aesar was once the ingulvie, Brân the Blessed? (Comment 6)

When new regions are conquered, their gods, or duplicates of them, are sent to this temple, that the people from those nations, visiting the metropolis, might have their accustomed images before which to bow. Sometimes, they pull down one idol and set up another, or merely change its name. The sweet little niche of Vesta is now possessed by the Sun, and Marcellian and Marcus replaced Romulus and Remus (Comment 7). And as these gods are in the Place of the Skull, so it is in other temples that stand in Roma.

© Old photo of the Pantheon, by Marie L. Hughes, 1944

The Place of the Skull, now called the Pantheon. Note the shadow of its domed roof falling on the wall of the building to the left. It is one of the best-preserved buildings in Rome today and at one stage in its existence, it was entirely covered in soil, making a man-made hill.

I have just returned from the temple of Jupiter Feretrius, where I witnessed a ceremony which I will describe to you. As the morning here is regarded as the most propitious part of the day, their great ceremonies are all ended before noon. The priest entered by a door from the library, dressed in a cream robe called *alba,* and ascended by a few steps to the altar. He wore, also, a tunic of various colours (A coat of many colours?). His head was shaven, which struck me as singular, and he had upon his breast a richly decorated covering called a pectoral. He wore also a veil. The whole dress struck me as very fanciful, nor could you conjecture, save from his head and face, whether he was a man or a woman. When he had washed his hands, he marched around the altar, and, having made obeisance before it, he stood fronting the people. Lighted tapers covered the altar. The servants and inferior priests burned incense, while the priest made many prostrations.

When the ceremony was ended, the head of the god in whose honour it was performed was carefully locked in a little box, and then the priest dismissed the people with these words, *Missio est*. And after being sprinkled by the inferiors with water mingled with salt, which is called 'lustralis aqua' or holy water, they left the temple, smiling and talking, and apparently gratified. And, with little variation, this is a picture of what I have witnessed in all the temples I have yet visited. The sacrifices, as I had supposed, did not always consist of slain animals; sometimes nothing is offered but a little round wafer, which is called *mola*, and the offering of which, as they declare, removes the sins of the people. This was instituted by Numa, and is called 'the unbloody sacrifice'.

I find also here a belief of a state somewhere between hell and the Elysian Fields, where the souls of the departed go which were not bad enough for hell nor good enough for heaven. I know not whether they borrowed this doctrine from Vergilius Maro (Virgil), who is held here in great repute, and who taught it; or whether it was older than Maro. Probably he only embodied what was a popular superstition in his fine poem. But the use which the priests make of it has saddened me with their want of dishonesty. They pretend to the power of abridging the awful sufferings of souls in this intermediate place by prayers and sacrifices, and for which they charge very high prices when the people are able to pay. In this way the priests here draw enormous revenues from the living for the saving of the souls of the dead. They speculate on the sorrows of the living; and from hearts broken by afflictions and trials they draw some of their chief revenues. They are impostors who live by defrauding the community.

Now, sir, if you will turn to the history of Roma at the date of this letter, you will find that I have given you an exact account, as far as such an account can be drawn in the short time here, and at the time selected. Whatever may be your private views, you would prefer the name of Druidism to the traditions of the Sybils. But I may weary you with these details which I make, and which you must read with sorrow. This is a wicked city, and its priests are the most wicked of its people. It is a most superstitious city … it has an atmosphere of horror … O, sir, will you not join me in a prayer in remembrance of Lezae of Mona ... Very truly your friend, Brí Leith of Mona, in Roma'.

Summary of Comments

Comment 1: The book of Genesis records that 'there were giants on the earth in those days' (Genesis 6:4) and they were still in existence in the 16th Century. Michelangelo complained bitterly about the toilet habits of 'ugly giants' living in hovels outside the Sistine Chapel while he was painting its ceiling. They 'stooled' under his scaffold and the stench, he said, was 'insufferable' (*The Writings of Michelangelo,* Pietra de Monic, France, 1878).

Comment 2: The Khrestians were still active in Antioch at the time of Emperor Julian (c. 363). Antioch was the Mithraic religious centre for centuries, a fact that was to have profound consequences for the whole character of later Christianity.

Comment 3: Early Christian churchmen called themselves 'little fishes', confirmed by Bishop Tertullian (c. 210) who wrote: 'We little fishes according to our Big Fish, are born in water'.

Comment 4: After the death of Julius Caesar in 44 BC, Mark Antony announced to the Senate that an old priestly Order called *The Repellers of Wolves* was to regroup. Very little is known of them, but it seems that they wore pure white hooded togas after Initiation, and were opposed to particular religious teachings.

Comment 5: Suetonius records that 'Aesar is the Etruscan for 'god' ... C being the Roman numeral 100' (*The Twelve Caesars,* Suetonius, pg, 104, The Penguin Classics, translated by Robert Graves, 1958). Excluding the first letter in Caesar's name, the remainder of the word had great significance in the community and held a divine status. He was subsequently venerated as the *Divine Julius* but was not honoured in the Pantheon at the time of Arch-Druid Brí Leith's visit. It seems that a special temple was set aside for his worship.

Comment 6: Mentioned earlier was Sir Francis Bacon's thirty-three-letter cipher in the Shakespearean Folio that says; THE PLACE OF THE SKULL WAS THE HOME OF GOD. He knew that the now-called Pantheon was built especially to house the gods and Brí Leith believed that Bran the Blessed was one of those gods. The name Aesar was given to Gaius Julius (Iulius) after his deification, and thus he became Julius Aesar. The Roman numeral 'C' for 100 was then added, and the name change became Caesar (100 Aesars and Julius was the first?). Brí Leith questioned whether the human head was that of Brân the Blessed, who in Druidic mythology was sixteen feet tall. That strange head is the subject of my next book, *The Secret Gospel Ciphers*.

Comment 7: The fact that busts of Mary's twins replaced Romulus and Remus reveals that, because they were the bonded 'sons of God' (through Tiberius to the deified Augustus), they had been individually deified after their death and honoured in the Pantheon. That conclusion is maintained today in the records of Catholicism with Marcellian and Marcus noted as being twin Saints of 'noble birth'. A First Century Roman Emperor deified the twins, not a Christian pope, for the construct of Christianity had not yet begun.

In 325, Constantine apotheosised the twin 'gods' as one entity, effectively introducing good and evil into the Roman religion. The book of Genesis (2:17) mentions the 'tree of knowledge of good and evil' in the Garden of Eden, and if you eat of the tree 'you will be like God, knowing good and evil'. Twin conflicts were biblical understandings of the times and may have originated from the Romulus and Remus dispute, or from the Old Testament story of Jacob and Esau. God loved Jacob, and hated Esau (Malachi 1: 2-3, Romans 9: 10-13), and that concept was fulfilled in the combined story of Rabbi Jesus and Judas Khrestus in Constantine's *New Testimonies*.

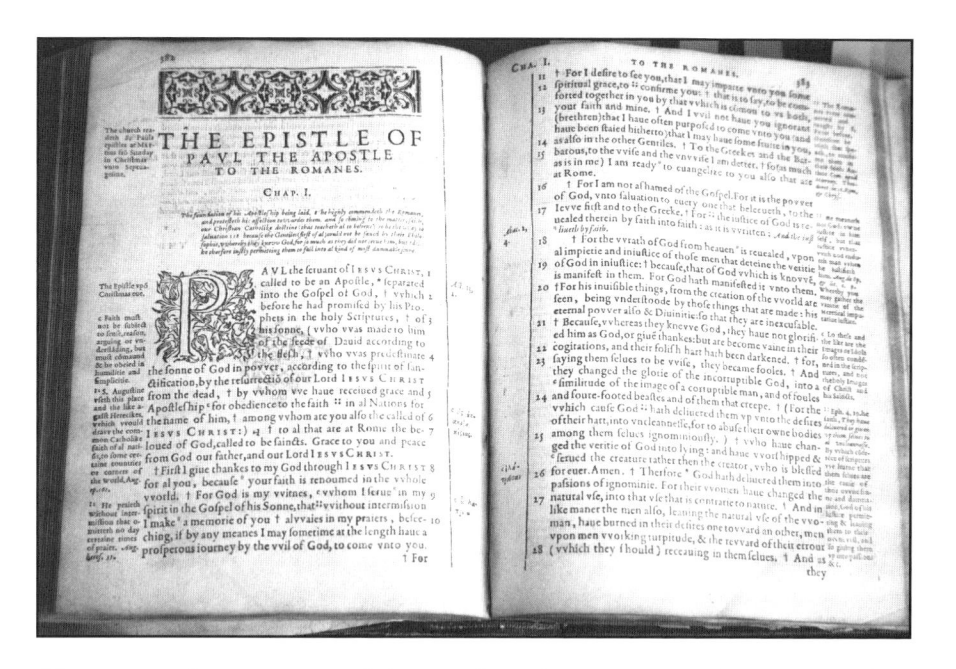

The opening forst two pages of the Epistle to the Romans in the FIRST Vulgate shows the general good condition of this old Bible. It is in this New Testament Epistle that the twin concepts of Christianity today are found.

Overview of the 'Letter from Rome'

In this description of the Roman church at the end of the First Century, several things stand out. Firstly, Jesus Christ is not mentioned but Mary's twins are honoured as gods. There is no mention of Paul's missionary message reaching Rome, yet the church maintains that he arrived there in 58, and died seven years later. Neither is there any allusion of a Christian community in Rome at that time, confirming the opinion of the Harvard Theology Review mentioned in Chapter 8. Importantly, there is no mention of St Peter being the first pope, nor allusion to a new religion associated with the Pontifex Maximus. The church claims that Peter died in 64, and if the Pontifex Maximus mentioned in this letter, living some 26 years later, was St Peter's successor, he was worshipping Jupiter, not Jesus Christ. The tradition that makes Peter the founder of the church of Rome depends only on the writings of Irenaeus (*Adverse Haeresies*, iii; 3, 2) who alluded to a journey 'to that other place' by Peter but did not say where.

Ancient Rome

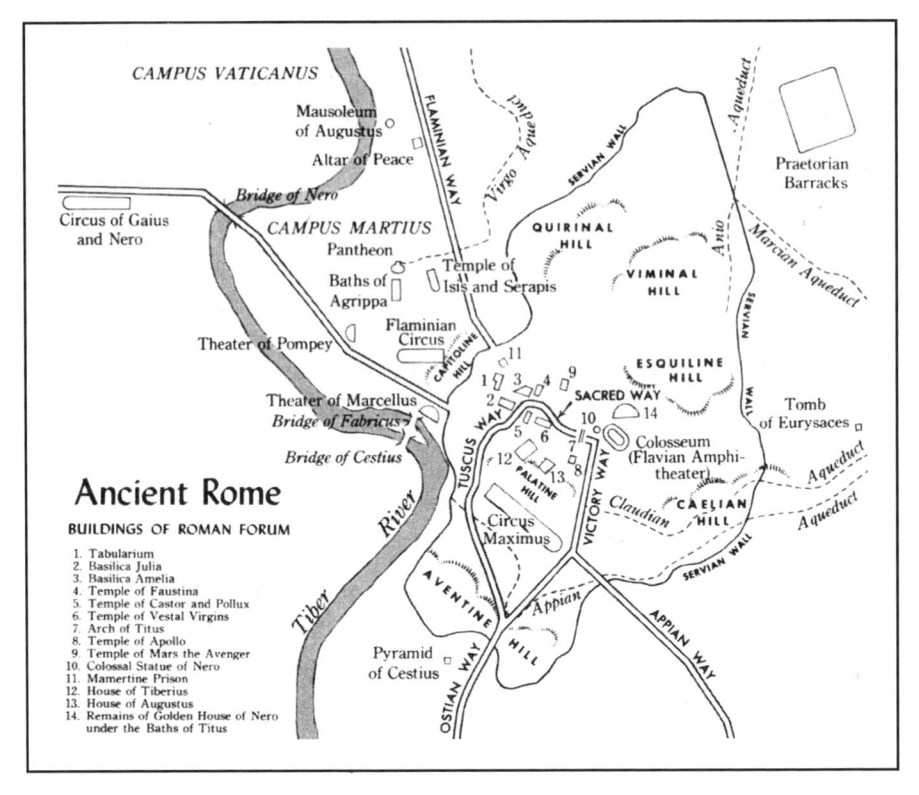

BUILDINGS OF ROMAN FORUM

1. Tabularium
2. Basilica Julia
3. Basilica Amelia
4. Temple of Faustina
5. Temple of Castor and Pollux
6. Temple of Vestal Virgins
7. Arch of Titus
8. Temple of Apollo
9. Temple of Mars the Avenger
10. Colossal Statue of Nero
11. Mamertine Prison
12. House of Tiberius
13. House of Augustus
14. Remains of Golden House of Nero under the Baths of Titus

© ABS, 1955

In the early 1940's, Pope Pius XII ordered an ancient cemetery under St. Peter's basilica to be scientifically excavated and the team found a series of twenty one mausolea facing southward onto a Roman street. The excavations resulted not in the discovery of apostle Peter's bones, as claimed by Pope Paul VI on June 26, 1965, but as the spot assumed in the 16th Century to be his First Century resting place. Opponents argue that Peter, allegedly crucified as a convicted criminal by Emperor Nero was not entitled to burial but more importantly, Peter was never in Rome anyway … church records claim that he went to Britain.

In 306, Eusebius compiled a list of earlier bishops of Rome but never mentioned Peter among them. However, he did say that Peter travelled to Britain (*Metaphrastes ad 29 Junii*, Menaloggi Graeceorum) and archaeological evidence confirms his record. The discovery at Whithern in Lincoln of a headstone on a grave now called the 'Peter Stone' supports Eusebius' statement, and nullifies the church claim that Peter is buried in Rome. It is a rough pillar, around four feet high and fifteen inches wide and the inscription in despoiled Roman capitals reads: 'LOE (VS) S (ANC) TI PETRI APVSTOLI', 'The place of Peter the apostle'.

The more important point, however, is that the false education of the public is in larger part due to a concealment of the fact that the real origin of Christianity had nothing to do with a divine Jesus Christ and a revelatory message, but is based on a fabricated and glorified literature that originated with the amalgamation of the lives of Mary's twin sons.

CHAPTER 37

Conclusion

Gospel evidence revealing that Jesus had a twin brother strikes at the very roots of Christian belief, for it shows that there is no validity, originality, or importance in the church's message, nor in its biblical texts. It also reveals that there was no supernatural Jesus Christ and, therefore, no genuine Christianity.

'All religions die of one disease, that of being found out'.

(Oscar Wilde, 1894)

The end, thanks be to God.

BIBLIOGRAPHY

This is a list of principal authorities consulted, referred to, or quoted in the preceding work. The Author wishes to express his grateful acknowledgment to the help he has received from the following books, and thank the authors, translators and publishers for making such works available.

Special note:

Due to mergers, closure or relocation of some publishing houses, efforts to trace some copyright owners proved difficult. If such works are referenced in this book, copyright is hereby acknowledged and grateful appreciation is extended to those persons whose thoughts and talents assisted in the development of this book. Any omissions, errors or oversights should be brought to the attention of the Author for correction and appropriate acknowledgment in reprints.

About Jerome, Bishop Jewell's works, London Folio, 1611
About the 'Books of Hystaspes' (Quoted by Justin Martyr), Chicago Public Library
Acta Archelai, The Dialogue Between Manes and Archelaus (issued by Hegemonius), trans. 1806
A Compendious History of the Council of Trent, B.W. Matthias, M.A., Dublin, 1832
Acta Concilii Niceni, Colon 1618
Acts of Justin (Martyr)
Acta of Pilate (sometimes called the *Gospel of Nicodemus*)
Against Heresies (Adv. Haer.), Irenaeus (*Against Heresies* was originally called *The Detection and Overthrow of False Gnosis* and was re-titled at the Council of Trent)
A Gospel of Shame, Elinor Burkett and Frank Bruni, Viking 1993
A History of the Council of Trent, Thomas Nelson and Sons, 2 Vols, Hubert Jedin (Trans. D. E. Graf), 1949
A Life of Constantine (7th Ed.), Dean Dudley, Attorney at Law, 1925, Ill. USA
Against Marcion (Adv. Marc.), Tertullian, MS. 1727

Against the Ebronites (Contra Ebronites), St. Epiphanius
Against the Gentiles (Adv. Gentiles), Tertullian
Analects of Confucious, The
Ancient Christian Writers, Trans. J. H. Crehan, the Newman Press, c. 1900
Ancient Rome, Rodolfo Lanciani, Boston, 1889
Ancient Secret, The, Flavia Anderson, Victor Gollancz Ltd, London, 1953
Annales Ecclesiastici (12 Vols.), Cardinal Caesar Baronius, Vatican librarian and church historian, 1538-1607
Ante Nicene Library, The, (ANL) A collection of writings of early churchmen prior to the Council of Nicaea, Edited by the Rev. Professor Roberts, D.D, and Principal James Donaldson, L.L.D, St. Andrews. 24 Vols. (Includes additional volumes of recently discovered manuscripts), circa 1900; also, American Reprint, eight volumes, The Christian Literature Publishing Co., Buffalo, NY, 1885. *The Nicene and Post-Nicene Fathers,* cited as N&PNF; First and Second Series; many volumes; same publishers.
Antioch, the Mithraic City, Rev. Leonard B. Ralston, Berkeley Square, London, 1921
A Patriotic Greek Lexion, Ed. G. Lampe, Oxford, 1961
Apology of Bishop Jewell, London Folio xxii, 1595
A Preliminary Dissertation about the Authors of the Bible, Bishop Lewis Du Pin, Third Edition, London, 1696
Archbishop Ussher's Works, 8 Vols, London 1613
Authentic and Acknowledged Standards of the Church of Rome, The, J. Hannah D.D., 1844

Bea-Methodius (Bermechobus), Supposed writings of St. Methodius of Olympus (d. 311)
Behold a Pale Horse, William Cooper, Light Technology Publishing, 1991
Beveridge's Pandecta Canonum, includes 60 Canons of the Synod of Laodicea still extant in original Greek
Bible and its Painters, The, Bruce Bernard, Orbis Publishing, 1988
Bible Criticism (2 Vols.), Professor Samuel Davidson D.D. LC.D, Contributor to *Encyclopedia Britannica*
Bible Fraud, The, Tony Bushby, 2001 (Website; www.thebiblefraud.com)
Bible Myths and Their Parallels in Other Religions, Reverend T.W. Doane, 1882
Bibliotheca Veterum Patrum, 28 Vols., Patristic writings of the Latin Church, 1765
Biblitheca sanctorum, Rome 1965, V1, 1132-7
Bishop Jewell's History of the Church, Reeves, London, 1611
Book of Enoch, The, Oxford Clarendon, U.K. 1912, Dr. Richard Lawrence's translation
Book of the Church, The, Bishop R. Southerly, Fourth Ed., London, 1837, *etiam,* 1841
Book of the Entrance to Eternal Life, The, Ani, Royal Scribe, Alexandrian Library, Egypt
Book of the Roman Catholic Church, Charles Butler, 8 Vols., 1825
Books of Alexander, The, Questions he asked the Brahmans; first published circa 1490, Alexandrian Library, Alexandria, Egypt
Bryant's Analysis of Ancient Mythology
Bull of Pope Pius, VII, To the Primate of Poland, Section 2, 3

BIBLIOGRAPHY

Butler's Lives of the Saints, Rev. Alban Butler, 1926

Cannibalism: The Religious Significance, Eaton University Press, USA, 1943
Cardinal Bembo, His Letters and Comments on Pope Leo X, 1842 Reprint
Catalogue of the Greek and Latin Papyri in the John Ryland's Library, by C. H. Roberts, c. 1934
Catholic History, Dom Arnold Wion, Benedictine historian, 1596
Cave's Primitive Christianity, William Cave, D.D. 1682, reprinted by Akerbar in 1790
Censoring of Diderot's Encyclopedia and the Re-established Text, The, D. H. Gordon and N. L. Torrey, NY, 1947
Christ in Art, Mrs. Jameson, British Library
Christian Forgeries, Major Joseph Wheless, Judge Advocate, Idaho, 1930
Christna Et Le Christ, Translated from the Hari-Purana, by Jacolliot
Church of the Cymry, Rev. W. Hughes, undated
Church Sex Crimes, Tristan Rankine, Awareness Quest, Australia, 1995
Church of Rome, The, Rev. Charles Elliott, D.D, 1844
Church History, Socrates Scholasticus (the Scholar), Jenning's Trans., 1911
Ciceronians es, non Christianus
City of God, Augustine, from 1609 translation
City of Saints, The, Miscellaneous Tracts, Thomas Hawkings, c. 1890
Clement of Alexandria, Fragment from Cassiodorus, ANL
Codex of Hillel, 600 Manuscripts, first published in England in 1780
Codex Sinaiticus, 8th Ed., Prof. C. Tischendorf, The Letterworth Press, UK
Colloquies, Desiderius Erasmus, London, reprint 1878
Commentary and Notes on the Apostolic Epistles, James Macknight, London, 1821
Confessions of Augustine, Augustine, Library of the Fathers, Oxford Movement, 1838
Confessions of a French Catholic Priest, New York, Mathers, 1837
Confessions of Tertullian, Tertullian, The Ante Nicene Library, circa 1900
Constantine's Letter (in regard to having the first fifty copies of the New Testament written and bound)
Constantinople: Byzantium-Istanbul, D. Talbot Rice, London, 1965
Constitutions of Constantine
Constitutions of the Church, Vatican Council 1
Contra Celsum (Against Celsus)
Contradictions in the Bible, Prof. Eugene McArthur, Edinburgh, 1936
Controversy with Breckenridge, John A. Breckenridge, 1836
Corruptions of Councils, Dr Philip Morney, original publication in 1612; 1889 reprint
Council of Nicaea, The History of, Dean Dudley, first printed 1886, reprinted in 1965 by Health Research, California
Creators of the Renaissance, The, Lionello Venturi, Geneva, 1950
Creed of Nicene, The, Formulary (first printing 1807)
Crime and Immorality in the Catholic Church, Emmett McLaughlin, Catholic priest
Crucifixion of Truth, The, Tony Bushby, Joshua Books, Australia, First Published in March, 2005;

reprinted in June 2005 (Website; www.thebiblefraud.com)
Cyprian, Epist. 74, ed. Pamel. 1589

Dark Side of Christianity, The, Helen Ellerbe, Morningstar Books, USA, 1995
D'Aubigné, History of the Great Reformation, 3 Vols. J. H. Merle, London, 1840
Dead Sea Scroll Deception, The, Michael Baigent, Richard Leigh, Corgi Books, 1992
De Antiqua Ecclesiae Disciplina, Bishop Lewis Du Pin, Catholic historian, (Folio, Paris, 1686), English translation by J. H. C. Hopkins, D.D
Decisions of the Council of Trent, Edmund Gibson, Bishop of London, 1738
De Civitate Dei, Augustine, Bishop of Hippo
Delineation of Roman Catholicism, Rev. Charles Elliott, D.D., 1844
Descent of Manuscripts, The, Albert C. Clarke, University of Oxford, 1918
De Statu Mortuorum, Dr. Burnet, English author, c. 1840
Detection and Overthrow of False Gnosis, Irenaeus
De Viris Illustribus, 135, D. Vallarsi trans., Verona, 1734-42
Diegesis, The, Reverend Robert Taylor, Boston, 1873
Difficulties of Romanism, The, George Stanley Faber, London, 1826
Discovery of the Essene Gospel of Peace, 1989 Edition, Edmond Bordeaux Szekely
Doctrine of Justification, The, James Buchanan DD. LL.D (Reprinted 1977 from the 1867 version by T. T. Clarke, Edinburgh), Baker Book House, Grand Rapids, Michigan
Dungeons, Fire and Sword; The Knights Templar in the Crusades, John Robinson, Michael O'mara, London, 1994
Du Pin's Ecclesiastical History, Oxford, 1725

Early Christian Classics, 2 Vols., J. A. Robinson, 1916
Early History of the Ancient Israelites, The, Professor Thomas L. Thompson, E. J. Brill, Leiden, The Netherlands, 1992
Early Theological Writings, G.W.F. Hegal
Ecce Homo, Joseph Jobe, Macmillan, 1962
Ecclesiastical History, Mosheim, 6 Vols., London, 1825
Ecclesiastical History, Eusebius of Caesarea
Ecclesiastical History, Sozomen
Ecclesiastical Policy of the New Testament, The, Professor Samuel Davidson D.D. L.C.D
Eclectric Review, Melancthon, 1497-1560
Edgar's Variations of Popery, Second Edition, 1838
Edict of Callistus I, Bishop of Rome, 217-222
Edict of Callistus I, Commentaries, J. Cosin, Bishop of Durham, 1594-1672
Edicts of Justinian (Dictionaire de Theologie, 1920)
Eleusinian and Bacchic Mysteries, The, Thomas Taylor, 1875
End of Controversy, The, Dr. Milner, c. 1840
Epitome of the General Councils of the Church, from the Council of Nicaea, to the Conclusion of the Roman Council of Trent in the Year 1563, The, Reverend Richard Grier, D.D., 1828

BIBLIOGRAPHY

Erasmus, Desid, in Nov. Test. Annotations, Fol. Basil, 1542
Essene Origins of Christianity, The, E. B. Szekely, International Biogenic Society, 1989 *Essenes and the Vatican*, E. B. Szekely, International Biogenic Society, 1989 Edition
Eusebius of Caesarea, J. B. Lightfoot, World Publ. Co. 1962, NY (in *A Dictionary of Christian Biograph, Literature, Sects and Doctrines*, London 1880
Evargrius, A History of the Church from AD 431 to AD 594, E. Walford, Bonn's Ecclesiastical Library, London, 1851
Extermination of the Cathars, The, Simonde de Sismondi, 1826
Exhortation to the Heathen (Exhort), Clement of Alexandria

Fabiola, Cardinal Wiseman, undated
False Decretals, The, E. H. Davenport, Oxford, 1916
Far Hence Unto the Gentiles, Major Samuels, 1964
Fathers of the Church, (6 Vols.) Translated by Thomas B. Falls, Publ. Christian Heritage, Penns. 1938
Fathers of the Greek Church, The, Hans von Campenhausen, trans. Stanley Godman
Fides Regia Britannica, Cardinal Alford
Fifty Years in the Church of Rome, Chas. Chiniquy, First Printed 1885
First Gay Pope, The, Lyn Fletcher, Alyson Publications, 1992
First Apology and the Second Apology, The, Justin Martyr (Oxford University Trans.)
First Seven Ecumenical Councils, The, L. D. Davis, 1987
Five Centuries of Religion, G. G. Coulton, Cambridge University Press, 1923
Five Gospels, The, The Jesus Seminar, Macmillan Publishing Company, N.Y., 1993
Florence and Venice, H. A. Taine, New York, 1869
Forgery in the New Testament, S. Patrick, Shaftsbury Ave. Bloomsbury, London, 1952
Fourth Century Rumors About Christ, P. M. Cozzia-Leone, Archives de Louvre, 1857
Foxe's Book of Martyrs
Frenzy to Create a God, The, Development of New Testament texts, Rev. F.G. Miller (revised by Dr. A. Frenlon in 1907), U.K, 1895

Genesis of Christianity, Plummer, Edinburgh, 1876
Genuineness and Authenticity of the Gospels, Mr. B. A. Hinsdale (MA)
Glascock, Dr. Henry, (notes) McLaughlin Foundation, Los Angeles, 1996
Glimpses of Life Beyond Death, Tony Bushby, Joshua Books, Australia, 2004 (Website address, www.thebiblefraud.com)
Glories of Mary, Mother of God, The, Alphons de Ligorio, Dublin Ed, 1835
God's Book of Eskra
Good News of the Kingdoms, The, Mr. Norman Segal, Australia 1995
Gutenberg Revolution, The, John Man, Headline Book Publishing, London, 2003

Heresies (Epip., Haer), Epiphanius
Heresies (Hippo, Haer), Hippolytus
Heretic Popes, Rev. Charles Elliott, D.D, Wesleyan Conference Office, London, 1844

Herods, The, Dean Farrar, undated
Hidden Vatican Files, The, Inside Information From the Secret Church Archives, from an exclusive manuscript written by a Catholic priest and released to Tony Bushby by his widow. Publ. Date, 2006
History in the Encyclopedia, D. H. Gordon and N. L. Torrey (NY. 1947)
History of the Bible, Bronson C. Keeler, C. P. Farrell, Publ 1881, Reprint 1965 by Health Research
History of Literature, The, Freculphus apud Godwin
History of the Papacy During the Reformation, Mandell Creighton, London, 1882
History of Popery, The, 2 Vols. London, 1735
History of Purple as a Status Symbol in Antiquity, M. Reinhold, Brussels, 1970
History of the Christian Church, Philip Schaff, D.D., Ms. No. 283, Chicago Public Library
History of the Christian Church, H. H. Milman, D.D. 1871
History of the Christian Religion (to the year 200), Judge C. B. Waite, 6th Ed. 1908
History of the Culdees, Jamieson
History of Dominic, Castiglio, Venice 1529
History of the Knights Templar, The, Charles G. Addison, First Publ. 1842, Republished by Adventures Unlimited, 1997
History of the Popes, B. Maclean (Ferrier), 1907
History of the Popes, Leopold von Ranke, London, 1878
History of the Popes from the Foundation of the See of Rome to the Present Time, The, Archbishop Bower, 3rd Edition, London, 1750
History of the Vulgate, Paolo Sarpi, Translated by Brent, London, 1676
Holy Blood and the Holy Grail, The, Michael Baigent, Richard Leigh and Henry Lincoln, Corgi Books, 1990
Holy Place, The, Henry Lincoln, Jonathon Cape, London, 1991
Homosexuality in the Church, Confidential Diocesan Report to the Bishops (UK) 1994
How the Great Pan Died, Edmond S. Bordeaux, Mille Meditations, 1968
Hyptatia, Pagan Origins of Christianity, Dean, 1792

Index Librorum Prohibitorum, Antwerp, 1571
Indian Review, The, Del Mar, 1903
Indulgences, Their Origin, Nature and Development, Quaracchi, 1897
In God's Name, An Investigation Into the Murder of Pope John Paul I, David Yallop, Corgi Books, London 1984
Inquisition, The, Michael Baigent and Richard Leigh, Penguin Books, 2000
Inquisition and Liberty, G. G. Coulton, London, 1938
Institutes of Christian History, Johann Mosheim, 1755
Introduction To The New Testament, Professor Davidson, (MS 104)
Index of Prohibited Books, 'By Command of the Present Pope Gregory XVI', London, 1840
Index Expurgatorius Vaticanus, Edited by R. Gibbings, B.A., Dublin, 1837
Intellectual Development, Dr. James McCabe, Bloomsbury, 1927
Irenaeus, A. Stieren, Leipzig, 2 Vols. 1848

BIBLIOGRAPHY

Irenaeus of Lyons, trans. John Keble, London 1872
Irenaeus, writings in the ante-Nicene Fathers, N.Y. 1926
Isis Unveiled, H. P. Blavatsky, 2 Vols. Theosophical University Press, California, 1976

Jasher (Yasher), 1751 (twice mentioned in the Old Testament), oldest known version is called *The Essene Book of Genesis* and is held in the Vatican Archives (E. B. Szekely)
Jebamoth, The
Jerome, A Summary of his Three Writings, Prof. Isaac Muir, 1889
Justin Martyr, writings contained in the ante-Nicene Fathers, N.Y. 1926
Justinian and Theodora, Robert Browning, Thames and Hudson, London, 1987

Key for Catholics, Richard Baxter, London 1839
Knights Templar, The, Stephen Howarth, Collins, London, 1982
Koran, the Holy, translated by A. Yusuf Ali, Publ. By Amana Corp., Maryland, USA
Koran, The, translated by George Sale, Frederick Warne and Co., London, 1734
Krata Repoa (or, Initiation into the Ancient Mysteries of the Priests of Egypt), C. F. Koppen and J. W. B. Von Hymmen, Berlin, 1782

Lead Us Not Into Temptation, Jason Berry, Doubleday, NY, 1992
Lectures on the Council of Trent, J. A. Froude, New York, 1896
Lectures on the Doctrine of the Catholic Church, Wiseman, 2 Vols., London, 1836
Leonardo da Vinci, Sigmund Freud, New York, 1947
Letters of Jerome, The (Library of the Fathers)
Letter to Heliodorus, originally written in 374 by Jerome
Letter to the Bishops of Egypt and Libya
Liber Pontificalis, Duchesne, Undated, but c. 1900
Liberty, Bishop Jeremy Taylor, 15 Vols. Heber's Ed., 1822
Library of the Bulls, The
Library of the Fathers, The, 'Damasus', Oxford, 1833-45
Life and Pontificate of Leo X, 2 Vols, William Roscoe, London, 1853
Life of Constantine, Attributed to Eusebius
Life of Lardner, by Dr. Kippis
Life of Michelangelo Buonarroti, J. A. Symonds, Modern Library, c. 1883
Life of St. Francis, Demonoligia
Life of Vespasian, Suetonius, Second Century Roman historian
Literary Policy of the Church of Rome, The, Rev. Mr. Mendham, Second Ed., 1840
Literary Source Book of the Italian Renaissance, M. Whitcomb, Philadelphia, 1900
Lives of the Most Eminent Painters, Sculptors, and Architects, Giorgio Vasari, 1907
Lives of the Popes, Mann, c. 1905
Lives of the Roman Pontiffs, The, Bartolomeo Platina (1421-81), Vatican librarian
Lives of the Saints, The, Reverend S. Baring Gould, 16 Vols. 1872
London Quarterly Review, John W. Burgon, Dean of Chichester, 1883

Lost and Hostile Gospels, Reverend S. Baring Gould, circa 1872
Lost Gods, John Allegro, Publ. by Michael Joseph Ltd, London, 1977
Lost Scrolls of the Essene Brotherhood, The, E. B. Szekely, International Biogenic Society, 1989 Edition
Lucrezia Borgia, Ferdinand Gregorovius, London, 1901

Magical Mystical Sites, Elizabeth Pepper and John Wilcock, Sphere Books Ltd, London, 1976
Mahabharata, The Hindu Epic, trans., Minisus, London, 1910
Martin Luther and the Reformation, Chas Beard, London, 1896
Medici, The, G. F. Young, Modern Library, undated
Medicine Chest, St Epiphanius
Meditations, Marcus Aurelius
Mentality of the Clergy, The, Psychologist Quarterly, Professor R. L. Hugo, Calif. 1969
Messiah Myth, The, Professor Thomas L. Thompson, Basic Books (a member of the Perseus Group), New York, 2005
Michelangelo and the Pope's Ceiling, Ross King, Random House, London, 2002
Monumental Christianity, J. P. Lundy, 1876
Mysteries of Catholicism, The, G. H. Pember, MA, Oliphants Ltd, London, 1942

Name of the Furies, The, Eumenides
Nazareth, the City, Dr. Stanton, Gemma, London, circa 1905
Nexus New Times, Nexus Magazine Pty Ltd, Australia, ed. Duncan M. Roads

Of the Five Plagues of the Church, Count Antonio Rosmini, priest, 1848
Old Christian Literature, Van Manen of Leyden (contributor to *Encyclopedia Biblica,* circa 1860)
Old Christian Texts, A Collection, M. Collins, London, 1890
Old Church Records, Thomas Harding, Antwerp, (Bibliotheca Alexandrina), 1565
Oldest Manuscripts in New Zealand, The, David M. Taylor, 1955
On God's Government (De Gubernationale) Salvanius of Marseilles, circa 450, Trans. by E.V. Sanford; found in the 'Records of Civilization, Sources and Studies', published by Columbia University
On the Errors of the Trinity, Michael Servetus
On the Government of the Ancient Church, William Cave, D. D. London, 1683
On the Roman Forgeries in Councils, Thomas Comber, D. D. London, 1689
On the Veiling of Virgins, Tertullian
On the Work of Monks, St Augustine, circa AD 450
Oracles of Callistus I, translated by Victor Germaine, 1822
Origen Against Celsus, translated by James Bellamy, London, 1660
Origen, De. Princip., Commentary on Rome
Origin of Religion Belief, Draper
Orosius, Paulus, Fourth Century church historian who records extracts from Josephus's writings that are not present in the modern text of Josephus
Orthodox Corruption of Scripture, The, Prof. Bart D. Ehrman

BIBLIOGRAPHY

Panegyric on the Emperor Trajan, Pliny the Younger, Roman Senator, c. 112
Paraphrase and Commentary on the New Testament, 2 Vols. London, 1703
Pastoral Theology, Professor J. Beck, 1910
Petrus Cluniacensis, Peter, Abbot of Cluny, c. 1310
Pilgrimage to Rome, Rev. Seymour, 1832
Poedagogus (or Instructor), Clement of Alexandria
Prescriptions of Tertullian
Primitive Christianity, Professor Rudolf Bultman, The Fontana Library, 1956
Printer's Marks, W. Roberts, G. W. Bell and Sons, London, 1892

Queen Mabel, Percy Bysshe Shelley, 1813

Rape Crisis Centre Report on the Church, Victoria, Australia, 1994
Raphael, Eugene Muntz, London, 1882
Records of Events, Marcellinus Ammianus, in the Loeb Classical Library
Rectification of Names, The, E. S. Burt, Mentor Books, New York, 1949
Reformation, The, Dr. Will Durant, Simon and Schuster, New York, 1957
Regio Fides, Griffiths (one of the most learned Roman Catholic historians)
Religion of the Romans, New York ed., Adams, 1826
Renaissance Painting, Barron's
Repellers of Wolves, John Telfer, Pre-publication manuscript, 2005
Revelationum, Lib, 1, cap. X, Rome, St. Bridget of Sweden, reprint 1628
Roman Emperors, The, Michael Grant, George Weidenfeld and Nicholson Limited, 1985
Roman Martyrology, British Library, London
Roman Myths, Jane F. Gardner, British Museum, 1993
Roman State and Christian Church, (A collection of legal documents, 3 Vols; Vol. 3 contains translations of all Emperor Justinian's religious legislation, with full discussions), London, 1966
Romer's Egypt, Book Club Associates, by arrangement with Michael Joseph Ltd and the Rainbird Publishing Group Ltd, 1982
Rousseau and Revolution, Will and Ariel Durant, Simon and Schuster, New York, 1967

Sacred Geography, British Library, London, author unknown, c. 1704
Sayings of the Christian Priests, Rev. J. Desmond, W. D., Russell Square, London, 1936
Scorpiace, Tertullian
Scribes and Correctors of the Codex Sinaiticus, H. J. M. Milne and T. C. Skeat, British Museum, London, 1938
Scrolls of Nebeseni, The, Priest of Memphis, Alexandrian Library, Egypt, c. 500 BC
Second Marriage a Species of Adultery, Tertullian
Secret in the Bible, The, Tony Bushby, Joshua Books, Australia, 2003; Website: www.thebiblefraud.com
Secrets of Rennes-Le-Chateau, Lionel and Patricia Fanthope, Samuel Weiser, Inc. USA, 1992
Secrets of the Christian Fathers, J. W. Sergerus, 1685, reprint 1897
Secret History of the Court of Justinian, Procopius, publ. by the Athenian Society in 1896

Secreta Monica, The (The Secret Instruction), English reprint, 1857
Secret Teachings of All Ages, Manly P. Hall, Philosophical Research, The Society Inc., L.A., Calif. 1901
Servetus and Calvin, R. Willis M.D., London, 1877
Sibylline Oracles, Extant are Nos. 1, 2, 3, 4, 5, 6, 7, 8, 11, 12, 13, 14
Sibyllini Libra
Soliloquies of Augustine, R. E. Cleveland, London, Williams and Norgate, 1910
Source Book of Medieval History, Frederic Ogg, New York, 1907
Stromata (or *Miscellanies*), Clement of Alexandria, held in the Florence MS.
Summa Theology, St. Thomas Aquinas
Sungods in Mythology, Dr. J. L. C. Lugo, Vienna, c. 1870
Supremacy of the Pope, Samuel Edgar, 2nd Edition, London, 1838

Talmud in History, The, G. R. S. Mead, B.A., M.R.A.S., London and Benares, 1903
Telling Lies for God, Professor Ian Plimer, Random House, 1994
Temples, Tombs and Hieroglyphs, Barbara Mertz, Victor Gollancz Limited, London, 1964
Testament of Christian Civilization, The, Joseph McCabe, Watts and Co. London, 1946
Theological Tracts, 'On Councils', 6 Vols., London, 1791
Theological Works, Isaac Barrow, Oxford, 1830
Theophilus to Autolycus, Theophilus of Antioch
Testament of Solomon, The, Ed. C. McCown, Leipzig, 1922
The Constantine Constitutions
The Creed and Oath of Pope Pius IV, bearing the date November 1564
The Records of Rome, 1868, British Library
The 'Terrible Secret' of Christianity, Tony Bushby, for publication in 2006
The Twilight of Christianity, Dr. H. Elmer Barnes, c. 1930
Three Early Doctrinal Modifications of the Text of the Gospels, The Hibbert Journal, London, 1902
To His Wife, Tertullian, circa 210
Trias Thaumaturga, John Colgan

Uncertain History of Christian Beginnings, The, J. Patterson, Auckland, New Zealand
Unknown Books of the Essenes, The, E. B. Szekely, International Biogenic Society, 1989
Unpublished records of Josephus, The (Freiburg), Tony Bushby

Valleus' Notes (Valleus Paterculus), (Acta Pilati)
Vatican Billions, The, Avro Manhattan, Paravision Books, London, 1972
Venetian Painters, F. J. Matther, New York, 1936
Vicars of Christ, Peter de Rosa, Crown Publishers, New York, 1988
Victims of the Marmertine, The, Rev. A. J. O'Reilly, D.D., undated but pre-1929
Vindicae Ecclesia Anglicanne, Robert Southey, London, 1826
Volume Archko, archaeological writings of the Sanhedrin and Talmud of the Jews
Vulgar Verses, Rev. Joseph Burke, London, 1840

When Women Where Priests, Karen Jo Torjesen, HarperSanFrancisco, 1995
When Women Ruled the World, Julie Halligan, pre-publication manuscript, 2005
Why Councils Differed, George Campbell, McDougal Press, Aberdeen, 1816
Wisdom of the Ancients, The, Sir Francis Bacon, 1619, reprint by Berington, 1894
Works of Nathaniel Lardner, D.D. 10 Vols. Bloomsbury, London, 1824
World's Sixteen Crucified Saviours, The, K. Graves, Banner of Light Publishing Co., 1900
Writings of Michelangelo, The, Pietra de Monic, France, 1878
Writings of Saint John of Damascus, The, F. H. Chase, publ. By 'Fathers of the Church'
Writings of Saint Justin Martyr, The, trans. T.B. Falls, publ. Christian Heritage

The Library of the Fathers

A series of English translations of selected writings of the church fathers. The first volume to appear was *The Confessions of Augustine,* 1838 (Published by the Oxford Movement 1833-45) and includes a later attachment called *Sayings of the Fathers.*

The writings of Dr. Constantine Von Tischendorf

(Available in the British Library, London)
Alterations to the Sinai Bible; Are Our Gospels Genuine or Not? Codex Sinaiticus; The Authenticity of Our Gospels; The Origin of the Four Gospels; The Various Versions of the Bible; When Were Our Gospels Written?

Encyclopedias and dictionaries consulted

A Basic Jewish Encyclopedia, Rabbi Harry A. Cohen, Ph. D, Wyndham and Stacey Ltd, London, 1965
A Dictionary of Biblical Tradition, David Lyle Jeffrey, William B. Eerdman's Publishing Co., Grand Rapids, Michigan
A Dictionary of Universal Knowledge for the People, Lippincott and Co. 1877
Ancient Egyptian Dictionary, R. Johnson and E. Rumbel (in Cairo Library)
An Illustrated Encyclopedia of Mysticism and The Mystery Religions, J. Ferguson, Thames and Hudson, London, 1976
Annals Ecclesiastici, J. D. Mansi and D. Georgius, 38 Vols. Lucca, 1738-59
An Expository Dictionary of Biblical Words, W. E. Vine, M.A., Merrill F. Unger and William White Jnr., Thomas Nelson Publ. 1984
Bingham's Antiquities of the Christian Church, Straker's Ed. 1840, London
Blair's Chronological Tables
Bushby's Encyclopedia of Christian Cover-ups, pre-publication manuscript, 2006
Catholic Encyclopedia, The, 15 volumes, plus index, 1907-1914
Catholic Encyclopedia, The, published under the Imprimatur of Archbishop Farley; New York, Robert Appleton Co., 1907-9
Catholic Encyclopedia, The, Robert C. Broderick, Thomas Nelson Publ. 1976
Classical Dictionary, William Smith, Harper and Brothers, New York, 1877

Code of Canon Law, The, The Canon Law Society of America, 1985
Companion Encyclopedia of Theology, Routledge, 1995
Decrees of the Ecumenical Councils (2 Vols.), Sheed and Ward
Devil's Dictionary, The, Ambrose Bierce, circa 1900
Dictionaire de Theologie, 1920
Dictionary of Beliefs and Religions, Wordsworth Reference, Publ. by Wordsworth Editions Ltd, England, 1995
Dictionary of the Bible, Grant and Rowley; 2nd Ed., 1963
Dictionary of Christian Antiquities, ed. Smith and Cheetham, London, 1875
Dictionary of Classical Mythology, Religion, Literature and Art, Oskar Seyffert, Random House, 1995
Dictionary of Greek and Roman Antiquities
Dictionary of Islam, London, 1895
Dictionary of Proper Names and Places in the Bible, O. Odelain and R. Seguinean, 1981
Dictionary of Rare Words, Isaac Burrows, Cambridge, 1830
Dictionary of Sects, Blunt
Dictionary of the Bible, original edition by James Hastings D.D., revised by F.C. Grant and H. H. Rowley, 1963
Diderot's Encyclopedia, 1759
Encyclopedia Biblica, four volumes; Adam & Charles Black, London, 1899; American Reprint, The Macmillan Co., New York, 1914
Encyclopedia Britannica, Edinburgh Edition, Printed for A. Bell and C. Macfarquar, 3rd Edition in 18 Volumes, 1797
Encyclopedia Britannica, 18 Volumes, James Moore's Dublin Edition, 1790-97
Encyclopedia Britannica, 9th Edition, 24 Volumes, A. and C. Black, 1875-1889
Encyclopedia Britannica, particularly Volumes 8, 9, 10 and 11
Encyclopedia Dictionary of the Bible, McGraw, New York 1963
Encyclopedia Ecclesiastica, Prompta Biblioth, Lucii F. Ferraris, Francof, 1781
Encyclopedia Judaica (16 volumes), Ed. Cecil Roth, Jerusalem, 1974
Encyclopedia Judaica Jerusalem, 1971
Encyclopedia of Catholic Doctrine, 1997
Encyclopedia of Catholicism, 1989
Encyclopedia of Early Christianity, Everett Ferguson (Ed.), St. James Press, Chicago and London, 1974
Encyclopedia of Freemasonry, Albert Mackey, MD, McClure Publishing, 1917
Encyclopedia of Religion and Ethics, Edited by James Hastings, T. & T. Clark, Edinburgh, 1914
Encyclopedia of the Early Church, English Trans. 1992
Encyclopedia of the Roman Empire, Matthew Bunson, Facts on File, NY. 1994
Encyclopedias, Their History Throughout the Ages, 1966
Funk and Wagnell's New Encyclopedia, 1988
Funk and Wagnell's New Standard Dictionary, 1913
Harper's Bible Dictionary, Paul J. Achtemeier, Harper and Row, 1985
Historical Dictionary of the Orthodox Church, Prokurat, Golitizin, Peterson, Scarecrow Press Inc. 1996
Jewish Encyclopedia, N.Y. 1903

Lakeland Bible Dictionary, Zondervan Publ. House, 1966
London Encyclopedia
Modern Catholic Encyclopedia, The, The Liturgical Press, 1994
New American Cyclopedia, The, circa 1890
New Bible Dictionary, Inter-Varsity, Leicester, England, 1986
New Catholic Encyclopedia (N.C.E.), 1976 volume
New Dictionary of Theology, Inter-Varsity, Leicester, England, 1988
New Encyclopedia Britannica, 1987
New Jewish Encyclopedia, The
New Larousse Encyclopedia of Mythology, 1984
Our Sunday Visitor's Catholic Encyclopedia, 1986 Edition
Oxford Classical Dictionary, The, 1949
Oxford Dictionary of Popes, The, Oxford University Press
Oxford Dictionary of the Christian Church, Cross 1974, 1997
Oxford Icelandic Dictionary
Papal Pronouncements (2 Vols.), The Pierian Press, 1990
Popular and Critical Bible Encyclopedia, Samuel Fallows, Chicago, 1919
Smaller Classical Dictionary, 1910
Tanner's Notitia Monastica, 1744
Theology Dictionary of the New Testament, W. M. B. Eerdman's Publ. Co., U.S.A. 1981
The Universal Jewish Encyclopedia, New York
Vines Expository Dictionary of New Testament Words, W. E. Vine, M.A. 1996
Webster's Unabridged Dictionary
Wade's British Chronology

Bibles used as comparative references

Alexandrian Bible, translation by Tischendorf
American Standard Version by the American Revision Committee, 1901
Anonymous Bible, The, 1762, 'In this Bible an attempt was made to correct the text of the King James Version' (Extract from Preface, by F. S. Paris)
Bear Bible, The,
Bezae Bible, The
Bible of St. John, The, 1690
Bible of the Church, 1765
Bible in Verse, The, 4 Vols., 1778
Bishop's Bible, The, 1608 Edition
Chaloner-Douay Version of the Catholic Vulgate
Christian's Divine Bible, Corrected by Henry Southwell, London, 1773
Constantine Bible, The
Ethiopian Bible
First Catholic Bible in the English Language, The, 1563

Fool Bible, The, Printed during the reign of Charles 1, the text of Psalm 14:1 read, 'The fool has said in his heart there is a god'. The printer was fined ?3000 and all copies withdrawn
Forgotten Sins Bible, See Luke 7:47 (1638)
Good News Bible, The, Today's Version (English), 1976
Gospel of Thomas the Twin
Interlinear Translation of the Greek Scriptures, The, 1969
Jefferson Bible, The
Jerusalem Bible, The, 1966
Judas Bible, The, Jesus is called Judas at Matthew 26:36
King James Bible (K.J.B.), 1611, revised 1881-1885; 1901; 1946-1952; 1971
Latin Vulgate, Trans. R. Challoner, 1609; 1749; 1750; 1752; 1764; 1772
Matthew Bible, The
Mount Sinai Manuscript of the Bible, (British Museum, addit. MS. 43725), 1934
New American Bible, The, St. Joseph Edition, 1970
New English Bible, The (three variations)
New International Version, The, 1973
New Testament According to the Eastern Text, George M. Lamsa
Poor Man's Bible, The, 1806
Priest's Bible, The
Printers' Bible, 1702
Profit Bible, Oxford edition (1711)
Revised Standard Version, Catholic Edition, 1966
Roman Bible, The
St Augustine's Bible
Syrian Bible, The
The Common Translation Corrected, Oxford, 1718-1724
Universal Bible, 1766
Variorum Teacher's Edition, The, Eyre & Spottiswoode
Vatican Bible, The

INDEX

A

A coded alphabet in secret books	50
A traditional Islamic saying	41
A veil of secrecy	50
Acacius, a bear trainer	205
Achment, Sultan Abdoul	324
Acta Cunobeline	160, 176
Acts of the Apostles	81, 108, 316-319, 324, 325
canonical version of	317
false speeches in	318
earliest known Greek text	319
earliest known version of verse	37, 319
forged nature of	319
written falsely	319
suppressed chapter of	320
suppressed version of	324
Acts of Thomas	38, 39, 54, 100, 102, 103, 277
two messiahs recorded in the	38, 39, 54
Adoration of the Magi	246, 252
Aesar	169, 331, 332, 335, 336
Against Celsus	44, 83
Agbad, Emperor	292
Agrippa	45, 98, 142, 332
Albigensians	217, 218
Alcuin	162, 210, 211
Alexander the Historian	190
Alexandria	51, 167, 178, 184, 317, 343
collection of scrolls from	279
Allegro, John	136
Ambrose of Milan	79, 106, 320
Ambrosias	44
Amiatino Gospel	295
Amis and Amiles	210
Amphilochius, Bishop of Iconium	289
Anastasius II, Emperor	210
Anglesey	156, 322, 327
Anglican Bishop of Birmingham, Hugh Montefiore	193
Anointing was an ancient custom	67
Antioch	51, 61, 81, 108-110, 184, 200, 279, 335
patriarchs of	215
on the Orontes	328
Apollonius	58, 318
Apollonius of Tyana	125, 143
Aponas, an astrological writer of the 13th Century	265
Apostolic Constitutions	79
Arch-Druid Brí Leith	327, 335
Asaia, the Essaian	318
Asmodeus	277
Associated Press	294
Athena	269, 270
Augustine, Saint	44, 106, 200, 202, 230, 243, 263, 303
Augustus, Emperor	45, 46, 107, 108, 114, 142, 172, 265
Avalon, Isle of	156

B

Babylonian fish-god, Oannes	330
Babylonian Sanhedrin	47, 48, 92, 147, 148, 152

Baibars, the self-proclaimed sultan of Egypt	61	Botticelli, Sandro	246
Bale, John	240	Brân Adamnán, Abbot of Mona	327
Bandello	250	Brân the Blessed	332, 336
Barabbas	97	British Library Newspaper Division	223
definition of	97	British Museum	45, 62, 106, 164, 166, 228, 324
Bardesanes (154-222)	38	Trustees of	113
Barker, Robert	264	Bull of Two Swords	221
Bartholomew	222	Bultman, Rudolf	188
Basilica of St Paul's Outside-the-Walls	33	Byzantine Museum	62
Basilides	60, 61, 99, 100	Byzantium	182, 206, 213
Bellarmine, Robert	290, 293		
Bellini, Giovanni	247	**C**	
Bendigeid Vran	62	C. S. Sonnini	324
Bernice	46	Caecilian of Carthage	168
Beroaldo, Filippo	241	Caligula	94, 95, 96, 98
Bertoldo di' Giovanni, a pupil of Donatello	280	Callistus	318
Bethany	120	Cana	17, 123, 124
Mary of	76, 118	Capital Initial Code	270, 272
Mary Magdalene, nee	119	Cardinal Augustinus Bea of Germany	295
Bethany Group	153-160, 175, 316, 320	Cardinal Caesar Baronius	61, 154, 165, 176, 215, 236, 239, 240, 291, 293, 310
Bible Fraud, The	4-9, 43, 46, 48, 55, 62, 84, 89, 122, 139, 161, 165, 265, 272	Cardinal Calandrini	303
Bishop Frotheringham	242	Cardinal Caraffa	299
Bishop Fulbertus	304	Cardinal Charles Borromeo	258
Bishop Grosseteste	220	Cardinal Gasparo Contarini	281
Bishop Jeremy Taylor	303, 304	Cardinal Giovanni del Monte	282
Bishop Lewis Du Pin	88, 170, 241, 299	Cardinal il Vecchio	293
Bishop Platina	312	Cardinal Jovius	239
Bishop Rieux of Toulouse	84	Cardinal Lodovico	250
Bishop Theodoret of Antioch	322	Cardinal Molano	259
Bishop Victor of Tunnunum	210	Cardinal of Santaquatro	236
Boadicea, Queen	164	Cardinal Pietro Bembo	20, 60, 239, 240, 243, 244
Bodleian Codex	300	Cardinal Porizetti	238
Bomberg, Daniel	299	Cardinal Pucci	237
Book of Elxai	60	Cardinal Sadoleto	239, 243
Book of Enoch	34, 50, 63, 64	Cathars	217, 218, 219, 277
Book of James	23, 316, 325	Catholic Encyclopedia	35, 39, 49, 52, 71, 80, 83, 87, 88, 89, 91, 98, 100, 102, 105, 126, 127, 134, 143, 153, 154, 155, 159, 163, 166, 168, 178, 179, 180, 184, 186, 200, 201, 202, 212, 215, 218, 219, 220, 221, 222, 232, 237, 239, 242, 256, 283, 284, 287, 289, 294, 298, 299, 305, 307, 308, 309, 310,
Book of Revelation	76, 185, 202, 255, 305, 317		
Book of the Popes	310, 311		
Book of Thomas, the Contender	39		
Books of Alexander	343		
Born of Fornication	96		

INDEX

	311, 312, 316, 317, 318, 353, 356		177, 179, 184, 201, 258-260,
new	91, 135, 143, 167, 168, 183, 290, 317, 318		282-284, 286, 292, 297, 298, 301-304
Catholic Encyclopedia, new	49, 71	Crescentis, a Roman family	213
Caulacu	61, 99	Cristofano Robetta	260
Celestial Judgments	154	Crucifixion of Truth, The	25, 185, 255, 318
Celsus	43, 44, 83, 128	Crucifixion of young women	224
Cerinthus	317, 318	Culdee church	157-159, 161, 162
Charlemagne, Emperor	210	Culdees, the	157-159, 161, 162, 175
Charnel-houses	328	Cumbrian Abbey records	160, 161
Children being crucified	224	Cumbrian Archives	327
Christians were called Galileans	80, 107, 108	Cumbrian monastery	41, 87, 274
Chrysostom	103	Cumbrian Volumes	160
Claudia Procula	99	Cunobeline. *See also* Acta Cunobeline	
Clement of Alexandria	124, 151, 194, 305, 316, 344, 346, 351, 352	Curiones	330
		Cypros of Petra	48
Clementine Vulgate	293	Cyrenius, Governor of Syria	74
Codex Atlantico	249	Cyril of Jerusalem	79, 183
Codex Laudianus	319	Cyrus, the father of Mary	119, 122
Codex Nazaraeus	150		
Cod-head	330	# D	
Coel 11, King	164	da Firenze, Andrea	221
College of Essenes	51	Damascus Document	55
Community Rule	54, 55, 69	Damianius	60, 159
Comparing an old Bible with a new version	41, 308	Damianius, Saint	61
		De Grimm, Baron	223
Congregation of the Index	297	Dead Sea Scrolls, the	37, 38, 52-55, 66-69, 70, 79, 117, 136, 189, 300, 309
Constantine Von Tischendorf	23, 128, 190, 305, 307, 344	Deception of Sylvester	214
Constantine, Donation of	215	Deesis	61
Constantine, Edict of	36	Delatores	95
Constantine, Emperor	59, 107, 135, 164, 170, 171, 173, 178, 183, 187, 215, 285, 312, 336	Denarnaud, Marie	277
		Desiderius Erasmus	304, 312
Constantine, King	165, 166, 173, 181, 183, 312	Diderot, Denis	312, 313
Contra Celsus	44	Diderot's Encyclopedia	22, 25, 39, 88, 200, 210, 212, 216, 219, 227, 231, 232, 235, 242, 243, 288, 293, 299, 312, 313, 344, 355
Cosimo de' Medici	279		
Cosmas	61	Didymus	34
church of	61	Greek work for twin	
Cosmas, Saint	61, 62	Didymus Judas Thomas	35, 37, 38, 59, 325
Council of Nicaea, The	19, 34, 36, 42, 82, 160, 164, 168, 169, 170, 173, 178, 182, 184, 202, 289, 306, 317, 318	Didymus, the Twin	34, 38
		Dies Irae	55
Council of Trent	21, 39, 163, 164, 173,	authorship of	256

Diocletian	59, 106, 159, 166		125, 155, 167-170, 176, 177, 179, 180, 187, 264, 289, 317, 318, 338
Diocletian persecution	159		
Diodorus Siculus	113, 139	Evangelium Joannis de obitu Mariae	39
Dioscuri, the	61	Expurgatory Index	302, 305
Discovery of a tombstone at Bingerbruck	42, 43, 46	Ezra	63, 137
Dissolution of Monasteries	159	**F**	
Divine Julius	169-172, 174, 175, 183, 234, 335	False Isidorian Decretals	214
Dominic	218, 219	Feciales	330
Dominic de Guzman	218	Ferguson	1990, 38, 302, 363
Donatus	166	Fifth Ecumenical Council of Constantinople	161, 207
Donna Lucrezia	230	FIRST Vulgate	22, 26, 27, 29, 32, 34, 41, 64, 65, 97, 116, 153, 196, 295, 296, 315, 316, 324-326, 337
Douay Bible	315		
Double of Jesus Christ, the	34, 39, 41, 284, 316, 322		
Durant, Dr Will	109, 222	English-language	25, 34, 177, 276, 283, 284
E		Forbidden to be read the word of God	199
Ebionites	54, 152	Index of Prohibited Books	297
Edessa	38, 103	writings of St. Augustine	303
Egyptian Book of the Dead	130, 132	Forged Decretals of Gratian	219
Egyptian Museum at Cairo	63	Forgery Mill, The church	307
Elliott, Reverend Charles	83, 214, 223, 242, 301, 302, 303, 305	Francis Bacon, Sir	35, 63, 262, 263, 265, 269-272, 277, 336
Emperor Constantius 'the Pale'	164	Franciscan friars in hell	246
Encyclopedia Britannica new	356	Fratres Ambervales	330
		Frederick II	220
Encyclopedia Brittanica	35, 80, 86, 115, 118, 161, 170, 184, 208, 210, 212, 222, 235, 236, 290, 304, 307-309, 342, 355	Frumentarii, the	95
		G	
Encyclopedia of Early Christianity, Everett	38, 83, 87, 289, 302, 355	Galilee	49, 55, 74, 75, 76, 88-91, 94, 119
		Galilee, upper	88, 91, 98
Ephraem the Syrian	38	Gamaliel of Jabneh	115
Epiphanius, Riddle of	44	Geoffrey of Monmouth	149
Epiphanius, Saint	44, 45, 60, 63, 68, 86, 176, 199, 317	Gethsemane	94, 188
		Ghirlandaio	227, 260
Erasmus	304, 305, 319	Gildas the Wise	112, 157
Essenes	15, 16, 47, 48, 50-53, 55, 66-70, 76, 79, 102, 115-117, 125, 136, 152, 190, 193, 317	Giotto di Bondone	154
		Giovanni Angelo De' Medici	283
order of	318	Giovanni de' Medici	234, 236, 280
Eulogomenopolis	216	Giulia Farnese	232, 233
Eusebius	34, 44, 51, 61, 82, 83, 117,	Giulio de Medici	237

INDEX

Give me this stranger	101
Glastonbury	113, 114, 156, 160, 322
Glastonbury Abbey	155, 157
Golgotha	99, 133
Good Wednesday	132
Gospel Jesus Christ	49, 92, 97, 98, 101, 126, 143, 194, 196
Gospel of Cerinthus	318
Gospel of Hidden Knowledge	36
Gospel of Mark, original version of	35
Gozzoli, Benozzo	246
Grand-Pontiff of the Order of the Temple	226
Graziano, Giovanni	216
Gregory of Nazianzus	103
Gregory of Tours	103
Grottaferrata Theofilatto	216
Grotto of the Initiates	131
Guicciardini, the historian of Florence	233, 234
Gundafor of the Acts of Thomas	102
Gundafor, King of the Indians	102

H

Hadrian, Emperor	73, 172
Harvard Theology Review	80, 337
He will be called son of God	54
Head of the Essene Community	68-70
Hecebolus	205
Heitmers	241
Helena	135, 164, 182
Helena, Empress	164, 165
Henry IV, King	157, 222
Henry Peacham's *Minerva Britannia*	269
Herod, King	48, 52, 73, 74
Herodotus	58, 113, 273, 328
Hidden Information	50, 148, 270, 272
Hidden Mother	39
Hierocles, Governor or Bithymia	125
Hieronymus Wierix	224
Hillel, the Elder	115
Hippolytus of Rome	60, 289
History of the Christian Church, Philip Schaff	40, 201
Homily on the Life of a Pilgrim	38
Horus the Krst	63
House of Boethus in Babylon	115
House of Herod	48, 51
Hugh de Payens	226

I

Iacopo Sadoleto	239
Iesou Iulus Xristou	62
Index Expurgatorius	83, 84, 208, 209, 302, 304, 305
Inquisition, Roman	22, 83, 303
Inquisition, The	219, 227, 240, 292, 297-300, 302- 304
Interpolations by Christians	83
Invention of the Cross	17, 135
Ioudas Khrestus	60
Ioudas Te'oma	59
Irenaeus	61, 81, 99, 105, 126, 143, 150, 151, 155, 165, 176, 289, 305, 316, 337
Isabella d' Este Gonzaga, Marchesa of Mantua	247
Isca Dumnoniorum	160
Italian Renaissance	245

J

Jacob and Esau	101, 336
Jacob became Israel	57
James the Younger	32, 119
James, Gospel of	32, 122
Jerome	19, 30, 89, 103, 106, 200-205, 207, 263, 282, 286, 287, 290, 292, 295, 304, 311, 319, 320, 322
Jesew Cryst	62
Jesus Christ	6, 13, 34, 35, 39, 45, 49, 51, 54, 60, 62, 64, 68, 78, 79, 81-83, 87, 89-92, 97-99, 101, 123, 126, 133, 135, 143, 150, 151, 161, 163, 168, 169, 173, 177-181, 185, 187-189, 191-196, 198, 212, 217, 218, 238, 256, 258, 272-274, 277, 279, 280, 287, 289, 290, 300, 306, 307, 312, 319, 337, 339, 340
Jesus is called 'Cresceus'	61, 65

Jesus Khrestus 171, 173, 177, 183
Jesus was the son of a certain Julius 43, 44
whose surname was Panthera
Jesus, Rabbi 60, 102, 116, 117, 120-129, 132, 142, 144-152, 159-161, 165, 171, 173, 175-177, 180, 188-190, 193, 196, 211, 212, 216, 217, 221, 224, 275, 285, 299, 325, 336
Jesus, 'the human one' 49
Jesus, the Kryst 62, 63, 68
Jesus, the Magician 43, 125, 126
Johann Burchard 229, 230, 232
John the Baptist 66-71, 76, 117, 142, 150, 196, 247, 256, 258, 259
   anointing of 67
   regarded as the messiah 67, 68
John, Gospel of 34, 41, 107, 130, 150, 185, 218, 269, 289, 290, 317, 318
Joseph ben Matthias 58
Joseph of Arimathea 60, 76, 90, 97-101, 112, 113, 142, 144, 154-156, 159
Joseph with Jesus and the Geminius' 40
Josephus 50-52, 58, 68, 70, 74-76, 78, 79, 82-84, 87, 89-91, 95, 116, 117, 143, 146, 170, 181, 190
Joses 32-34, 325
Judas ben Halachmee 47, 60
Judas Iscariot 89, 95, 96, 250
Judas Khrestus 16, 82, 84, 86-104, 120, 124, 144, 152-154, 165, 171, 173, 175, 181, 188-193, 196, 211, 212, 216, 217, 219, 221, 224, 241, 285, 302, 336
Judas Maccabeus 51
Judas the Galilean 16, 75, 76, 78-80, 82
Judas Thomas, the Twin. *See also* Judas, the twin
Judas, called Thomas 32-35, 38, 39, 41, 42, 48, 49, 55, 57-59, 66, 69, 70, 75, 76, 102-104, 146
Judas, Epistle of 34
Judas, the Twin. *See also* Judas Thomas, the Twin
Jude 32, 34, 366
Jude, Epistle of 34, 363

Jude, the son of Ezekias 74, 366
Julian 107, 108
Julian, Emperor 68, 107-109, 219, 335
   Arguments of 68
Julius Caesar 73, 142, 166, 169, 170, 172, 177, 335, 336
Jupiter Feretrius 333
Justin Martyr 64, 105, 125, 127, 180, 305
Justinian 205, 206, 207, 208

K

Kashmir 103, 104
Khrestians 17, 81, 82, 84, 86, 88, 90, 94, 105-111, 152, 197, 328, 335
King James 1 262, 263
King James Bible, The 21, 97, 162, 186, 199, 262-264, 267, 270
King Solomon 55, 67, 89, 130, 272, 273
Knights Templar 21, 41, 57, 134, 226, 227, 260, 262, 268, 270, 272, 273, 277
Knox, Professor John, of the Union 290
Theological Seminary
Koran, The 61, 100
Krishna 63, 64, 143, 171, 174, 175, 177, 187
Krst 62-64, 68, 141, 177, 366
Krst John the Baptist 68

L

Laurentius Pucci 236
Lazarus 118, 119, 126, 154, 155, 195, 287
Legally called, 'the sons of God' 55
Leonardo da Vinci 1, 196, 228, 229, 245-252, 258, 260, 261, 328
Life of Rabbi Jesus 60
Llandeilo Fawr 327
Lord Bacon's Cypher 272
Lorenzo de' Medici 280
Lorenzo di Pierfrancesco de Medici 256
Lorenzo the Magnificent 280
Lost Wisdom of Antiquity 268
Lucian of Antioch 289
Lucian of Samosata 107

INDEX

Lud	148, 149, 316, 321
Lud, King	149
Lud's Town	149
Ludgate	149, 316, 321

M

Mad Meletius	184
Madonna with Two Children	260
Maelgwyn of Llandaff, Lord of Anglesey and Snowdonia	156
Magna Carta	327
Manawydan	60
Mar Saba Monastery	194, 195
Maran, Revelations of	60
Marcarius of Jerusalem	181
Marcellian	59, 275, 332, 336
Marcellinus Ammianus	86, 110
Marcellus	175, 176
Marcus	59, 161, 172, 175, 180, 332, 336
Marcus Aurelius, Emperor	105, 172
Marcus Tullius Tiro became Cicero	58
Marie Negre Dables, Dame de Hautpoul	277
Mark, Gospel of	19, 27, 35, 69, 139, 180, 192, 194, 195, 320
Mars	60, 85, 319, 330, 331, 332
Mars Hill in Athens	319
Martin Luther	238, 281
Mary Eucharis	106, 122
Mary Magdalene	17, 106, 118-123, 149, 154-156, 272, 277
Mary Magdalene, Gospel of	106, 120
Mary of Bethany	76, 118, 119
Mary of Egypt	122
Mary of Magdala	76, 277
Mary of the Herod clan	95
Mattathias	51
Matthew, Gospel of	26, 33, 49, 71, 77, 90, 117, 118, 124, 137, 186, 192, 202
Mehgheehlla Scroll, the	47, 60, 61
Mendip Hills	114
Message of John Concerning the Death of Mary, the	39, 41

Messina	213
Michelangelo	1, 21, 121, 228, 229, 233, 234, 245, 250, 253-256, 258, 261, 280, 335
the writings of	335
Michelet, French historian	245
Militia of Jesus Christ	20, 218
Millias, John Everett	252
Minucius Felix	105, 106
Mithraic Father of Rome	16, 97, 98
Mohammad	100
Mona	322, 327, 335
Moses	55, 116, 122, 130, 273
Moses, Law of	46, 55, 69, 70, 96, 116, 118, 120, 123, 147, 189
Museo Gregoriano	125
Mysterious Ones	51

N

Nabatean Arabs	48, 89
Nabateans	48
Nag Hammadi	35, 38, 39
Nag Hammadi Scrolls	35, 309
Naked man to naked man	195
Nantes, Edict of	222
Nathanael	56
National Gallery of London	258
Nazarenes	80, 92, 190, 317
Nazareth	133
Nazars	190
Nero, Emperor	86, 338
Nero, Marcellian Iulus Claudius	59
Nero, Marcus Iulus Claudius	60
Nero, Tiberius Julius Claudius	46
New Learning	284, 288, 309
New Rome	182
New Testimonies	173, 177, 178, 274, 318, 336
Niccolo de' Niccoli	280
Nicholas, Archbishop of Westminster	298
Nicodemus, Gospel of	128
Nineteen Eighty-Four	313
Notavitch, Nicolas	104

O

Office of the Inquisition, the	303
Old Testament	38, 52, 54, 63, 67, 68, 77, 79, 83, 89, 101, 116, 122, 124, 133, 142, 148, 189, 190, 202, 205, 255, 268, 273, 274, 300, 315, 324, 336
Origen of Alexandria	44, 83, 208
Osius	167
Out of the Flaminian Gate	298

P

Pacino da Bonaguide	227
Pagan origin of Christ	81
Palazzo del Belvedere	228
Palermo Stone	63
Palsgate Testimonies	160
Pantheon	142, 332, 333, 335, 336
Panthers, The	141
house of	46
Paul	51, 57, 66, 68, 115, 116, 123, 124, 196, 243, 287, 289, 316, 318-324, 337
Paul's Field	322
Paul's journey to Britain	316
Paulus Orosius, a Fourth Century church historian	84
Peter de Rosa	177, 291
Peter, Gospel of	36, 98, 100, 101
Petronius Arbiter Elegantiarum	90
Philip, Gospel of	120
Philo	50, 52, 76, 98, 143, 181
Pinhas	148
Place of the Skull, the	17, 133, 274, 332, 333, 336
Pliny	40, 47, 52, 76, 143, 181, 190, 241
Polycarp	61, 65
Polydore Vergil	60, 159
Pontelli, Baccio	254
Pontifex Maximus of the Seven Hills	329
Pontifical Biblical Commission	135, 294
Pontius Pilate	85, 90, 98, 99, 101, 109, 128, 146
Pope Alexander VI	20, 22, 228-232, 242, 286, 297, 299
Pope Benedict IX	216
Pope Benedict XIII	60
Pope Benedict XIV	135
Pope Boniface VIII	220, 221
Pope Celestine V	276
Pope Clement VII	237
Pope Clement VIII	291-293, 301
Pope Clement XIII	25, 312
Pope Damasus	198-201, 207, 286, 298, 311
Pope Gelasius I	297
Pope Gregory IX	219, 220
Pope Gregory VII	217, 220
Pope Gregory XIII	213
Pope Innocent III	217-219
Pope John VIII	212
Pope John XXII	185
Pope John XXIII	224
Pope Julius II	228, 232-236, 247, 254, 256
Pope Leo the Great	240
Pope Leo X	20, 60, 228, 234-239, 257, 280, 306
Pope Leo XIII	294
Pope Licius III	217
Pope Paul III	281-283
Pope Paul VI	295, 298
Pope Pius IV	21
Pope Pius V	213
Pope Pius VII	223
Pope Sixtus V	22, 25, 177, 258, 288-291, 293, 295, 301
Pope Sylvester I	215
Pope Sylvester III	216
Porphyry	82, 181
Prince Bohemond	61
Prince Linus, son of King Caradoc	175
Procopius of Caesarea	205
Pseudo-Areopagitell Forgeries	215
Publius Licinius Gallienus, Emperor	160
Publius Maro, became Virgil	58
Publius Petronius	143, 181
Puget, Pierre	259

INDEX

Q

Quindecemviri	330
Quintus Curtius Rufus	143
Quirinius	174
Qumran	51-54, 66, 69, 71, 72, 190

R

Rabbi Gamaliel Hillel	116
Raphael	21, 228, 229, 233, 237, 243, 245, 250, 256-258, 261
Raphinus	321, 323
Ravenna	196, 206
Red-light districts	55
Remus	174, 332, 336
Rennes-le-Chateau	276, 277
Repellers of Wolves, the	331, 335
Roma	160, 221, 328, 330, 332, 334, 335
Roman historian, Publius Cornelius Tacitus	40
Roman Imperial Secret Service, The	16, 94, 95
Romulus	174, 328, 332, 336

S

Sabinius, the Bishop of Hereclea	139, 168
Sacred Lakes	130
Sacred Marriage	61
Safed Scroll	47, 48, 50, 61
Salome, and the severed head of John the Baptist	70
Salvianus	110
Sanhedrin, the	18, 46, 92, 97, 115, 146-148
Santa Maria delle Grazie in Milan	250
Sauniere, Berenger	276
Schonfield, Hugh	49, 66, 67, 192
Scopetine	227
Secret Archives of the Vatican	178, 185, 295
Secret Gospel, The	195, 336
Secret in the Bible, The	5-7, 9, 25, 37, 134, 145, 152, 272, 273
Secret knowledge	36, 64, 121, 126, 151, 227
Secret of the Kingdom of God	37, 196
Seleucus	319, 320
Septemviri	330

Septimius Severus	172
Seraglio Bible, The	19, 178, 295
Shiemon ben Azzai	45
Sibyl of Tarquin	76, 255
Sibylline Books, The	18, 165, 173
Silvanius	58, 59
Simeon bar Cochba	53, 71, 72, 74
Simon	32-34, 57, 119, 124, 128, 325
Simon Magi	127, 128
Simon of Cyrene	99-101
Seizure of	98
Simon of Petra	90, 96, 124, 128
Simon Peter	89, 90, 192, 312
Simon the Zealot	92
Sinai Bible, The	92, 118, 123, 124, 192, 287
Sistine Chapel, the	227, 254-256, 335
Sixth Ecumenical Council in 680AD	135
Sixtus' Vulgate	22, 288, 290-292
Smedley, William T	263
Smith, Professor Morton	43, 126, 194, 195
Socrates Scholasticus	110, 176, 302
Sodales	330
Solomon Romano	300
Sophronius Eusebius Heironymus	200
St. Paul's Cathedral	149, 321
Stada was Yeshu'a ben Panthera's (Jesus') mother	47
Star Chamber	332
Suetonius	70, 73, 86-88, 94, 142, 143, 169, 181, 335
Sulpice, Saint	276
Symmachian Forgeries, The	214
Szekely, Edmond Bordeaux	84, 295
Szekely, Edmond Bordeaux	178

T

Tacitus	45, 70, 73, 85-88, 95, 143, 181, 241, 280
Taliesin, the Welsh Prince-Bard	112
Talmud	15, 42, 45-48, 60, 92, 146, 148, 150, 151, 299-301
Temple of Caesar	170
Tenvantius	122, 149

Tenvantius, King	122, 157
Tertullian	105, 127, 151, 175, 176, 335
Testimony of Flavius, The	82, 83
The Alexandrian scrolls	279
The Church Militant and Triumphant	221
The discovery at Whithern, in Lincoln	338
The one who art mother of twin young ones	39
Theodora	205-208
Theodosius I, Roman Emperor	109, 110, 183, 184, 198
This narrative was kept a closely guarded secret for 32 years	54
Thomas is Greek for 'twin'	41
Thomas, Gospel of	35- 37, 39, 41, 101, 125, 160, 191, 192, 277, 320
Three Chapters, The	207, 208
Throat-cutters	218
Thucydides Sallustius	143
Tiberius Julius Abdes Panthera	42, 46
Tiberius, Emperor	41, 46, 87, 94, 98, 142
Toma Khrestus	59
Tomas de Torquemada	299
Torah	50, 115, 116, 144-148, 268
Trogus Pompeius	125
True Discourse, the	43, 44
Trypho, a Jewish academic	64
Twin Judas Twin	35, 37
Twin Saints of 'noble birth'	336
Two Innocents	227

U

Urbino	237, 244, 256

V

Vagabond monks	111
Vanozza Catanei	230
Vasari, Giorgio	213, 231, 246, 247
Vatican Hill	228
Vergilius Maro	334
Verses for the Vulgar	200, 201, 282, 326
Vespasiano da Bisticci	279
Vestal Virgins	331
Virgin Mary	32, 119, 123, 232, 233, 249
Virgin of the Stairs, the	253, 280
Visigoths	277
Vittorio Eliano	300

W

War Scroll, the	76, 77
Watson, Dr. Richard, a disillusioned Christian historian,	169
Westphalia	241
Why Jesus was regularly called Panthera	43-46
Wilde, Oscar	340
William Shakespeare	262, 271
Wisdom of the Ancients, Sir Francis Bacon	35, 63

X

Xavier	292

Y

Yeshai ben Halachmee	47, 61
Yeshu'a ben Panthera	42, 47, 60
See also Yeshu'a ben Stada	
Yeshu'a ben Stada	46, 47, 60
See also Yeshu'a ben Panthera	
Yesu Hesus Cunobeline	62
Young, Robert	307

Z

Zachaeus	155
Zealots	92, 100, 152
as robbers	90, 92, 100
Zeus	105, 169, 171, 189

THEY LIED TO US IN SUNDAY SCHOOL

By Ian Ross Vayro

Ian Ross Vayro gives us the facts in a way that is impossible to dispute.

There is much more to those quaint Bible stories than we might have been led to believe.

Ian is trained in Archaeology and Ancient History and he has spent a lifetime studying Theology.

'The conclusions of Ian Ross Vayro expose the lies, fraud and so called infallible truths of Organised Religion.'
Tony Bushby

Joshua Books
JoshuaBooks.com